NATIONAL AUDUBON SOCIETY

FIELD GUIDE TO
New England

D0062162

Peter Alden
Brian Cassie   Richard Forster
Richard Keen   Amy Leventer
Wendy B. Zomlefer

Alfred A. Knopf, New York

This is a Borzoi Book.
Published by Alfred A. Knopf, Inc.

Prepared and produced by
Chanticleer Press, Inc., New York.

Printed and bound by
Dai Nippon Printing Co., Ltd., Hong Kong.

First Edition
Published May 1998
First Printing

Library of Congress Cataloging-in-Publication Data

National Audubon Society field guide. New England / Peter Alden
. . . [et al.]. — 1st ed.
    p.   cm.
  Includes index.
  ISBN 0-679-44676-1
  1. Natural history—New England.   I. Alden, Peter.   II. National
Audubon Society.
QH104.5.N4N38   1998
508.74—dc21   97-31241

Front cover: Moose, Baxter State Park, Maine
Spine: Schoodic Point, Maine
Back cover: Crescent moon and Venus at dawn; Musk Mallow; Cedar
  Waxwing; eastern shoreline of Monhegan Island, Maine
Table of Contents: Waterfall, Macedonia Brook State Park; Common Tern;
  full moon; American Copper; lighthouse, Machias Seal Island, Maine
Title Page: Dorr Mountain and the Tarn in fall, Acadia National Park, Maine
Pages 8–9: Clay cliffs at Gay Head, Martha's Vineyard, Massachusetts
Pages 74–75: Moose drinking from a pond
Pages 376–377: Kees Falls, White Mountain National Forest, Maine

National Audubon Society

The mission of NATIONAL AUDUBON SOCIETY, founded in 1905, is to conserve and restore natural ecosystems, focusing on birds, other wildlife, and their habitats for the benefit of humanity and the earth's biological diversity.

One of the largest, most effective environmental organizations, Audubon has more than 550,000 members, numerous state offices and nature centers, and 500+ chapters in the United States and Latin America, plus a professional staff of scientists, lobbyists, lawyers, policy analysts, and educators. Through our nationwide sanctuary system we manage 150,000 acres of critical wildlife habitat and unique natural areas for birds, wild animals, and rare plant life.

Our award-winning *Audubon* magazine, published six times a year and sent to all members, carries outstanding articles and color photography on wildlife and nature, and presents in-depth reports on critical environmental issues, as well as conservation news and commentary. We also publish *Field Notes,* a journal reporting on seasonal bird sightings, and *Audubon Adventures,* a children's newsletter reaching 450,000 students. Through our ecology camps and workshops in Maine, Connecticut, and Wyoming, we offer professional development for educators and activists; through Audubon Expedition Institute in Belfast, Maine, we offer unique, traveling undergraduate and graduate degree programs in Environmental Education.

Our acclaimed *Wild!Life Adventures* television documentaries, airing on TBS Superstation and in syndication, deal with a variety of environmental themes, and our children's series for the Disney Channel, *Audubon's Animal Adventures,* introduces family audiences to endangered and threatened wildlife species. Our weekly birding series *All Bird TV,* which airs on Discovery's Animal Planet Channel, provides viewers with birding tips and takes them to some of the greatest bird locations in the United States. Other Audubon film and television projects include conservation-oriented movies, electronic field trips, and educational videos. National Audubon Society also sponsors books and interactive programs on nature, plus travel programs to exotic places like Antarctica, Africa, Australia, Baja California, Galápagos Islands, and Patagonia.

For information about how you can become an Audubon member, subscribe to *Audubon Adventures,* or to learn more about our camps and workshops, please write or call:

NATIONAL AUDUBON SOCIETY
Membership Dept.
700 Broadway
New York, New York 10003
212-979-3000
http://www.audubon.org/

Contents

Part One: Overview

Part Two: Flora and Fauna

Part Three: Parks and Preserves

Appendices

Natural Highlights

For the naturalist, outdoors enthusiast, and scenery watcher, New England has as much variety and spectacle as any spot on the continent. Comprising the 66,608 square miles of Connecticut, Maine, Massachusetts, New Hampshire, Rhode Island, and Vermont, New England is warmed by balmy summer breezes and blasted by the most ferocious winds ever recorded on the planet. It is home to rare and endangered flora and fauna and abundant marine life, delicate wildflowers and enormous breaching baleen whales, alpine meadows and patches of Eastern Prickly Pear cacti. Because of the great diversity it offers, New England is a naturalist's paradise.

Mount Katahdin, Maine

Mountains

The first sunlight reaching the United States each morning falls upon the summits of Mount Katahdin, an isolated peak in the Maine wilderness, and Mount Desert Island's Cadillac Mountain. New England's mountains, the ancient Greens, the majestic Whites, and the jagged Taconics, may not reach the lofty heights of western chains (though they did eons ago), yet their grandeur and wildlife and their recreational aspects make them as beloved to New Englanders as the Rockies are to westerners.

View from summit of Mount Greylock, Massachusetts

Woodlands

New England's spectacular autumn leaf show, which is unparalleled in the world, highlights the region's woodlands. During other seasons, naturalists may spot up to 30 species of wood warblers, several dozen types of mushrooms, and fascinating mammals, from the pesky Eastern Gray Squirrel to the enormous Moose.

Coastlines

Throughout the year, New England's sea-coasts are bountiful and beautiful. Spring tides and storms offer superb beachcombing. Summer skies fill with terns. Fall brings extensive bird, butterfly, and dragonfly migrations. In winter, the region is visited by spectacular numbers of Common Eiders and other sea ducks, and many large local populations of Harbor Seals.

Acadia National Park, Maine

Island off Massachusetts coast

Islands

From Maine's tiny Potato Island to the vacation meccas of Nantucket and Martha's Vineyard in Massachusetts, New England's islands are home to diverse animal and plant life. The unspoiled nature of the hundreds of smaller islands is their great attraction.

Housatonic River

River Valleys

A determined Housatonic River canoeist paddling south from Pontoosuc Lake in Pittsfield, Massachusetts, will pass oxbows, marble outcrops, and countless fields and riparian woodlands before emerging at Long Island Sound in Connecticut. Other New England river valleys—such as the Connecticut, Allagash, Merrimack, French, and Lamoille—offer equally lovely vistas.

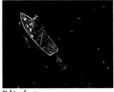

Fishing boat

Offshore Waters

New England's offshore waters, accessible by hundreds of commercial whale-watching and fishing boats, are extraordinarily rich in marine life. Several species of whales and large flocks of oceanic seabirds may greet the warm-weather visitor to Cox's Ledge (south of Rhode Island), Stellwagen Bank (off the Massachusetts coast), or the Bay of Fundy (off northeastern Maine).

Topography

Inland New England is dominated by the Appalachian mountain range. Elevations increase gradually northward from the Connecticut shore through the Berkshire Hills of western Massachusetts and Vermont's Green Mountains. The highest clusters of peaks—several over 5,000 feet in elevation—are in the White Mountains of New Hampshire. Other ranges extend northeastward through Maine. A relatively flat glacial outwash plain covers parts of Rhode Island and southeastern Massachusetts, meeting the sea in sweeping sand beaches. Farther north the coast turns mainly rocky, and along its entire length there are many peninsulas and islands. The Connecticut River is New England's longest, but the Merrimack in New Hampshire and Massachusetts and the Penobscot, Kennebec, Saco, and Androscoggin in Maine are also extensive. Vermont's Lake Champlain is the largest lake, followed by Lake Winnipesaukee in New Hampshire and Moosehead Lake in Maine. Thousands of smaller lakes and ponds dot the landscape.

1. Lake Champlain

This large freshwater lake, on the Vermont–New York border, is 125 miles long and up to 14 miles wide, with a maximum depth of 399 feet. Whale bones discovered near its shores in 1848 provide evidence that the lake was once filled with seawater.

2. Mount Washington

At 6,288 feet, Mount Washington, in the Presidential Range of New Hampshire's White Mountains, is the tallest peak in New England. Formed 380 million years ago, the ridge is composed of very compacted and resistant schist.

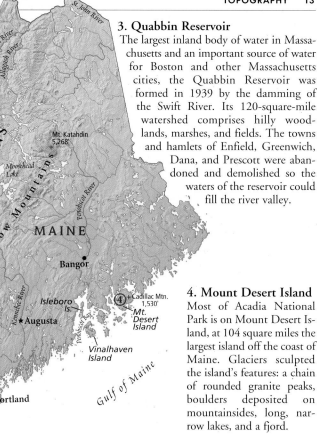

3. Quabbin Reservoir

The largest inland body of water in Massachusetts and an important source of water for Boston and other Massachusetts cities, the Quabbin Reservoir was formed in 1939 by the damming of the Swift River. Its 120-square-mile watershed comprises hilly woodlands, marshes, and fields. The towns and hamlets of Enfield, Greenwich, Dana, and Prescott were abandoned and demolished so the waters of the reservoir could fill the river valley.

4. Mount Desert Island

Most of Acadia National Park is on Mount Desert Island, at 104 square miles the largest island off the coast of Maine. Glaciers sculpted the island's features: a chain of rounded granite peaks, boulders deposited on mountainsides, long, narrow lakes, and a fjord.

5. Narragansett Bay

Narragansett Bay is part of a coastline that was flooded when sea levels rose as the glaciers melted at the end of the last ice age. The bay's numerous inlets and passages are mainly aligned in a north–south direction, the result of glacial drainage guided by the original bedrock structure.

6. Connecticut River

The Connecticut River rises in a series of lakes in New Hampshire near the Canadian border and flows southward along old fault lines, forming the state line between New Hampshire and Vermont. It then cuts through Massachusetts and Connecticut and empties into Long Island Sound, amid vast salt marshes, at Old Saybrook—flowing a total of 407 miles. The Connecticut River drains approximately 11,000 square miles, nearly one-third of New England's landscape.

Ocean and Coast

The New England coastline is indented with estuaries, bays, peninsulas, and headlands, and dotted with near-shore islands. The shoreline totals 5,400 miles with all its irregularities, compared with a point-to-point distance of about 570 miles. Connecticut has sandy beaches, protected from the Atlantic Ocean by New York's Long Island. Farther east, in Rhode Island, there are beaches, a few rocky headlands, and rocky islands in Narragansett Bay. In southeastern Massachusetts, the Elizabeth Islands buffer sandy beaches that continue as Cape Cod, where high dune systems and saltwater marshes are found along with high bluffs and sand cliffs that rise as much as 175 feet from some beaches. North of Boston, sandy beaches are underlain by pebbles and gravel; winter storms often remove the sand, leaving behind a cobbly beach. Cape Ann, a rocky granite promontory, extends almost 15 miles out into the Atlantic. The varied coast of Maine encompasses broad, sandy beaches between prominent headlands, drowned river valleys reaching inland, rocky peninsulas, and an offshore maze of hundreds of small rocky islands.

THE CHANGING SHAPE OF CAPE COD

New England's energetic fall and winter weather, typified by strong nor'easters blowing out of the North Atlantic, erodes some parts of the coast and deposits sand at others. Waves that strike the beach at an angle move sediment along the coastline, gradually extending the length of a spit, a process known as longshore drift. A single large storm, however, can breach a spit in a matter of hours. In recent years, the area around Wellfleet has lost shoreline at a rate of about 3 feet per year, while Provincetown Spit, Nauset Spit, and South Monomoy Island have been steadily lengthened.

Early Shoreline
Present Shoreline
→ Longshore Drift

Portland

Great Bay

Portsmouth

Isles o Shoals

Newburyport

Ca Ar

Gloucester

Salem

Boston   Massachuse Bay

Plymouth

Mount Hope Bay

Providence   New Bedford

Greenwich Bay

Narragansett Bay

Newport   Buzzards

Mystic   Vineyard Sound

New London   Rhode Island Sound

New Haven   Niantic Bay   Block Island Sound   Martha Vineyar

Plum Island

New Haven Sound   Block Island

Bridgeport

Long Island Sound

Along the New England coast, the tidal range—from low to high tide—varies from only about 3 feet in New London, Connecticut, to about 20 feet in Eastport, Maine. The Atlantic Ocean off New England is an excellent environment for fish and other sea creatures, which spawn in the coastal salt marshes and over the shallow banks offshore.

Bay of Fundy

Eastport

Bar Harbor

Frenchman Bay

Mt. Desert Island

Rockland

Penobscot Bay

Deer Isle

Isle au Haut

Vinalhaven Island

Matinicus Island

Bath

Monhegan Island

lf of aine

Offshore Waters

The oceanic waters off New England are influenced by the interaction of relatively warm waters in the central Atlantic and two major currents. An expanse of water in the Central Atlantic called the Sargasso Sea is an isolated lens of warm, clear water about 3,500 feet deep, trapped by the clockwise circulation system of the North Atlantic. Forming the western margin of these warm waters is the Gulf Stream, a warm current about 60 miles wide and up to 2,000 feet deep, that starts in the Gulf of Mexico and flows north until, above Cape Hatteras, North Carolina, it broadens, becomes more diffuse, and veers northeastward away from the coastline; at the latitude of Newfoundland, it continues eastward as the North Atlantic Drift. Eddies or loops can break off from the Gulf Stream, sending toward New England rings of warm water that can persist for several months. Meanwhile, the Labrador Current travels southward along the coast of Nova Scotia, bringing cool, nutrient-rich water from the Canadian Arctic. As a result of these complex and variable influences, ocean temperatures can vary significantly—in late summer by as much as 15 degrees—between southern and northern New England.

wagen ank

Provincetown

Cod y

Cape Cod

arnstable

Monomoy Islands

Nantucket Sound

Channel

Nantucket Island

Nantucket Shoals

Georges Bank

The Sculpting of the Landscape

The New England landscape was first molded by plate tectonic activity and later reshaped as rivers sliced through the bedrock, eroding material and carrying vast amounts of sediment to the sea. This process began 450 million years ago when North America collided with northwest Africa. During the last 2 million years, glacial ice repeatedly scoured the surface, exposing the underlying bedrock.

Plate Tectonics

According to the theory of plate tectonics, earth's surface is broken into a dozen major plates that constantly move as a result of convection currents generated by the planet's internal heat. Three types of motion occur along the boundaries of these plates.

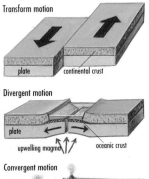

Transform boundaries, or fault lines, where plates are laterally sliding past each other, are the sites of earthquakes. At **divergent** plate boundaries, the plates move away from one another, or rift apart. Magma (molten rock) rises from within the earth and fills the void that was created, solidifying under the ocean as new seafloor or on land as a rift valley. At **convergent** plate boundaries, two plates collide, causing a buckling of the continental crust and/or forcing one plate beneath the other in a process called subduction, which can result in earthquakes and volcanoes. All the major mountain chains, including the Appalachians, and 80 percent of earth's volcanoes are located along convergent plate boundaries. Convergence events that create mountains are called orogenies.

A Rift Valley

The birth of the Atlantic Ocean was associated with rifting, the tearing apart of earth's crust, about 225 million years ago. The geologic Connecticut Valley, which extends from just south of the Vermont–Massachusetts border to Long Island Sound, was formed by the same divergent forces. If rifting had continued in the area of today's valley, the coastline would lie to the west and the valley would be part of the ocean floor. In the Connecticut Valley the rift was filled in with "brownstone" sedimentary rock (a sandstone) interlayered with basalt, a volcanic rock.

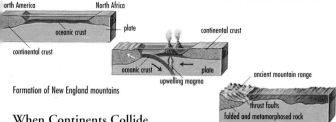

Formation of New England mountains

When Continents Collide

North America converged with northwestern Africa three times. In the Taconic Orogeny, about 450 million years ago, thrust faulting moved huge slabs of rock hundreds of miles westward from the point of collision, forming a mountain range perhaps as tall as today's Himalayas that wind and water have since worn down into the Berkshire Hills and Taconic Mountains. Some 380 million years ago, during the Acadian Orogeny, collision again occurred, causing volcanic extrusions (solidification of lava on earth's surface) and granitic intrusions (solidification of rock below the surface); such granites form the core of many White Mountain peaks. In the Alleghenian Orogeny, 300 million years ago, Africa again struck a glancing blow, leaving behind land that became part of the New England coast.

METAMORPHIC FOLDS

Great compressional forces, such as those that occur when continents collide, result in the deformation and metamorphism of rocks. Under such conditions, minerals in the rocks are recrystallized, or changed into different minerals, a process that may produce bands of color in the rock. Dramatic contortions of rock called metamorphic folds are exposed in roadcuts throughout New England.

Metamorphic rocks at Pemaquid Point, Maine

Long Rock Point, Vermont

THRUST FAULTING

In thrust faulting, thin slices of earth's crust are moved long distances as part of a collision between plates. During the Taconic Orogeny, older and lighter-colored rock called dolomite was thrust westward over younger, darker sediment composed of black shale at Long Rock Point, on Lake Champlain near Burlington, Vermont. Evidence of the thrust faulting appears as a sharp boundary made of crushed and contorted rock.

MONADNOCKS

Mount Monadnock (New Hampshire), Mount Ascutney (Vermont), and Wachusett Mountain and Mount Greylock (Massachusetts) are monadnocks, huge chunks of erosion-resistant rock that remain above broad, flat land worn away by water, wind, and glaciers.

Mount Ascutney, Vermont

Erosion by Glaciers

During the most recent ice age, which ended about 10,000 years ago, the glacier that covered most of New England, called the Laurentide Ice Sheet, was about a mile thick at its maximum. As the ice expanded and retreated, it scoured surfaces, sculpted bedrock, and captured eroded debris and deposited it elsewhere. The New England landscape retains abundant evidence of glacial erosion in the form of majestic cirques, aretes, U-shaped valleys, and a fjord. Exposed bedrock surfaces are often covered with glacial striations (scratches), oriented parallel to the direction of the flow, that formed as the glacier moved across the landscape.

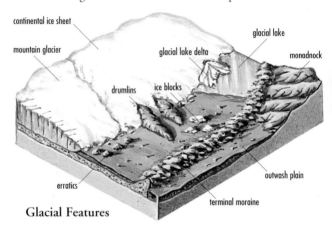

continental ice sheet

mountain glacier

glacial lake delta

glacial lake

monadnock

drumlins

ice blocks

erratics

outwash plain

terminal moraine

Glacial Features

Types of Glaciers

Glaciers are masses of ice that move or spread over land. Ice sheets are continent-size glaciers that slowly advance outward from the center of ice accumulation. Even outside of ice ages, smaller mountain glaciers (or valley glaciers) form in cold, high mountains when accumulated snow compresses into ice and begins to move; like rivers of ice, mountain glaciers travel downhill. During the last ice age, the Laurentide Ice Sheet and smaller mountain glaciers both played dramatic roles in sculpting the New England landscape.

Roche moutonnée (the Beehive) at Acadia National Park, Maine

ROCHES MOUTONNEES

Roches moutonnées, or sheepbacks, are carved knobs of bedrock, elongated in the direction of ice flow. The size of these formations varies from small to massive. Roches moutonnées are found on many small islands off the Maine coast, especially near Bath, as well as in Massachusetts along I-91 in the Connecticut Valley.

Glacial Waterways

Toward the end of the last ice age, Lake Champlain was connected to the St. Lawrence River as an inland arm of the Atlantic Ocean. This configuration, called by geologists the Champlain Sea, resulted when the Laurentide Ice Sheet depressed the underlying land and altered water flow and drainage patterns. As the glacier retreated, meltwater filled valleys that, when blocked at one end, became glacial lakes. One such body of water, named Lake Hitchcock, extended along the Connecticut Valley for 150 miles from Lyme, New Hampshire, to Rocky Hill, Connecticut. The lake grew until, about 10,000 years ago, it breached a natural dam at its southern end, and the Connecticut River reoccupied its pre-glacial course.

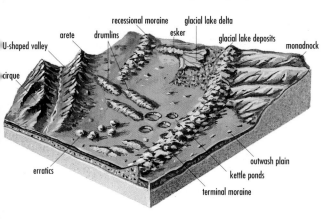

U-SHAPED VALLEYS

Franconia Notch, New Hampshire

As mountain glaciers move across the landscape, V-shaped valleys previously created by running water are rounded into U-shaped structures with flat floors and steep sides. New Hampshire's notches—such as Crawford, Franconia, and Pinkham—are examples. Along the coast, floors of U-shaped valleys may erode below sea level and become flooded with seawater when the ice retreats, forming a fjord, an inlet with parallel walls that often extend far below the water surface. Somes Sound, a deep fjord, nearly divides Maine's Mount Desert Island in two.

CIRQUES AND ARETES

Mount Katahdin, in Maine, has a knife-edge ridge, or arete, formed when glaciers carve out valleys on either side of a ridge. At the head of these valleys, the glaciers sculpted amphitheater-like hollows called cirques, such as Huntington Ravine and Tuckerman Ravine, on the slopes of Mount Washington in New Hampshire.

Mount Katahdin, Maine

Deposits Left by Glaciers

As glaciers retreated (melted back) from the New England land-scape, they deposited geologic debris that is seen today in such formations as glacial erratics, kettle ponds, drumlins, and eskers, as well as in such larger land forms as moraines and outwash plains. Kames, formed by streams of melting glacial ice that deposited mud and sand along the ice front, appear as isolated, flat-topped hillocks or terraces "hanging" on valley walls. Deposits left at deltas leading into glacial lakes are the source of the sand and gravel that is one of New England's major mineral resources.

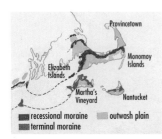

recessional moraine   outwash plain
terminal moraine

The Glaciers' Advance

Cape Cod and the islands of Martha's Vineyard and Nantucket mark the limit of the glaciers' advance in New England. Forming the spines of both Martha's Vineyard and Nantucket are *terminal moraines,* originally composed of a rubbly mix of rocks and sand pushed ahead of the advancing ice sheet and deposited when it began to retreat. A second line of *recessional moraines,* deposited during a pause in the retreat of the ice, formed the Elizabeth Islands southwest of the Cape, plus a high ridge across the base of the peninsula and bluffs along the Cape's north shore. South of the moraines lie *outwash plains,* formed when meltwater flowed in large volume from the glaciers and spread gravel, sand, and mud out into flat, level terrain. The southern coastal areas of the two islands and much of the outer Cape (north of its "elbow") are outwash plains.

Glacial Erratics

Glacial erratics are boulders carried by a glacier and deposited as it retreated. One of the largest known erratics, near Madison, New Hampshire, is 83 feet long and weighs 5,000 tons. Scientists believe this rock originated 2 miles north of its present location. Other notable glacial erratics include Doane Rock (Cape Cod National Seashore), Bartlett Boulder and Sawyer Rock (New Hampshire), Monhegan Rock (near Montville, Connecticut), and the granite erratic on Cadillac Mountain (Maine), shown here.

Kettle Ponds

Kettle ponds, such as Walden Pond, near Concord, Massachusetts, are sites on moraine and outwash plains where blocks of stagnant ice broke off from the retreating ice sheet at the end of the last glacial period. The ice blocks were buried as glacial meltwater carrying debris away from the ice sheet built up plains of outwash material around and over them. The ice blocks melted, and the sediment burying them collapsed. The resulting depressions in the

Walden Pond, Massachusetts

sand were filled with the meltwater and continue to be replenished by precipitation and groundwater. Hundreds of kettle ponds dot the New England landscape.

Hingham Bay, southern end of Boston Harbor

Drumlins

Bunker Hill, Breeds Hill, Dorchester Heights, and the islands of Boston Harbor are clusters of drumlins. These masses of glacial debris are small, streamlined, asymmetrical hills shaped like the bowl of an upside-down spoon and tailing off in the direction in which the glacier traveled. Generally only 50 to 150 feet high and a few thousand feet long, drumlins are often easiest to see from the air.

Eskers

The Whalesback at Aurora, Maine, is an esker—a long, sinuous ridge composed of sand and gravel deposited by meltwater streams flowing in tunnels along the bottom of a melting glacier. Eskers stand as much as 50 feet above the surrounding landscape.

Esker at Aurora, Maine

Fossils

A fossil is any indication of past plant or animal life, including petrified wood, dinosaur bones, ancient seashells, footprints, or casts in the shape of an animal left in rock after the organism itself disintegrated. Almost all fossils are discovered in sedimentary rocks, usually in areas that were once underwater, which explains why many fossils are of aquatic species. Much of New England's ancient sedimentary rock was eroded by rivers or glaciers or underwent metamorphosis, which usually destroys fossils the rocks contain. Thus the region has few fossils. The two most common fossil-containing rock types in New England are shale and sandstone.

Dinosaur Tracks

The earliest documented discovery of fossil evidence of dinosaurs anywhere in the world was a set of footprints found in 1802 by a farmer's son in 200-million-year-old red sandstone near South Hadley, Massachusetts. Because scientists of the time had no knowledge of dinosaurs, the three-toed tracks were presumed to have been made by giant birds.

DINOSAUR FOOTPRINT
The photo above shows the 15″-wide footprint of a dinosaur of the genus *Eubrontes*—large, flesh-eating reptiles that lived 200 million years ago. Some 500 dinosaur footprints can be seen at Dinosaur State Park in Rocky Hill, Connecticut.

FAVOSITE FOSSILS
Fossils of two species of *Favosites,* commonly known as honeycomb coral, can be found in limestones in the Franconia, New Hampshire, area. This colonial coral, an important reef builder about 400 million years ago, lived in tropical marine waters.

FOSSILIZED FISH
Fossilized fish are common in dark shale along the bed of the Connecticut River, especially below the dam at Turners Falls, Massachusetts. Some 200 million years ago, the river was a lake whose waters were often low in oxygen, resulting in incomplete decomposition of organic matter and thus an abundance of preserved fish skeletons.

PETRIFIED TREE TRUNKS
At Odiorne Point, in coastal Rye, New Hampshire, a forest that was submerged when the sea level rose at the end of the last major glacial period is visible during very low tides. The lower portions of tree trunks and whorls of roots are preserved as rocks on the floor of the cove.

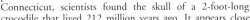

A GALLOPING CROCODILE

In March 1995, in rock exposed in a roadcut near Cheshire, Connecticut, scientists found the skull of a 2-foot-long crocodile that lived 212 million years ago. It appears closely related to a species whose fossilized remains were found in 1894 in Scotland, which at one time was joined to North America in the supercontinent known as Pangaea. The little crocodile walked on four fairly long legs and could truly gallop, with all four feet off the ground at once.

FOSSIL SEASHELLS

Several groups of fossil seashells are found in New England, including fossil bivalves, gastropods, and cephalopods. Areas where seashell fossils are found were once below sea level. The clay pits in Danvers, Massachusetts, have many 500-million-year-old bivalve fossils, including *Portlandia arctica,* and 225-million-year-old specimens can be found in the vicinity of Mount Tom, Massachusetts.

TRILOBITES

Extinct marine arthropods, trilobites generally occurred in shallow water. Members of the genus *Paradoxides,* which lived 400 million years ago, were among the largest trilobites, growing sometimes to several feet in length. Although it is unusual for fossils to be preserved in metamorphic rock, trilobite fossils have been found in outcrops of argillite, a metamorphosed mudstone, in Braintree and Quincy, Massachusetts.

Fossil Collections in New England Museums

DINOSAUR STATE PARK, ROCKY HILL, CT
A geodesic dome houses 500 tracks made by 20-foot-long dinosaurs 200 million years ago, as well as dioramas, murals, and a geologic time line.

PEABODY MUSEUM OF NATURAL HISTORY, YALE UNIVERSITY, NEW HAVEN, CT
Wide range of dinosaur fossils, including a skeleton of an *Apatosaurus.*

DINOSAUR HALL, SPRINGFIELD SCIENCE MUSEUM, SPRINGFIELD, MA
Connecticut Valley fossils, including dinosaur tracks, plus full-size replicas of a *Tyrannosaurus rex,* a *Stegosaurus* skeleton, and a *Coelophysis,* an early dinosaur that lived in the valley.

MUSEUM OF COMPARATIVE ZOOLOGY (PART OF THE MUSEUM OF CULTURAL AND NATURAL HISTORY), HARVARD UNIVERSITY, CAMBRIDGE, MA
Vertebrate and invertebrate fossils, including early mammals, a *Triceratops* skull, and a 42-foot-long *Kronosaurus,* a swimming reptile that pursued cephalopod prey in ocean waters.

PRATT MUSEUM OF NATURAL HISTORY, AMHERST COLLEGE, AMHERST, MA
Many fossils (including an enormous mastodon skeleton), plus partial skeletons of *Triceratops* and *Diplodocus,* and the first and one of the largest collections of dinosaur footprints found in North America.

MUSEUM OF NATURAL HISTORY, ROGER WILLIAMS PARK, PROVIDENCE, RI
More than 2,500 plant fossils, most of Rhode Island origin.

Minerals

Minerals, the building blocks of rocks, are naturally occurring inorganic, crystalline substances with characteristic chemical compositions and structures that determine their appearance. A mineral may be a single native element, such as copper or gold, or a compound of

Garnet

elements. Minerals are recognized by such physical properties as hardness, cleavage or fracture (the ways they can break), luster (the way the surface reflects light), and crystal structure. Color may be an unreliable identifying feature, since minor impurities can cause significant color variations.

QUARTZ

Crystals are six-sided, with pyramidal ends. Many colors: white, gray, red, purple, pink, yellow, green, brown, black; transparent or milky; glassy luster. One of the most common minerals; abundant in New England's intrusive igneous rocks, such as granite, and on many beaches, such as Ogunquit Beach in Maine, which is mostly clean quartz sand.

COPPER

Copper-red or pale rose-red on a fresh surface, but quickly tarnishes to copper-brown; metallic luster. Fairly soft; can be scratched by a knife. Common in volcanic rocks. First American mining company worked copper deposits near East Granby, Connecticut, as early as 1706.

TALC

Pearly whitish to pale green; feels greasy. One of the softest minerals; easily scratched by a fingernail. Used in talcum powder and, when found in massive units as "soapstone," by sculptors. Associated with metamorphic rocks such as schist and marble. Mined in Connecticut and Vermont.

RHODONITE

Distinctive pink color; near right-angle cleavage. Associated with metamorphic rocks such as marble. Massive form usually cut by narrow veins of dense, black manganese oxide. Found in Betts Manganese Quarries in Plainfield, Massachusetts.

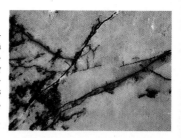

PYRITE

Golden or pale yellow; metallic luster. Occurs in many shapes—cubes and octahedra—but can be massive, occurring in nodules or flat disks. Crystal faces often marked with tiny parallel lines. Often called "fool's gold." Common in all rock types.

LIMONITE

Opaque and dull; yellow-brown. Does not form crystals; occurs as shapeless masses. Open-pit mining of limonite—chemically the same substance as rust—was an important early American mining industry; deposits were converted to pure iron. Extensive beds at Salisbury and Kent, Connecticut, and in Berkshire County, Massachusetts.

MICA

Composed of atoms arranged in perfect sheets; aggregations can be broken into flat, paper-thin plates. **Muscovite** (left): clear to white or gray tinged with yellow, green, brown, red, or violet; once used to make windows. **Biotite** (right): darker black, brown, reddish brown, or green; has greater iron and magnesium content. Both types abundant in metamorphic rock, such as schist, and igneous rock, such as granite. Shiny, flake-like minerals in rock are usually mica.

TOURMALINE

Crystals are round-triangular in cross section; often have vertical striations (lines). May be black, brown, blue, pink, red, green, or multi-colored. Gem-quality crystals—usually coal-black and shiny—common in coarse-grained granite of Maine.

GARNET

Typically reddish-brown gemstone. Hard and resistant to erosion. Formed in rocks that have undergone significant metamorphism, this "index mineral" helps geologists determine pressure and temperature of metamorphism that has taken place in surrounding rock. Pinkish color of Popham Beach, near Bath, Maine, is due to high proportion of tiny garnet fragments in sand.

Rocks

A given rock may be composed of only one mineral or may be an aggregate of different minerals. Rocks provide a tangible record of many geologic processes that are impossible to observe directly—for example, the melting of rocks in earth's interior. The identification of rocks can sometimes be difficult, but clues are provided by their constituent minerals, grain size, and overall texture.

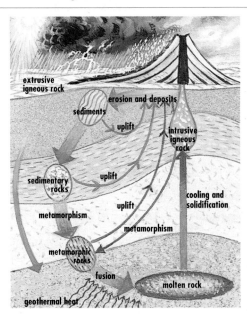

The Rock Cycle

The three basic classes of rocks undergo processes that convert them from one form to another. *Igneous* rocks form through solidification of molten material from earth's interior. Extrusive igneous rock forms on earth's surface through volcanic activity; intrusive igneous rock solidifies below the surface. *Sedimentary* rocks form from consolidation of layers of sediment (fragments of older, weathered rock ranging in size from submicroscopic particles to boulders, and/or organic or chemical matter) deposited at earth's surface. *Metamorphic* rocks form when existing rocks are transformed through heat and/or pressure. Deep within the earth, metamorphic rock is fused into molten rock. As the small arrows on the drawing indicate, the complete cycle can be interrupted at any point. New England has an abundance of metamorphic and igneous rock and very little sedimentary rock. Plate-tectonic collisions resulted in great pressure (metamorphism) and the volcanic release of lava (igneous rock), and millions of years of river erosion and the more recent glaciers removed great amounts of sediment.

Bedrock Geology

Bedrock is continuous solid rock either exposed at earth's surface or covered by soil and sediment. Most New England bedrock is hidden by glacial clay, sand, gravel, and outwash. Along the western border of New England, bedrock is mainly the metamorphic rocks slate and marble. Most central and coastal New England bedrock is comprised of a wider variety of metamorphic rocks, including slates, schists, gneisses, marbles, and quartzites. Throughout the Connecticut Valley of southern New England, basalts and sandstones are the most common bedrock. New England bedrock is characterized by numerous igneous intrusions, many composed of granite.

Oldest Rock

The oldest rocks in New England are a circular arrangement called the Chain Lakes Massif, located northwest of Eustis, Maine, along the Quebec border; similar rocks occur on Isleboro Island, Maine. These gneisses (coarse-grained rocks with a banded appearance), dated at 1.6 billion years, are a highly metamorphosed part of the foundation of North America.

GRANITE

Intrusive igneous rock. *Appearance:* speckled pink, white, and gray-black; large, coarse-grained crystals. *Constituent minerals:* quartz (clear to white), feldspar (pink or white), and dark-colored mica. A common New England rock type, found in much of coastal Maine and White Mountains of New Hampshire.

BASALT

Extrusive igneous rock, formed as lava erupts at or near earth's surface. *Constituent minerals:* feldspar and pyroxene. *Appearance:* dark green to black; very fine-grained; shape depends on where rock came to surface. **Columnar basalt** (top): geometrically shaped pillars formed at or near surface; common in Connecticut Valley. **Pillow basalts** (bottom): sac-shaped lumps formed as lava rose through earth's crust and chilled rapidly in cold seawater; can be seen on Barred Islands in Penobscot Bay, Maine, and in Connecticut Valley in Massachusetts and Connecticut.

CONGLOMERATE

Sedimentary rock; often called puddingstone. *Constituent material:* rounded boulders, gravels, and pebbles cemented together when sediments are buried. *Appearance:* multi-colored; large-grained; overall texture often bumpy; individual grains smooth. Common on south side of Blue Hills (where Routes 128 and 28 cross south of Boston) and atop Mount Battie in Camden Hills State Park, Maine.

SANDSTONE (BROWNSTONE)

Sedimentary rock. *Appearance:* brownish red in New England (thus the name "brownstone"), from iron oxides that cement together dominant *constituent minerals:* sand-size quartz and feldspar grains. Features preserved in sandstone—such as ripple marks, cross-bedding, and raindrop impressions—provide clues about the environment in which the sediment accumulated.

SHALE

Fine-grained sedimentary rock. *Constituent minerals:* mixture of clay minerals, quartz, mica, and feldspar. *Appearance:* usually grayish to black; often finely layered; splits easily along relatively flat planes. Forms in aquatic environments; often contains fossils. Black shale, common in the Connecticut Valley, contains some of the few fossils found in New England.

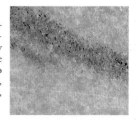

SLATE

Smooth, hard metamorphic rock originating as compacted shale. *Appearance:* color depends on *constituent minerals:* red and purple slate has abundant iron oxides; green slate has high amounts of chlorite. Cleaves (breaks) readily into sheets. Quarried in Monson, Maine, and in Taconic Mountains of southwestern Vermont.

MARBLE

Metamorphosed limestone; in New England, dates from 450 million years ago. *Appearance:* fine- to medium-grained; normally white, but accessory minerals may produce colors—black, green, red, and yellow to brown—that often occur in spots, blotches, or veins. Mined in Milford, Connecticut, and Green Mountains of Vermont.

SCHIST

Metamorphic rock common in Appalachians; formed from such other rocks as shale, sandstone, conglomerate, basalt, slate, and granite. *Appearance:* color depends on constituent materials: can be blue, green, or other colors; medium- to coarse-grained; breaks into thin, wavy sheets. *Constituent minerals:* half are platy minerals (those that separate into flat sheets), usually micas (muscovite and biotite); also quartz, feldspar, chlorite, and garnet.

Can be seen in greenish roadcuts on Route 16 in New Hampshire (between West Ossipee and Chocorua); on I-93 throughout New Hampshire; on I-89 between Burlington and Montpelier, Vermont; and on I-95 around Portland, Maine. Highest peaks of White Mountains are made of schist.

Habitats

Depending on the meaning assigned to the word "habitat"—a definition on which few authorities agree—New England has anywhere from a few habitats to hundreds of them. We have chosen to present nine widespread, characteristic natural environments, the majority of which are common to all New England states, with exceptions: Vermont is the only state in the region without a seacoast, and the three southern New England states have no alpine areas within their boundaries and almost no northern coniferous forest—a mere touch at the top of the tallest peaks in Massachusetts.

The northern broadleaf forest is geographically the largest forest type in the region; along with the southern New England forest it makes up most of the land area in New England. The 20th century has seen a great change in distribution of New England habitats, with the gradual reforestation of much of the region, as well as degradation and loss of wetlands, expansion of suburbs, and the extensive disappearance of open areas. Still, New England remains a landscape that is rich in habitat variety and suitable for a lifetime of exploration.

The habitats pictured below and types of natural communities included within each are described on the pages that follow.

NORTHERN CONIFER FORESTS AND ALPINE REGIONS

NORTHERN BROADLEAF FORESTS

SOUTHERN NEW ENGLAND FORESTS

OPEN AREAS

FRESHWATER WETLANDS

OPEN INLAND WATER AND WATERWAYS

SEACOASTS

OCEANS AND BAYS

CITIES AND SUBURBS

Northern Conifer Forests and Alpine Regions

New England's coniferous woods are so dark and thick in parts that all animal sound seems to issue from the only open areas available, the treetops. Cape May, Blackpoll, and Blackburnian Warblers sing their high-pitched songs from the tips of spruces in early summer, and Red Squirrels fuss at almost everything in their arboreal territories. Generations of Moose have traveled the well-worn trails. At the higher elevations, on the Mount Katahdin tableland and in the Green and White Mountains, isolated populations of glacial-era plants and animals—such as Bigelow's Sedge and the Mount Katahdin race of the Polixenes Arctic butterfly—exist in a glorious and fragile alpine environment.

Spruce forest, Cathedral Woods, Monhegan Island, Maine

Spruce-Fir Forests

Growing in the coolest, wettest corners of New England, spruce-fir forests (often called boreal forests) occupy three distinct regions: high mountains from northwestern Maine to southern Vermont, boggy peatlands in the same range, and the fog-shrouded coast of eastern Maine. The coastal forests are dominated by Red and White Spruces, those surrounding bogs by Black Spruces and Tamaracks, and the mountain forests by Balsam Firs and Red Spruces. These dark coniferous woodlands—foresters call conifers "softwoods"— are almost devoid of ground cover vegetation, as little light penetrates the thick evergreen groves. The attractive Bunchberry is one species that thrives in the highly acidic soil in these low-light surroundings. Spruce Grouse survive in these dark groves by eating conifer needles, while wood warblers and insects abound in summer. No New England forest is more fragrant.

Krummholz, Mount Washington, New Hampshire

Krummholz

Krummholz (German for "crooked wood") is the very tangled, stunted, low-growing forest that exists on mountain slopes in a narrow belt just below the tree line. Krummholz grows only as tall as the insulating snow layer permits, usually only a few feet; high winds and bitter winter temperatures prevent growth above this level. Few birds inhabit the krummholz, a harsh environment for much of the year. One that nests here exclusively is Bicknell's Thrush; from late May through July its song is the characteristic sound of this forest type. Higher peaks in all three northern New England states have trails leading up into the krummholz.

Alpine Zone

Once you pass the tree line, you are in the alpine zone. Sedges, lichens, and dwarf wildflowers abound in this most hostile of New England environments. The animals here are mainly invertebrates that spend most of their lives in hibernation, with perhaps a few-week summer breeding period. New Hampshire's Presidential Range has nearly 8 square miles above timberline, including Mount Washington's Alpine Gardens, where hardy wildflowers and the blackish-grayish White Mountain race of the Melissa Arctic butterfly can be seen. Other alpine areas occur atop Vermont's Mount Mansfield and Camel's Hump and on Maine's Mount Katahdin.

Alpine zone, Mount Washington, New Hampshire

Northern Broadleaf Forests

Northern Broadleaf Forests

Northern broadleaf forest covers most of Maine and Vermont, two-thirds of New Hampshire, and the Berkshire Hills in western Massachusetts. Dominated by maples, birches, and American Beech—broadleaf trees for which the forest is named—it commonly includes such conifers as Eastern Hemlocks, Eastern White Pines, and spruces. One of the great glories of the New England scene is its fall foliage, and this is the forest that produces the most spectacular display. From mid-September through mid-October, maples take on brilliant orange and red hues, while birches and beeches turn radiant yellow and gold (see page 102 for a description of how leaves turn color and a map of fall foliage periods in New England). Those who know the northern broadleaf woods visit them at other seasons as well, for they are marvelous year-round.

Maple-birch-beech woods along Howe Brook Trail, Baxter State Park, Maine

Maple-Birch-Beech Woods

The forest floor beneath this deciduous woodland holds a dark, fertile soil rich in minerals and humus. A comparatively open canopy allows sunlight to stream down upon the thick mat of forest leaf litter, establishing a rich, open environment perfect for the growth of numerous shrubs, wildflowers, and tree seedlings. Woodland butterflies such as the White Admiral can be abundant in summer. This forest is home to a full complement of vertebrates, from Red Efts (Eastern Newts) to Yellow-bellied Sapsuckers to Common Porcupines. Black Bears, White-tailed Deer, and Moose forage extensively here.

White Pine Woods

Eastern White Pines

Eastern White Pines grow scattered about the northern broadleaf forest, especially in New England's central regions, and often occur in quite extensive stands on drier, sandier soils. Do not expect a richness of plant diversity here, for the pine needles that carpet the forest floor are low in phosphorous, calcium, and potassium, elements essential to plant growth. A few species adapted to this acidic environment, such as the Canada Mayflower, occur in abundance. Eastern White Pines provide perfect nest sites for several hawk, owl, and woodpecker species, and food for the immature stages of hundreds of species of beetles, moths, and other insects.

Hemlock Woods

Whereas Eastern White Pines prefer sunnier, drier, sandier sites, Eastern Hemlocks reach their greatest abundance in cool, moist areas, and commonly occur throughout most regions of the northern broadleaf forest. Near the southern reaches of the forest, however, Eastern Hemlocks are much more common in cold, dark ravines and on shaded hillsides. The inquisitive, noisy Red-breasted Nuthatch may be heard among the hemlock boughs. Hemlocks can grow to majestic size if spared the ravages of fire, which is much more devastating to them than it is to broadleaf trees such as Red Maples and oaks, which easily sprout back to life from burned stumps; a serious fire will wipe out hemlocks for decades.

Eastern Hemlock woods in spring, Petersham, Massachusetts

Southern New England Forests

Hike through any of the forests of southern New England and chances are you eventually will find your path blocked by a lichen-covered stone wall. The trademark New England stone walls that cross untold miles of upland woodlands speak of the drama of the changing landscape—of the innumerable fieldstones left by the scouring glaciers, of the clearing of the original forests by farmers, of the subsequent abandonment and regrowth of the land. These woods, which are primarily a mixture of broadleaf and coniferous trees, are a patchwork of southern and northern species, comparatively short and open in places, tall and dense in others. Mushrooms of every description and reintroduced Wild Turkeys are two features of the landscape. As their name suggests, these forests cover almost all of Rhode Island, Connecticut, and Massachusetts, except for the Berkshire Hills, as well as a few low-lying, southern areas of Vermont, New Hampshire, and Maine.

Great Bay National Wildlife Refuge, Newington, New Hampshire

Transition Forests

A transition forest is just what its name implies, a transitional blend zone between southern and northern New England forest types. Oaks, birches, maples, and Eastern White Pines grow in different parts of the forest, which occurs in a diagonal band from northwestern Connecticut to southwestern Maine, with northward tongues well up the Merrimack and Connecticut River valleys. Resident White-tailed Deer, Common Raccoons, and Eastern Gray Squirrels abound. The songs of the Black-throated Green Warbler, Black-throated Blue Warbler, and Solitary, Red-eyed, and Yellow-throated Vireos, which glean arboreal insects and their larvae, may be heard throughout these woods from May to July.

Oak-Hickory Forests

Chestnut Oaks, Barkhamsted, Connecticut

Spreading across Connecticut, Rhode Island, eastern Massachusetts, and a bit north along the coast, this is a modern forest, grown up on post-agricultural land in the 20th century. Various oaks and hickories dominate the open, relatively dry woods canopy, while Sassafras is common in the understory. Ground cover includes native ferns, wildflowers, shrubs, and, in places, invasive introduced species. Japanese Barberry, armed with spines and doggedly aggressive, forms an impenetrable shrub layer in some parts of this forest. Eastern Screech-Owls find deer mice, Southern Flying Squirrels, woodland moths, and earthworms aplenty for feeding their broods. Virginia Opossums—active, like owls, mainly at night—may sometimes be glimpsed padding along woodland paths.

Pine-Oak Woods

An impoverished, sandy soil keeps the variety of trees to a minimum in the pine-oak woodlands that are characteristic of Cape Cod and that also spread across much of southeastern Massachusetts and north-central Rhode Island. Tall Pitch Pines and small, multibranched Bear Oaks often occur together and greatly outnumber all other species. The name Pitch Pine refers to the high resin content of the knotty wood; the American colonists produced turpentine and tar they used for axle grease from this species. The Eastern Towhee and the Fowler's Toad race of Woodhouse's Toad share the woodland floor with the Trailing Arbutus, or Mayflower, whose pinkish-white blossoms herald the New England spring.

View from Rattlesnake Ledge, West Greenwich, Rhode Island

Open Areas

Most of the Northeast's drier open areas are communities kept open in some part by the hand of humankind. (Such areas, known as uplands, are above the water table, while wetlands are on a level with it.) Perhaps more than any other regional habitat, open areas are disappearing in the face of rampant development. Grassland sparrows, Upland Sandpipers, and much of the unique grassland flora are all under siege; carefully maintained short-grass airstrips at military bases are the last strongholds for these species. The Massachusetts Audubon Society and other environmental groups are developing strategies for saving this most endangered of New England habitats.

Heathland, Nantucket Island, Massachusetts

Heathlands

Dominated by shrubs and wildflowers of the heath family, New England heathlands are the preferred habitat of several declining birds, such as the graceful Northern Harrier, the Grasshopper Sparrow, and the Short-eared Owl. The blueberry barrens of easternmost Maine and the moors of outer Cape Cod and its nearby islands are fine examples of heathlands. Members of the heath family can tolerate salt spray and poor soils while nonheath species cannot, so coastal heathlands remain open naturally.

Hay and Dairy Fields

Visit a New England hay or dairy field in June and the sweeping grasses, lively daisies, ebullient Bobolink choruses, and delicate Common Ringlet butterflies will bring the wildlife potential of open, grassy meadows into clear focus.

Vermont dairy field

Daniel Webster Wildlife Sanctuary, in Marshfield, Massachusetts, has these species, plus many open country predators, from Coyotes to Short-eared Owls. Both the Common Ringlet and the Coyote have expanded their ranges into New England in recent years.

Corn field with Canada Geese

Corn Fields

Corn fields from Vermont to Connecticut provide autumn and winter grazing areas for thousands of resident, migrant, and wintering Canada Geese. Mice and voles use these fields and provide food for owls and foxes. Flocks of Horned Larks and migrating American Pipits also are fond of corn stubble.

Abandoned Fields

Throughout New England, untended fields resprout naturally from generations of viable seeds lying in the soil. Within a few seasons, a patch of seemingly barren ground can be rife with grasses and wildflowers, tiny shrubs and saplings, and in-vertebrate and vertebrate ani-

New Hampshire field

mals. Especially in eastern and southern parts of New England, Little Bluestem grass and Eastern Red Cedar trees sprout up in post-agricultural fields. Little Bluestem supports the cater-pillars of moths and butterflies, while Eastern Red Cedar is a superb site for songbirds. Eastern Cottontails, Woodchucks, and mice move in when grasses have grown sufficiently to provide food and cover. A score of late-summer and fall goldenrod species thrive in this habitat.

Logan Airport, Boston, Massachusetts

Airports

Dotted across the region, airfields are the prairies of present-day New England. Expanses covered with closely cropped or mown grass replicate land kept open and free of brush by naturally occurring fires. The larger airports, some monitored by wildlife agencies, provide much-needed habitat for breeding grassland songbirds, such as Grasshopper Sparrows and Upland Sandpipers, and for win-tering Snowy Owls. These uncommon species have their most con-centrated New England populations in such fields.

Power-line Corridors

Cleared of woody vegetation on a regular basis, power-line corridors are becoming one of the region's most important open spaces. Many scrub-lov-ing birds, such as Indigo Buntings, Blue-winged War-blers, and Prairie Warblers, find the habitat suits them,

Power-line corridor in western Vermont

providing excellent cover and food resources; these species and oth-ers prefer open scrub that is adjacent to woodlands and fairly swarm to power-line corridors because of this. Power-line swaths can be good for butterfly watching, too, as their openness encourages the growth of adult and larval food plants, such as Spotted Joe-Pye-weed and Meadowsweet.

Freshwater Wetlands

Wetlands recharge our water tables, absorb and hold flood waters, filter out water impurities and pollutants, and provide shelter and food for an array of animals from tadpoles to Great Blue Herons. Botanists search out rare orchids and bizarre insect-eating plants in wetlands. Amphibian and dragonfly lovers find the creatures that attract them in wetlands, and birders look for furtive rails and bitterns there. Getting around on foot in the muck of swamps and marshes can be a tricky business, but walking is sometimes eased by raised paths or boardwalks. In the end, the rewards are always worth the effort. Wetlands of all types occur in every New England state.

Freshwater Marshes

Marsh, Baxter State Park, Maine

The wettest New England wetlands, marshes generally have shallow standing water throughout the year and always have saturated soils and few or no trees. Marshes form along slow-moving streams and at pond and lake borders throughout the region. They may be alkaline or acidic, and large or quite compact. Marsh plants, generally herbaceous, may be emergent (rooted in shallow water) or floating species; the greatest number are reeds, sedges, rushes, and grasses. Cattails are one of the most common marsh plants but in many areas are being muscled out by the non-native, invasive Purple Loosestrife and Common Reed. Fragmentation (through construction of roads and buildings) and degradation (from introduced plant species and pollution) threaten marshes, but the habitat continues to support many vertebrates, including most frogs and the Red-winged Blackbird, and vast numbers of invertebrates. The most conspicuous marsh insects are flies (including mosquitoes) and dragonflies.

Bogs

Wet, spongy areas rich in plant residues, bogs are home to unique life forms, which is why they are beloved by naturalists. Bogs form where water accumulates and sits. Lack of water movement produces low oxygen levels and high acidity, conditions few plants can tolerate. Carnivorous and other bog plants, such as Northern Pitcher Plants, sedges, heaths, and *Sphagnum* mosses, are chemically adapted to survive in this

Bog, Great Wass Island Preserve, Maine

Swamp, Green Mountain National Forest, Vermont

nutrient-poor environment and often grow in a thick mat. New England bogs are an excellent habitat for Four-toed Salamanders and dragonflies, including species that are otherwise rare in the region. Northern New England is the region's best bog country. *Note:* The possibility of falling through the mat is small, but it is wise to explore bogs with a companion.

Swamps

While swamps, freshwater wetlands with shrubs or trees, occur throughout New England, Red Maple swamps, named for their dominant tree species, are the most common wetlands in the southern part of the region. There are 300,000 acres of Red Maple swamp in Massachusetts alone, and 200 vertebrate and more than 400 plant species occur in this richly diverse environment. Skunk Cabbage blossoms with the earliest thaws, while the Cinnamon Fern's massive fronds add to the swamp's summer splendor. Rhode Island's Great Swamp is a fine place to get acquainted with the habitat, as is the Hockomock Swamp of southeastern Massachusetts.

Moist meadow, Moosehorn National Wildlife Refuge, Maine

Moist Meadows

Drier than marshes and with many more grasses than sedges, moist meadows are unequaled as insect study sites, with damselflies, dragonflies, and butterflies especially prominent. Nodding Ladies' Tresses, which flower in these meadows in late summer, are one of New England's most common orchids. Moist meadows may be flooded only in spring, gradually drying out during summer, when streams and rainwater keep the soils damp. Many of these meadows, kept open by earlier agricultural practices, are gradually being overgrown and are disappearing from the landscape.

Open Inland Water and Waterways

It may well be impossible to tally up all of New England's rivers, streams, lakes, and ponds. The glaciers transfigured this land, leaving thousands upon thousands of troughs, valleys, basins, and other low spots in their wake. Over the years these depressions filled with water; some of them evolved into major rivers and others into untold numbers of nameless ponds and streams. Waterways and their surrounding bottomlands are tremendously important to the survival of the vast majority of the region's wildlife. These immensely productive systems are critical to fishes, amphibians, certain mammals, such as beavers, muskrats, and otters, and legions of aquatic invertebrates. Their edges provide nesting and feeding grounds for migrating and breeding birds, from Spotted Sandpipers to Great Blue Herons. Perhaps nowhere in the world do Ospreys nest as densely as upon nesting platforms in Massachusetts' Westport River.

Pond at Waseeka Wildlife Sanctuary,
Hopkinton, Massachusetts

Ponds

Shallower and sometimes more ephemeral than lakes, and typically with abundant plant life, ponds are home to a sometimes bewildering array of life, including the handsome Northern Water Snake and the surpassingly beautiful Fragrant Water-lily. A pail of pond water with some bottom sediment is likely to reveal an amazing miniature pondscape, replete with tadpoles, fingernail clams, leeches, snails, water striders, and dragonfly naiads.

Lakes

From sprawling Lake Champlain to the more modest lakes of southern New England to Allagash Lake in the northern Maine wilderness, the region is rich in lakes. It is depth rather than surface area that distinguishes a lake from a pond: a lake is a still body of water deep enough so that at least some part does not receive sunlight on the bottom, making plant growth impossible. Lakes are prime habitat for Common Loons, migrant and nesting waterfowl, and all of the region's large freshwater game fishes.

Squam Lake, New Hampshire

Macedonia Brook State Park, Kent, Connecticut

Streams and Brooks

Ecologists call them first, second, and third order streams, but New Englanders refer to most of them as brooks or creeks. Beloved for trout as well as for spring-flowering Jack-in-the-pulpits, New England brooks offer some of the most splendid settings in the region—trout, as the saying goes, don't live in ugly places. Smaller and shallower than rivers, streams and brooks and creeks provide living quarters for stonefly and mayfly larvae, brook salamanders, crayfishes, and Minks. Speckled Alders may hide a family of Yellow Warblers or a Smooth Green Snake within their thick, sheltering branches.

Rivers

Rivers and their valleys are the region's natural transportation system, used for travel by Native Americans, modern New Englanders, and migrating fishes and birds alike. Elegant willows drape the banks of many New England rivers. New Hampshire's Nashua River Basin is a glowing example of restoration and preservation of the historical and scenic elements of a river ravaged by pollution and neglect.

Parker River, Massachusetts

Seacoasts

New England coastal profiles present dramatically different outlines—the northern coastlines are frequently jagged, rocky headlands, while to the south, warm-water bays and sandy beaches are characteristic. Myriad rock-loving barnacles and Blue Mussels give way to beds of Eastern Oysters as one heads southward. Cape Cod National Seashore, Acadia National Park, and many national wildlife refuges preserve the richness of the region's coastal environments. With 250,000 acres of coastal wetlands, New England supports an impressive variety of shoreline flora and fauna.

Swans Island, Maine

Rocky Shores

Seaweed-covered rocky shorelines, with their full complement of organisms, including Blue Mussels, Northern Rock Barnacles, and sea stars, all of which can take the steady pounding of North Atlantic waves, are a major feature of the New England coastline from eastern Maine south to Boston. Tidepools—gullies and depressions left filled with seawater when the tide recedes—offer shelter for marvelous sea anemones and nudibranchs. Various green algae are common and provide food for grazing invertebrates, including periwinkles. Double-crested Cormorants, common from April to November, rest and feed along much of New England's rocky coastline.

Barrier Beaches

American Beach Grass, Beach Heath, Beach Plum, and other hardy vegetation grip the sand, hold the dunes in place, and help keep 300 miles of New England barrier beaches intact. These beaches—low-lying strips of land that lie parallel to the main coast, sometimes as offshore formations but more often attached to the mainland at one or both ends and backed by marshes—help hold back the Atlantic during nor'easters and provide habitat for rare nesting birds. They occur mainly to the south of Cape Elizabeth, Maine; the granite bedrock of the coast farther north rarely erodes, providing little sediment to form sandy beaches and dunes. Piping Plovers and Least Terns have to cope with marauding gulls and ever-increasing human populations along New England's barrier beaches, but are surviving.

Cape Cod: Outer Nauset Beach protects Pleasant Bay

Scarborough Marsh, Scarborough, Maine

Salt Marshes

Behind the barrier beaches and along the estuaries, salt marshes—low-growth habitats that are made up mainly of nonwoody plants and that are regularly inundated with salt water—are the region's dominant coastal wetlands, especially in southern New England. The flushing action of the tides, which drains the marsh of harmful wastes and then re-floods it with nutrients, is what makes this one of the richest habitats on earth. The greater part of a salt marsh, flooded only during the highest monthly tides and called the *high marsh,* is carpeted by Saltmeadow Cordgrass. Look here for the lovely Sea Lavender and jettisoned exoskeletons of Atlantic Horseshoe Crabs. The *low marsh,* at the edge of the flats, is flooded twice daily; its dominant vegetation is the noticeably taller Saltmarsh Cordgrass. Recognized as an invaluable nursery ground for countless sea fishes, mollusks, shrimp, and crabs, salt marshes are feeding grounds for a host of aquatic and terrestrial predators; these marshes also generate nutrients that flow into nearby bays and coastal areas.

Tidal flats, Cape Cod National Seashore

Tidal Flats

At low tide, vast expanses of tidal flats, both sandy and muddy, stretch outward from estuary shorelines in a broad intertidal zone (the area between the high- and low-tide lines). Resident creatures of the flats have to be burrowers to escape twice-daily exposure to air and the ravenous appetites of migrant shorebirds like the Black-bellied Plover. Soft-shelled Clams and duck clams of the genus *Macoma* are locally abundant. Among the region's best tidal flats are those at the Monomoy National Wildlife Refuge on Cape Cod, the Joppa Flats along the Merrimack River in Newburyport, Massachusetts, and the flats at Milford Point, Connecticut.

Oceans and Bays

New England coastal waters, from the fog-shrouded Bay of Fundy to the placid harbors of Long Island Sound, host legions of animals, microscopic to colossal. The great jutting arm of Cape Cod is the natural boundary between northern and southern waters; ocean temperatures average 10 degrees higher on the south side of the Cape than to the north. Many marine organisms living from Labrador south and from North Carolina north reach their range limits here. Within genera and families there are often cold-water species found in waters from the Cape north, and other warmer-water species from the Cape south. Unfortunately, the history of these marine creatures and their habitats is one of exploitation, and it is only recently that strict environmental regulations have been enacted to help protect this extraordinarily rich environment.

Harbor at Newburyport, Massachusetts

Bays and Inlets

The New England coastline is punctuated along its length with a dizzying number of inlets and bays, many of which form natural harbors. Maine, with a point-to-point coastal length of 230 miles, has an actual mainland shoreline of approximately 3,500 miles when the extent of all of the peninsulas, coves, and bays, wandering in and out in every compass direction, is tallied. New England's in-shore waters harbor large populations of that most famous and delicious of crustaceans, the lobster. Common Eiders raft by the hundreds in shoals and bays through the winter months.

Coastal Islands

Small coastal islands, many only a few acres in extent, some barely more than a sand spit, have proven critical to the survival of New England terns, shorebirds, and herons during the breeding season. Away from dogs, foxes, raccoons, and other land predators, the colonies thrive. Most colonies are regularly monitored, and many are carefully protected by state and federal agencies. Maritime

Monomoy Island, Massachusetts

vegetation, such as the Beach Rose, is the critical holdfast that keeps sandy islands from being swept away by storm tides and winds.

Shallow Banks

A submarine topography of ledges, banks, basins, and channels provides ideal conditions for concentrating huge numbers of plankton and small fishes. Throughout the year, storms and steady rushing currents force upwellings that bring rich concentrations of these foods to the ocean surface, and whales and seabirds from as far away as Antarctica travel to Stellwagen Bank off the Massachusetts coast to feast on them. Whale-watching boats naturally target the same area. Georges Bank, a sandbank approximately 100 miles off the Massachusetts coast and roughly 65 feet below the sea surface, has historically been one of the most productive fishing grounds off the East Coast. A local spinning current corrals a combination of cold, nutrient-rich waters from the north and warmth from the central Atlantic Ocean and Gulf Stream, creating a hospitable environment for 100 species of fish and dozens of other species, including marine birds, whales, dolphins, and porpoises. (For information on the overfishing that has led to severe depletions and recent efforts to protect fish populations, see page 240.)

Humpback Whales

Cities and Suburbs

Eastern and southern New England have had burgeoning populations for almost 400 years, and suburban sprawl has settled across a large part of the land. Much wildlife has retreated in the face of skyscrapers, strip malls, and housing complexes, but even in the biggest cities Black-capped Chickadees visit third-story window feeders and Common Nighthawks and Killdeers transform flat-topped gravel roofs into nesting territories. Homeowners may complain about Woodchucks and Eastern Gray Squirrels and even flocks of boisterous Common Grackles, but each year's sales of garden seedlings and wild bird feed set records and help ensure that the not-so-wild suburbs will continue to attract their share of adaptable wildlife.

New England summer garden

Gardens

Gardens are not essential environments for any native New England species but are wonderful places to enjoy butterflies and other insects and, of course, flowers and shrubs throughout the seasons. Flowering shrubs provide nest sites, shelter, and food for birds, while Bee Balms, Black-eyed Susans, and other flowers attract butterflies and occasional Ruby-throated Hummingbirds. Two of a number of good places to learn about gardening with native plant species are the New England Wildflower Society's Garden in the Woods, in Framingham, Massachusetts, and Gilsland Farm, just north of Portland, Maine.

Urban Parks

City planners have saved a bit of New England nature for city dwellers, with parks, arboretums, and even garden cemeteries integrated into the urban landscape. Two of the most notable landscape

Swan Point Cemetery, Providence, Rhode Island

Female Peregrine Falcon on nest

designers were Frederick Law Olmsted and Charles Eliot, who laid out Boston's "Emerald Necklace" green spaces. Massive songbird flights, called warbler waves, can be seen in May at such urban oases as East Rock Park in New Haven, Connecticut, Swan Point Cemetery in Providence, Rhode Island, Forest Park in Springfield, Massachusetts, and Mount Auburn Cemetery in Cambridge, Massachusetts.

Buildings and Bridges

By 1966 Peregrine Falcons, because of DDT poisoning, had completely disappeared as a breeding bird in the East. In recent years, wildlife biologists have coaxed Peregrines into nesting successfully on bridges and tall buildings in New England and elsewhere. Other species, such as the cacophonous European Starling, find nesting and roosting sites among urban structures large and small. Chimney Swifts, visiting New England after spending the winter feeding over South American forests and savannas, depend on city and suburban chimneys for nest sites.

Suburban Backyards

Through the use of native and ornamental plantings, man-made pools, and feeding stations, suburban properties attract a surprising range of wildlife. Backyard wildlife spotting is a popular hobby, and wildlife agencies have taken advantage of this, gathering valuable data through surveys of backyard mammals, birds, and insects.

European Starling at nest box

The Effects of Humans

New England's primeval forests, with their soaring Eastern White Pines and magnificent American Chestnuts, thrived until 400 years ago. Since the first Europeans set foot here, this corner of the continent has undergone cataclysmic change. In a matter of generations, European settlers transformed, completely and irrevocably, lands the Native Americans had scarcely altered in 10,000 years. The fields that replaced the forests, the wildflowers that grow in the fields, the insects that visit the wildflowers—in these and myriad other features, New England's landscape, fauna, and flora have been greatly transfigured. The effects of human activities shown here are but a few of thousands.

Beaver lodge, Holderness, New Hampshire

The Beaver and Man

American Beavers were once abundant in New England. From 1631 to 1636, some 12,500 pounds of beaver pelts were shipped to England from the Plymouth colony alone. However, overtrapping took its toll: by 1700 beavers were virtually eliminated from all but the northernmost areas of New England. One result: the ponds that drained when thousands of unmaintained beaver dams collapsed became fertile land for farming. Today tens of thousands of beavers have returned to New England from adjoining regions, and once again beaver dams are part of the landscape.

The Gypsy Moth

Number 27 Myrtle Street, Medford, Massachusetts, was home to Leopold Trouvelot, introducer of the Gypsy Moth to North America. Experimenting with the European moths in the 1860s, he allowed some to escape, and the rest, as foresters and homeowners throughout the region know, is sad history. Gypsy Moth caterpillars, unlike most lepidopterans, feed on an enormous range of plants—they can strip hundreds of species of trees, vines, shrubs, wildflowers, and even aquatic plants of their foliage. If an outbreak of the moths is severe, trees may be killed within a year or two.

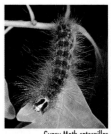

Gypsy Moth caterpillar

Introduced Plants and Animals

European Skipper

New England's successfully introduced species of plants and animals have arrived over the course of four centuries. The plants are perhaps best thought of as "alien" rather than "introduced," as they generally came as stowaway seeds that took root along roadsides and train tracks and near ports, then naturalized in open country over the years. Most New England alien plant species, including many clovers, the Oxeye Daisy, dandelions, hawkweed, Queen Anne's Lace, and Yarrow, are European in origin. Some escaped garden flowers, and trees such as the Blue Spruce and the Apple, have also spread across the region. Nearly 1,000 introduced plant species have become naturalized in New England. Many animals were deliberately introduced, often to be hunted (Ring-necked Pheasant) or fished (Largemouth Bass), or to eat city insects (European Starling and House Sparrow), or to benefit growers (Honey Bee). Unintentionally introduced animals include the abundant European Skipper and the Japanese Beetle.

The Effects of Introduced Species

Introduced species of animals and plants tend to change the landscape, sometimes dramatically and often for the worse. The European Starling is arguably New England's most common bird, and its aggressiveness has made life more demanding for smaller species such as Eastern Bluebirds. Purple Loosestrife, with its tenacious root system, is crowding out native wetland plants and changing the face of many freshwater marshes by turning

Purple Loosestrife

them into biologically unproductive monocultures. Other invasive exotics may feed on native species or carry diseases and parasites for which local organisms have few or no defenses.

The Felling of the Forests

The rigors of the New England environment, coupled with an unromantic, theological view of man's place in the wilderness, put early European settlers to work clearing the land and imposing an Old World landscape of orderly fields and town commons. The cutting of trees for fuel, but one element of the process, consumed a quarter billion cords of wood by 1800. In the 19th century, the advance of the railroads and invention of the steam sawmill sounded the death knell of New England's great surviving primeval forests. The last large stand of such forest, a 300-acre broadleaf tract in Colebrook, Connecticut, was cleared in 1913.

Conservation

In 1835, French visitor Alexis de Tocqueville wrote of the attitudes of Americans: "In Europe people talk a great deal of the wilds of America, but the Americans themselves never think about them; they are insensible to the wonders of inanimate nature, and they may be said not to perceive the mighty forests that surround them till they fall beneath the hatchet." After centuries of devastation, the notion of conservation evolved slowly, to be sure, but the health of the environment is now a key issue in all New England states.

Thoreau's cabin at Walden Pond, Concord, Massachusetts

Early Voices for the Land
The voices of New England Transcendentalist authors Ralph Waldo Emerson and Henry David Thoreau were largely lost on a 19th century hell-bent on industrialism. Emerson, in *Nature,* and Thoreau, in *Walden* and *A Week on the Concord and Merrimack Rivers,* among other works, wrote simply and eloquently of the need for a balance between humankind and nature. George Perkins Marsh, a transplanted Vermonter writing in Italy, expressed similar sentiments in *Man and Nature.*

Baxter State Park, Maine

One Man's Gift
For two decades, Percy Baxter tried to convince the state of Maine to protect the Mount Katahdin region as a state park, but his advice went unheeded. Finally, in 1930, he bought almost 6,000 acres that included most of the mountain and gave it to the state. By the 1960s, he had purchased more than 195,000 additional acres and deeded them to Maine to be kept wild forever. Baxter State Park is a magnificent testimony to one person's indefatigable conservation efforts. Thousands of others have contributed to the conservation movement on a lesser scale.

Huntington Ravine, White Mountains

The Weeks Act

The Weeks Act of 1911 made it possible for the federal government to purchase large tracts of timberland and watershed in the East from large public and private landholders. New England's national forests—the nearly 800,000-acre White Mountain National Forest and the 350,000-acre Green Mountain National Forest—directly resulted from this monumental piece of environmental legislation.

The Audubon Society Movement

The National Audubon Society has more than 30 chapters in Connecticut, Maine, and Vermont, and most New England states have Audubon organizations. The oldest and largest is the Massachusetts Audubon Society. Founded in 1896, Mass. Audubon ushered in the movement to protect threatened species and environments and to educate New Englanders about their natural heritage.

Common Tern

Cleaning New England's Rivers

Riparian corridors are enormously productive biologically and tragically abused ecologically. No U.S. ecosystem has suffered as much in the 20th century. Grassroots organizations are leading campaigns to restore rivers and streams across New England. National legislation has been critical to river restoration, while regional programs such as Adopt-a-Stream, developed by the Massachusetts Department of Fisheries, Wildlife, and Environmental Law Enforcement, have blossomed with the support of participating action committees and individuals. Such programs create public awareness and advocate for civic action.

Endangered and Recovering Species

A number of factors have critically affected the species balance of New England plants and animals since European settlement. Habitat modification has been the largest single factor in the reduction or loss of species. Hunting, pathogens (such as Dutch Elm disease and chestnut blight), pesticides, and pollutants have all contributed as well. On the positive side, modern hunting and fishing regulations, legislation, and conservation efforts on behalf of threatened and endangered species have allowed many populations of organisms to survive.

Legislation to Protect Species

The federal Endangered Species Act (1973) provides special protection to the rarest species; it prohibits trade in endangered species and subspecies or their products, and requires that federal agencies assess the impact on wildlife of proposed projects. According to the act, an endangered species or subspecies is one in danger of extinction throughout all or a significant part of its range. A threatened species is one likely to become endangered within the foreseeable future. The National Audubon Society keeps a Watch List of species that are in danger of reaching threatened or endangered status.

Plymouth Gentian

Threatened and Endangered Plants

Hundreds of New England plant species are threatened, among them the alpine-zone Robbins' Cinquefoil, an inconspicuous, yellow-flowered New England endemic (meaning it is found only here), the striking Plymouth Gentian, which grows on coastal plains, and the Spreading Globeflower, limited to four Connecticut sites. Changes in land use and natural plant succession contribute most to the disappearance of uncommon species, though a few showy or specialized plants have been subjected to unscrupulous collecting. Organizations such as the New England Wildflower Society lead the way in protecting the region's native flora through education and propagation programs.

Wood Duck

Recovering Species

The hurricane of 1938 devastated New England and wiped out most natural Wood Duck nest sites (hollows in old trees). An ambitious nesting box program since then has resulted in thousands of successful Wood Duck nestings yearly. Two other birds, the Bald Eagle and Peregrine Falcon, by the 1960s driven to near extinction in North America because of DDT poisoning, now have much healthier New England populations because of long-term programs in which introduced young birds are raised with human assistance at a site where it is hoped they will return to nest. Even the widespread and common White-tailed Deer is a study in recovery. Earlier New Englanders had hunted Whitetails off the map, but hunting restrictions have made them abundant once again.

Extinct and Extirpated Species

New England has had its share of extinctions. The Passenger Pigeon, arguably the most abundant bird species ever, was hunted (for food) into oblivion, as were the Great Auk, Labrador Duck, and Sea Mink. Locally extirpated are the Gray Wolf, Walrus, Eastern Woodland Caribou, Wolverine, and Elk. The Mountain Lion, known in New England as the Catamount, was last recorded in the region in 1881, at Barnard, Vermont.

Reforestation

Although between 1875 and 1925 the region saw its second great forest harvest, this time of second-growth timber, New Englanders were largely abandoning farm life by the early 1900s, and the landscape was again taking on a wooded appearance. States that had been three-quarters denuded by 1850 (Connecticut, Rhode Island, Massachusetts, and Vermont) were on their way to being three-quarters treed by the middle of the 20th century. Today New England is once again known for its glorious trees.

Paper Birches

Weather

New England's location at an atmospheric crossroads—halfway between the equator and the North Pole and at the meeting of landmass and sea—is the dominant factor controlling its climate. Arctic cold waves, mild breezes from the distant Pacific (modified by their long journey across the continent), moist subtropical air off the nearby Gulf Stream, and fog-laden air from the North Atlantic all converge on the region to breed a great variety of weather.

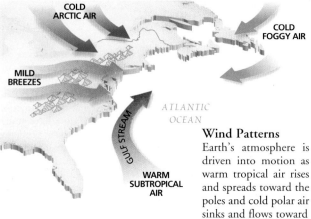

Wind Patterns

Earth's atmosphere is driven into motion as warm tropical air rises and spreads toward the poles and cold polar air sinks and flows toward the equator. Earth's rotation warps this north–south exchange of warm and cold air into vast wind patterns, including the prevailing westerlies, a broad west-to-east air current that flows over the United States and southern Canada. Most of New England's weather approaches from the west, even its notorious nor'easters.

Tracing a Nor'easter

A nor'easter can dump many inches of rain (or a foot or more of snow) across much of New England and whip the coastline with gale-force winds (39 mph or much higher).

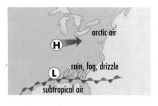

THE STAGE IS SET

All nor'easters feature an arctic high from the north and warm subtropical air (a low) from the south, with a front separating them. Before the storm system develops the front may remain stationary for a while, producing light rain or snow or heavy thunderstorms.

THE STORM BUILDS

As the storm system starts spinning in a counterclockwise direction, a warm front to the east marks the leading edge of northbound warm air. As it rises over the colder, denser air to its north, the gently rising warm air produces

Highs and Lows

Embedded in the prevailing westerlies are a succession of whirls and eddies: systems of high pressure (fair weather) and low pressure (cloudiness, high humidity, stormy weather) that form and dissipate along fronts, which are the boundaries between warm and cold air masses. Winds blow in a circular pattern around the center of Northern Hemisphere weather systems: either counterclockwise (as seen from above) in a low-pressure system or clockwise in a high-pressure system. In New England, low-pressure systems often form along a front between arctic air to the north and subtropical air from the Gulf Stream to the south. High-pressure systems may arrive from the arctic reaches of Canada and Siberia, bringing bitter cold in winter and refreshing air in summer, or cross the continent from the Pacific Ocean, bringing milder weather. During autumn months, a mild high-pressure system may become entrenched over New England, bringing pleasant "Indian summer" days.

How Storms Come and Go

While most New England storms arrive from the west, including the Canadian midwest (in the form of Alberta clippers, named for their rapid motion), and from the southern plains (Colorado lows), they may also approach from the Gulf of Mexico and the Caribbean. "Back-door" fronts, cold fronts that slip southwest from the North Atlantic, can bring sudden chill and fog in spring and relief from the heat in summer. In late summer and fall, New England is occasionally hammered by hurricanes from the south. Nor'easters, so named because northeasterly winds blow onshore from a low off the coast, may form off New England's coast or they may originate over the Gulf of Mexico, the Appalachians, or even far inland, around Colorado. Several nor'easters pound New England in an average year.

steady rain or snow. Meanwhile, west of the center, arctic air plunges south behind a cold front, along which heavier cold air shoves like a wedge beneath the warm and usually moist air. Forced upward, the warm air expands and cools, its moisture condensing into clouds, rain, or snow.

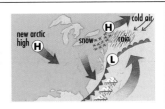

THE END OF THE STORM

After several hours, the center of low pressure passes, generally to the east or northeast, followed by the cold front, which may set off brief but heavy showers, squalls, and thunderstorms. As the storm departs, in-flowing high pressure brings clearing, colder weather

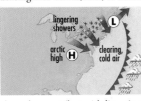

along the coast (but with lingering precipitation and clouds over the mountains and east of the Great Lakes), one or more days of fair skies, and eventually southerly winds ahead of the next storm.

Over the course of a year, New England may experience just about every kind of meteorological phenomenon, from blizzards to 100-degree heat waves.

Rain

A given location in New England gets 20 to 30 thunderstorms annually. Overall precipitation (rain, snow, sleet) is fairly evenly distributed throughout the year. Annual amounts range from 32 inches in northern Vermont to 50 inches in western Massachusetts to a high of 90 inches atop Mount Washington in New Hampshire.

Lightning

Lightning is an electrical discharge between one part of a cloud and another, between two clouds, or between a cloud and earth. In a typical year, lightning strikes New England about 350,000 times, and perhaps ten times as many flashes arc across the sky without touching the ground.

Snow

Annual snowfall amounts range from 24 inches in southern Connecticut to more than 120 inches atop Mount Washington. Although inland and highland areas receive much more snow than the coastal sections, the coast is more likely to be hit by individual large storms that dump more than a foot of snow in a day or two.

- 100 inches or more
- 60 to 100 inches
- 36 to 60 inches
- 24 to 36 inches

Record-setting New England Weather

WORST HURRICANE September 21, 1938. 186 mph winds at Blue Hill near Boston. 600 people killed, most from flooding in Connecticut River Valley and from storm-surge flooding along coasts of Connecticut, Rhode Island, and New York's Long Island.

WORST TORNADO June 9, 1953. Worcester, Massachusetts. 90 killed.

HIGHEST TEMPERATURE August 2, 1975. 107° F at Chester, Massachusetts.

LOWEST TEMPERATURE January 23, 1857. −52° F at Bath, Maine.

GREATEST BLIZZARD March 11–14, 1888. 50″ of snow at Middletown, Connecticut.

WORST FLOODING August 1955. Back-to-back hurricanes Connie and Diane, arriving four days apart, each dumped up to a foot of rain on Connecticut River Valley. 82 dead and $831 million damage.

WORST ICE STORM November 26–29, 1921. Ice 3″ thick on wires in Worcester, Massachusetts.

HIGHEST WIND EVER RECORDED ON THE PLANET April 12, 1934. 231 mph at the summit of Mount Washington.

Tornadoes

On average, nine tornadoes per year touch down in New England, most within a "tornado alley" that stretches from northern Connecticut to southeastern New Hampshire. Within this small area, the frequency of tornadoes per square mile rivals that of the much larger tornado alley of the central United States.

Ice Storms

When warm air aloft overruns a mass of cold air clinging to the ground, the result can be rain that falls as liquid but freezes on contact with everything it touches—grass, trees, roads, and wires; the resulting ice coating is called glaze. Minor ice storms, also known as freezing rain, coat the southern New England coast two to four times a year, while some valleys in the White Mountains may get freezing rain a dozen or more times.

Sleet

The conditions that create ice storms can also generate sleet. If the cold air mass near ground level is deep enough, the falling rain may freeze solid before reaching the ground, resulting in tiny ice pellets that resemble small hailstones. Sleet, usually mixed with snow, rain, or freezing rain, occurs 8 to 12 times a year across New England.

Hurricane Bob, August 19, 1991

Hurricanes

While a full-strength hurricane (a storm with winds over 73 mph) strikes New England only about every five years, nearly every year hurricanes that hit elsewhere bring substantial rains; nearly one-fourth of New England's late-summer rainfall comes from such storms. Memorable hurricanes that have hit the region include the hurricane of 1938, Hurricane Carol in 1954, and Hurricane Bob in 1991.

Seasons

New England experiences seasonal changes as pronounced as any on the planet. In most locales, the highest and lowest temperatures of the year span a 100-degree range. The region's location halfway between the equator and the North Pole makes it particularly sensitive to the changing angles of sunlight striking the ground over the course of a year, which is what causes the change of seasons.

As earth moves around its orbit, its 23.4-degree tilt on its axis means that for part of the year the Northern Hemisphere is inclined toward the sun and the sun's rays shine on it more directly; for part of the year it is tilted away from the sun and the sun's rays are more oblique. The latitude that receives the greatest heat from the sun is farther north during the summer months (though earth's surface—land and sea—takes a while to warm up, so that early August is actually hotter than late June). Atmospheric currents, such as the prevailing westerlies, in turn shift to the north. Higher sun angles and longer days in the Arctic during summer take the bite out of the polar air masses and decrease the heat difference between the tropics and the North Pole, weakening heat-driven currents.

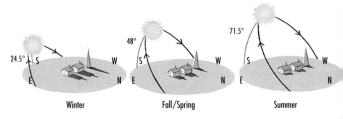

At 42° N latitude (the latitude of Plymouth, MA), the noontime sun at the winter solstice has an altitude above the horizon of only 24.5°; at the spring and fall equinoxes, its altitude is 48°; and at the summer solstice, the noontime sun rises 71.5° above the horizon.

White-tailed Deer

Spring

Spring officially begins on or about March 21, called the spring (or vernal) equinox, when the sun appears directly overhead at noon at the equator. In spring, the first incursions of mild air from the Gulf Stream and the Gulf of Mexico arrive in New England, but the Arctic can still send south bitter-cold air masses, and the clash provides some of the most violent weather of the year. March is often wintry, with nor'easters bringing cold rain and snow. In April and May, passing showers are followed by brisk sunny days.

Summer

The sun reaches its peak over the Northern Hemisphere around June 21, the longest day (that is, daylight period) of the year, known as the summer solstice. As the sun's more direct rays heat the high Arctic, tempering New England's source of cold air, and the

Lowbush Blueberry

"Bermuda High" expands inland from the Atlantic Ocean, the region experiences periods of heat and humidity. Cold fronts may skirt northern areas, holding humid air at bay and occasionally even bringing frost. In southern New England, cold fronts are much less frequent; on many days the only relief comes from sea breezes or thunderstorms bred from the humid air. Midsummer daytime temperatures average 80 degrees or higher across most of New England.

Autumn foliage, Brunswick, Maine

Fall

As it does at the spring equinox, the sun "crosses" the equator again at the fall (or autumnal) equinox, around September 22. Mid-September usually brings the first freeze of the season to uplands in Maine, Vermont, and New Hampshire, and cool air over the continent meeting warmer air from the Gulf Stream often breeds the season's first nor'easter. By the end of October, every area of New England is likely to have had a freeze. Autumn also brings Indian summer—spells of sunny, warm days after the first freeze. By early November, nor'easters have removed most of the autumn leaves from the trees.

Winter

Winter arrives on December 21, the winter solstice, but low temperatures and chilly rains and snow often make it feel like winter by early December. Inland and in the north, most precipitation falls as snow, while along the coast, rain or a mixture of sleet and snow is more likely. Late January often brings the season's coldest outbreak, and winter conditions generally persist into March.

Snowy Owl

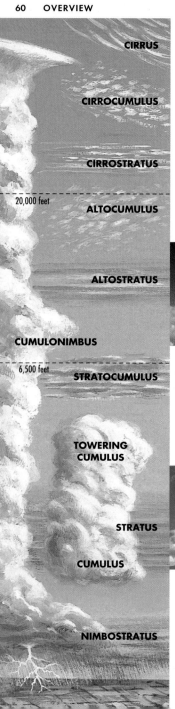

CIRRUS

CIRROCUMULUS

CIRROSTRATUS

20,000 feet

ALTOCUMULUS

ALTOSTRATUS

CUMULONIMBUS

6,500 feet

STRATOCUMULUS

TOWERING CUMULUS

STRATUS

CUMULUS

NIMBOSTRATUS

Typical Clouds

Clouds form when moist air is cooled, causing water molecules to condense into water droplets or ice crystals. While most types of clouds can be spotted over New England, the ones described here are among the most common. The illustration at left shows the relative common altitudes of the different cloud types; distances are not shown to scale.

CUMULONIMBUS
Tallest of all cloud types; commonly called thunderheads. Lower part composed of water droplets; fuzzy, fibrous top—the "anvil"—made of ice crystals. Produce lightning, thunder, heavy rain, and sometimes hail, high winds, or tornadoes.

LENTICULAR CLOUDS
Stationary, smooth-edged clouds that form at crests of air currents over mountainous terrain. Indicate high winds at mountaintop level and turbulence above mountains. Also common are more ragged **cap clouds**, formed directly on summits of higher mountains.

CUMULUS

Water-droplet clouds formed at tops of rising air currents set in motion by uneven heating of ground by sun. Domed tops, like bright white heads of cauliflower. Typical clouds of fine summer days, but can occur any time of year. More common over hilly or mountainous terrain.

TOWERING CUMULUS

Cumulus clouds grow into towering, or swelling, cumulus if atmospheric moisture is sufficient and it is much warmer at ground level than in the air aloft. May produce light showers, which in turn can develop into thunderstorms—watch for rapid billowing in tops.

CIRRUS

High (5 miles or more), thin, wispy clouds made of ice crystals; may be seen in any season, anywhere in region. In winter, cirrus thickening from west or south may signal approaching rain or snow; however, cirrus often come and go without bringing any lower clouds or rain.

ALTOSTRATUS

Middle-level clouds, mainly of water droplets; usually appear as featureless gray sheet covering sky. Thickening, low altostratus from west or south often bring steady widespread rain or snow within hours. May be seen in New England at any time of year; most common in winter.

FOG

Clouds formed at ground level; occurs up to 100 days per year in some areas. **Advection fog:** forms when humid air overruns cold surfaces, like ocean water; common on coast. **Radiation fog:** caused by overnight cooling of still air; burns off as sun rises; common in interior valleys.

STRATUS AND NIMBOSTRATUS

Stratus: low, indistinct, gray water-droplet clouds, usually covering sky in calm conditions; common in summer along coast; may become fog if close to ground. **Nimbostratus:** stratus clouds from which precipitation falls; almost always present during steady snow or rain.

Our Solar System

The sun, the nine planets that revolve around it, and their moons make up our solar system. Venus, Mars, Jupiter, and Saturn are easily visible to the naked eye; Mercury, Uranus, Neptune, and Pluto are more difficult to see. Other objects in our solar system are transient: the wide orbits of comets make them rare visitors near earth, and meteors flash brightly for only seconds before disappearing.

Sky-observing in New England

About half the nights in New England are clear enough for viewing the sky. Stars and planets are much more visible when there is little moonlight. Nights with low humidity and air pollution (such as after cleansing rains and winds) are best. Areas away from the lights of large urban centers—such as northern New England, outer Cape Cod, and offshore islands—offer optimum conditions.

FULL MOON

The full moon rises at sunset and sets at dawn. It is highest in the sky in December, up to 77 degrees above the horizon in southern New England (in summer it rises only about 25 degrees). Some lunar features show up best when the moon is full: the dark "seas" (hardened lava flows) and the "rays" of bright material splattered from craters. Craters and mountain ranges are best seen before and after full moon, when the angle of sunlight throws them into relief; look especially near the terminator, the dividing line between the moon's day and night sides. Because the moon is locked in earth's gravitational grip, the same side of the moon always faces us.

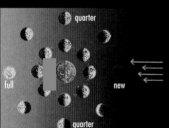

PHASES OF THE MOON

As the moon makes its monthly orbit around earth, the illuminated lunar surface area appears to grow (wax), shrink (wane), and even disappear (at new moon). The center of the illustration shows the phases, with sunlight coming from the right. The outer drawings show how the moon looks from our perspective on earth.

VENUS

Cloud-shrouded Venus alternates between being our "morning star" and "evening star," depending on where it is in its orbit. This brilliant planet usually outshines everything in the sky except the sun and moon. As it circles the sun, Venus displays phases, which can be viewed through a small telescope or high-power binoculars.

Venus (left) and the moon

MARS

Every 25½ months, when earth is aligned between Mars and the sun, Mars is closest to us and at its brightest and most colorful, appearing orange-red to the naked eye. At this time, called opposition (opposite in the sky from the sun), Mars rises at sunset and remains in the sky all night. Bright white polar caps and dusky surface markings may be glimpsed through a small telescope at opposition. Mars rivals Jupiter in brightness at opposition, but fades somewhat at other times.

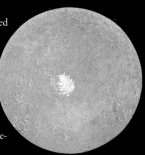

JUPITER

Visible in our morning sky for about five months at a stretch and in our evening sky for five months, Jupiter appears brighter than any star in the night sky at all times. The largest planet in our solar system, it has a diameter of 88,850 miles, 11.2 times that of earth. Jupiter's four largest moons—Ganymede, Io, Europa, and Callisto—can often be spotted with binoculars.

Jupiter (top) and moons

SATURN

Visible most of the year, Saturn appears to the naked eye as a slightly yellowish, moderately bright star. A small telescope reveals its rings, composed mainly of rocky chunks of ice, and the two largest (Titan and Rhea) of its more than 20 known moons.

METEORS

These "shooting stars" are typically chips ranging from sand-grain to marble size that are knocked off asteroids (tiny planets) or blown off comets and burn up as they strike our atmosphere. The strongest annual meteor showers are the Perseids, which peak around August 12, and the Geminids, which peak around December 13.

COMETS

Comets are irregular lumps of ice and rock left over from the formation of the solar system. Occasionally a notable comet approaches the sun as it travels in its far-ranging orbit. The sun's energy vaporizes the comet's surface, generating a tail of gas and dust that may be millions of miles long.

Comet Hale-Bopp, 1997

Stars and Deep-sky Objects

As earth orbits the sun in its annual cycle, our planet's night side faces in steadily changing directions, revealing different stars, constellations, and views of our own Milky Way. People in ancient times named constellations after mythological figures and familiar creatures whose shapes they saw outlined by the stars. The best known of these constellations lie along the ecliptic, the imaginary line that traces the apparent path of the sun through the sky. Earth, our moon, and other planets orbit in nearly the same plane, all traveling along a band roughly 16 degrees wide centered on the ecliptic and called the zodiac. (The zodiac is traditionally divided into 12 segments, but 13 constellations actually intersect it.)

Modern constellations are simply designated regions of the celestial sphere, like countries on a map. Most constellations bear little resemblance to their namesakes. Beyond the approximately 6,000 stars visible to the naked eye lie other fascinating deep-sky objects—star clusters, galaxies, nebulas (gas clouds)—that can be seen, some with the naked eye and others with binoculars or a small telescope.

The Zodiac

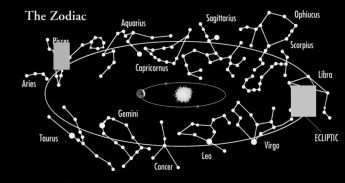

Ophiucus · *Sagittarius* · *Aquarius* · *Pisces* · *Scorpius* · *Capricornus* · *Libra* · *Aries* · *ECLIPTIC* · *Gemini* · *Taurus* · *Virgo* · *Leo* · *Cancer*

Seasonal Sky Maps

The following pages show star maps for each of the four seasons, drawn at a latitude of 45 degrees north for the specific times and dates given. (If you wish to observe at a different time or date, note that the same stars appear two hours earlier each month or one hour earlier every two weeks.) The map for each season is divided into four quadrants: northeast, northwest, southeast, and southwest. Start by facing the direction in which you have the clearest view. If your best view is southeastward, use the southeast map. The maps plot the constellations and major stars; the wavy, pale blue areas represent the band of the Milky Way; the zenith, the point directly overhead, is indicated. The key to finding your way around the sky is to locate distinctive constellations or star groups (a few are described at right), then to use them to find others. The maps do not chart the planets of our solar system, whose positions change continually. Their locations are often listed in newspapers in the weather section.

WINTER: ORION

On winter nights, we look outward through a spiral arm of our disk-shaped galaxy. Many hot, young blue or white stars (such as Sirius, Rigel, and Procyon), along with some older, cooler yellow and reddish stars (Betelgeuse, Capella, and Aldebaran), dominate the sky. New stars are being born in the Orion Nebula, a mixture of young stars, gases, and dust visible to the naked eye or with binoculars as a fuzzy area in Orion's sword, which hangs from his belt.

SPRING: THE DIPPERS

The spring sky features the well-known Big Dipper, part of the constellation Ursa Major, the Great Bear. The two stars at the end of the Big Dipper's bowl point almost directly at Polaris, the North Star, a moderately bright star (part of the Little Dipper, or Ursa Minor) that lies slightly less than 1 degree from

the true north celestial pole. Polaris sits above the horizon at an altitude equal to the observer's latitude (42 to 45 degrees in New England).

SUMMER: MILKY WAY

During the summer months, earth's dark side faces toward the bright center of the Milky Way, making that hazy band of light a dominant feature in the sky. A scan with binoculars through the Milky Way from Cygnus to Sagittarius and Scorpius reveals a dozen or more star clusters and nebulas. High to the northeast, the hot, white stars of the Summer Triangle—Vega, Deneb, and Altair—are usually the first stars visible in the evening.

FALL: ANDROMEDA GALAXY

On autumn evenings, earth's night side faces away from the plane of our galaxy, allowing us to see other, more distant ones. The Andromeda Galaxy can be found northeast of the Great Square of Pegasus, just above the central star on the dimmer northern "leg" of Andromeda. (On the Fall Sky: Southeast map the galaxy is near the first D in Andromeda.) Appearing as an elongated patch of fuzzy light, it is 2.4 million light years away.

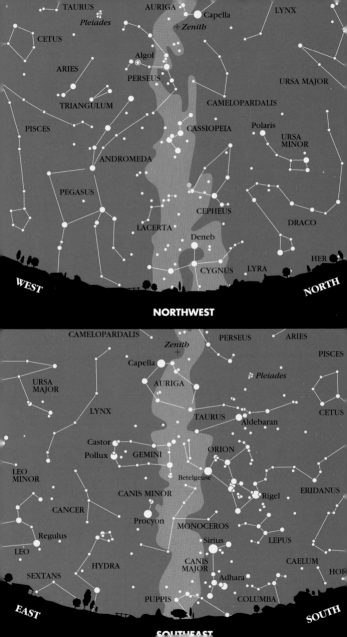

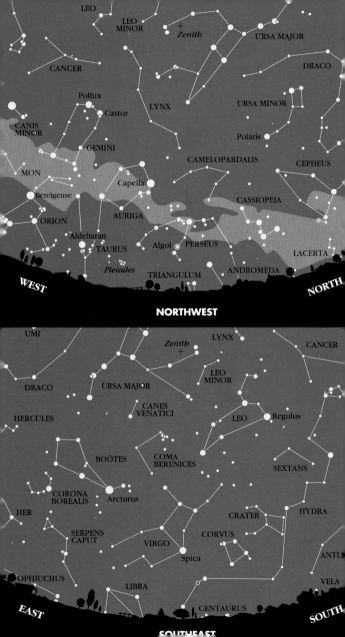

March 1, midnight; April 1, 10 P.M. (11 P.M. DST); May 1, 8 P.M. (9 P.M. DST)

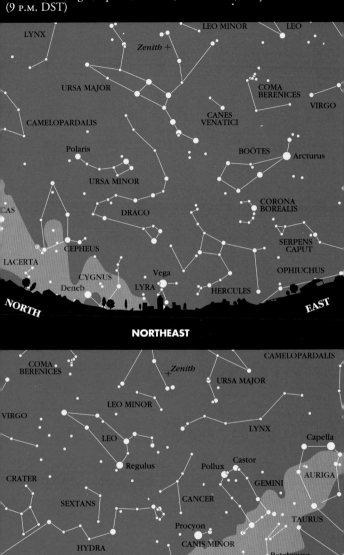

LYNX

LEO MINOR

LEO

Zenith +

URSA MAJOR

COMA BERENICES

VIRGO

CANES VENATICI

CAMELOPARDALIS

Polaris

BOÖTES

Arcturus

URSA MINOR

CORONA BOREALIS

CAS

DRACO

SERPENS CAPUT

LACERTA

CEPHEUS

OPHIUCHUS

CYGNUS

Vega

Deneb

LYRA

HERCULES

NORTH

EAST

NORTHEAST

COMA BERENICES

CAMELOPARDALIS

Zenith +

URSA MAJOR

LEO MINOR

VIRGO

LYNX

Capella

LEO

Castor

Regulus

Pollux

AURIGA

CRATER

GEMINI

SEXTANS

CANCER

TAURUS

Procyon

HYDRA

CANIS MINOR

Betelgeuse

ANTLIA

MONOCEROS

PYXIS

PUPPIS

ORION

VELA

CANIS MAJOR

Sirius

LEPUS

SOUTH

WEST

SOUTHWEST

The Summer Sky

The chart is drawn for these times and dates but can be used at other times during the season

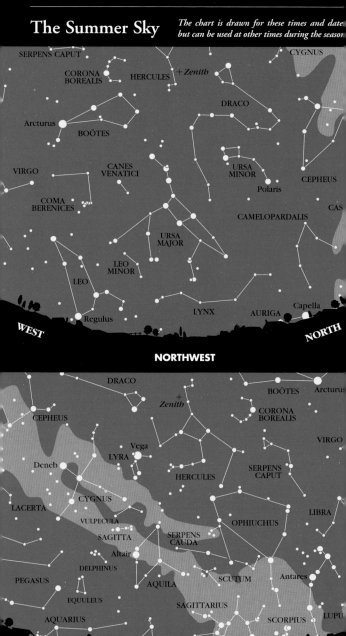

September 1, midnight (1 A.M. DST); October 1, 10 P.M. (11 P.M. DST); November 1, 8 P.M.; December 1, 6 P.M.

NORTHEAST

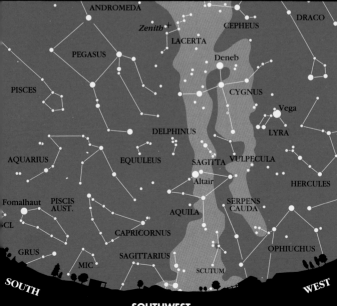

SOUTHWEST

Flora and Fauna

How to Use the Flora and Fauna Section

Part Two of this book presents nearly 1,000 of the most common species found in New England, beginning with mushrooms, algae, lichens, ferns, and other spore plants, and continuing with large and small trees, wildflowers, invertebrates (mostly seashore creatures and insects), fishes, amphibians, reptiles, birds, and mammals. Flora species are presented alphabetically by family name. Fauna species are sequenced according to their taxonomy, or scientific classification. The classification and the names of species in this guide are based on authoritative sources when these exist for a given group.

Introductions and Other Essays

Most major sections of Part Two—for example, trees, wildflowers, marine invertebrates, birds—have an introduction, and some groups within the larger sections are also described in brief essays. The introductions should be read along with the species accounts that follow, as they present information that is fundamental for understanding the plants or animals in question. For groups without introductory essays, shared features are sometimes given in the opening sentence of the first species in the sequence.

Names

Each account begins with the common name of the species. Common names can change and may differ in other sources; if a species has a widely used alternate name, that is given within quotation marks, directly below the common name. The scientific species name, shown below the common name, is italicized (alternate scientific names are also sometimes listed). In a few cases (some flowers and invertebrates), organisms are best known on the genus level and are presented as such here. For example, the Periodical Cicadas are presented as a group: the *Magicicada* species. Below the scientific name is the name of the group (class, order, family) with which the species is most commonly associated.

Description

The species accounts are designed to permit identification of species in the field. An account begins with the organism's typical mature or adult size: length (L), height (H), diameter (D), tail length (T), and/or wingspan (WS). The size is followed by the species' physical characteristics, including color and distinctive markings. We use the abbreviations "imm." (immature) and "juv." (juvenile). The term "morph" describes a distinctive coloration that occurs in some individuals.

Other Information

For every species, the typical habitat is described. Other information may also be given, such as seasonality (bloom times of flowers or periods of activity for mammals) or the need for caution (species that can cause irritation, illness, or injury). Similar species are sometimes described at the end of an account. The range (the area in which the species lives) is not stated if the species occurs through-

adult   immature

Names
AMERICAN ROBIN
Turdus migratorius
THRUSH SUBFAMILY

Description
10″. Male breast and sides rufous-orange; back and wings gray-brown; head blackish, with broken white eye ring; throat striped; bill yellow; tail black, with tiny white corners; vent white. Female head and back duller brown. Tail fairly long. Imm. buffy white below with heavy blackish spots; pale buffy scaling on back. In spring and summer, an earthworm specialist. In fall and winter, roams in berry-searching flocks, forms large communal roosts.

Other Information
VOICE Song: prolonged, rising and falling *cheery-up cheery-me*. Calls: *tut tut tut* and *tseep*. **HABITAT** Woods, shrubs, towns. **RANGE** Mar.–Nov.: all N. Eng. Dec.–Mar.: some in s N. Eng.

out New England; the one exception to this rule is the birds, for which the range is always given. The term "local" means that a species occurs in spotty fashion over a large area, but not throughout the entire area. In describing the geographic range of species, we use the abbreviations e (east), w (west), n (north), s (south), c (central), and combinations of these (sc for south-central). For state names, we use the two-letter postal codes.

Readers should note that color, shape, and size may vary within plant and animal species, depending on environmental conditions and other factors. Bloom, migration, and other times can vary with the weather, latitude, and geography.

Classification of Living Things

Biologists divide living organisms into major groups called kingdoms, the largest of which are the plant and animal kingdoms. Kingdoms are divided into phyla (or divisions, in plants), phyla are divided into classes, classes into orders, orders into families, families into genera (singular: genus), and genera into species. The species, the basic unit of classification, is generally what we have in mind when we talk about a "kind" of plant or animal. The scientific name of a species consists of two words. The first is the genus name; the second is the species name. The scientific name of the Meadow Jumping Mouse is *Zapus hudsonius. Zapus* is the genus name, and *hudsonius* is the species name.

Species are populations or groups of populations that are able to interbreed and produce fertile offspring themselves; they usually are not able to breed successfully or produce fertile offspring with members of other species. Many widespread species have numerous races (subspecies)—populations that are separated from one another geographically; races within a species may differ in appearance and behavior from other populations of that species.

Flora

The flora section of this guide includes flowering and nonflowering plants as well as algae and mushrooms, which are no longer considered part of the plant kingdom. Botanists are developing new classification systems that place most algae outside of the green plants group. Mushrooms are covered here because they are somewhat plant-like in appearance and are often found on plants or plant matter.

In this guide, we begin with mushrooms, followed by algae and lichens. The next group is the nonflowering spore plants such as mosses, clubmosses, horsetails, and ferns. Trees follow, beginning with conifers, then large broadleaf trees, and finally small broadleaf trees and shrubs. Wildflowers, including flowering vines, grasses, and water plants in addition to terrestrial herbaceous plants, end the flora section.

In most of the flora subsections, species are grouped by family. The families are sequenced alphabetically by the English family name. The measurements given in the species accounts are typical mature sizes in New England. Colors, shapes, and sizes may vary within a species depending on environmental conditions. Bloom times vary throughout the region (northern Maine can be several weeks behind Connecticut and Massachusetts) and can also be affected by the weather conditions in a given year. The geographic range is specified only when the species is not found throughout the entire region of New England.

Users of this guide are warned against eating or otherwise consuming any plants or parts of a plant (including fiddleheads or berries or other fruits) or any mushrooms based on the information supplied in this guide.

Mushrooms

The organisms known as fungi—including molds, yeasts, mildews, and mushrooms—range from microscopic forms to mammoth puffballs. Unlike plants, they do not carry out photosynthesis, and thus must obtain food from organic matter, living or dead. The fungi in this book are of the type commonly known as mushrooms.

Most mushrooms that grow on the ground have a stalk and a cap. The stalks of different species vary in shape, thickness, and density. There is often a skirt-like or bracelet-like ring midway up or near the top of the stalk, and the stalk base is often bulbous or sometimes enclosed by a cup at or just below the surface of the ground. Bracket (or shelf) mushrooms, which grow on trunks or logs, are often unstalked or short-stalked. A mushroom's cap may be smooth, scaly, warty, or shaggy, and its shape may be round, flat, convex (bell- or umbrella-shaped), or concave (cup- or trumpet-shaped). The caps of many species change as they mature, from closed and egg-shaped to open and umbrella-like; the cap color may also change with age.

Fungi reproduce through the release of single-celled bodies called *spores*. Many mushrooms bear their microscopic, spore-producing structures on the underside of the cap, either on radiating blade-like gills or within tiny tubes that terminate in pores. In others, the spore-producing structures line the inside of a cup-shaped cap or are located in broad wrinkles or open pits on the sides or top of the cap. Puffball mushrooms produce their spores within a ball-shaped body; the spores are released when the mature ball breaks open at the top or disintegrates.

In the accounts that follow, sizes given are typical heights (for stalked species) and cap widths of mature specimens.

CAUTION
Of the many hundreds of mushroom species occurring in New England, at least 10 are deadly poisonous to eat, even in small amounts, and many others cause mild to severe reactions. The brief descriptions and few illustrations in this guide do not provide adequate information for determining the edibility of mushroom species. Inexperienced mushroom-hunters should not eat any species they find in the wild.

Parts of a Mushroom

KING BOLETUS
Boletus edulis
BOLETUS FAMILY
H 7″; W 8″. Cap round, spongy; muffin-like; reddish brown, slightly sticky, cracks in dry weather. Stalk very stout, whitish to beige, club-shaped to bulbous; upper ⅓ white-webbed; base enlarged. Cap underside has minute white pores. **SEASON** June–Oct. **HABITAT** Various woods; often under conifers, birches, aspens.

FLY AMANITA
"Fly Agaric"
Amanita muscaria var. *formosa*
AMANITA FAMILY
H 6"; W 6". Cap umbrella-shaped, yellow or orange, with flaky white warts. Stalk stout, white, usu. with skirt; base bulbous. Gills white. **CAUTION** Deadly poisonous. **SEASON** June–Sept. **HABITAT** Woods, pastures.

DESTROYING ANGEL
Amanita virosa
AMANITA FAMILY
H 6"; W 4". Entirely white. Cap umbrella-shaped, with ragged edges. Stalk tall with tattered skirt, bulbous base. **CAUTION** Deadly poisonous. **SEASON** June–Oct. **HABITAT** Broadleaf woods, pastures.

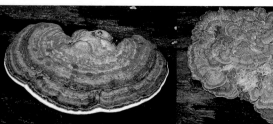
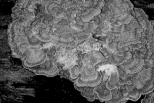

ARTIST'S FUNGUS
Ganoderma applanatum
BRACKET FAMILY
W 11". Cap flat to convex, semicircular to fan-shaped; grayish brown with concentric zones of brown and gray; hard, stalkless, attached directly to wood. Cap underside white, bruises brown, with pores. **SEASON** Year-round. **HABITAT** Living or dead broadleaf trees.

CHICKEN MUSHROOM
"Sulphur Shelf"
Laetiporus sulphureus
BRACKET FAMILY
W 7". Cap flat, fan-shaped; orange, with yellow lobed edge; stalkless, attached directly to wood. Cap underside yellow, with tiny pores. Forms overlapping clusters or rosettes. **SEASON** May–Nov., mainly autumn. **HABITAT** Living or dead trees.

BIRCH POLYPORE
Piptoporus (Polyporus) betulinus
BRACKET FAMILY
W 7". Cap flat to slightly convex, semi-circular to kidney-shaped, with edge rolled under; white to brown; hard. Underside white to light brown, with pores. Stalk absent or very short and on cap edge. **SEASON** Year-round. **HABITAT** Trunks of living or dead birches.

CHANTERELLE
Cantharellus cibarius
CHANTERELLE FAMILY

H 3″; W 3″. Entirely orange or yellow. Cap usu. trumpet-shaped, wavy-edged. Stalk thick, tapers toward base. Gills thick, ridge-like, extend down stalk. Takes many different forms; some are considered distinct species. **SEASON** July–Aug. **HABITAT** Woods.

COLLARED EARTHSTAR
Geastrum triplex
EARTHSTAR FAMILY

W 1″ (ball); L 2″ (lobes). Round, light brown ball; tough, darker outer layer splits into 4–8 curled-under, pointed lobes that form star shape; inner ball releases spores via nipple-like opening at top. **SEASON** Aug.–Oct. **HABITAT** Open broadleaf woods.

ALCOHOL INKY
Coprinus atramentarius
INKY CAP FAMILY

H 4″; W 2″. Cap bell-shaped, with pleated edge; gray to brownish, shiny; dissolves at maturity. Stalk slender, white, hollow. Gills white to inky-blackish. Forms large clusters. **SEASON** May–Sept. **HABITAT** Grass, wood debris; common in towns.

MEADOW MUSHROOM
Agaricus campestris
MEADOW MUSHROOM FAMILY

H 2½″; W 3″. Cap flat, white to grayish or gray-brown; smooth or silky-scaled; ragged-edged. Stalk stout, often tapered toward base, with ragged skirt. Gills bright pink to dark brown. **SEASON** May, Aug.–Sept. **HABITAT** Meadows, pastures.

MORELS
Morchella species
MOREL FAMILY

H 4″; W 1½″. Cap conical, honey-combed with deep, irreg. pits; yellowish brown; hollow. Stalk whitish, hollow, enlarged at base. Spores produced in pits on cap. **SEASON** May–June. **HABITAT** Recently burned or disturbed ground; old apple orchards.

GIANT PUFFBALL
Calvatia gigantea
PUFFBALL FAMILY
W 13″. Large, round, white to brownish ball with cracking surface; attached to ground by short, root-like cord. Top breaks up to release spores. **SEASON** June–Oct., esp. late summer. **HABITAT** Grasslands, open woods.

EMETIC RUSSULA
Russula emetica
RUSSULA FAMILY
H 3½″; W 2″. Cap flat, with sunken center; red, shiny, brittle. Stalk stout, brittle, hollow, white. Gills white. **CAUTION** Poisonous. **SEASON** Aug.–Sept. **HABITAT** Soil, well-decayed wood in forests.

OYSTER MUSHROOM
Pleurotus ostreatus
TRICHOLOMA FAMILY
H 1½″; W 5″. Bracket. Cap fan- or funnel-shaped, wavy-edged; white, gray, or brown. Stalk absent or very short, curved, whitish, attached to one side of cap, velvety at base. Gills whitish, extend down stalk. Forms overlapping clusters. **SEASON** May–Nov. **HABITAT** Trunks, logs, stumps of broadleaf trees.

Algae

Algae are a diverse array of organisms ranging from microscopic unicellular forms to large seaweeds. Three groups of algae are included in this guide: red algae, yellow-brown algae, and green algae. (In this section, the species are presented in these large groupings rather than by family or order.) Red algae and yellow-brown algae occur almost exclusively in salt water. Green algae most often live in fresh water but are also found in salt water and on land. In fact, land plants evolved from certain kinds of green algae.

The selected algae in this guide are all sizable marine plants commonly known as seaweeds. All have stalks, leaf-like structures called *fronds* (sometimes with air bladders that keep them afloat), and a pad-, disk-, or root-like structure called a *holdfast* with which they attach to a *substrate* such as sand, rock, shells, a pier, or some other surface. Some species tend to become detached from the substrate and float freely. In the accounts that follow, sizes given are lengths of mature specimens, unless otherwise noted.

IRISH MOSS
Chondrus crispus
RED ALGAE
4″. Deep reddish purple to pink or yellow-green. Fronds multi-forked, flat, stiff; often curly at tips; grow in bush-like clusters. Attached to rocks. **HABITAT** Tidepools, shallow waters of rocky shores, intertidal zone.

DULSE
Palmaria palmata
RED ALGAE
12″. Reddish purple. Fronds long, broad, flat, slimy, each forked into several lobes. Attached to rocks or shells; often exposed at low tide. **HABITAT** Intertidal zone to deep offshore waters.

SEA LETTUCE
Ulva lactuca
GREEN ALGAE
D 24″. Green, shiny. Fronds thin ruffled sheets; roundish to irreg. in outline. Attached to rocks and pilings; sometimes free-floating. **HABITAT** Oceanside rocks, mudflats.

KNOTTED WRACK
Ascophyllum nodosum
YELLOW-BROWN ALGAE
6′. Olive green. Fronds smooth, flat, irregularly branched; interrupted by oval air bladders; in Jan.–Apr. have oval, yellowish, stalked reproductive organs. Free-floating, or attached to rocks or piers. Sways in water at high tide; drapes over rocks at low tide. **HABITAT** Quiet shores.

BLADDER ROCKWEED
Fucus vesiculosus
YELLOW-BROWN ALGAE
24″. Olive green. Fronds long, flat, rubbery; branched in twos; edges bumpy, lined with oval air bladders. Attached to rocks and piers. **HABITAT** Rocky shores exposed to waves; intertidal zone.

NORTHERN KELP
Laminaria longicruris
YELLOW-BROWN ALGAE
15′. Brownish green. Fronds long, tough, hollow stalks with long, leaf-like blades with somewhat ruffled edges. Attached to rocks by large fibrous holdfast. **HABITAT** Intertidal zone. **RANGE** South to RI.

Lichens

A lichen is a remarkable dual organism made up of a fungus and a colony of microscopic green algae or cyanobacteria ("blue-green algae"). Such a relationship—dissimilar organisms living in intimate association—is known as *symbiosis* and may be detrimental to one of the participants (parasitism) or beneficial to both (mutualism). In a lichen, the fungus surrounds the algae and absorbs water, minerals, and organic substances from the substrate (soil, rock, tree bark) it is growing on; the algae supply carbohydrates produced by photosynthesis. It is not definitely known whether symbiosis in lichens is mutually beneficial or mildly to wholly parasitic.

Lichens occur in a wide range of habitats, including some of the harshest environments on earth, such as deserts and the Arctic (where they serve as the primary food of reindeer and caribou), and can also be found in forests, along roadsides, on buildings and other man-made structures, and on mountaintops. They can withstand extreme variations in temperature and other harsh conditions. During droughts they dry up but do not die; they rapidly absorb water when it does become available, springing back to life. Lichens range widely in color, occurring in white, black, gray, and various shades of red, orange, brown, yellow, or green. Their color often varies dramatically with moisture content.

Most lichens grow very slowly, about ¹⁄₂₅ inch to ½ inch per year, and can have extremely long lifetimes: specimens estimated to be at least 4,000 years old have been found. Many lichens have special structures for vegetative reproduction: tiny fragments that break off easily or powdery spots that release powdery balls of algae wrapped in microscopic fungal threads. In others, the fungal component produces spores carried on conspicuous fruiting bodies, which may be cup-like, disc-like, or globular.

Lichens are an important source of food and nesting material for many mammals and birds. Humans have used lichens as food, medicine, dye, and fiber, and as natural tools for monitoring the environment: lichens are sensitive indicators of air quality and ecosystem continuity.

In the accounts that follow, sizes given are typical heights (H) and/or widths (W) of mature specimens.

RING LICHEN
Arctoparmelia centrifuga

W 6″ (outermost ring). Concentric rings or bands; older parts olive green, newer growth yellowish; white below. Rings form when oldest parts fall away; new growth often begins again inside rings. **HABITAT** Exposed rocks.

DOG LICHEN
Peltigera canina

W 6″. Blue-gray (dry) to brown (wet) rosette of leathery, crinkled lobes; underside felt-like, veined, with tufts of root-like strands. Fruiting bodies brown, on extensions of lobes. **HABITAT** On ground or mossy rocks in woods.

MAP LICHEN
Rhizocarpon geographicum

W 2″. Thin, yellow to yellow-green crust, with black outline; black cracks containing black, disc-shaped fruiting bodies. **HABITAT** Bare rocks, esp. mountaintops.

BRITISH SOLDIERS
Cladonia cristatella

H ¾″. Tufts of yellowish gray-green, branched, somewhat scaly stalks topped with round, scarlet fruiting bodies. **HABITAT** On soil or wood in open areas.

PYXIE CUP
Cladonia pyxidata

H 1″. Patches of frilly, gray-green to olive scales topped by miniature goblets that are bumpy or scaly inside (and sometimes outside) and may have small brown dots and brown, globular fruiting bodies on rims. **HABITAT** On soil or rock.

REINDEER LICHEN
"Reindeer Moss"
Cladina rangifera

H 4″; W 2″. Silver-gray; resembling many-branched miniature trees, with "twigs" tending to face same direction. Fruiting bodies brown, rare. Used in model railroads and architectural models to represent trees. **HABITAT** On sand, soil in open areas.

Spore Plants

Spore plants are green land plants such as mosses, clubmosses, horsetails, and ferns (ferns are introduced separately on page 88) that reproduce from spores rather than seeds. Among the earliest evolved land plants still present on earth, these plants do not produce flowers or fruits. The most conspicuous part of their reproduction is the *spore,* a reproductive cell that divides and eventually develops the structures producing the sperm and egg, which fuse to form a new adult plant.

Mosses are feathery, mat-forming plants typically found in shady, damp to wet habitats. When "fruiting," their spores are released from a lidded capsule often elevated on a wiry brown fertile stalk. Mosses typically absorb water and nutrients directly from the environment, as they lack a sophisticated vascular system for conducting water and nutrients internally.

Like ferns and trees, clubmosses and horsetails have well-developed vascular systems. Clubmosses often look like upright green pipe cleaners or tiny conifers rising from the ground in shady woodlands. When fruiting, their spores are produced in tiny but visible sacs, called *sporangia,* between the leaves. In some species the leaves and sporangia are densely clustered into a long, narrow, cone-like structure. Horsetails have conspicuously jointed stems with whorls of tiny, scale-like leaves and branches at most joints. Sporangia are produced along the edges of umbrella-like structures clustered into a cone-like configuration atop a brownish, whitish, or green stem. In the accounts that follow, the size given is the typical height of a mature specimen.

HAIRCAP MOSS
"Goldilocks"
Polytrichum juniperinum
MOSS CLASS
9″. Green carpet of tall erect stalks with stiff pointed leaves. Fertile stalks reddish, each topped with golden-brown, cylindrical capsule. **HABITAT** Disturbed soil in woods, on bog edges.

PEAT MOSSES
"Sphagnum Mosses"
Sphagnum species
MOSS CLASS
12″. Yellow-green to red mats of long spongy stalks with thick, whorled branches covered with tiny, scale-like leaves. **HABITAT** Swamps, bogs, ponds, streams; sometimes floating.

STAGHORN CLUBMOSS
"Ground Pine"
Lycopodium clavatum
CLUBMOSS FAMILY

8″. Green horizontal stalks with erect forked branches covered with tiny, erect, needle-like leaves. Fertile stalks erect, each topped with 1–3 yellowish spore cones. **HABITAT** Sandy woods and thickets.

TREE CLUBMOSS
"Ground Pine"
Lycopodium obscurum
CLUBMOSS FAMILY

8″. Green, erect, tree-like, with many flat forking branchlets covered with tiny, needle-like, flattened leaves. Spore cones yellowish, un-stalked; several atop upper branches. **HABITAT** Moist open woods, bogs.

FIELD HORSETAIL
Equisetum arvense
HORSETAIL FAMILY

20″. Stems erect, rough, green, with many rosettes of long ascending branches. Fertile stems pale brown, unbranched, stout, each topped with brown spore cone in spring. **HABITAT** Woods, fields, swampsides.

WATER HORSETAIL
Equisetum fluviatile
HORSETAIL FAMILY

3′. Stems erect, slender, green; unbranched or with many narrow branches in whorls along mid-stem. Fertile stems usu. branchless, each topped with brown spore cone. **HABITAT** Swamps, ponds, ditches.

Ferns

Ferns, the largest group of seedless vascular plants still found on earth, are diverse in habitat and form. In New England they occur mainly in shady forests and near fresh water, but several fern species thrive in open sunny areas. Most ferns grow in soil, often in clumps or clusters; some species grow on rocks or trees, and a few float on water.

Ferns have a stem called a *rhizome* that is typically thin and long and grows along the surface or below the ground. The rhizome bears the roots and leaves, and lives for many years. Fern leaves, called *fronds,* are commonly compound and may be *pinnate* (divided into *leaflets*), *bipinnate* (subdivided into *subleaflets*), or even *tripinnate* (divided again into *segments*); they are often lacy or feathery in appearance.

Frond types

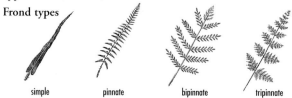

simple   pinnate   bipinnate   tripinnate

Ferns reproduce through the release of spores from tiny sacs called *sporangia,* which commonly occur in clusters *(sori)* on the underside of the frond. The sori may cover the entire frond underside, may form dots or lines, may occur only beneath the frond's curled-under edges, or may be covered by specialized outgrowths of the frond. Fronds that bear sporangia are called fertile fronds; those that do not are called sterile fronds. In some species the sterile and fertile fronds differ in size and shape.

Some ferns are evergreen, but the foliage of most New England ferns dies back each year with the autumn frosts. Each spring the rhizome gives rise to coiled tender young fronds called *fiddleheads.* Fiddleheads of some ferns are popular delicacies, but identification is difficult: the shoots of some deadly poisonous flowering plants (including various poison hemlocks) can be mistaken for fern fiddleheads, and many fiddleheads are edible at certain stages and poisonous at others. Only local experts should collect fiddleheads for consumption.

In the accounts that follow, sizes given are typical mature heights. For an explanation of leaf shapes, see page 134.

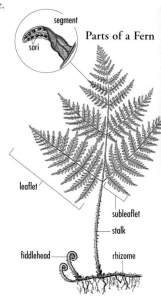

Parts of a Fern

segment
sori
leaflet
subleaflet
stalk
fiddlehead
rhizome

HAY-SCENTED FERN
Dennstaedtia punctilobula
BRACKEN FAMILY

24″. Stalks hairy. Fronds delicate, sticky-hairy; tripinnate, with about 20 or more pairs of lance-shaped leaflets, each with several ovate to lanceolate subleaflets. Fronds grow in line above creeping rhizome. Sori in cup-like structures along leaflet edges. **HABITAT** Sandy fields, woodland clearings.

BRACKEN
Pteridium aquilinum
BRACKEN FAMILY

3′. Stalks rigid. Fronds divided into 3 broadly triangular, stalked, bi- or tripinnate leaflets, each with many pinnate subleaflets. Sori are dots on curled-under leaflet edges. Forms large weedy colonies. Highly variable species, found worldwide. **HABITAT** Fields, woodland clearings.

NORTHERN MAIDENHAIR
Adiantum pedatum
MAIDENHAIR FERN FAMILY

18″. Stalks purple-black, wiry, forked. Fronds bipinnate; fan out in delicate whorls. 5–6 leaflets per stalk fork, each with several fan-shaped to oblong subleaflets with scalloped or incised edges. Sori on curled-under leaflet edges. **HABITAT** Woods, moist ground, rock faces.

NEW YORK FERN
Thelypteris noveboracensis
MARSH FERN FAMILY

20″. Stalks slender. Fronds bipinnate, with 20 or more pairs of lance-shaped leaflets; subleaflets many, oblong to linear. Sori few, near leaflet edges, under kidney-shaped flaps. **HABITAT** Sunny clearings in moist woods, thickets.

COMMON POLYPODY
"Rock Cap Fern"
Polypodium virginianum
POLYPODY FERN FAMILY

8″. Stalks slender. Fronds pinnate, with 10–20 pairs of linear, wavy-edged leaflets. Fronds grow in line from creeping rhizome. Sori in 1 row on each side of leaflet midrib. **HABITAT** Rocks and logs in moist woods.

CINNAMON FERN
Osmunda cinnamomea
ROYAL FERN FAMILY

4'. Stalks covered with cinnamon-brown wooly hairs. Fronds bipinnate with many oblong, pinnate, many-lobed leaflets. Fertile fronds (appear before sterile fronds) have club-shaped, seed-like clusters of sori. **HABITAT** Moist woods, streamsides, swamps.

ROYAL FERN
Osmunda regalis var. *spectabilis*
ROYAL FERN FAMILY

5'. Stalks erect, yellowish. Fronds bipinnate, with 6 or more pairs of leaflets, each with 5–7 oblong subleaflets. Fertile leaflets contracted, with sori that form conspicuous clusters atop fronds. **HABITAT** Swamps, marshes, streamsides, moist woods.

INTERRUPTED FERN
Osmunda claytoniana
ROYAL FERN FAMILY

30". Stalks slender, arched. Fronds bipinnate, with 18 or more pairs of lance-shaped leaflets and many subleaflets. Fertile fronds interrupted in middle by 4 or more pairs of fertile leaflets with sporangia clustered along edges; middle bare after spring spore season. **HABITAT** Moist woods, swamps, roadsides.

NORTHERN LADY FERN
Athyrium filix-femina var. *angustum*
WOOD FERN FAMILY

24". Stalks fragile. Fronds tripinnate, with 20 or more pairs of lance-shaped leaflets; subleaflets deeply cut into segments. Sori under rectangular to horseshoe-shaped flaps, in 1 row on each side of leaflet midrib. **HABITAT** Shady woods, swamps.

SPINULOSE WOOD FERN
"Florist's Fern"
Dryopteris carthusiana
WOOD FERN FAMILY

30". Stalks rough. Fronds tripinnate, with many pairs of leaflets; subleaflets cut into toothed segments. Sori under kidney-shaped flaps, in 1 row on each side of leaflet midrib. **HABITAT** Moist woods, marshes, swamps.

COMMON OAK FERN
Gymnocarpium dryopteris
WOOD FERN FAMILY

10". Stalks slender, scaly at base. Fronds divided into 3 broadly triangular leaflets, lower 2 tripinnate, upper 1 bipinnate; subleaflets deeply cut into blunt segments. Few sori on each side of leaflet midrib. **HABITAT** Rocky slopes in cool woods.

CHRISTMAS FERN
Polystichum acrostichoides
WOOD FERN FAMILY

21". Stalks stout, scaly. Fronds pinnate, with many pairs of lance-shaped toothed leaflets, each with prominent, ear-like projection at base. Sori usu. cover frond underside. Evergreen. **HABITAT** Woods, streamsides.

OSTRICH FERN
Matteuccia struthiopteris var. *pensylvanica*
WOOD FERN FAMILY

4'. Sterile fronds ostrich-plume–like, bipinnate, with many pairs of leaflets; subleaflets linear. Fertile fronds dark brown, stiff, lyre-shaped; leaflets and sori form dark brown clusters of pod-like structures. **HABITAT** Moist woods, swamps, streamsides.

SENSITIVE FERN
Onoclea sensibilis
WOOD FERN FAMILY

25". Stalks stiff, brittle. Sterile fronds leathery, pinnate, with about 12 pairs of wavy-edged leaflets. Fertile fronds a brown cluster of bead-like sori and modified leaflets. **HABITAT** Moist woods, swamps.

Trees and Shrubs

Trees and shrubs are woody perennial plants. Trees typically have a single trunk and a well-developed crown of foliage, and grow to at least 16 feet tall; some attain heights of more than 100 feet. Shrubs are usually less than 20 feet tall and often have several woody stems rather than a single trunk. This book covers two major categories of trees and shrubs. Conifers begin on page 95. Broadleaf trees and shrubs begin on page 101.

Individual tree sizes vary according to age and environmental factors. The heights given in the following sections are for average mature individuals in New England; younger trees and those exposed to harsh conditions are smaller; older specimens may attain greater heights in optimal conditions. Trunk diameter, which also varies greatly within a species, is cited only for very large species.

Identifying a Tree

Trees can be identified by three key visual characteristics: crown shape (illustrated below), bark color and texture, and leaf shape and arrangement (illustrated on page 134). Below are common crown shapes for mature conifers and broadleaf trees. These shapes are idealized and simplified for illustrative purposes. The first line of each species account describes the tree's shape in these terms.

pyramidal   conical   columnar   spreading

rounded   vase-shaped   broad

The roots, trunk, and branches of most trees and shrubs are covered in bark, a protective layer consisting mainly of dead cells. The bark of young trees often differs in color and texture from mature bark. As a tree grows, the bark splits, cracks, and peels. In some trees, such as birches, the bark peels horizontally. In cedars the bark shreds in vertical strips. In many trees the bark may develop furrows, ridges, or fissures, may break up into plates, or may flake off. The species accounts describe mature bark unless otherwise noted.

Beneath the bark is the wood, most of which is dense, dark, dead tissue (heartwood) that provides structural support for the plant. Between the heartwood and the bark are many pale, thin layers of living tissue (including sapwood) that transport water and minerals, and produce new wood and bark. Concentric rings, each representing a period (often a year) of growth, are visible in cut trunks and branches.

Shapes of Common New England Trees

The following are illustrations of the shapes of 48 common New England species. They represent individuals growing in good conditions and with plenty of space. The shapes of individual trees vary tremendously; those growing in a grove or forest, for instance, may not have these shapes at all.

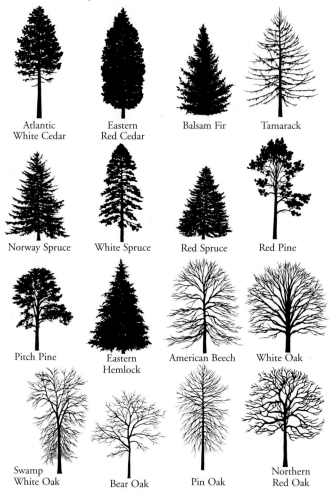

Atlantic
White Cedar

Eastern
Red Cedar

Balsam Fir

Tamarack

Norway Spruce

White Spruce

Red Spruce

Red Pine

Pitch Pine

Eastern
Hemlock

American Beech

White Oak

Swamp
White Oak

Bear Oak

Pin Oak

Northern
Red Oak

Chestnut Oak

Post Oak

Yellow Birch

Paper Birch

Gray Birch

Eastern
Hop Hornbeam

Flowering
Dogwood

Black Tupelo

Northern
Hackberry

American Elm

American Holly

Horse
Chestnut

Sassafras

American
Basswood

Yellow Poplar

Striped Maple

Norway Maple

Red Maple

Silver Maple

Sugar Maple

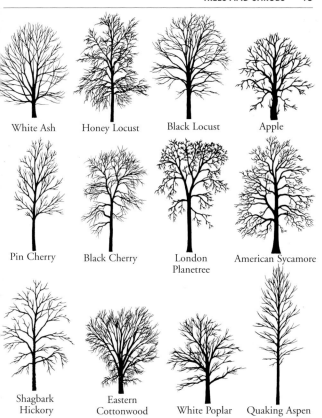

White Ash   Honey Locust   Black Locust   Apple

Pin Cherry   Black Cherry   London Planetree   American Sycamore

Shagbark Hickory   Eastern Cottonwood   White Poplar   Quaking Aspen

Conifers

Gymnosperms ("naked seeds") are trees and shrubs that produce exposed seeds, usually in cones, rather than seeds that are enclosed in an ovary, as in the angiosperms (flowering plants). Conifers, ginkgos, and cycads are all gymnosperms. New England's native gymnosperms are all conifers.

Commonly called "evergreens" and known in the timber industry as "softwoods," conifers are the most numerous and widespread gymnosperms found on earth. Their leaves are needle-like (long and slender) or scale-like (small and overlapping), typically evergreen, and well adapted for drought and freezing temperatures, thanks to a thick waxy coating and other protective features.

A distinctive characteristic of conifers is the cone, a reproductive structure comprised of a central axis with spirally arranged scales bearing pollen or seeds. A single tree usually has both pollen-bearing (male) and seed-bearing (female) cones; male cones are usually carried on lower branches, or lower down on the same branches as females. Male cones appear in spring, shed pollen, and soon fall from the tree. Female cones are larger, more woody, and have scales that protect the seeds until the cones expand to release them; this often occurs in the autumn of the second year after the formation and pollination of the cones. Unless otherwise specified, the cones described in this guide are female.

Most conifer species in New England—pines, larches, hemlocks, spruces, and firs—belong to the pine family. In our area, those commonly known as pines (genus *Pinus*) bear long needles in bundles of two to five; cones vary widely among different species. Other pine family members found in New England have much shorter needles. Larches bear needles in brush-like clusters that are deciduous (shed seasonally) and that turn yellow in autumn; cones are upright, stalked, and round to egg-shaped. Hemlocks bear needles on woody cushions and have small cones at the branch tips. Spruces have rough twigs, hanging cones, and sharp, four-sided needles borne on tiny, raised, woody pegs. The true firs (those of the genus *Abies*) are characterized by upright cones and needles arising from tiny depressions on the branches.

Other conifers in New England include those of the cypress family (such as the Atlantic and Northern White Cedars, the Eastern Red Cedar, and the Common Juniper) and the yew family. Most members of the cypress family have narrow, scale-like leaves covering their branches; their small cones are round, bell-shaped, or (in the junipers) fleshy and berry-like. Yews have needles in two opposite rows and bear seeds not in cones but individually and surrounded by a fleshy, cup-shaped, berry-like structure called an aril.

Typical tree shapes are illustrated on pages 92–95, and leaf shapes, including the needles and scale-like leaves of conifers, are shown on page 134. Unless otherwise noted in the individual species description, needle or scale color is green, fading to yellowish or brown when shedding, and cone color is brown.

NORTHERN WHITE CEDAR
"Eastern Arborvitae"
Thuja occidentalis
CYPRESS FAMILY

45′. Crown narrow, conical; branches short, spreading. Leaves tiny, pointed, flat scales. Cones ½″, tulip-shaped, light blue or brown, upright. Bark thin, shreddy, reddish brown. **HABITAT** Swamps, bogs. **RANGE** Mainly n N. Eng.

ATLANTIC WHITE CEDAR
Chamaecyparis thyoides
CYPRESS FAMILY

60′. Crown conical or rounded; branches slender, horizontal. Leaves dark blue-green, tiny, overlapping, scale-like; cover twigs. Cones tiny, egg-shaped, purplish to brown. Bark shreddy, in long loose strips, reddish brown. **HABITAT** Swamps, bogs. **RANGE** s ME and south, mainly on coastal plains.

EASTERN RED CEDAR
Juniperus virginiana
CYPRESS FAMILY

40′. Crown narrow, compact, columnar. Leaves tiny, scale-like, cover twigs. Cones tiny, berry-like, dark blue. Bark thin, shreddy, reddish brown. **HABITAT** Open areas, old fields, roadsides.

COMMON JUNIPER
"Pasture Juniper"
Juniperus communis
CYPRESS FAMILY

H 4′; W 10′. Usu. a spreading shrub; rarely a small tree. Needles ½″, sharp, curved, in whorls of 3. Cones tiny, berry-like, bluish. Bark shreddy, red-brown or gray. **HABITAT** Pastures, old fields, rocky slopes.

BALSAM FIR
Abies balsamea
PINE FAMILY

50′. Crown narrow, pyramidal, pointed. Needles ¾″, curved upward, in 2 rows per twig; aromatic. Cones 3″, cylindrical, purplish, upright, on highest branches. Bark thin, smooth, blistered, scaly, brown. Only fir native to N. Eng. **HABITAT** Boreal forests. **RANGE** n N. Eng.

TAMARACK
"American Larch"
Larix laricina
PINE FAMILY

80′. Crown pyramidal to conical; thin, open. Needles 1″, in soft, brush-like clusters. Cones ½″, egg-shaped, yellow-brown, upright. Bark scaly, thin, reddish brown. **HABITAT** Bogs, swamps, watersides, upland areas. Widely planted **European Larch** *(L. decidua)* is similar but has hairy cones.

NORWAY SPRUCE
Picea abies
PINE FAMILY

80′. Crown pyramidal; branches long. Needles ¾″, sharp, pointed. Cones 5″, cylindrical, slightly pointed, yellow-brown, hang down. Bark scaly, reddish brown. **HABITAT** Cultivated stands, towns.

WHITE SPRUCE
Picea glauca
PINE FAMILY

75′. Crown conical, often slender. Needles ½″, blue-green; exude skunk-like odor when crushed. Cones 2″, cylindrical, light brown, hang from branch tips. Bark smooth or scaly, thin, gray to brown. **HABITAT** Watersides, bogs, boreal forests. **RANGE** n N. Eng.

BLACK SPRUCE
Picea mariana
PINE FAMILY

40′. Shrub-like at tree line. Crown irreg., conical; branches short. Needles ½″, on yellow-brown twigs. Cones 1″, egg-shaped, gray, hang down; often clustered at treetop. Bark thin, scaly, gray to black. **HABITAT** Mainly bogs. **RANGE** n N. Eng.

BLUE SPRUCE
"Colorado Spruce"
Picea pungens
PINE FAMILY

90′. Crown pyramidal; foliage dense. Needles 1″, blue-green to silvery blue, sharp. Cones 3″, cylindrical, light brown. Bark scaly, furrowed, gray to brown. **HABITAT** Cultivated stands, towns.

RED SPRUCE
Picea rubens
PINE FAMILY

65′. Crown pyramidal to conical. Needles ½″, mostly sharp. Cones 1½″, cylindrical, reddish brown, hang down. Bark thin, scaly, gray to reddish brown. Most common native spruce; forms pure stands in rocky areas. **HABITAT** Mainly mtns. **RANGE** n and w N. Eng.

RED PINE
Pinus resinosa
PINE FAMILY

70′. Crown broad, irreg. or rounded; branches spreading. Needles 6″, 2 per bundle. Cones 2″, egg-shaped, light brown. Bark thick, scaly, reddish-brown plates. **HABITAT** Well-drained, sandy areas. **RANGE** n N. Eng. and south to n and w MA, nw CT.

PITCH PINE
Pinus rigida
PINE FAMILY

55′. Crown broad, rounded or irreg. Needles 4″; 3 per bundle; stout, stiff; also occur in tufts on trunk. Cones 2″, egg-shaped, yellow to brown. Bark thick brown to gray plates. **HABITAT** Sandy and rocky areas. **RANGE** c and s N. Eng.; esp. common on Cape Cod.

EASTERN WHITE PINE
Pinus strobus
PINE FAMILY

H 100′; D 3′6″. Crown broad to irreg.; branches nearly horizontal. Needles 4″; 5 per bundle. Cones 6″, curved, yellow-brown to gray. Bark furrowed, scaly, blackish gray. Largest, most common N. Eng. conifer. **HABITAT** Moist sandy soil, rocky slopes, swamps.

EASTERN HEMLOCK
Tsuga canadensis
PINE FAMILY

H 70′; D 30″. Crown pyramidal; top and branches slender; branches drooping. Needles ½″, flat, flexible, with 2 white stripes underneath; spread in 2 rows on slender, rough twigs. Cones ¾″, elliptical, brown; hang at twig ends. Bark brown; furrowed in scaly ridges. **HABITAT** Ravines, rocky outcrops, north-facing slopes.

SCOTCH PINE
Pinus sylvestris
PINE FAMILY

50′. Crown rounded, irreg. Needles 2¼″, twisting, sharp, blue-green, 2 per bundle. Cones 2″, egg-shaped, yellow-brown. Bark plated, brown or gray. **HABITAT** Cultivated stands, towns.

CANADA YEW
"American Yew"
Taxus canadensis
YEW FAMILY

5′. Low straggly shrub. Needles ¾″, pointed, green, flattened in 2 rows. Bark shreddy, reddish brown. **CAUTION** Needles and red "berries" of all yews are poisonous. **HABITAT** Cool, moist, mixed woods.

Broadleaf Trees and Shrubs

Trees belonging to the angiosperm (flowering plant) group are called broadleaf trees because their leaves are generally broad and flat, in contrast to the needle-like leaves of most conifers. Whereas the seeds of conifers and other gymnosperms are exposed, those of angiosperms are enclosed in an ovary that ripens into a fruit. The fruit may take the form of an edible drupe or berry, such as a cherry or mulberry, a hard-cased nut, the paired winged seeds of a maple, or a dried-out seedpod, such as that of a locust tree.

In warmer regions of North America, many broadleaf species (known in the timber industry as "hardwoods") maintain active green leaves year-round, but in New England most flowering trees and shrubs are deciduous, shedding their leaves for the winter because the leaves cannot survive long periods of freezing weather. A prominent exception is the American Holly, which retains its shiny green leaves all winter.

The individual species descriptions in this guide note leaf color only if it is not green. The term "turn" indicates the fall color of the leaves. The various types of leaf arrangements and shapes mentioned in the species descriptions are illustrated on page 134, between the trees and wildflowers sections. As most broadleaf trees bear their leaves in an alternate arrangement, only exceptions are noted in the species descriptions. Leaf measurements indicate length unless otherwise stated. Leaflet measurements are given for compound leaves.

Illustrations of flower types and parts, and a discussion of flower structure and function, are given on pages 135–137, at the beginning of the wildflowers section. Because the flowers of many trees are inconspicuous, only prominent ones are emphasized in the species accounts. In New England, trees generally flower from early April to mid-May (Connecticut, Rhode Island), mid-April to late May (Massachusetts), or late April to early June (Vermont, New Hampshire, Maine). Tree bloom dates are included only if they differ from these typical ranges. Fruits of broadleaf trees mature in New England mainly from July to October (a week to four months after the flowers). Months of maturation are given only for edible fruit.

To facilitate identification, we have grouped descriptions of large broadleaf trees (which begin on page 103) separately from small broadleaf trees and shrubs (which begin on page 121).

The Fall Foliage of New England

Deciduous trees change color elsewhere in the world, but no other region can match New England in species diversity and the resulting dramatic display of fall color, which annually attracts legions of admirers. Maples, Sassafras, hickories, sumacs, and some oaks turn various shades of brilliant red, red-purple, orange, and yellow—often with leaves of different colors on a single tree—while birches, aspens, beeches, and willows exhibit a range of golden hues. The map below shows typical fall foliage "peak" periods.

Late September
Early October
Mid-October
Late October

Each blaze of color represents a subtle change in leaf chemistry. In late summer, leaves begin forming layers of cells at the leafstalk base that will help the leaf detach and heal the resulting scar on the branch. As these layers grow, the veins of the leaves become clogged. The dominant pigment of the green leaf, chlorophyll, is no longer renewed and disintegrates rather quickly, revealing the yellow and orange pigments that had been masked by the chlorophyll. Under the right conditions, some species convert colorless compounds in their leaves into new red, scarlet, and purple pigments. Because these red pigments require high light intensity and elevated sugar content for their formation, the colors appear following a period of bright autumn days and cool nights, which prevent accumulated sugar from leaving the dying leaf.

The best autumn leaf colors follow a summer with plentiful rainfall, which promotes the formation of abundant leaf sugars. Leaves remain attached longer in relatively dry and warm autumn weather, while heavy winds, downpours, and early frosts may cause premature leaf drop.

AMERICAN CHESTNUT
Castanea dentata
BEECH FAMILY

20′. Formerly large, abundant; wiped out by disease; now found in N. Eng. only as sprouts from bases of long-dead trees; rarely live long enough to fruit. Leaves 7″, oblong, pointed, toothed; turn yellow. Bark smooth. **HABITAT** Mainly hillsides in mixed woods. **RANGE** All ex. n ME.

AMERICAN BEECH
Fagus grandifolia
BEECH FAMILY

80′. Crown rounded. Leaves 4″, elliptical, toothed, turn yellow or brown, often last into winter. Bark smooth, light gray. Fruit light brown, prickly; ¾″ burs split in fall to reveal 2–3 triangular, brown, ½″ beechnuts. Often forms stands. **HABITAT** Upland slopes, well-drained lowlands.

Oaks

Oaks, a large genus *(Quercus)* of the beech family numbering several hundred species, are widely distributed in temperate regions of the Northern Hemisphere. Eleven species form a major component of the deciduous hardwood forest in New England. The durable, straight-grained wood of many oak species is valued as timber.

Highly variable in shape, oak leaves may be deeply lobed or unlobed, toothed or untoothed; different shapes sometimes occur on a single tree. Many oak species are evergreen in warmer climates, but all are deciduous in New England. Newly emerged leaves in the spring are often reddish; mature leaves often turn red or yellow in the autumn. Many dead leaves remain attached to the branches until early winter or even throughout winter. Oak flowers are minute, greenish, simple in structure, and unisexual. Flowers of both sexes occur on the same tree. Male flowers are clustered into slender pendulous spikes called catkins, which produce copious pollen. Female flowers occur singly or in short spikes at leaf axils; after fertilization, each tiny pistil develops within one or two years into an acorn with a scaly cap.

WHITE OAK
Quercus alba
BEECH FAMILY

H 90'; D 3'6". Crown rounded; branches stout, numerous, wide-spreading. Leaves 7", with 5–9 rounded lobes; turn dull red or bronze. Bark scaly, shallowly furrowed, light gray. Acorns 1¼", oblong; cap shallow, warty. **HABITAT** Riversides, sandy areas, dry hillsides. **RANGE** c and s N. Eng.

SWAMP WHITE OAK
Quercus bicolor
BEECH FAMILY

60'. Crown rounded, open; branches mostly droop. Leaves 6", with 5–10 rounded lobes per side; shiny above, white-hairy below; turn red or brown. Bark furrowed, gray-brown. Acorns 1¼", egg-shaped; cap deep. **HABITAT** Streamsides, swamps. **RANGE** w VT and sw ME and south to coastal plains of CT.

SCARLET OAK
Quercus coccinea
BEECH FAMILY

70'. Crown rounded, open. Leaves 7", with 7–9 deep, widely spaced lobes with bristly toothed tips; shiny, turn scarlet. Bark furrowed into scaly ridges or plates, dark gray. Acorns 1", egg-shaped, with faint rings; cap deep. **HABITAT** Slopes, ridges. **RANGE** c and s N. Eng.

BEAR OAK
"Scrub Oak"
Quercus ilicifolia
BEECH FAMILY

15'. Small rounded tree or much-branched shrub. Leaves 3", usu. with 5 shallow lobes with bristly toothed tips; turn yellow-brown. Bark furrowed, scaly, gray. Acorns ½", egg-shaped, vertically striped; cap deep. **HABITAT** Sandy barrens, rocky ridges. **RANGE** c and s N. Eng.; abundant on Cape Cod and Islands.

PIN OAK
Quercus palustris
BEECH FAMILY

60′. Crown spreading; dead branchlets project from trunk like pins. Leaves 5″, with 5–7 deep, widely spaced lobes with bristly toothed tips; shiny, turn red or brown. Bark rough, dark gray. Acorns ½″, roundish; cap shallow, thin, saucer-shaped. **HABITAT** Moist areas, esp. riversides and streamsides. **RANGE** CT, RI, w MA.

NORTHERN RED OAK
Quercus rubra
BEECH FAMILY

65′. Crown rounded; branches stout, spreading. Leaves 7″, with 7–11 shallow lobes with bristly toothed tips; dull green, turn dark red. Bark furrowed into scaly ridges, dark gray. Acorns 1″, egg-shaped; cap shallow, broad. Often in pure stands. **HABITAT** Hillsides, lowlands.

CHESTNUT OAK
Quercus prinus
BEECH FAMILY

60′. Crown spreading, irreg. Leaves 6″, with 10–16 rounded teeth per side; turn yellow. Bark thick, furrowed, gray. Acorns 1¼″, egg-shaped; cap deep, thin, warty. **HABITAT** Well-drained lowlands, rocky ridges. **RANGE** From sw ME south.

POST OAK
Quercus stellata
BEECH FAMILY

45′. Crown spreading. Leaves 5″; 5 lobes form cross shape; leathery, hairy, gray-green below; turn brown. Bark scaly, furrowed, light gray. Acorns 1″, oval; cap deep. **HABITAT** Floodplains, drier ridges. **RANGE** Coastal plains of s CT, RI, se MA.

BLACK OAK
Quercus velutina
BEECH FAMILY

60′. Crown spreading, open. Leaves 7″, with bristle-tipped lobes shallower than those of Scarlet Oak; turn dull red or bronze. Bark blackish, deeply furrowed in long ridges. Acorns ¾″, oval; cap shallow, rough-scaled, flat-based. **HABITAT** Sandy, rocky, and clay hillsides; uplands. **HABITAT** s ME to s N. Eng.

YELLOW BIRCH
Betula alleghaniensis
BIRCH FAMILY

80′. Cylindrical; crown rounded. Leaves 4″, elliptical, toothed; bases often notched; turn bright yellow. Bark when young silver-gray to yellowish, peeling in thin, curly, papery strips; becomes reddish-brown, scaly plates. Cones 1″, oval, brownish, scaly, upright. **HABITAT** Moist mixed woods, woodland edges, swamps.

SWEET BIRCH
"Black Birch"
Betula lenta
BIRCH FAMILY

60′. Crown broad, rounded. Leaves 4″, elliptical, long-pointed, toothed; bases unequal; turn bright yellow. Bark smooth, shiny, slaty (young); blackish- or reddish-brown scaly plates (mature). Cones 1″, oblong, brown, upright. **HABITAT** Woods, north-facing slopes. **RANGE** Common in s N. Eng., rarer north to s ME.

PAPER BIRCH
"White Birch"
Betula papyrifera
BIRCH FAMILY

70′. Crown narrow, open. Leaves 3″, ovate, long-pointed, toothed, turn light yellow. Bark when young chalky to creamy white, with thin, horizontal stripes, peels in papery strips to reveal orange inner bark; later brown, furrowed. Cones 1¾″, cylindrical, brown, scaly, hanging. **HABITAT** Upland woods, clear-cut and burned areas. **RANGE** Most common in w and n N. Eng.

GRAY BIRCH
Betula populifolia
BIRCH FAMILY

30′. Crown open, conical, often bushy; branches droop to ground. Leaves 3″, triangular, toothed, turn yellow. Bark smooth, brownish (young) or grayish-white with many horizontal lines (mature). Cone 1″, cylindrical, brown, scaly. **HABITAT** Clearings, burned areas, roadsides.

AMERICAN HORNBEAM
"Musclewood"
Carpinus caroliniana
BIRCH FAMILY

20′. Crown broad, rounded; trunk fluted, muscular-looking, short, often forked. Leaves 3″, elliptical, toothed, parallel-veined, turn orange or scarlet. Bark smooth, gray. Fruit tiny, hairy, greenish nutlets, with 3-pointed, leaf-like scale; in 3″ clusters. **HABITAT** Streamsides, wooded ravines. **RANGE** c ME and south.

EASTERN HOP HORNBEAM
Ostrya virginiana
BIRCH FAMILY

25′. Crown rounded; trunk fluted, muscular-looking. Leaves 3½″, ovate or elliptical, toothed, turn yellow. Bark scaly, furrowed in wide ridges, gray-brown. Fruit many tiny nutlets in papery, light brown sacs, in hanging, hop- or cone-like, 2″ clusters. **HABITAT** Upland woods.

POISON SUMAC
Toxicodendron (Rhus) vernix
CASHEW (SUMAC) FAMILY

20′ (tree); 8′ (shrub). Crown narrow; often a shrub. Leaves 12″, pinnately compound, with 5–13 ovate, pointed, untoothed leaflets, each 3½″; stalks reddish; turn scarlet or orange. Bark smooth or warty, dark gray. Flowers tiny, greenish; in 8″ open branching clusters. Berries tiny, yellowish white; in 8″ open hanging clusters of 100 or more. **CAUTION** Do not touch; oils very dangerous. **HABITAT** Swamps. **RANGE** c and s N. Eng.

FLOWERING DOGWOOD
Cornus florida
DOGWOOD FAMILY

25′. Crown spreading. Leaves 4″, opposite; elliptical, pointed; veins curved; turn red. Bark small squarish plates, reddish brown. Flowers tiny, yellow; in dense head encircled by 4 white, 2″ petal-like bracts with pink notches. **HABITAT** Broadleaf woods, yards. **RANGE** sw ME and south.

BLACK TUPELO
"Blackgum"
Nyssa sylvatica
DOGWOOD FAMILY

70′. Crown dense, conical. Leaves 6″, elliptical to obovate, glossy, turn bright red. Bark plated, deeply furrowed, gray. Fruit ½″, berry-like, deep blue. **HABITAT** Floodplains. **RANGE** c and s N. Eng.

NORTHERN HACKBERRY
Celtis occidentalis
ELM FAMILY

35′. Crown rounded; branches often bushy "witches' brooms" deformed by mites and fungi. Leaves 3″, ovate, toothed; bases asymmetrical; turn yellow. Bark gray, smooth with corky ridges (young), or scaly (mature). Fruit ½″, cherry-like, red to purple. **HABITAT** Bottomlands, ridges. **RANGE** s N. Eng. (local).

SLIPPERY ELM
Ulmus rubra
ELM FAMILY

70′. Crown broad, open, flat-topped. Leaves 6″, toothed, elliptical; bases asymmetrical; very rough above; turn yellow. Bark deeply furrowed, plated, gray-brown; inner bark slippery, fragrant. **HABITAT** Wooded slopes, valleys. **RANGE** From se ME south.

SIBERIAN ELM
Ulmus pumila
ELM FAMILY

60′. Crown rounded, open. Leaves 2″, elliptical, smooth, toothed; turn yellow. Bark rough, furrowed, gray-brown. Introduced from Asia as blight-resistant replacement for American Elm; tolerates poor soil, pollution. **HABITAT** Cities, towns.

AMERICAN ELM
Ulmus americana
ELM FAMILY

90′. Crown vase-shaped; trunk forks into many upwardly angled branches that droop at ends. Leaves 5″, asymmetrical, elliptical, toothed, turn yellow. Bark gray, furrowed into interlocking ridges. Dutch Elm disease, spread by beetles, killed most trees from 1930 to 1960. **HABITAT** Floodplains, woodland edges.

AMERICAN HOLLY
Ilex opaca
HOLLY FAMILY

40′. Crown narrow, rounded, dense. Leaves 3″, elliptical, spiny-toothed, stiff, shiny, evergreen. Bark smooth to warty, light gray. Fruit ½″, berry-like, red; lasts into winter. **HABITAT** Coastal plains. **RANGE** s CT and RI and east to se MA and Martha's Vineyard (local).

HORSE CHESTNUT
Aesculus hippocastanum
HORSE CHESTNUT FAMILY

50′. Crown spreading, rounded. Leaves opposite, palmately compound fans of 5–7 obovate, toothed, pointed leaflets, each 7″; on 5″ stalk; turn yellow. Bark furrowed, scaly, gray-brown. Flowers 1″, white with red or yellow dots; in 10″ upright clusters. Fruit 2″ spiny green balls; contain shiny, brown, chestnut-like seeds. **CAUTION** Seeds poisonous. **HABITAT** Towns. **RANGE** c and s N. Eng.

SASSAFRAS
Sassafras albidum
LAUREL FAMILY

40′. Tree or thicket-forming shrub; crown spreading. Leaves 5″, 1-, 2-, or 3-lobed; turn red, orange, yellow (various colors on same tree). Bark thick, furrowed, gray-brown. Fruit ½″, oval, shiny, dark blue on thick red stem; clustered. **HABITAT** Moist, sandy woodland openings and edges. **RANGE** c and s N. Eng.

AMERICAN BASSWOOD
Tilia americana
LINDEN FAMILY

80′. Crown dense, rounded. Leaves 5″, broadly ovate or rounded, coarsely toothed; bases asymmetrical; turn yellow. Bark thick, tough, gray, furrowed. Fruit ½″, nut-like, in cluster hanging on long stalk from leaf-like bract. **HABITAT** Moist valleys and uplands, towns. **RANGE** c ME and south.

YELLOW POPLAR
"Tulip Tree"
Liriodendron tulipifera
MAGNOLIA FAMILY

100′. Crown rounded; trunk tall, straight. Leaves 5″, with 4 pointed lobes, basal pair wider and straight-based; long-stalked; turn yellow. Bark thick, furrowed, dark gray. Flowers large (2″ by 2″), tulip-shaped; 6 rounded green petals, orange at base; solitary at branch tips. **HABITAT** Wooded wetlands, slopes, gardens. **RANGE** CT, w RI, w VT.

SWEET BAY MAGNOLIA
Magnolia virginiana
MAGNOLIA FAMILY

20′. Crown narrow, rounded. Leaves 6″, oblong, thick; shiny above, whitish below; turn brown. Bark smooth, gray, aromatic. Flowers 2½″, white, cup-shaped, with 9–12 petals; fragrant. **HABITAT** Coastal plains, swamps; riversides, pondsides. **RANGE** s N. Eng (local).

Maples

Maples comprise a large family of trees (and occasionally shrubs) native to the temperate zone of the Northern Hemisphere. They are a major component of the deciduous hardwood forest that covers vast areas of North America. Seven maple species occur in New England, where they are essential to the brilliance of the fall foliage. Maples have considerable economic value as cultivated ornamental trees, as timber, and as the source of maple syrup.

Maples are characterized by their distinctive leaves, flowers, and fruit. The leaves are deciduous; those of most New England species are palmately lobed (hand-shaped). Maple flowers—typically small and yellow, greenish, or reddish—are arranged along the branches in variously shaped bunches (fascicles). Most distinctive is the flat, boomerang-shaped maple fruit (the samara), commonly known as a *key,* which is composed of two winged portions linked together at their bases. When it detaches from the tree, the key twirls in the air like a helicopter propeller. The precise shape of the key and the spread of the V-shaped angle between the wings distinguish each maple species.

STRIPED MAPLE
Acer pensylvanicum
MAPLE FAMILY

25′. Crown open, irreg.; trunk has vertical white stripes. Leaves 6″, with 3 pointed, finely toothed lobes; paler below; turn yellow. Bark smooth or rough, greenish brown, striped. Key 1¼″; wings at 140-degree angle. **HABITAT** Cool, moist, upland woods. **RANGE** n NH and south to c CT.

NORWAY MAPLE
Acer platanoides
MAPLE FAMILY

60′. Crown rounded, dense. Leaves 6″, opposite, 5-lobed, sharply and irregularly toothed; turn bright yellow. Red-leaved form (pictured at left) rare. Bark narrowly furrowed, ridged; gray or brown. Key 2″; wings at 160-degree angle. **HABITAT** Towns, roadsides.

RED MAPLE
Acer rubrum
MAPLE FAMILY

70′. Crown narrow or rounded, compact. Leaves 3½″, opposite, 3- to 5-lobed, irregularly toothed, whitish-hairy below, red-stalked; turn red, some orange or yellow. Bark furrowed, scaly, gray. Key 1″, reddish; wings at 60-degree angle. Often first tree to show fall color, in late Aug. **HABITAT** Swamps, streamsides; slopes in mixed woods.

SILVER MAPLE
Acer saccharinum
MAPLE FAMILY

70′. Crown spreading, open, irreg.; trunk short, stout, forked. Leaves 5″, opposite, with 5 deep, pointed lobes (middle one often 3-lobed), toothed, silvery white below; stalk reddish; turn pale yellow. Bark gray, furrowed in long shaggy ridges. Key 2″; wings at 90-degree angle. **HABITAT** Watersides, bottomlands.

Maple Sugaring

As New England's bitter winter yields to spring, usually in late February or early March, temperatures frequently rise above freezing during the day and drop back below freezing at night. For centuries, this has heralded the beginning of the annual maple harvest, a flurry of activity that lasts anywhere from three to eight weeks and produces New England's world-famous maple syrup and other confections.

Sap is the watery fluid circulating nutrients through a plant's vascular system. Carbohydrates formed by photosynthesis are stored in plants mainly in the form of starch; in maple trees during winter, some of this starch is converted to sugar and dissolved in the sap. Temperatures fluctuating above and below freezing raise the pressure inside the tree; only when pressure is high will sap flow strongly from the tree.

In New England, sap is usually drawn from Sugar Maples. To collect the sap, maple farmers tap a metal spout called a spile into a hole drilled in a mature tree (about 40 years old). The sap drips into a bucket; each hole yields about 10 gallons of sap (about 98 percent water, 2 percent sugar), which is then boiled down into one quart of syrup (33 percent water, 67 percent sugar).

SUGAR MAPLE
Acer saccharum
MAPLE FAMILY

80'. Crown rounded, dense. Leaves 5", opposite, with deep, long-pointed, few-toothed lobes; multi-colored in fall (red, orange, yellow; pictured on page 425). Bark deeply furrowed, gray. Key 1¼"; wings at 60-degree angle. **HABITAT** Valleys, mtns., woods, field edges. **RANGE** All N. Eng., ex. sandy coastal areas.

MOUNTAIN MAPLE
Acer spicatum
MAPLE FAMILY

25'. Small tree or shrub; crown vase-shaped. Leaves 4"; opposite, with 3–5 short, toothed lobes; rough above, hairy below; turn orange or red. Bark scaly, furrowed, thin, gray-brown. Key 1"; wings at 90-degree angle. **HABITAT** Moist rocky hills, mtns. **RANGE** n and w N. Eng.

WHITE MULBERRY
Morus alba
MULBERRY FAMILY

40'. Crown rounded. Leaves 5", broadly ovate, coarsely toothed, usu. asymmetrically lobed; turn golden. Bark furrowed into scaly ridges, gray-brown. Fruit ¾", blackberry-like; white, red, or black; edible, ripe July–Aug. **HABITAT** Roadsides, cities, woodland edges.

BLACK ASH
Fraxinus nigra
OLIVE FAMILY

50'. Crown narrow, rounded. Leaves 14", opposite, pinnately compound, with 7–11 lanceolate, stalkless, finely toothed leaflets, each 4"; turn brown or yellow. Bark corky, with small plates that rub off easily; gray. Fruit 1¼" broad, 1-winged key. **HABITAT** Streamsides, swamps, floodplains. **RANGE** n and c N. Eng. (local).

WHITE ASH
Fraxinus americana
OLIVE FAMILY

70'. Crown rounded or conical, dense. Leaves 10", opposite, pinnately compound, with usu. 7 ovate or elliptical, toothed leaflets, each 4", whitish below; turn purplish or yellow. Bark gray, deeply furrowed into forking ridges. Fruit 1½", single-winged key; in hanging clusters. **HABITAT** Valleys, upland slopes.

GREEN ASH
Fraxinus pennsylvanica
OLIVE FAMILY

60'. Crown rounded or irreg., dense. Leaves 8", opposite, pinnately compound, with usu. 7 lanceolate, short-stalked, shiny leaflets, each 4"; turn yellow. Bark furrowed, gray. Fruit 2", very narrow, 1-winged key; in dense hanging clusters. **HABITAT** Streamsides, swamps.

HONEY LOCUST
Gleditsia triacanthos
PEA (LEGUME) FAMILY

80'. Crown broad, open, flat-topped; trunk and branches have bunches of long branched spines. Leaves 8", pinnately or bipinnately compound, with many oblong leaflets, each 1"; turn yellow. Bark deeply furrowed, gray-brown. Flowers ½" yellowish bells in short clusters. Fruit 16" black, twisted pods; shed unopened. **HABITAT** Towns, gardens, streamsides, waste areas. **RANGE** s N. Eng.

BLACK LOCUST
Robinia pseudoacacia
PEA (LEGUME) FAMILY

50′. Crown rounded, irreg., open; trunk crooked, spiny. Leaves 10″, pinnately compound, with 7–19 oval leaflets, each 1½″; fold at night; turn yellow. Bark light gray, deeply furrowed into forking ridges. Flowers fragrant, white, ¾″ pea-flowers in 8″ drooping clusters. Fruit 4″ brown or black, flat, hanging pods. **HABITAT** Sandy, rocky areas; open areas; woods.

AILANTHUS
"Tree of Heaven"
Ailanthus altissima
QUASSIA FAMILY

60′. Crown spreading, rounded, open. Leaves 24″, pinnately compound, with 13–25 lanceolate leaflets, each 4″, with toothed, uneven bases; turn yellow. Bark rough, furrowed, light brown. Flowers tiny, yellow, in 8″ branched clusters; often fetid. Fruit 1½″ pinkish pods in clusters. Can grow from cracks in concrete. **HABITAT** Towns. **RANGE** c and s N. Eng.

DOWNY SERVICEBERRY
"Shadbush"
Amelanchier arborea
ROSE FAMILY

30′. Crown rounded. Leaves 2½″, ovate or elliptical, finely toothed, turn yellow to red. Bark furrowed, gray. Flowers 1¼″ white, with 5 narrow petals; clustered at branch ends. **HABITAT** Riversides, moist slopes.

COCKSPUR HAWTHORN
Crataegus crus-galli
ROSE FAMILY

20′. Thicket-forming. Crown broad; trunk short, stout, with branched spines; branches densely tangled, thorny (all typical for hawthorns). Leaves 2½″, obovate, toothed near tips, turn orange and red. Bark scaly, gray or brown. Flowers ½″, white, 5-petaled, clustered. One of many N. Eng. hawthorns. **HABITAT** Old fields, pastures. **RANGE** w N. Eng.

SWEET CRAB APPLE
Malus (Pyrus) coronaria
ROSE FAMILY

25′. Crown broad, open; trunk short. Leaves 3″, ovate, toothed, turn yellow. Bark furrowed, scaly, red-brown. Flowers 2″, white or pink, with 5 rounded petals; cover outer branches. Apples 1″, yellow, edible, ripe late summer. **HABITAT** Woodland edges, gardens.

APPLE
Malus sylvestris (Pyrus malus)
ROSE FAMILY

30′. Crown rounded; trunk short. Leaves 3″, ovate, wavy-edged, toothed, gray-hairy below, turn yellow. Bark scaly, flaky, gray. Flowers 2″, pinkish-white, with 5 rounded petals. Apples 3″, yellow or red, edible, ripe Sept.–Oct. **HABITAT** Roadsides, woodland edges, fields.

AMERICAN PLUM
Prunus americana
ROSE FAMILY

25′. Thicket-forming; crown broad; trunk short. Leaves 3½″, elliptical, long-pointed, toothed, leathery, turn yellow. Bark scaly, brown. Flowers 1″, with 5 white petals, bright red sepals below; in small clusters; foul-smelling. Plums 1″; skin reddish purple; flesh yellow, edible; ripe July–Aug. **HABITAT** Watersides. **RANGE** s N. Eng.

PIN CHERRY
"Fire Cherry"
Prunus pensylvanica
ROSE FAMILY

20'. Crown narrow, rounded, open. Leaves 4", lanceolate, finely toothed; turn yellow. Bark papery, red-brown to gray, with horizontal lines. Flowers ½", with 5 white rounded petals; clustered. Cherries tiny, red; flesh sour, edible (ripe July–Aug.), pits inedible. **HABITAT** Clearings.

BLACK CHERRY
Prunus serotina
ROSE FAMILY

40'. Crown rounded. Leaves 5", elliptical, toothed, with curled edges, tapered tip; turn yellow and/or red. Bark scaly, dark gray to black. Flowers ½", with 5 white rounded petals; in 5" clusters. Cherries ½", dark red to blackish; flesh edible (ripe Aug.), pits inedible. N. Eng.'s largest native cherry. **HABITAT** Old fields, woodland edges.

AMERICAN MOUNTAIN ASH
Sorbus americana
ROSE FAMILY

25'. Crown spreading. Leaves 7", pinnately compound, with 11–17 lanceolate, finely toothed leaflets, each 3"; turn yellow. Bark thin, smooth, gray, with short horizontal lines. Flowers tiny, white; in dense, flat-topped, 5" clusters. Berries tiny, red, in clusters of 100 or more. **HABITAT** Swampsides, mountainsides.

LONDON PLANETREE
Platanus x acerifolia
SYCAMORE FAMILY

70'. Crown vase-shaped. Leaves 8", incl. long stalk; palmately 3- or 5-lobed, maple-like; turn brown. Bark smooth, with pale silvery-green, gray, and brown patches; peels in large flakes. Fruit 1" bristly brown balls on long stalks. Widely cultivated, pollution-tolerant hybrid of American Sycamore and Oriental Planetree. **HABITAT** Towns.

AMERICAN SYCAMORE
Platanus occidentalis
SYCAMORE FAMILY

H 90'; D 3'6" or more. Crown broad, open; trunk massive. Leaves 6", incl. long stalk; broadly ovate, maple-like, with 3–5 shallow lobes; turn brown. Bark smooth; silvery-white base overlaid with peeling patches of darker gray and brown. Fruit 1" brown balls. Among N. Eng.'s largest broadleaf trees. **HABITAT** Streamsides, lakesides, floodplains. **RANGE** s ME and south to s N. Eng.

PIGNUT HICKORY
Carya glabra
WALNUT FAMILY

60'. Crown spreading, irreg. Leaves 8", pinnately compound, with 5 pointed, finely toothed, lanceolate leaflets, each 5"; turn yellow. Bark light gray, rough, furrowed in forking ridges. Flowers tiny, greenish; males in slender, drooping catkins. Fruit 2" thin, pear-shaped, green to dark brown husks; contain thick-shelled nuts. **HABITAT** Upland woods. **RANGE** MA, CT, RI.

SHAGBARK HICKORY
Carya ovata
WALNUT FAMILY

60'. Crown narrow, irreg. Leaves 11", pinnately compound, with 5 elliptical, pointed, finely toothed leaflets, each 5"; turn golden. Bark long curling strips; light gray. Fruit 2½", roundish, thick, green to brown or black husks; contain edible nuts; ripe Oct. **HABITAT** Bottomlands, rocky hillsides in mixed woods. **RANGE** c and s N. Eng.

MOCKERNUT HICKORY
Carya tomentosa
WALNUT FAMILY

60′. Crown rounded. Leaves 12″, pinnately compound, with 7 or 9 elliptical, stalkless, finely toothed leaflets, each 5″; hairy below; aromatic when crushed, turn yellow. Bark gray, furrowed into interlocking ridges. Fruit 1¾″, oval to round, thick brown husks; contain thick-shelled edible nuts; ripe Oct. **HABITAT** Moist hillsides. **RANGE** MA, CT, RI; Connecticut River valley halfway up VT/NH border.

EASTERN COTTONWOOD
Populus deltoides
WILLOW FAMILY

90′. Crown open, spreading; trunk massive, forked. Leaves 5″, incl. long stalk; triangular, with straight base, pointed tip; toothed, shiny; turn yellow. Bark thick, rough, deeply furrowed, light gray. Fruit: ½″, light brown, elliptical capsules, arranged in 8″ catkins; release cottony seeds in late spring. **HABITAT** Riversides, floodplains, sandbars in rivers. **RANGE** w N. Eng.: local, mostly Housatonic, Connecticut, and Farmington River valleys.

WHITE POPLAR
Populus alba
WILLOW FAMILY

65′. Crown rounded, irreg. Leaves 3″, with 3–5 gently pointed lobes; undersides white, felt-like; turn reddish. Bark pale gray, mostly smooth (furrowed, rough at tree base). Fruit 2″ catkins of tiny, egg-shaped capsules; contain cottony seeds. Grows rapidly; spreads by root sprouts, becoming a weed tree. **HABITAT** Towns, parks.

BIGTOOTH ASPEN
Populus grandidentata
WILLOW FAMILY

50′. Crown narrow, rounded. Leaves 3½″, ovate, with coarse, curved teeth; stalks long, slender, flat; turn yellow or reddish with yellow veins. Bark furrowed, brown. Fruit 2½″ catkins of tiny, narrow, conical, green capsules; release many cottony seeds. **HABITAT** Sandy uplands, streamsides, abandoned fields, burned areas.

QUAKING ASPEN
Populus tremuloides
WILLOW FAMILY

50′. Crown narrow, rounded. Leaves 2½″, nearly round, with tiny point, finely toothed; stalks slender, flat; turn golden-yellow. Bark yellowish to dark gray, usu. thin, smooth, with warty patches (furrowed on very large trunks). Fruit tiny, narrow, green capsules in drooping 4″ catkins; release cottony seeds. Leaves "quake" in slightest breeze. **HABITAT** Woodland edges, burned and clear-cut areas.

BLACK WILLOW
Salix nigra
WILLOW FAMILY

75′. Crown narrow or irreg.; has 2–5 leaning trunks; new twigs reddish. Leaves 4″, narrowly lanceolate, finely toothed, shiny; turn light yellow. Bark dark brown or blackish, furrowed into scaly ridges. N. Eng.'s largest willow. **HABITAT** Watersides.

WEEPING WILLOW
Salix babylonica
WILLOW FAMILY

40′. Crown open, irreg.; trunk short, broad; branches very long, drooping, yellow-green. Leaves 4″, narrowly lanceolate, with long-pointed tips, finely toothed; turn yellow. Bark gray, rough, deeply furrowed. **HABITAT** Watersides, roadsides.

Small Broadleaf Trees and Shrubs

To facilitate identification, we have separated most small broadleaf trees and shrubs from the large broadleaf trees. The species in this section generally reach an average mature height of 20 feet or less.

Although there is no scientific difference between trees and shrubs, trees typically have a single woody trunk and a well-developed crown of foliage, whereas shrubs usually have several woody stems growing in a clump. Many of New England's small trees and shrubs have beautiful and conspicuous spring flowers and/or colorful late-summer or autumn fruits. Flower and leaf arrangements and shapes are illustrated on pages 134–135. The majority of species covered here are deciduous; evergreens are noted as such.

SPECKLED ALDER
Alnus rugosa
BIRCH FAMILY

12′. Clump-forming shrub or small tree with 1–2 trunks. Leaves 3″, in 3 rows, elliptical, irregularly toothed, with sunken veins above; turn yellow. Bark smooth, gray, speckled with white. **HABITAT** Streamsides, lakesides, swamps.

GLOSSY BUCKTHORN
Rhamnus frangula
BUCKTHORN FAMILY

16′. Open, rounded shrub or small tree. Leaves 2½″, elliptical, glossy, with straight, parallel veins; stalks reddish; turn yellow. Bark thin, warty, grayish. Berries tiny, red or black, clustered. **HABITAT** Roadsides, open woods, clearings.

STAGHORN SUMAC
Rhus typhina (hirta)
CASHEW (SUMAC) FAMILY

18′. Tall shrub or small tree with upright branches; crown open, flat, irreg. Leaves to 18″, pinnately compound, with 11–31 lanceolate, toothed, 4″ leaflets, turn red. Bark smooth or scaly, dark brown; twigs velvety. Flowers tiny, yellowish green, in 6″ upright clusters; bloom June–July. Berries tiny, red, hairy, in 6″ upright oval clusters at branch tips; last into winter. **HABITAT** Old fields, woodland edges, roadsides.

WINGED SUMAC
"Dwarf Sumac"
Rhus copallina
CASHEW (SUMAC) FAMILY

10′. Shrub or small tree with stout spreading branches. Leaves 10″, pinnately compound, with 7–23 lanceolate shiny leaflets, each 2½″ and on winged axis; turn crimson. Bark smooth, light gray-brown. Flowers tiny, greenish white, in 3″ conical clusters atop branches; bloom July–Aug. Berries tiny, reddish, hairy, in 3″ conical clusters. **HABITAT** Dry woods, clearings, roadsides. **RANGE** s and c N. Eng.

SMOOTH SUMAC
Rhus glabra
CASHEW (SUMAC) FAMILY

10′. Large shrub or small tree with open flat crown. Leaves 12″, pinnately compound, with 11–31 lanceolate, toothed leaflets, each 3″; turn red or orange. Bark smooth, brown; twigs gray or red. Flowers tiny, yellowish green, in 7″ open clusters; bloom June–July. Berries tiny, red, hairy, sticky; in 8″ upright, dense, conical clusters. **HABITAT** Old fields, woodland edges, roadsides. **RANGE** s and c N. Eng.

ALTERNATE-LEAF DOGWOOD
Cornus alternifolia
DOGWOOD FAMILY

20′. Crown flat-topped, spreading; branches horizontal. Leaves 4″, elliptical, with curved veins; clustered at twig ends; turn yellow or red. Bark smooth, green on branches; furrowed, gray on trunk. Flowers tiny, white, in loose, flat-topped, 2″ clusters. **HABITAT** Woods.

GRAY DOGWOOD
"Gray-stemmed Dogwood"
Cornus racemosa
DOGWOOD FAMILY

9′. Rounded shrub; forms large clumps. Leaves 3″, opposite, elliptical, with curved veins; turn maroon. Bark scaly, gray-brown. Flowers tiny, white, red-stalked, in 2″ conical clusters; bloom May–June. Berries tiny, white, red-stalked. **HABITAT** Streamsides, woodland edges, roadsides.

RED OSIER DOGWOOD
Cornus stolonifera (sericea)
DOGWOOD FAMILY

8′. Thicket-forming shrub; red branches conspicuous in winter. Leaves 3″, opposite, elliptical or ovate, pointed, toothless, with curved sunken veins; turn reddish. Bark smooth, glossy reddish. Flowers tiny, white, in upright, flattish, 2″ clusters. **HABITAT** Streamsides, moist woods.

SHEEP LAUREL
"Lambkill"
Kalmia angustifolia
HEATH FAMILY

30″. Rounded evergreen shrub. Leaves 2″, mostly in whorls of three; oblong; lower ones hang down. Bark smooth, brown. Flowers ½″, deep pink, saucer-shaped, in round clusters; stamens pop out when touched; bloom May–Aug. **HABITAT** Bogs, shrubby swamps, pastures.

MOUNTAIN LAUREL
Kalmia latifolia
HEATH FAMILY

10′. Many-stemmed, rounded evergreen shrub or small tree with crooked trunk. Leaves 3″; alternate, opposite, or in threes along twigs; crowded at tips; elliptical, thick, stiff. Bark shreddy, rusty. Flowers ¾″, white or pink, with red dots; saucer-shaped; stamens pop out when touched; in upright branched clusters. **HABITAT** Mixed woods, heaths. **RANGE** c and s N. Eng.

LABRADOR TEA
Ledum groenlandicum
HEATH FAMILY

3′. Low evergreen shrub. Leaves 2″, alternate along twigs, crowded at tips; lanceolate, with curled-down edges; wooly, brown below; fragrant. Twigs hairy, reddish. Flowers ½″, white, 5-petaled; in erect clusters at branch tips. **HABITAT** Bogs, moist shores, mountaintops. **RANGE** c and n N. Eng.

RHODORA
Rhododendron canadense
HEATH FAMILY

3′. Many-branched, rounded shrub. Leaves 1¼″, alternate along twigs, crowded at tips, oblong. Bark smooth, gray. Flowers 1½″, rose-purple, with 3 unequal petals; in small clusters. **HABITAT** Bogs, moist slopes, open mountaintops. **RANGE** w and n N. Eng.

ROSEBAY RHODODENDRON
"Rosebay" "Great Laurel"
Rhododendron maximum
HEATH FAMILY

15′. Large, thicket-forming, evergreen shrub; crown rounded; trunk short, crooked. Leaves 6″, alternate along twigs, crowded at tips, oblong, thick. Bark scaly, thin, red-brown. Flowers 1½″, white or pink, waxy, in upright clusters; bloom June–July. **HABITAT** Moist woods, streamsides in hills, swamps. **RANGE** s ME and south (local).

PINK AZALEA
"Pinxter Flower"
Rhododendron nudifolium
HEATH FAMILY

6′. Open, rounded, shrub. Leaves 3″, alternate along twigs, crowded at tips, oblong, pointed, hairy-edged; turn yellow. Bark smooth, brown. Flowers 2″, usu. pink, with long curved stamens; clustered at twig tips. **HABITAT** Swamps, bogs, woodland clearings. **RANGE** s N. Eng. (local).

WHITE SWAMP AZALEA
"Swamp Honeysuckle"
Rhododendron viscosum
HEATH FAMILY

6′. Many-branched, rounded shrub. Leaves 2″, alternate along twigs, crowded at tips, obovate. Twigs hairy, grayish. Flowers 2″, white, trumpet-shaped, sticky, fragrant; clustered at branch tips; bloom June–Aug. **HABITAT** Swamps, pondsides.

LOWBUSH BLUEBERRY
Vaccinium angustifolium
HEATH FAMILY

16″. Small rounded shrub; forms thickets. Leaves ¾″, oblong, turn red. Flowers tiny, white to pink bells; grow in clusters; bloom May–June. Berries ½″, waxy blue, edible; ripe July–Aug. **HABITAT** Mtn. slopes, lowland barrens.

HIGHBUSH BLUEBERRY
Vaccinium corymbosum
HEATH FAMILY

10′. Large, rounded, multi-stemmed shrub. Leaves 2¼″, elliptical, hairy below, turn bronze or red. Flowers tiny white bells in short clusters; bloom May–June. Berries ½″, dark blue dusted whitish, edible; ripe June–Aug. **HABITAT** Shrubby swamps, meadows, dry hillsides.

LARGE CRANBERRY
Vaccinium macrocarpon
HEATH FAMILY

12″. Trailing, woody, evergreen shrub; forms dense creeping masses. Leaves ¾″, oval, leathery. Stems smooth, wiry, reddish. Flowers ½″, with 4 curled-back petals; white above, pink below, with long orange stamens over red center; on thin orange stalks; bloom June–Aug. Berries ¾″, dark red, edible; ripe Sept.–Oct. **HABITAT** Open bogs, lakesides.

WINTERBERRY
Ilex verticillata
HOLLY FAMILY

7'. Rounded shrub or small tree with short, low-branching trunk. Leaves 2", oblong, finely toothed, not spiny; turn brown to black. Bark smooth, dark gray. Berries tiny, red, in rows along leaf axils, conspicuous into winter. Deciduous, unlike other hollies. HABITAT Swamps, damp thickets, pondsides.

AMERICAN ELDER
"American Elderberry"
Sambucus canadensis
HONEYSUCKLE FAMILY

12'. Tall shrub with spreading branches. Leaves 7", opposite, pinnately compound, with 5–11 oblong toothed leaflets, each 4"; turn greenish yellow. Bark smooth with raised dots, light gray-green. Flowers tiny, white; in 8" flat-topped clusters; bloom June–July. Berries tiny, purplish black, in flat clusters; used for jelly, wine; ripe July–Sept. HABITAT Open areas near water.

MAPLE-LEAF VIBURNUM
Viburnum acerifolium
HONEYSUCKLE FAMILY

4'. Low shrub. Leaves 3½", opposite, 3-lobed, toothed; turn purplish pink. Bark warty, gray or dull brown. Flowers tiny, white, in 2" round clusters; bloom May–July. Berries tiny, glossy black, in 3" clusters on upright stalks. HABITAT Broadleaf woods. RANGE All N. Eng., ex. se MA.

HOBBLEBUSH VIBURNUM
Viburnum alnifolium
HONEYSUCKLE FAMILY

6′. Shrub; branches bend to ground and take root. Leaves 8″, opposite, round, short-pointed, finely toothed; turn orange or red. Stems smooth, brown. Flowers white, in 6″ clusters; outer ones 1″, inner ones tiny. Berries tiny, red to black. **HABITAT** Cool woods to 3,000′. **RANGE** w and n N. Eng.

NANNYBERRY
Viburnum lentago
HONEYSUCKLE FAMILY

20′. Shrub or small tree with short branching trunk. Leaves 3½″, opposite, elliptical, finely toothed, shiny above; turn red or orange. Bark furrowed into scaly plates, gray, has skunk-like odor. Flowers tiny, white, in 5″ clusters; bloom May–June. Berries ½″, blue, red-stalked, in flat clusters. **HABITAT** Woodland edges, rocky hillsides, streamsides. **RANGE** w and n N. Eng.

NORTHERN ARROWWOOD
Viburnum recognitum
HONEYSUCKLE FAMILY

7′. Much-branched, thicket-forming shrub with many shoots from base. Leaves 3″, opposite, ovate, large-toothed; turn shiny red. Bark smooth, gray. Flowers tiny, white, in upright 3″ clusters; bloom May–July. Berries tiny, dark blue, in 3½″ clusters of 30 or more. **HABITAT** Moist low areas. **RANGE** c and s N. Eng.

CRANBERRY VIBURNUM
"Highbush Cranberry"
Viburnum trilobum
HONEYSUCKLE FAMILY

10′. Shrub with spreading branches. Leaves 3″, opposite, with 3 wide, serrated, pointed lobes; turn reddish. Bark smooth, gray. Flowers white, in 3″ clusters; inner ones tiny, outer ones ¾″. Berries ½″, bright red, translucent, juicy; used in preserves; ripe late summer, last to early winter. **HABITAT** Streamsides, wooded hillsides. **RANGE** w and n N. Eng.

SPICEBUSH
Lindera benzoin
LAUREL FAMILY

9′. Rounded shrub; branches spreading to upright. Leaves 4″, oblong, turn yellow. Bark smooth, greenish brown. Flowers tiny, yellow, in clusters along twigs; bloom in April. Berries ½″, oval, red, in groups of 1–5. Most parts spicy-fragrant. **HABITAT** Swamps, moist woods. **RANGE** All N. Eng., ex. n ME.

BUTTONBUSH
"Honey-balls"
Cephalanthus occidentalis
MADDER FAMILY

12′. Multi-stemmed shrub; branches many, crooked. Leaves 4″, opposite and whorled, ovate or elliptical, with pointed tip. Bark scaly, gray-brown. Flowers tiny, white, in 1½″ pincushion-like balls; bloom June–Aug. Fruit 1″ rough brown balls of tiny nutlets. **HABITAT** Swamps, streamsides, pondsides.

BEACH PLUM
Prunus maritima
ROSE FAMILY

6′. Rounded shrub; branches many, upright. Leaves 2″, elliptical, finely toothed; turn yellow. Bark smooth, blackish. Flowers ½″, white, with 5 petals; line branches; bloom early June. Plums 1″, round, purple, edible; ripe Sept.–Oct. **HABITAT** Coastal dunes.

COMMON CHOKECHERRY
Prunus virginiana
ROSE FAMILY

18′. Shrub or small tree; often forms thickets. Leaves 2½″, elliptical, finely toothed; turn yellow. Bark smooth to scaly, gray-brown. Flowers ½″, white, 5-petaled, in 4″ clusters; bloom May. Berries ½″, red to blue-black, in grape-like clusters; flesh edible (July–Aug.), pits inedible. **HABITAT** Hilly streamsides, clearings, roadsides.

MULTIFLORA ROSE
Rosa multiflora
ROSE FAMILY

10′. Dense rounded shrub; stems long, arching. Leaves 4″, pinnately compound, with 7–11 ovate toothed leaflets, each 1″; have fringed appendages; turn yellow. Bark smooth, gray to reddish. Thorns sparse, curved, flattened. Flowers 1¼″, white, 5-petaled, fragrant, at stem ends; bloom June–July. Fruit many ½″ round scarlet rose hips. **HABITAT** Fields, roadsides. **RANGE** s N. Eng.

SWAMP ROSE
Rosa palustris
ROSE FAMILY

5′6″. Multi-branched shrub. Leaves 4½″, pinnately compound, with 5–7 oval, finely toothed leaflets, each 1½″; turn yellow. Stems smooth, green. Thorns sparse, strong, paired at leaf nodes. Flowers 2¼″, pale rose-pink, 5-petaled; bloom June–Aug. Fruit few ½″ ovate, scarlet, bristly rose hips. **HABITAT** Swamps, marshes, woodland watersides.

BEACH ROSE
Rosa rugosa
ROSE FAMILY

4′. Dense, clump-forming shrub with arched branches. Leaves 6″, pinnately compound, with 7 heavily wrinkled, obovate, toothed leaflets, each 1¼″; turn yellow. Bark brown, densely covered with straight sharp spines. Flowers 4″, deep pink, with 5 petals; bloom June–Oct. Fruit few 1″ bright red, globular rose hips with long sepals. **HABITAT** Seaside thickets, roadsides.

VIRGINIA ROSE
Rosa virginiana
ROSE FAMILY

4′. Low shrub, often in clumps. Leaves 5″, pinnately compound, with 5–9 elliptical toothed leaflets, each 1½″; have flared appendages at bases; turn yellow. Bark greenish brown. Thorns mostly short, straight; a few heavy, curved. Flowers 2½″, with 5 pale pink petals, yellow stamens; bloom June–July. Fruit ½″ red round rose hips. **HABITAT** Pastures, clearings, thickets.

HIGHBUSH BLACKBERRY
"Common Blackberry"
Rubus allegheniensis (argutus)
ROSE FAMILY

8′. Thicket-forming bramble with upright, arched stems. Leaves 5″, palmately compound, with 3 or 5 toothed leaflets, each 2″; turn orange. Stems smooth or fluted, gray-brown. Thorns taper from stout base to fine point. Flowers 1″, white, 5-petaled; bloom May–July. Berry 1″, oval, black when ripe (Aug.), edible. **HABITAT** Clearings, old fields.

WILD RED RASPBERRY
Rubus idaeus
ROSE FAMILY

5′. Bramble; stems erect, round, white-dusted. Leaves 5″, pinnately compound, with 3–7 sharply toothed leaflets, each 2½″; turn yellow. Stems brown or red. Thorns small, many. Flowers ½″, white, 5-petaled, in clusters of 2–5 at branch tips; bloom May–June. Berries ¾″, rosy pink, edible; ripe July–Sept. **HABITAT** Roadsides, old fields.

SWEET FERN
Comptonia peregrina
WAX-MYRTLE (BAYBERRY) FAMILY

3′. Low-growing shrub; branches fern-like. Leaves 5″, linear, with 10–20 rounded lobes per side; turn brown. Stems reddish, smooth. Fruit ¾″, green bristly bur; each encloses 1–4 edible nutlets; ripe July–Aug. Leaves very aromatic. **HABITAT** Clearings, pastures, disturbed woods.

SWEET GALE
Myrica gale
WAX-MYRTLE (BAYBERRY) FAMILY

3′. Shrub with erect branches. Leaves 2″, obovate, toothed at tips. Stems whitish gray to brown. Fruit tiny yellowish nutlets in cone-like clusters. **HABITAT** Marshes, bogs, swamps.

NORTHERN BAYBERRY
Myrica pensylvanica
WAX-MYRTLE (BAYBERRY) FAMILY

6′. Dense rounded shrub. Leaves 3″, obovate; fragrant; turn bronze. Stems smooth, with irreg. resinous bumps, gray-brown. Berries tiny, silvery, wax-covered; in grape-like clusters lining stems below leaves. **HABITAT** Dry sandy areas, coastal and inland.

SWEET PEPPERBUSH
Clethra alnifolia
WHITE ALDER FAMILY

6′. Tall, multi-branched, leafy shrub. Leaves 2½″, obovate, coarsely toothed on outer half. Stems smooth, flaky, gray-brown. Flowers ⅓″, white, with 5 petals, 10 long stamens; in 8″ upright spikes; powerfully scented; bloom late July–Sept. **HABITAT** Coastal wetlands; swamps. **RANGE** Coastal plains from s ME south.

BEBB WILLOW
Salix bebbiana
WILLOW FAMILY

18′. Much-branched shrub or small tree with rounded crown. Leaves 3″, oblong, finely toothed, wavy-edged; turn yellow. Older bark rough, furrowed, gray; often has diamond-shaped patterns caused by fungi. **HABITAT** Lakesides, swamps, meadows; forms thickets in uplands after fires.

PUSSY WILLOW
Salix discolor
WILLOW FAMILY

10′. Multi-stemmed shrub or small tree with open, rounded crown. Leaves 3″, lanceolate, silvery below; turn yellow. Bark smooth to scaly, gray; twigs smooth, brown. Flowers tiny, clustered into 2″ hairy silvery catkins; bloom late Feb.–Apr., long before leaves. Fruit ½″ capsules; contain downy seeds; ripen in spring, before leaves. **HABITAT** Meadows, bogs, riversides.

WITCH HAZEL
Hamamelis virginiana
WITCH-HAZEL FAMILY

15′. Scraggly shrub or small tree with broad open crown and multiple trunks. Leaves 4″, obovate, with uneven bases, scallop-toothed; turn yellow. Bark smooth or scaly, gray. Flowers 1″, yellow, with thin, ribbon-like petals; bloom Oct.–Nov. Fruit ½″ light brown, egg-shaped capsules; eject black seeds as far as 20′. **HABITAT** Woods, streamsides.

Leaf Shapes

scales

needles in bundle

needles in cluster

linear

oblong

lanceolate

oblanceolate

obovate

ovate

rounded

heart-shaped

arrowhead-shaped

elliptical

toothed

lobed

palmately lobed

pinnately lobed

palmately compound

pinnately compound

bipinnately compound

Leaf Arrangements

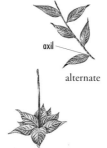

axil

alternate

opposite

whorled

basal

clasping

sheathing

Flower Types

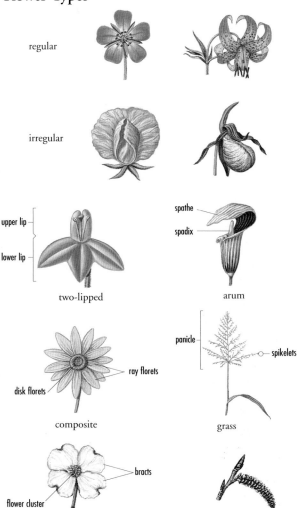

regular

irregular

upper lip
lower lip

two-lipped

spathe
spadix

arum

disk florets
ray florets

composite

panicle
spikelets

grass

bracts
flower cluster

bracts and flower cluster

catkin

Flower Cluster Types

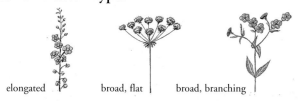

elongated

broad, flat

broad, branching

Wildflowers

New England has more than 2,000 species of flowering plants in more than 100 families. This section covers a broad selection of common and interesting wildflowers, including vines, grasses, and water plants.

The term "wildflower" has many connotations: one person's wildflower is another person's weed—a plant growing where it's not wanted. For the purposes of this field guide, wildflowers are defined as relatively small, noncultivated flowering plants that die back after each growing season.

The wildflowers included here are mainly herbaceous (nonwoody); some are woody but too small to be placed with the shrubs; a few have a woody base with herbaceous stems. These plants come in many forms. Many have a single, delicate, unbranched, erect stem terminated by a single flower or a flower cluster. Some have very robust stems, others are many-branched and shrubby. In some, the stems trail along the ground, sometimes spreading by runners. Those known as "vines" have a long, slender, often flexible stem that either trails on the ground or climbs, sometimes with tendrils to hold it in place. Plants of the grass family have erect, jointed stems and blade-like leaves; some other plants, such as rushes and sedges, are described as grass-like because they have narrow leaves and slender stems. Aquatic plants are adapted to life in or along water.

Wildflowers are most often identified by features of their flowers. The flowers or flower clusters may be borne in the leaf axils along the main stem or on branches off the stem. Modified leaves called *bracts* are often situated at the base of the flower or flower cluster. Flowers are typically composed of four sets of parts. The outermost set in a "complete" flower is the green, leaf-like *sepals* (known collectively as the *calyx*) that protect the often colorful second set—the *petals*. The next set is the *stamens*, the "male" part of the flower, each consisting of pollen sacs *(anthers)* typically on a stalk *(filament)*. The innermost set is the "female" part of the flower, with one or more *pistils,* each of which typically has a swollen base, the *ovary* (containing the ovules that after fertilization become the seeds), and a stalk *(style)* topped by the pollen-collecting *stigma.* The fruit develops from the ovary, forming a covering for the seed or seeds. The form of the fruit varies from species to species.

Parts of a Flower

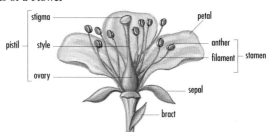

Although many plants have flowers with both stamens and pistils, some species have unisexual flowers that may occur on the same or separate plants. Many wind-pollinated species, such as Common Ragweed, grasses, and cattails, have reduced flowers that often lack petals and/or sepals. These wind-pollinated flowers tend to be inconspicuous, unlike flowers that need to attract insects for pollination. Seed dispersal is often aided by animals: migrating birds and other animals eat fruit or seeds whole and disperse seeds in their droppings; fruits that are bur-like or covered with various kinds of sticky hairs attach to animals on contact and later fall off or are shed along with fur. Plants such as dandelions and hawkweeds bear tiny fruits that have parachute-like tops and are carried by the wind far from the parent plant.

Flowers of a few representative types are illustrated on page 135. The buttercup and the lily are *regular* flowers: their parts radiate in a wheel-like (radially symmetrical) fashion. Pea and orchid flowers are commonly encountered flowers of *irregular* shape. Many plants in the lobelia, mint, and snapdragon families have tubular, *two-lipped* flowers. The tiny flowers of the arum family are clustered on a club-like *spadix,* which is usually enfolded by a leaf-like *spathe.* The *composite* "flower" of the daisy or aster is actually a head of many flowers: tiny tubular *disk florets* form a disk in the center, encircled by petal-like *ray florets.* (Dandelions and hawkweeds have flower heads made up of all ray florets; true thistles have all disk florets.) Grasses have tiny, reduced florets enclosed in scale-like bracts; these are organized in overlapping arrangements called *spikelets,* which typically form a larger, often plume-like arrangement called a *panicle.* Dogwood "flowers" in fact consist of a dense head of tiny flowers encircled by several large, petal-like *bracts.* The tiny unisexual flowers of oaks and many other species of trees and shrubs are clustered into slender spikes called *catkins.* Many plants bear flowers in clusters along or atop the stems or branches. Flower clusters take many forms, such as small round bunches, elongated spikes, feathery plumes, and broad, flat-topped or branching arrangements.

In the accounts that follow, sizes given are typical heights of mature specimens.

ARROWHEAD
"Big-leaved Arrowhead"
Sagittaria latifolia
ARROWHEAD FAMILY

3′6″. Flowers ⅔″, white, 3 petals around green button with yellow stamens; in whorls of 3 on tall stalk. Leaves 12″, usu. arrowhead-shaped. Roots bear edible tubers that rise to surface in fall. **BLOOMS** July–Sept. **HABITAT** Shallow water, ditches.

SKUNK CABBAGE
Symplocarpus foetidus
ARUM FAMILY

24". Shell-like 6" spathe, mottled brownish purple and green; encloses knob-like spadix covered with tiny flowers. Leaves very large, cabbage-like, veined; unfurl from tight roll after flowering. Smells like decaying meat, attracts pollinating insects. **BLOOMS** Feb.–Apr. **HABITAT** Swampy woods.

SWEETFLAG
"Calamus"
Acorus calamus
ARUM FAMILY

4' (leaves above water). Spadix 3", yellow, dotted with tiny greenish flowers in diamond-shaped patterns, angled; juts outward halfway up stalk, below leaf-like spathe. Stems and leaves stiff, sword-like. Berries small, gelatinous. **BLOOMS** June–July. **HABITAT** Marshes, other watersides.

WATER ARUM
"Wild Calla"
Calla palustris
ARUM FAMILY

12". Yellow spadix partly clasped by broad, white, 2" spathe, with pointed tip and rolled edge; on thick stalk separate from those bearing leathery, heart-shaped leaves. Resembles calla lily growing in water. **BLOOMS** June–July. **HABITAT** Bogs, pondsides.

JACK-IN-THE-PULPIT
Arisaema triphyllum
ARUM FAMILY

24". Spathe ("pulpit") hood-like, green, often maroon-striped; curves over fleshy, finger-like green spadix ("jack"). Leaves large, 3-parted, tall-stalked; 1 or 2 per plant. Berries shiny red, clustered. **CAUTION** Eating berries causes mouth irritation; touching roots can blister sensitive skin. **BLOOMS** May–June. **HABITAT** Woods.

ARROW ARUM
Peltandra virginica
ARUM FAMILY

24″. Colony-forming. Erect, wavy-edged, 6″ spathe curls around pale yellow, rod-like, tapering spadix. Leaves large (1′), arrowhead-shaped, fleshy, prominently veined, long-stalked. Berries greenish or blackish; clustered. **BLOOMS** May–July. **HABITAT** Marshes, pond-sides; esp. common along waterways.

COMMON RAGWEED
"Hayfever Weed"
Ambrosia artemisiifolia
ASTER FAMILY

3′. Coarse, hairy, branched stems bear tiny, inconspicuous greenish flowers in open clusters of 3″ spikes. Leaves light green, deeply bipinnately dissected into many lobes, each 4″. Wind-borne pollen among primary causes of hay fever. **BLOOMS** July–Sept. **HABITAT** Fields, waste areas, roadsides.

Plants That Cause Allergies

An allergy is a sensitivity in certain individuals to ordinarily harmless substances. "Allergy plants" include those that produce airborne pollen, which causes hay fever in susceptible individuals (reportedly at least 10 to 20 percent of the population). The cold-like symptoms include respiratory irritation, sneezing, and eye inflammation, and may lead to more serious conditions such as ear infections and asthma.

Allergy plants typically have inconspicuous flowers that produce copious pollen. They include various grasses and trees (such as pines and oaks), as well as the most common agents of hay fever in the United States: the infamous ragweeds (*Ambrosia* species). The amount of pollen in the air generally peaks at three times during the year, depending on the plant species in bloom: early spring (mainly early-flowering trees), midsummer (mainly grasses, some other herbaceous plants, and a few late-flowering trees), and fall (ragweeds and a few other plants).

Some plants are unfairly blamed for allergies. For example, the conspicuous, insect-pollinated goldenrods (*Solidago* species) are not responsible for late-summer–autumn allergies; ragweed is probably the culprit.

WHITE SNAKEROOT
Ageratina altissima (Eupatorium rugosum)
ASTER FAMILY

3'. Solitary or clustered, firm, smooth, branching stems bear tiny, white, rayless flowers in flat, fuzzy, 2" clusters. Leaves ovate, sharply toothed. Fruit tiny, seed-like, with white bristles. **CAUTION** Cows eating this plant give toxic (potentially fatal) milk. **BLOOMS** July–Oct. **HABITAT** Shady woods.

YARROW
Achillea millefolium
ASTER FAMILY

24". Gray-green, leafy, usu. hairy stems topped with tiny white or pink flowers in dense, flat-topped, 3" clusters. Leaves very finely dissected, fern-like, gray-green, stalkless, soft; pleasantly aromatic when crushed. Formerly used for a wide variety of medicinal purposes. **BLOOMS** June–Sept. **HABITAT** Fields, roadsides.

DUSTY MILLER
Artemisia stelleriana
ASTER FAMILY

24". Mat-forming. Tiny yellow flowers bloom atop erect spikes. Leaves white-wooly, broadly rounded, deeply multi-lobed. **BLOOMS** May–Sept. **HABITAT** Sandy beaches, coastal dunes.

MUGWORT
Artemesia vulgaris
ASTER FAMILY

4'. Flowers tiny, erect, button-like, yellow-green, aromatic, in 3" clusters. Leaves deeply toothed and lobed, downy underneath. **BLOOMS** July–Sept. **HABITAT** Waste areas.

HEATH ASTER
Aster ericoides
ASTER FAMILY

3'. Bushy, colony-forming. Flowers ½", with many white rays around yellow center; in branched clusters of many dozens. Leaves linear, hairy, stiff. **BLOOMS** Aug.–Oct. **HABITAT** Dry fields, roadsides.

CALICO ASTER
Aster lateriflorus
ASTER FAMILY

4'. Shrubby. Flowers tiny, daisy-like, with white to pale purple rays around yellow to reddish-purple center; dozens borne on one side of each branch. Leaves lanceolate, toothed. **BLOOMS** Aug.–Sept. **HABITAT** Fields, thickets.

SPOTTED KNAPWEED
Centaurea maculosa
ASTER FAMILY

3'. Flowers 1", thistle-like, lavender, with forked outer rays and black-tipped bracts. Stems hairy, wiry, many-branched. Leaves deeply cut. **BLOOMS** July–Aug. **HABITAT** Fields, roadsides.

STIFF ASTER
Aster linariifolius
ASTER FAMILY

18". Clump-forming. Flowers 1", with blue-violet rays around yellow center; dozens borne at stem ends. Leaves linear, rigid. **BLOOMS** Aug.–Oct. **HABITAT** Fields, dry rocky areas.

NEW ENGLAND ASTER
Aster novae-angliae
ASTER FAMILY

5'. Flowers 1", with many pale blue or violet rays around yellow or bronze center; many clustered at branch ends. Stems hairy. Leaves lanceolate, crowded, clasping. **BLOOMS** Aug.–Oct. **HABITAT** Meadows, moist roadsides.

PURPLE-STEMMED ASTER
"Bristly Aster" "Swamp Aster"
Aster puniceus
ASTER FAMILY

6'. Flowers 1½", with many light violet to bluish rays around yellow disk; few per branch. Stems and leaves usu. rough. **BLOOMS** Aug.–Oct. **HABITAT** Swamps, wet thickets.

NODDING BUR MARIGOLD
Bidens cernua
ASTER FAMILY

3'. Flowers 1¼", with 6–8 yellow rays around bulbous center; sometimes rayless; nod with age. Leaves lanceolate, toothed, stalkless. Barbed, seed-like fruits stick to fur, clothing. **BLOOMS** Aug.–Sept. **HABITAT** Pondsides, moist meadows.

CHICORY
Cichorium intybus
ASTER FAMILY

3′. Flowers 1½″ wide, stalkless, with bright blue, toothed rays; close at midday. Basal leaves dandelion-like; stem leaves linear, clasping. **BLOOMS** July–Sept. **HABITAT** Fields, roadsides.

CANADA THISTLE
Cirsium arvense
ASTER FAMILY

4′. Many fringy, rounded, 1″, pale purple-pink flowers atop smooth, much-branched stems. Leaves lanceolate, deeply cut, spiny. **BLOOMS** June–Sept. **HABITAT** Fields, roadsides.

BULL THISTLE
Cirsium vulgare
ASTER FAMILY

6′. Flowers rose-purple, 2″; each atop a spiny, bulbous, green base with yellow-tipped bracts. Stems spiny-winged. Leaves pinnately lobed, spiny, pale to wooly underneath. N. Eng.'s prickliest thistle. **CAUTION** Handle with gloves. **BLOOMS** July–Sept. **HABITAT** Fields, roadsides.

HORSEWEED
Conyza canadensis
ASTER FAMILY

5′. Erect, bristly, leafy stems bear tiny greenish-white flowers in branching clusters among upper leaves. Leaves linear. **BLOOMS** July–Sept. **HABITAT** Bare soil, open areas.

DAISY FLEABANE
Erigeron annuus
ASTER FAMILY

4′. Hairy, leafy, branching stems bear dense clusters of ¾″ flowers with many short white, pink, or purple rays tightly packed around yellow disk. Leaves lanceolate, toothed. **BLOOMS** June–Sept. **HABITAT** Fields. **Philadelphia Fleabane** ("Common Fleabane," *E. philadelphicus*): 3′; flowers 1″; leaves hairy, oblong or ovate, toothed or untoothed, upper ones clasping; blooms May–Aug.

ORANGE HAWKWEED
"Devil's Paintbrush"
Hieracium aurantiacum
ASTER FAMILY

15″. Single stems bear ¾″, orange, dandelion-like flowers with toothed rays; buds surrounded by black hairy bracts. Leaves hairy, elliptical, in rosette at stem base. **BLOOMS** June–Aug. **HABITAT** Fields, roadsides. **Yellow Hawkweed** ("King Devil," *H. caespitosum* or *pratense*): 24″, has yellow flowers clustered on hairy stalks; large, oblong, stiff-hairy leaves; blooms May–Sept.

SPOTTED JOE-PYE-WEED
Eupatorium maculatum
ASTER FAMILY

4′. Sturdy, hairy, purple or purple-spotted stems end with tiny, pink-purple flowers in flat, fuzzy 5″ clusters. Leaves lanceolate, toothed, whorled. **BLOOMS** July–Sept. **HABITAT** Moist meadows, thickets.

LANCE-LEAVED COREOPSIS
"Tickseed"
Coreopsis lanceolata
ASTER FAMILY

20″. Colony-forming. Flowers 2½″, tall-stalked, yellow; rays toothed at tips. Leaves linear, sometimes lobed at bases. **BLOOMS** June–July. **HABITAT** Sandy fields, roadsides.

BONESET
Eupatorium perfoliatum
ASTER FAMILY

4′. Thick hairy stems seemingly grow through leaves. Flowers tiny, fuzzy, white, in dense flat clusters. Leaves lanceolate, wrinkly, toothed. **BLOOMS** July–Sept. **HABITAT** Moist meadows.

DWARF DANDELION
Krigia virginica
ASTER FAMILY

11″. Solitary, many-rayed yellow flower at the end of each slender stem. Leaves lanceolate, toothed or lobed, in rosette at stem base. **BLOOMS** Apr.–Aug. **HABITAT** Dry sandy fields, open woods.

COMMON BURDOCK
Arctium minus
ASTER FAMILY

4'. Bushy. Flowers ¾", thistle-like, pink or purple; surrounded by hook-tipped bracts. Upper leaves ovate, lower leaves heart-shaped; wooly underneath. Prickly flower heads catch on fur, clothing. **BLOOMS** July–Oct. **HABITAT** Fields.

ROUGH-LEAVED SUNFLOWER
"Woodland Sunflower"
Helianthus strumosus
ASTER FAMILY

6'. Flowers 3½", yellow, with several rays around yellow disk. Stems usu. smooth. Leaves ovate or lanceolate, rough; pale and hairy underneath. **BLOOMS** Aug.–Sept. **HABITAT** Open woods.

OXEYE DAISY
Leucanthemum vulgare
ASTER FAMILY

24". The familiar field daisy. Flowers 2", composed of white rays around yellow disk; solitary on erect stem. Leaves dark green; coarsely lobed; many lobed. **BLOOMS** June–July. **HABITAT** Fields.

BLACK-EYED SUSAN
Rudbeckia hirta
ASTER FAMILY

3'. Flowers 3", composed of long, yellow, daisy-like rays around brown central cone; solitary on slender, rough, hairy stems. Leaves lanceolate to ovate, hairy; lower ones toothed; arranged in rosette at stem base. **CAUTION** Stem and leaves very bristly, may irritate skin. **BLOOMS** June–Sept. **HABITAT** Fields.

PEARLY EVERLASTING
Anaphalis margaritacea
ASTER FAMILY

24". Slender erect stems end in flat-topped clusters of tiny globular flowers, each made up of many petal-like, papery white bracts around yellow center. Leaves linear, wooly underneath. **BLOOMS** July–Sept. **HABITAT** Open areas.

SALTMARSH FLEABANE
Pluchea odorata (purpurescens)
ASTER FAMILY

3'. Erect, camphor-scented. Flowers tiny, cup-like, pink-purple; in flat 2" clusters. Leaves variable, often ovate and slightly toothed. **BLOOMS** Aug.–Sept. **HABITAT** Saltmarsh edges. **RANGE** Coastal, s ME and south.

GOLDEN RAGWORT
Senecio aureus
ASTER FAMILY

24". Smooth, branching. Flowers ¾", daisy-like, yellow; in branched, flat-topped clusters. Basal leaves heart-shaped, stem leaves finely cut. **BLOOMS** May–July. **HABITAT** Swamps, moist woods, meadows.

CANADA GOLDENROD
"Meadow Goldenrod"
"Tall Goldenrod"
Solidago canadensis
ASTER FAMILY

4'. Plume-like, pyramidal clusters of tiny yellow flowers at branch ends. Stems hairy at top. Leaves lanceolate, sharp-toothed, 3-veined, crowded. One of more than a dozen goldenrods found in N. Eng. **BLOOMS** Aug.–Oct. **HABITAT** Meadows, roadsides, open woods.

LANCE-LEAVED GOLDENROD
Solidago (Euthamia) graminifolia
ASTER FAMILY

3'. Flat clusters of tiny yellow flowers at branch ends. Stems smooth or downy. Leaves linear, pointed, parallel-veined. Fragrant. **BLOOMS** July–Oct. **HABITAT** Fields, saltmarsh edges.

BLUE-STEMMED GOLDENROD
Solidago caesia
ASTER FAMILY

3'. Small scattered tufts of tiny yellow flowers. Stems smooth, purplish, unbranched, white-powdered. Leaves slim, pointed, toothed, stalkless. **BLOOMS** Aug.–Oct. **HABITAT** Woods, thickets.

ROUGH-STEMMED GOLDENROD
Solidago rugosa
ASTER FAMILY

5'. Plume-like clusters of tiny yellow flowers on upper side of branches. Stems rough-hairy. Leaves broad, tapering, wrinkled, deep-toothed, hairy. **BLOOMS** July–Oct. **HABITAT** Fields, roadsides, edges of woods.

SEASIDE GOLDENROD
Solidago sempervirens
ASTER FAMILY

4'. Tall. Club- or plume-like clusters of tiny yellow flowers on arched branches. Stems smooth, stout. Leaves fleshy, slim, untoothed, smooth, clasping. **BLOOMS** Aug.–Oct. **HABITAT** Coastal marshes, sand dunes.

PRICKLY SOW-THISTLE
Sonchus asper
ASTER FAMILY

4'. Flowers 2", dandelion-like, yellow. Stems smooth, angled. Leaves prickly-edged, lanceolate, with downward-curled basal lobes, clasping. **BLOOMS** July–Sept. **HABITAT** Open areas.

COMMON TANSY
Tanacetum vulgare
ASTER FAMILY

3'. Erect, colony-forming. Flowers tiny, yellow, button-like, in dense flat-topped clusters. Leaves fern-like, dark green; very aromatic. **CAUTION** Poisonous. **BLOOMS** July–Sept. **HABITAT** Open areas.

COMMON DANDELION
Taraxacum officinale
ASTER FAMILY

10". Flowers 1½", yellow, 1 per stem; each ripens into fluffy, white, globular seed ball. Stem hollow, juice milky. Leaves deeply and irregularly toothed, in rosette at stem base. The everyday lawn weed. **BLOOMS** Apr.–Sept. **HABITAT** Lawns, fields.

NEW YORK IRONWEED
Vernonia noveboracensis
ASTER FAMILY

5′. Tall erect stems, branched toward top, with open clusters of tiny, frilly-spiky, deep lavender or violet flowers at branch ends. Leaves lanceolate, finely toothed. **BLOOMS** Aug.–Oct. **HABITAT** Moist areas. **RANGE** s N. Eng.

COLTSFOOT
Tussilago farfara
ASTER FAMILY

8″. Clump-forming. Each scaly stalk has single yellow, 1″, dandelion-like flower. Leaves large, heart-shaped, toothed, whitish underneath, upright; appear after flowers. Among N. Eng.'s earliest blooming wildflowers. **BLOOMS** Mar.–May. **HABITAT** Moist areas, roadsides.

YELLOW GOATSBEARD
"Meadow Salsify"
Tragopogon pratensis
ASTER FAMILY

24″. Flowers 2½″, yellow, dandelion-like, with green, long-pointed bracts; close at midday; 1 per stem; each ripens into very large seed ball. Stem smooth, juice milky. Leaves grass-like, clasping. **BLOOMS** June–Aug. **HABITAT** Fields.

INDIAN TOBACCO
Lobelia inflata
BELLFLOWER (BLUEBELL) FAMILY

3′. Flowers tiny, pale blue-violet, 2-lipped, with long-pointed, green sepals; each base becomes inflated seedpod. Stems hairy. Leaves ovate, toothed. **CAUTION** Poisonous. **BLOOMS** July–Sept. **HABITAT** Fields, roadsides.

COMMON BELLFLOWER
"Garden Bellflower"
Campanula rapunculoides
BELLFLOWER (BLUEBELL) FAMILY

3′. Flowers 1½″, blue, bell-shaped, with 5 pointed lobes and 5 bent-back green sepals; in showy, 1-sided spikes. Lower leaves heart-shaped. Often escapes garden cultivation. **BLOOMS** July–Aug. **HABITAT** Fields, roadsides.

HAREBELL
"Bluebell"
Campanula rotundifolia
BELLFLOWER (BLUEBELL) FAMILY

15". Flowers ¾", violet-blue, 5-lobed bells; nod on thread-like stalks. Stems wiry. Leaves mostly narrow, grass-like. **BLOOMS** June–Aug. **HABITAT** Rocky meadows. **RANGE** c and n N. Eng.

CARDINAL FLOWER
Lobelia cardinalis
BELLFLOWER (BLUEBELL) FAMILY

4'. Leafy erect stems bear slender spikes of showy scarlet flowers, each 1½", tubular, 2-lipped; upper lip 2-lobed, lower lip 3-lobed; stamens united into projecting tube. Leaves lanceolate, toothed. Name refers to bright red robes worn by Roman Catholic cardinals. **BLOOMS** July–Sept. **HABITAT** Wooded streamsides, moist meadows.

GREAT LOBELIA
Lobelia siphilitica
BELLFLOWER (BLUEBELL) FAMILY

3'. Flowers 1", bright blue, white-striped, 2-lipped, in long clusters at stem ends. Leaves oval, toothed. **BLOOMS** Aug.–Sept. **HABITAT** Lowland woods; meadows, swamps. **RANGE** w N. Eng.

WILD GINGER
Asarum canadense
BIRTHWORT FAMILY

9". Single, 1½", brownish flower, with 3 long-pointed lobes; close to ground. Leaves (1 pair), heart-shaped, dark, leathery, hairy. **BLOOMS** Apr.–June. **HABITAT** Woods.

ORIENTAL BITTERSWEET
"Asiatic Bittersweet"
Celastrus orbiculatus
BITTERSWEET FAMILY

L variable. Twining woody vine. Flowers tiny, green. Leaves round or ovate, toothed. Fruit scarlet, showy, in clusters from yellow leaf axils. **BLOOMS** May–June. **HABITAT** Woodland edges.

SWOLLEN BLADDERWORT
Utricularia inflata
BLADDERWORT FAMILY

8" (flower stalk). Flowers ¾" yellow, 2-lipped, on erect stalk that rises above water on wheel-like float of 6–8 inflated leafstalks. Carnivorous: air bladders on submerged leaves suck in minute prey. **BLOOMS** June–Aug. **HABITAT** Still water.

JAPANESE KNOTWEED
Polygonum cuspidatum
BUCKWHEAT FAMILY

6′. Bushy; forms dense stands. Flowers tiny, white, in 3″ spreading clusters at leaf axils. Stems reddish, bamboo-like. Leaves heart-shaped. **BLOOMS** Aug.–Sept. **HABITAT** Open areas, woodland edges.

PENNSYLVANIA SMARTWEED
"Pink Knotweed"
Polygonum pensylvanicum
BUCKWHEAT FAMILY

3′. Tiny, bright pink flowers in erect 2½″ spikes on sticky-haired stalks. Leaves slim, lanceolate, from knot-like stem joints. **BLOOMS** July–Sept. **HABITAT** Moist open areas.

SHEEP SORREL
Rumex acetosella
BUCKWHEAT FAMILY

10″. Flowers minute, reddish or greenish, in spikes up to ½ length of stem. Leaves arrowhead-shaped. Spreads vigorously. **BLOOMS** May–Sept. **HABITAT** Waste areas.

CURLY DOCK
Rumex crispus
BUCKWHEAT FAMILY

4′. Flowers tiny, greenish, in dense branching clusters. Stem single, erect. Leaves 8″, oblong or lanceolate, wavy-edged. Bears thousands of red or brown winged seedpods. **BLOOMS** June–Sept. **HABITAT** Fields.

AMERICAN BUR-REED
"Three-squared Bur-reed"
Sparganium americanum
BUR-REED FAMILY

24″. Erect, grass-like, aquatic. Zigzagging stalks bear 1″, ball-like heads of tiny green flowers. Leaves flat, narrow, blade-like, partly submerged. Often forms dense stands. **BLOOMS** May–Aug. **HABITAT** Shallow marshes, mud.

WHITE BANEBERRY
Actaea alba (pachypoda)
BUTTERCUP FAMILY

24″. Flowers tiny, white, clustered atop stems. Leaflets ovate, toothed. Berries white with black dot, red stalks. **CAUTION** Berries very poisonous. **BLOOMS** May–June. **HABITAT** Rich woods, thickets. **Red Baneberry** *(A. rubra)* is a bushier plant, with cherry-red berries.

WOOD ANEMONE
Anemone quinquefolia
BUTTERCUP FAMILY

8″. Single, white, 1″ flower, usu. with 5 petal-like sepals, often pink underneath. Stem slender. 1 whorl of 3 leaves, each divided into 3 toothed leaflets. Forms sizable stands. **BLOOMS** Apr.–June. **HABITAT** Open woods.

WILD COLUMBINE
Aquilegia canadensis
BUTTERCUP FAMILY

18″. Flowers 1½″, drooping, red and yellow bells, with long, red, upward-projecting spurs. Leaves light green, long-stalked, divided and subdivided into threes. **BLOOMS** May–June. **HABITAT** Rocky woods, ledges.

MARSH MARIGOLD
"Cowslip"
Caltha palustris
BUTTERCUP FAMILY

24″. Flowers 1½″, buttercup-like, shiny, bright yellow. Leaves heart-shaped, shallow-toothed, glossy, succulent. **BLOOMS** Apr.–June. **HABITAT** Streams, swamps, ditches.

GOLDTHREAD
Coptis groenlandica
BUTTERCUP FAMILY

5″. Flowers ½″, white, with several petal-like sepals; 1 per stalk. Runners yellow, thread-like. Leaves compound, with 3 shiny, toothed leaflets. **BLOOMS** May–June. **HABITAT** Bogs, swamps, mountaintops, cool woods.

ROUND-LOBED HEPATICA
Hepatica americana
BUTTERCUP FAMILY

5″. Flowers 1″, white, pink, lavender, or blue; 5–9 petal-like sepals; 1 per hairy stalk. Leaves rounded, 3-lobed; persist throughout winter. **BLOOMS** Apr. **HABITAT** Woods.

COMMON BUTTERCUP
"Tall Buttercup"
Ranunculus acris
BUTTERCUP FAMILY

2′. Flowers 1″, golden, with 5 glossy, overlapping petals. Stem erect, hairy, branching. Basal leaves deeply palmately divided. **BLOOMS** May–Aug. **HABITAT** Disturbed open areas, meadows.

CREEPING BUTTERCUP
Ranunculus repens
BUTTERCUP FAMILY
6". Flowers ½", yellow, shiny, with usu. 5 petals. Leaves blotchy, divided into 3 deeply cut, toothed leaflets; atop creeping runners from ground. **BLOOMS** May–Sept. **HABITAT** Disturbed open areas.

TALL MEADOW RUE
Thalictrum pubescens (polygamum)
BUTTERCUP FAMILY
5'. Tall, feathery. Flowers ⅓", white, bushy, clustered in plumes. Leaves bluish to olive, divided into many roundish, 3-lobed leaflets. **BLOOMS** June–Aug. **HABITAT** Meadows, swamps.

RUE ANEMONE
Thalictrum (Anemonella) thalictroides
BUTTERCUP FAMILY
8". 2–3 white to pink-tinged, 1" flowers, with 5–10 petal-like sepals. Stems slender. Leaves beneath flowers are 3-lobed, whorled. **BLOOMS** Apr.–May. **HABITAT** Woods. **RANGE** s ME and south.

EASTERN PRICKLY PEAR
Opuntia compressa (humifusa)
CACTUS FAMILY
10". Flowers 3", yellow, waxy. Stems flat, fleshy, bristle-tufted pads. Fruit reddish or purplish. N. Eng.'s only cactus. **CAUTION** Prickly. **BLOOMS** June–July. **HABITAT** Dunes, sandy places. **RANGE** Local on s coast to Nantucket, Cape Cod.

WATER HEMLOCK
Cicuta maculata
CARROT (PARSLEY) FAMILY
5'. Dome-shaped, loose, 4" clusters of many tiny white flowers. Stems smooth, sturdy, branched, magenta-streaked. Leaves doubly or triply divided into toothed, pointed leaflets. **CAUTION** All parts deadly poisonous. **BLOOMS** July–Aug. **HABITAT** Moist fields, swamps, thickets.

QUEEN ANNE'S LACE
Daucus carota
CARROT (PARSLEY) FAMILY
4'. Flat, lacy, 4" clusters of tiny white flowers, with purple floret at center and 3-pronged bracts below. Stems usu. hairy. Leaves very finely cut. **CAUTION** Poisonous; may irritate skin. **BLOOMS** June–Sept. **HABITAT** Fields, roadsides.

WATER PARSNIP
Sium suave
CARROT (PARSLEY) FAMILY

6′. Flat-topped, 2½″ clusters of tiny, dull white flowers. Stems ridged. Leaves pinnately divided into lanceolate, toothed leaflets. Fragrant. **BLOOMS** July–Sept. **HABITAT** Moist meadows, thickets, muddy shores.

GOLDEN ALEXANDERS
Zizia aurea
CARROT (PARSLEY) FAMILY

24″. Flat-topped, 2″ clusters of tiny, bright yellow flowers. Leaves 3-parted, redivided into several narrow, toothed, pointed leaflets. **BLOOMS** Apr.–June. **HABITAT** Meadows, moist woods.

Poisonous Plants

Poisonous plants are those that contain potentially harmful substances in high enough concentrations to cause injury if touched or swallowed. Determining whether a plant species is "poison" or "food" requires expertise. The information in this guide is not to be used to identify plants for edible or medicinal purposes.

Sensitivity to a toxin varies with a person's age, weight, physical condition, and individual susceptibility. Children are most vulnerable because of their curiosity and small size. Toxicity can vary in a plant according to season, the plant's different parts, and its stage of growth; and plants can absorb toxic substances, such as herbicides, pesticides, and pollutants from the water, air, and soil. The tasty-looking berry-like red fruit of yews, so often planted around schools, are highly toxic. Among the potentially deadly plants in New England are Jimson Weed, Mountain Laurel, Water Hemlock, various azaleas, and White Snakeroot.

Physical contact with plants that contain irritating resinous compounds causes rashes in many individuals. In New England, the main offender is the widespread Poison Ivy. The sap of several other plants, such as Celandine, can also cause dermatitis. Stinging Nettle is covered with hypodermic-like stinging hairs that actually inject pain-inducing substances when touched.

POISON IVY
Toxicodendron radicans
CASHEW (SUMAC) FAMILY

L/H variable. Climbing vine or erect or trailing shrub. Old stems hairy-looking, covered with fibrous roots. Flowers tiny, in yellowish-white 3″ clusters. Leaves variable; often palmately compound, with 3 ovate leaflets; dull or shiny; often red. Berries tiny, white. **CAUTION** Causes severe skin inflammation. Berries poisonous. **BLOOMS** May–June. **HABITAT** Thickets, trailsides.

BROAD-LEAVED CATTAIL
Typha latifolia
CATTAIL FAMILY

9'. Marsh-forming. Tall stiff stem ends in slender, yellowish, 4" tail (male flowers), with 6" brown cylinder (female flowers) just below. Leaves tall, blade-like, sheathing. **BLOOMS** May–July. **HABITAT** Watersides, ditches, marshes.

SPREADING DOGBANE
Apocynum androsaemifolium
DOGBANE FAMILY

3'. Bushy. Flowers ⅓", pink, bell-like, striped inside, fragrant; dangle from curved stalks. Stems have milky juice. Leaves smooth, ovate, bluegreen. Seedpods long, slender, paired. **BLOOMS** June–Aug. **HABITAT** Fields, roadsides.

PERIWINKLE
"Running Myrtle" "Vinca"
Vinca minor
DOGBANE FAMILY

6". Creeping evergreen. Flowers 1", pinwheel-like, purplish-blue with whitish star in center. Leaves ovate, shiny, dark green, paired. **BLOOMS** Apr.–May. **HABITAT** Gardens, roadsides, woods.

BUNCHBERRY
Cornus canadensis
DOGWOOD FAMILY

6". Flowers white, 1½", each made up of 4 petal-like bracts around greenish flower cluster; atop erect stems from creeping rootstock. Leaves ovate, in 1 whorl. Berries red. **BLOOMS** May–June. **HABITAT** Woods, bogs.

LESSER DUCKWEED
Lemna minor
DUCKWEED FAMILY

Green specks floating on water. Flowers minute, rare. Leaves tiny, round, flat, each with 1 thin 6" root below. Among the simplest, smallest, and most common flowering plants. Eaten by ducks. **HABITAT** Ponds, quiet rivers.

EELGRASS
Zostera marina
EELGRASS FAMILY

4'. Long, limp, tape-like leaves, partly submerged or floating. Flowers inconspicuous. One of very few flowering plants adapted to ocean water. Forms wildlife-rich sea meadows. **HABITAT** Ocean, below low-tide line.

FIREWEED
Epilobium angustifolium
EVENING-PRIMROSE FAMILY

5′. Tall single stem terminates in spike-like flower cluster, with drooping buds at tip. Flowers 1″, deep pink, with 4 roundish petals. Leaves narrow, linear. Slender, reddish, upward-angled seedpods below flower clusters release silky-haired seeds. **BLOOMS** June–Aug. **HABITAT** Clearings, roadsides, burned areas.

COMMON EVENING PRIMROSE
Oenothera biennis
EVENING-PRIMROSE FAMILY

5′. Flowers 1″, yellow, with 4 roundish petals around X-shaped stigma; lemon-scented; close at midday. Stems rough-hairy. Leaves lanceolate, toothed. **BLOOMS** June–Sept. **HABITAT** Open areas.

VIPER'S BUGLOSS
"Blueweed"
Echium vulgare
FORGET-ME-NOT FAMILY

30″. Hairy. Flowers ¾″, blue, with 5 lobes on tubular calyx; stamens reddish, projecting. Leaves oblong or lanceolate. **CAUTION** May irritate skin. **BLOOMS** June–Aug. **HABITAT** Fields, roadsides.

TRUE FORGET-ME-NOT
Myosotis scorpioides
FORGET-ME-NOT FAMILY

15″. Sprawling. Flowers tiny, light blue with golden "eye," in 2″ clusters at ends of small curved branches. Stems hairy. Leaves oblong, blunt, hairy, stalkless. **BLOOMS** June–Sept. **HABITAT** Watersides, ditches.

FRINGED GENTIAN
Gentianopsis crinita
GENTIAN FAMILY

24″. Flowers violet-blue, with 4 fringed, flaring petals; calyx has unequal pointed lobes; 1 atop each branch; open in sun, close at night. Leaves ovate to lanceolate, rounded at base, pointed at tip. **BLOOMS** Aug.–Oct. **HABITAT** Watersides, moist meadows. **RANGE** s ME (incl. Monhegan Is.) and south (local).

PLYMOUTH GENTIAN
"Marsh Pink"
Sabatia kennedyana
GENTIAN FAMILY

3'. Flowers 2", pink with yellow "eye" bordered in red; 8–12 petals. Leaves slender, lanceolate, unstalked. **BLOOMS** July–Sept. **HABITAT** Pondsides. **RANGE** Coastal RI and MA (local).

WILD GERANIUM
Geranium maculatum
GERANIUM FAMILY

20". Flowers 1¼", rose-pink, 5-petaled; in loose clusters at branch ends. Leaves toothed, deeply cut into 5 lobes. **BLOOMS** May–June. **HABITAT** Fields, open woods.

WILD SARSPARILLA
Aralia nudicaulis
GINSENG FAMILY

12". Hemispherical, 2" clusters of tiny greenish-white flowers under leafy umbrella. Single leaf divided into 3 groups of ovate, toothed leaflets. **BLOOMS** May–July. **HABITAT** Upland woods.

LAMB'S-QUARTERS
"Pigweed"
Chenopodium album
GOOSEFOOT FAMILY

3'. Spikes of minute greenish flowers in upper leaf axils. Stems branched, often red-streaked. Leaves diamond-shaped, toothed. **BLOOMS** June–Sept. **HABITAT** Farms, roadsides.

WILD CUCUMBER
"Balsam Apple"
Echinocystis lobata
GOURD FAMILY

L variable. Climbing vine, with tendrils and clusters of greenish-white flowers in leaf axils. Leaves palmate, maple-like. Fruit fleshy, green, prickly, 1½". **BLOOMS** Aug.–Sept. **HABITAT** Watersides, woodland edges.

VIRGINIA CREEPER
"Woodbine"
Parthenocissus quinquefolia
GRAPE FAMILY

L variable. Woody climbing vine. Flowers tiny, yellowish green, clustered. Leaves divided into 3–5 leaflets, each toothed, pointed; turn red. Berries purple-black. **BLOOMS** June–Aug. **HABITAT** Watersides, thickets, stone walls.

WILD GRAPES
Vitis species
GRAPE FAMILY

L/H variable. Climbing woody vine with large lobed or toothed leaves, twining tendrils, and shreddy bark. Flowers inconspicuous. Grapes purple. **BLOOMS** May–July. **HABITAT** Thickets, woodland edges.

WILD RICE
Zizania aquatica
GRASS FAMILY

8'. Flowers in broom-like, green (turning white), 24" panicles. Leaves 3', ribbon-like, with bases sheathing stems. **BLOOMS** June–Aug. **HABITAT** Shallow ponds, marshes.

SALTMARSH CORDGRASS
Spartina alternifolia
GRASS FAMILY

8'. Flowers in beige 8" panicles of upright spikelets. Leaves linear, flat, with bases sheathing round stems. Forms large colonies that force out other grasses. **BLOOMS** July–Sept. **HABITAT** Salt marshes. **Saltmeadow Cordgrass** *(S. patens),* 3'; has 12" brownish panicles of angled spikelets; in-rolled leaf edges; forms colonies, often flattened by wind.

COMMON REED
"Phragmites"
Phragmites australis (communis)
GRASS FAMILY

12'. Flowers in 12", reddish (turning silver), tufted panicles. Leaves linear, sharp, bluish. Often forms pure stands; invasive, replaces other marsh grasses, cattails. **BLOOMS** Aug.–Sept. **HABITAT** Brackish and freshwater marshes, ditches.

AMERICAN BEACH GRASS
Ammophila breviligulata
GRASS FAMILY

3'. Flowers in 16", erect, yellowish, narrow, free-standing panicles. Leaves tall, flat, stiff, narrow. Most common dune plant in N. Eng. Long roots stabilize sand. **BLOOMS** July–Sept. **HABITAT** Ocean-side dunes; shores of Lake Champlain, VT.

ROUND-LEAVED GREENBRIER
"Catbrier"
Smilax rotundifolia
GREENBRIER FAMILY

L variable. Thorny, woody, climbing vine. Flowers tiny, greenish, in small clusters. Leaves ovate, leathery; veins meet at leaf point. Berries blue. **BLOOMS** May–June. **HABITAT** Waterside thickets.

SPOTTED WINTERGREEN
Chimaphila maculata
HEATH FAMILY

10″. Flowers ⅔″, white or pink, waxy, with 5 folded-back petals around knobby pistil; fragrant. Leaves lanceolate, toothed; have white midvein; mostly whorled, evergreen. **BLOOMS** June–July. **HABITAT** Dry woods. **Pipsissewa** (*C. umbellata*) has less pointed leaves; blooms later (July–Aug.).

WINTERGREEN
"Checkerberry" "Teaberry"
Gaultheria procumbens
HEATH FAMILY

6″. Leathery-leaved, semi-woody, aromatic, evergreen shrub. Flowers tiny, waxy, white, 5-lobed bells. Leaves oval, slightly toothed, minty-scented. Berries scarlet; may persist through winter. Forms colonies via creeping, underground stem. **BLOOMS** Apr.–May. **HABITAT** Sandy woods.

SHINLEAF
Pyrola elliptica
HEATH FAMILY

10″. Elongated clusters of waxy, white, nodding, fragrant flowers, each ½″, with 5 thin petals around curved protruding style. Leaves dark olive, broad, oblong, basal, evergreen, red-stalked. **BLOOMS** June–Aug. **HABITAT** Woods.

INDIAN-PIPE
Monotropa uniflora
HEATH FAMILY

7″. Entire plant waxy, whitish. Flower ¾″, sometimes salmon-pink, with 4–5 petals, nodding; tops thick, translucent stem. Leaves scale-like. Saprophytic: gets nourishment from decayed organic matter. Turns black when picked. **BLOOMS** June–Sept. **HABITAT** Shady woods.

BEARBERRY
Arctostaphylos uva-ursi
HEATH FAMILY

8″. Trailing evergreen shrub. Flowers tiny white or pink bells, clustered at branch ends. Leaves small, glossy, leathery, paddle-shaped. Berries red. **BLOOMS** May–June. **HABITAT** Exposed rocky and sandy areas.

TRAILING ARBUTUS
"Mayflower"
Epigaea repens
HEATH FAMILY

10″. Flowers tiny, pink or white, tubular, 5-lobed, clustered. Stems woody, hairy, trailing. Leaves oval, leathery, evergreen. MA state flower; illegal to pick. **BLOOMS** Apr.–May. **HABITAT** Woods.

TWINFLOWER
Linnaea borealis
HONEYSUCKLE FAMILY

6″ (flower stalks). Dainty evergreen creeper. Flowers ½″, pinkish-white bells, in pairs atop slender stalks; fragrant. Stems hairy. Leaves oval. **BLOOMS** June–Aug. **HABITAT** Woods. **RANGE** n and w N. Eng.

LARGER BLUE FLAG
Iris versicolor
IRIS FAMILY

30″. Flowers violet-blue, 1 or more per sturdy stalk, each 3″, with petal-like parts in threes: sepals large, dark-veined, yellow-based; petals narrower, erect; styles 2-lobed, arched over sepals. Leaves sword-like, pale to grayish; rise from basal cluster. **BLOOMS** May–July. **HABITAT** Watersides, marshes.

YELLOW FLAG
Iris pseudacorus
IRIS FAMILY

30″. 1 or more showy yellow flowers on sturdy stalks among tall, sword-like leaves. Flowers 4″, with petal-like parts in threes: sepals large, back-curved; petals smaller, narrow, upright; styles fringed, arched over sepals. Leaves stiff, rise from basal cluster. Often forms clumps. Introduced from Europe as a garden plant; escaped cultivation. **BLOOMS** June–Aug. **HABITAT** Pondsides, streamsides, marshes, ditches.

POINTED BLUE-EYED GRASS
Sisyrinchium angustifolium
IRIS FAMILY

15″. Flowers ½″, blue; 3 petals, 3 petal-like sepals, all tipped with thorn-like point, atop long, flat, twisted, usu. branching stalks. Leaves grass-like, very narrow, linear. The various blue-eyed grasses are poorly named, as all of them are yellow-eyed and none belong to the grass family. **BLOOMS** May–July. **HABITAT** Moist meadows, shores.

SEA LAVENDER
"Marsh Rosemary"
Limonium carolinianum (nashii)
LEADWORT FAMILY

24″. Tiny, pale purple flowers along one side of diffuse wiry branchlets. Leaves broadly lanceolate, basal. Dresses coastal marshes in blue mist. Grossly overcollected. **BLOOMS** July–Sept. **HABITAT** Saltmarsh edges.

BLUEBEAD LILY
"Yellow Clintonia"
Clintonia borealis
LILY FAMILY

12″. Flowers 1″, yellowish green, bell-like, drooping, with 3 petals, 3 petal-like sepals, all curled, and 6 prominent stamens; 3–6 flowers per stem. Leaves oblong, bright, shiny, basal. Berries pure blue, shiny, oval, in clusters. **CAUTION** Berries poisonous. **BLOOMS** May–June. **HABITAT** Cool woods. **RANGE** w and n N. Eng.

TROUT LILY
"Dogtooth Violet"
Erythronium americanum
LILY FAMILY

10″. Flowers 1″, yellow inside, bronzy outside, solitary; nodding atop brownish stalk; 3 petals, 3 sepals, all swept back; 6 stamens with brownish or yellowish anthers. Leaves elliptical, mottled brownish, sheathe flower stalks. **BLOOMS** Apr.–May. **HABITAT** Moist woods and meadows.

CANADA LILY
Lilium canadense
LILY FAMILY

4′. Flowers 3″, yellow to orange, dark-spotted, nodding, 1 or more per stem. Leaves lanceolate, prickly-veined underneath, whorled. **BLOOMS** June–Aug. **HABITAT** Woods, moist meadows.

DAY LILY
Hemerocallis fulva
LILY FAMILY

3′. Leafless stalk rises from sword-like basal leaves, bears several tawny-orange, upward-facing, funnel-shaped flowers with erect, net-veined petals. Flowers 3½″; each lasts 1 day. Leaves 24″, narrow, pointed, channeled. Introduced as a garden plant; escaped cultivation. **BLOOMS** June–Aug. **HABITAT** Roadsides, meadows.

TURK'S-CAP LILY
Lilium superbum
LILY FAMILY

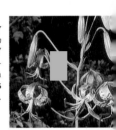

5′. Flowers 2½″, nodding, orange, with reddish-brown spots, curled-back petals, dangling brown anthers. Leaves lanceolate, whorled. **BLOOMS** July–Sept. **HABITAT** Woods, moist meadows. **RANGE** s N. Eng.

INDIAN CUCUMBER-ROOT
Medeola virginiana
LILY FAMILY

24″. Flowers ½″, yellowish green; dangle at center of upper leaf whorl. Stems often wooly. Leaves ovate or lanceolate. Berries bluish purple. **BLOOMS** May–June. **HABITAT** Moist woods.

CANADA MAYFLOWER
"Wild Lily-of-the-Valley"
Maianthemum canadense
LILY FAMILY

5″. Carpet-like colonies. Flowers tiny, white, star-like, in conical clusters. Leaves broad, pointed, with deeply cut bases. Berries white, ripen to red. **BLOOMS** May–June. **HABITAT** Upland woods.

WOOD LILY
Lilium philadelphicum
LILY FAMILY

30″. Flowers 2″, orange with purple-brown spots; face upward; 1–5 atop erect stalks. Leaves lanceolate, whorled. **BLOOMS** July–Aug. **HABITAT** Open woods. **RANGE** s and c N. Eng.

HAIRY SOLOMON'S SEAL
Polygonatum pubescens
LILY FAMILY

24″. Flowers ½″, bell-like, greenish white; dangle from leaf axils. Stems arched. Leaves ovate, stalkless, pale green, parallel-veined; hairy underneath. **BLOOMS** May–June. **HABITAT** Woods.

FALSE SOLOMON'S SEAL
Smilacina racemosa
LILY FAMILY

30″. Flowers tiny, white, fragrant, in pyramidal clusters atop angled, unbranched stems. Leaves elliptical, parallel-veined. Berries speckled green, ripen to red. **BLOOMS** May–July. **HABITAT** Woods.

PURPLE TRILLIUM
Trillium erectum
LILY FAMILY

12″. Single 2½″, foul-smelling flower with 3 purple-red petals alternating with 3 green, pointed sepals. Leaves large, diamond-shaped, dark green, net-veined; in whorl of 3. **BLOOMS** May–June. **HABITAT** Wooded hills.

LARGE-FLOWERED TRILLIUM
Trillium grandiflorum
LILY FAMILY

18″. Single 4″ flower, with 3 waxy, white or pink, wavy-edged petals. 1 whorl of 3 broadly ovate or diamond-shaped leaves. Berries red. **BLOOMS** June. **HABITAT** Moist woods. **RANGE** w N. Eng.

PAINTED TRILLIUM
Trillium undulatum
LILY FAMILY

16″. Single 2½″ flower, with 3 wavy-edged white petals, with pink or red marks at base. Leaves ovate, bluish, in whorl of 3. Berries shiny red. **BLOOMS** May. **HABITAT** Moist woods, swamps. **RANGE** Mainly w and n N. Eng.

SESSILE BELLWORT
"Wild Oats"
Uvularia sessilifolia
LILY FAMILY

9″. 1–2 creamy-yellow, narrow, nodding, 1″ bell-shaped flowers at tips of angled stems. Leaves oblong, unstalked, whitish underneath. **BLOOMS** Apr.–June. **HABITAT** Woods, thickets.

PURPLE LOOSESTRIFE
Lythrum salicaria
LOOSESTRIFE FAMILY

5′. Erect branching stems with 12′ spikes of pinkish-lavender flowers above paired or whorled, unstalked leaves. Flowers variably shaped, with wrinkled petals. Leaves lanceolate or linear, lower ones downy, clasping. Covers acres of wetlands; a spectacular sight when blooming, but tends to crowd out ecologically important native species. Introduced from Europe. **BLOOMS** July–Sept. **HABITAT** Marshes, pondsides, ditches.

SWAMP LOOSESTRIFE
"Water Willow"
Decodon verticillatus
LOOSESTRIFE FAMILY

7′. Flowers ½″, pink, with 5 wedge-shaped petals, in tufts at leaf whorls. Stems arched, intertwining. Leaves lanceolate. **BLOOMS** July–Aug. **HABITAT** Swamps, watersides. **RANGE** c ME and s NH and south.

BLUETS
Hedyotis (Houstonia) caerulea
MADDER FAMILY

6″. Patch-forming. Flowers ½″, pale blue with golden centers, tubular, 4-lobed. Basal leaves oblong, in tufts; stem leaves tiny. **BLOOMS** Apr.–June. **HABITAT** Open woods, fields.

PARTRIDGEBERRY
Mitchella repens
MADDER FAMILY

8″. Creeper. Flowers ½″, white or pinkish, waxy, 4-lobed funnels; fringed inside; paired at stem ends; fragrant. Leaves roundish, shiny, white-veined. Berries red, "2-eyed." **BLOOMS** June–July. **HABITAT** Woods.

SWAMP ROSE MALLOW
Hibiscus moscheutus (palustris)
MALLOW FAMILY

6′. Flowers 7″, hollyhock-like, pink with yellowish column of stamens; musk-scented. Leaves ovate, toothed; white-fuzzy underneath. **BLOOMS** July–Sept. **HABITAT** Marshes, streamsides. **RANGE** MA and south along coasts.

MUSK MALLOW
Malva moschata
MALLOW FAMILY

18". Flowers 1½", musky, pink or white, with notched, petals and bushy central column. Leaves intricately cut into very narrow lobes. **BLOOMS** July–Sept. **HABITAT** Fields, roadsides.

VIRGINIA MEADOW BEAUTY
Rhexia virginica
MEADOW-BEAUTY FAMILY

18". Flowers bright pink, with 4 rounded, slightly heart-shaped, often swept-back petals and 8 conspicuous, curly, yellow stamens; clustered at branch ends. Stems square, with wing-like angles. Leaves ovate, rounded at bases, toothed, strongly veined. Fruit urn-shaped capsules tipped with 4 points. **BLOOMS** July–Sept. **HABITAT** Sandy meadows, bogs, pondsides.

SWAMP MILKWEED
Asclepias incarnata
MILKWEED FAMILY

3'6". Flowers tiny, deep pink or rose-purple, in 3" clusters at branch ends. Stems branched; have milky juice. Leaves narrow, lanceolate. Seedpods long, pointed. **BLOOMS** June–Aug. **HABITAT** Watersides, moist meadows.

COMMON MILKWEED
Asclepias syriaca
MILKWEED FAMILY

4'4". Flowers tiny, purplish or pink, in rounded 2" clusters at leaf axils. Leaves broad-oblong, pale green; downy gray undersides and milky juice. Seedpods long, pointed, warty; release silky-hairy seeds. **BLOOMS** June–Aug. **HABITAT** Fields, roadsides.

ORANGE MILKWEED
"Butterfly Weed"
Asclepias tuberosa
MILKWEED FAMILY

23". Hairy. Flowers tiny, star-like, orange, in 2" clusters at branch ends. Leaves oblong, with watery juice. Seedpods narrow, hairy, erect. **BLOOMS** June–Sept. **HABITAT** Dry, open, sandy areas. **RANGE** c NE and south.

FRINGED POLYGALA
"Gaywings"
Polygala pauciflora
MILKWORT FAMILY

6". Flowers ¾", orchid-like, with 2 pink-purple wings flanking a bushy-tipped tube. Leaves oval, evergreen. **BLOOMS** May–June. **HABITAT** Woods. **RANGE** w and n N. Eng.

WILD BASIL
Clinopodium (Satureja) vulgaris
MINT FAMILY

15". Flowers ½", rose-purple, 2-lipped, in rounded wooly clusters in leaf axils and atop square, hairy stems. Leaves ovate, mostly un-toothed. **BLOOMS** June-Aug. **HABITAT** Thickets, woodland edges.

GROUND IVY
"Gill-over-the-ground"
Glechoma hederacea
MINT FAMILY

6". Flowers ¾", blue-violet, tubular, in leaf axils of upright branches. Stems creeping, square. Leaves roundish, scalloped, evergreen. **BLOOMS** Apr.–June. **HABITAT** Lawns, woods.

HENBIT
Lamium amplexicaule
MINT FAMILY

10". Flowers ⅔", lavender, 2-lipped, in leaf axils. Leaves roundish or ovate, scalloped; upper ones half-clasping, lower ones long-stalked. **BLOOMS** May–Sept. **HABITAT** Fields, roadsides.

WILD MINT
Mentha arvensis
MINT FAMILY

24". Flowers tiny, lilac or white, tubular, 4-lobed, in clusters at leaf bases; encircle weak, hairy, square stems. Leaves ovate; aromatic. **BLOOMS** July–Sept. **HABITAT** Moist areas, streamsides.

WILD BERGAMOT
Monarda fistulosa
MINT FAMILY

4'. Flowers 1", lavender, tubular, 2-lipped, in rounded clusters atop square stems. Leaves gray-ish green, lanceolate, toothed. **BLOOMS** July–Aug. **HABITAT** Open woods, fields.

SELF-HEAL
"Heal-all"
Prunella vulgaris
MINT FAMILY

12". Flowers ½", violet or pink, 2-lipped, with hood-like upper lip and fringed lower lip; in oblong heads atop square stems. Leaves ovate. **BLOOMS** June–Sept. **HABITAT** Fields, roadsides.

MARSH SKULLCAP
Scutellaria galericulata
MINT FAMILY

20". Flowers 1", bluish lavender, 2-lipped, with upper lip hooded, lower lip 3-lobed; in upper leaf axils. Stems square. Leaves lanceolate, toothed. **BLOOMS** July–Aug. **HABITAT** Moist meadows, swamps, watersides.

BLUE CURLS
Trichostema dichotomum
MINT FAMILY

20". Sticky. Flowers ¾", blue, 2-lipped, with upper lip 4-lobed, lower lip longer, white at base; stamens blue, long-curled. Stems hairy. Leaves lanceolate. **BLOOMS** Aug.–Sept. **HABITAT** Sandy areas. **RANGE** s and e N. Eng.

HEDGE BINDWEED
Calystegia (Convolvulus) sepium
MORNING-GLORY FAMILY

L variable. Smooth, twining vine. Flowers 3", funnel-shaped, 5-lobed, pink to white, white-striped. Leaves arrowhead-shaped. **BLOOMS** June–Sept. **HABITAT** Watersides, thickets.

COMMON WINTER CRESS
Barbarea vulgaris
MUSTARD FAMILY

18". Flowers tiny, bright yellow, cross-shaped; in many elongated 2½" clusters. Lower leaves pinnately lobed, with terminal lobe largest, rounded. Seedpods beaked. **BLOOMS** Apr.–June. **HABITAT** Open areas, moist roadsides.

AMERICAN SEA-ROCKET
Cakile edentula
MUSTARD FAMILY

12". Stems and leaves fleshy. Flowers tiny, pale lavender, 4-petaled. Leaves ovate to lanceolate, wavy-edged. Seedpods 2-parted, ovate, beaked. **BLOOMS** June–Sept. **HABITAT** Ocean beaches.

DAME'S ROCKET
Hesperis matronalis
MUSTARD FAMILY
3'. Flowers 1", purple, white, or pink, cross-shaped, 4-petaled, clustered at stem end. Leaves lanceolate, toothed. Seedpods long, pointed. **BLOOMS** May–July. **HABITAT** Fields, woods.

PEPPERGRASS
"Poor-man's Pepper"
Lepidium virginicum
MUSTARD FAMILY
16". Flowers tiny, white, cross-shaped, in ½" elongated clusters. Basal leaves toothed, lobed; stem leaves lanceolate. **BLOOMS** June–Oct. **HABITAT** Open areas, roadsides.

TRUE WATERCRESS
Rorippa nasturtium-aquaticum
MUSTARD FAMILY
10". Flowers tiny, white, in rounded clusters. Stems float or creep. Leaves have several oval leaflets, terminal one largest; often submerged. **BLOOMS** May–Aug. **HABITAT** Streams, springs.

WOOD NETTLE
Laportea canadensis
NETTLE FAMILY
3'. Flowers tiny, white, in clusters from leaf axils. Stems stout, with stinging hairs. Leaves thin, ovate, coarsely toothed, long-stalked. **CAUTION** Do not touch, hairs cause pain. **BLOOMS** July–Sept. **HABITAT** Watersides, woods.

CLEARWEED
Pilea pumila
NETTLE FAMILY
15". Flowers tiny, greenish white, in short curved clusters at leaf axils. Stems stout, translucent. Leaves ovate, veined, coarsely toothed. **BLOOMS** Aug.–Sept. **HABITAT** Shady gardens, woods.

STINGING NETTLE
Urtica dioica
NETTLE FAMILY
6'. Covered with stinging bristles. Flowers inconspicuous. Stems square. Leaves ovate, coarsely toothed, elm-like. **CAUTION** Do not touch; hairs cause pain. **BLOOMS** July–Sept. **HABITAT** Wetlands, woodland edges.

JIMSON WEED
Datura stramonium
NIGHTSHADE FAMILY

5'. Rank-smelling. Flowers 4", trumpet-shaped, white or violet. Stems often purplish. Leaves ovate, coarsely lobed. Fruit prickly, egg-shaped. **CAUTION** All parts extremely poisonous. **BLOOMS** July–Sept. **HABITAT** Fields.

BITTERSWEET NIGHTSHADE
Solanum dulcamara
NIGHTSHADE FAMILY

L variable. Climbing vine. Flowers ½", with 5 violet petals swept back from yellow central "beak," in loose clusters. Leaves 3-parted. Berries egg-shaped, shiny green, ripen to bright red. **CAUTION** Berries poisonous. **BLOOMS** June–Sept. **HABITAT** Thickets, woodland edges.

YELLOW LADY'S SLIPPER
Cypripedium calceolus
ORCHID FAMILY

23". Borne atop a leafy stalk are 1–2 fragrant flowers, each with a yellow, inflated, pouch-shaped lip petal. Lip 2", flanked by 2 spirally twisted, greenish-yellow to brownish-purple side petals and 2 greenish-yellow, lanceolate sepals (1 above lip, 1 below). Leaves 7", oval to elliptical, parallel-veined. Overpicked. **BLOOMS** May–June. **HABITAT** Bogs, limestone hills. **RANGE** w and n NE (local).

PINK LADY'S SLIPPER
"Pink Moccasin Flower"
Cypripedium acaule
ORCHID FAMILY

12". Colony-forming. Leafless stalk bears solitary flower with prominent pouch. Flower's distinctive inflated lip petal 2½" long, pink with red veins (occasionally pure white), deeply creased; sepals and side petals greenish brown, spreading. Leaves 7", oval, ribbed, dark above, silvery-hairy underneath; basal, paired. Does not transplant. **BLOOMS** May–June. **HABITAT** Woods, esp. under pines; bogs, rocky areas.

GRASS PINK
Calopogon pulchellus
ORCHID FAMILY

15″. 2–10 fragrant, upside-down orchids open sequentially up stalk. Flowers 1½″, pink, with uppermost petal yellow-bearded. 1 grass-like leaf. Do not pick. **BLOOMS** June–July. **HABITAT** Bogs, moist meadows.

RAGGED FRINGED ORCHID
Habenaria lacera
ORCHID FAMILY

18″. Flowers whitish green or creamy yellow; lip petal 3-parted, deeply fringed, with long curved spur at base. Lower leaves lanceolate, sheathing. **BLOOMS** June–Sept. **HABITAT** Bogs, moist meadows, fields, open woods.

NODDING LADIES' TRESSES
Spiranthes cernua
ORCHID FAMILY

18″. Flowers ½″, creamy-white, nodding; arranged in double spiral on seemingly twisted, slender spike; side petals and upper sepal unite to form hood over wavy-edged lower lip; fragrant. Basal leaves long, lanceolate; stem leaves small, scale-like. **BLOOMS** Aug.–Sept. **HABITAT** Moist meadows, thickets, riversides.

HELLEBORINE
Epipactus helleborine
ORCHID FAMILY

3′. Flowers ½″, greenish, tinged with purple; lower lip forms sac with pointed, under-turned tip; clustered in long terminal spike. Leaves broadly lanceolate, parallel-veined, clasping. The only nonnative orchid growing wild in N. Eng. **BLOOMS** July–Sept. **HABITAT** Woods, thickets, roadsides.

ROSE POGONIA
Pogonia ophioglossoides
ORCHID FAMILY

18″. Slender stem bears 1 sheathing leaf midway up; topped by 1¾″, solitary, rose-pink flower. Lip petal crested, fringed; 3 sepals form propeller shape; 2 ovate lateral petals overarch lip; 1 leaf-like bract below flower. Leaf 4″, ovate to broadly lanceolate. This and other wetland orchids suffer from degradation of habitat and overcollection. **BLOOMS** May–July. **HABITAT** Bogs, meadows, moist open woods.

GROUNDNUT
Apios americana
PEA (LEGUME) FAMILY

L variable. Climbing vine with short clusters of velvety, reddish-brown, fragrant, ½″ pea-flowers. Leaves divided into 5–7 ovate or lanceolate leaflets. **BLOOMS** July–Sept. **HABITAT** Watersides, woods.

YELLOW WILD INDIGO
Baptisia tinctoria
PEA (LEGUME) FAMILY

30″. Bushy. Loose elongated clusters of ½″ yellow pea-flowers at branch ends. Leaves sparse, grayish to bluish, divided into 3 ovate to wedge-shaped leaflets. **BLOOMS** May–Sept. **HABITAT** Dry fields. **RANGE** s N. Eng.

CROWN VETCH
Coronilla varia
PEA (LEGUME) FAMILY

18″. Sprawling or upcurving stems bear clover-like, pink-and-white 1″ flower clusters and many ovate paired leaflets. **BLOOMS** June–Sept. **HABITAT** Roadsides, fields.

SHOWY TICK TREFOIL
Desmodium canadense
PEA (LEGUME) FAMILY

4′. Plant erect, leafy, hairy; bears dense, elongated clusters of pink or rose-purple, ½″ pea-flowers atop stems. Leaves clover-like; divided into 3 oval leaflets. **BLOOMS** July–Aug. **HABITAT** Open woods, field edges.

BEACH PEA
Lathyrus japonicus
PEA (LEGUME) FAMILY

20″. Trailing vine often reaching tide line. Pink-lavender ¾″ pea-flowers in long-stalked clusters. Stems stout, angled. Leaves pinnately compound, with 6–12 thick, fleshy, oval leaflets; leafstalks have tendrils at ends, large arrowhead-shaped appendages at bases. Fruit elongated veiny pods. Found all over Western Hemisphere, from Greenland to Chile. **BLOOMS** May–Aug. **HABITAT** Beaches.

BIRD'S-FOOT TREFOIL
Lotus corniculatus
PEA (LEGUME) FAMILY
15″. Creeper. Flat-topped clusters of yellow ½″ pea-flowers at ends of low or prostrate stems. Leaves clover-like, with 2 small appendages at bases of leafstalks. **BLOOMS** June–Sept. **HABITAT** Meadows, roadsides.

WILD LUPINE
Lupinus perennis
PEA (LEGUME) FAMILY
20″. Upright elongated clusters of blue ½″ pea-flowers atop erect stems. Leaves palmately divided into 7–11 lanceolate leaflets. **BLOOMS** May–July. **HABITAT** Dry woods, fields.

ALFALFA
"Lucerne"
Medicago sativa
PEA (LEGUME) FAMILY
18″. Short spikes of dark blue-violet ½″ pea-flowers in short spikes on low or prostrate stems. Leaves clover-like, divided in threes. Seedpod coils into spiral. **BLOOMS** June–Sept. **HABITAT** Roadsides, fields.

RABBIT-FOOT CLOVER
Trifolium arvense
PEA (LEGUME) FAMILY
15″. Fuzzy, cylindrical ¾″ clusters of tiny, soft, grayish-pink flowers atop silky-hairy stems. Leaflets narrow, elliptical, in threes. **BLOOMS** May–Oct. **HABITAT** Dry open areas.

WHITE SWEET CLOVER
Melilotus alba
PEA (LEGUME) FAMILY
8′. Bushy. Flowers tiny, white, somewhat pea-like; fragrant when crushed; in slender, cylindrical 8″ clusters arising from leaf axils. Leaves pinnately compound, with 3 lanceolate, toothed leaflets. **BLOOMS** June–Sept. **HABITAT** Open areas. **Yellow Sweet Clover** *(M. officinalis)* is yellow-flowered, shorter (4′), more loosely branched plant; blooms May–Sept. Both species are cultivated as soil-enriching pasture crops and valued as honey plants.

PALMATE HOP CLOVER
Trifolium aureum (agrarium)
PEA (LEGUME) FAMILY

15". Roundish-oblong 1" heads of 20–40 tiny, yellow, clover-like flowers. Stems erect. Leaves divided into 3 wedge-shaped, stalkless leaflets. **BLOOMS** May–Sept. **HABITAT** Fields, roadsides.

RED CLOVER
Trifolium pratense
PEA (LEGUME) FAMILY

20". Dense, rounded 1" heads of tiny, magenta, pea-like flowers. Stems erect, hairy. Leaves divided into 3 oval leaflets, each marked with a pale V. **BLOOMS** June–Oct. **HABITAT** Open areas.

WHITE CLOVER
Trifolium repens
PEA (LEGUME) FAMILY

10". Flowers white, pinkish, or brownish; tubular; in somewhat spherical, ¾", stalked heads. Stems creeping. Leaves 3-parted, long-stalked. **BLOOMS** May–Oct. **HABITAT** Lawns, open areas.

COW VETCH
Vicia cracca
PEA (LEGUME) FAMILY

3'. Vine. Flowers ½", pink or lavender to blue-violet, tubular; crowded on long, 1-sided spikes. Leaves pinnately compound, with 8–12 pairs of leaflets on leafstalks topped with paired tendrils. **BLOOMS** June–Aug. **HABITAT** Fields, roadsides.

PICKERELWEED
Pontederia cordata
PICKERELWEED FAMILY

3'6". Flowers ⅓", violet-blue, 2-lipped, with yellow spots on upper lip; clustered in spikes. Stems mostly under water. Leaves large, heart-shaped. **BLOOMS** July–Aug. **HABITAT** Shallow water.

DEPTFORD PINK
Dianthus armeria
PINK (CARNATION) FAMILY

20". Flowers ½", deep pink, with 5 jagged-edged, white-dotted petals, atop slender stems. Leaves narrow, erect, needle-like. **BLOOMS** June–Aug. **HABITAT** Dry fields, roadsides.

RAGGED ROBIN
Lychnis flos-cuculi
PINK (CARNATION) FAMILY

30″. Flowers ½″, deep pink or white, raggedy, on delicate branched stalks. Stems thin, sticky above, hairy below. Leaves lanceolate, smaller ones higher on stem. **BLOOMS** May–July. **HABITAT** Fields, moist meadows. **RANGE** w and n N. Eng.

BOUNCING BET
"Soapwort"
Saponaria officinalis
PINK (CARNATION) FAMILY

24″. Flowers 1″, white or pinkish, with 5 scalloped petals; clustered atop thin branches; fragrant. Stems thick-jointed. Leaves lanceolate, parallel-veined, clasping. **BLOOMS** July–Sept. **HABITAT** Open areas.

WHITE CAMPION
"Evening Lychnis"
Silene latiflora (Lychnis alba)
PINK (CARNATION) FAMILY

3′. Flowers 1″, white or pinkish, with 5 deeply notched petals. Female flowers sweet-scented, with 5 curved pistils protruding from center; inflated sticky calyx has 20 dark veins and 5 curved teeth. Males, on separate plants, have slender 10-veined calyx, 10 stamens. Stems hairy, sticky, much-branched. Leaves ovate or lanceolate, hairy, paired. Blooms at night; attracts moths that pollinate flowers. **BLOOMS** May–Sept. **HABITAT** Open areas.

COMMON CHICKWEED
Stellaria media
PINK (CARNATION) FAMILY

8″. Flowers tiny, white, with 5 bisected petals and 5 longer green sepals. Stems weak, branched, trailing, with a hairy line. Leaves ovate, lower ones stalked, upper ones unstalked. **BLOOMS** Mar.–Oct. **HABITAT** Lawns, gardens.

BLADDER CAMPION
Silene vulgaris (cucubalus)
PINK (CARNATION) FAMILY

20″. Flowers ¾″, white, with lobed petals and protruding pistils on greenish, inflated, veined calyx; loosely clustered on upright branching stem. Leaves lanceolate or oblong. **BLOOMS** June–Sept. **HABITAT** Open areas.

NORTHERN PITCHER PLANT
Sarracenia purpurea
PITCHER-PLANT FAMILY

20″. Distinctive, vase-like leaves usu. contain water. Flowers 3″, purplish red, umbrella-shaped, nodding, long-stalked, with 5 petals, 4–5 petal-like sepals, expanded pistil. Leaves large, red-veined, curved to form hollow tube with flared lips and downward-pointing bristles. Carnivorous: insects lured by leaf color become trapped inside by hairs and eventually drown in water; plant absorbs nutrients as insects decompose. **BLOOMS** June–July. **HABITAT** Bogs.

ENGLISH PLANTAIN
Plantago lanceolata
PLANTAIN FAMILY

18″. Grooved stalks above leaf rosettes bear spherical or cylindrical, greenish-white heads of tiny, spirally arranged white flowers. Leaves lanceolate, ribbed. **BLOOMS** May–Oct. **HABITAT** Lawns, open areas.

COMMON PLANTAIN
"Broad-leaved Plantain"
Plantago major
PLANTAIN FAMILY

18″. Narrow, cylindrical, greenish-white spikes of minute flowers rise above basal set of large, ovate, strongly ribbed leaves. **BLOOMS** June–Oct. **HABITAT** Lawns, open areas.

POKEWEED
Phytolacca americana
POKEWEED FAMILY

8′. Bushy. Flowers tiny, white, in long clusters; pistil green, button-like. Leaves very large, oval. Berries purple-black; in drooping clusters on pink stalks. **CAUTION** Berries and root poisonous. **BLOOMS** July–Aug. **HABITAT** Woodland edges.

CELANDINE
Chelidonium majus
POPPY FAMILY

20″. Loose clusters of yellow, 4-petaled, ¾″ flowers on fragile stems. Leaves lobed, scalloped. **CAUTION** All parts toxic; yellow stem-juice irritates skin. **BLOOMS** May–July. **HABITAT** Woodland edges, roadsides, yards.

DUTCHMAN'S BREECHES
Dicentra cucullaria
POPPY FAMILY

10". ¾", pantaloon-shaped flowers are white with yellow tips, waxy, fragrant; dangle in clusters from arched leafless stalk. Leaves grayish fern-like; divided into many deeply cut leaflets. **BLOOMS** Apr.–May. **HABITAT** Woods, ledges.

BLOODROOT
Sanguinaria canadensis

POPPY FAMILY

6" (when blooming; taller later). Single 1½" flower per stalk, with 8–10 white petals around golden center. Stems underground; have red juice. 1 deeply lobed, toothed, pale grayish or bluish leaf; often embraces flower stalk. **BLOOMS** Apr.–May. **HABITAT** Woods.

WHORLED LOOSESTRIFE
Lysimachia quadrifolia
PRIMROSE FAMILY

20". Leaves and flowers in whorls of 4–5. Flowers ½", with 5 yellow petals that are dark red at bases and encircle 1 protruding pistil. Leaves lanceolate. **BLOOMS** June–Aug. **HABITAT** Open woods, moist meadows.

SWAMP CANDLES
Lysimachia terrestris
PRIMROSE FAMILY

3'. Erect stem topped with flower spike. Flowers ½", star-like, yellow; 5 petals, each with 2 red dots at base. Leaves lanceolate. **BLOOMS** June–Aug. **HABITAT** Marshes, watersides.

EASTERN STARFLOWER
Trientalis borealis
PRIMROSE FAMILY

8". Flowers ½", white, with 5–9 petals, stamens with golden anthers; paired on thread-like stalks atop stem. Leaves lanceolate, shiny, in star-shaped whorls. **BLOOMS** May–June. **HABITAT** Moist woods.

NARROW-LEAVED SPRING BEAUTY
Claytonia virginica
PURSLANE FAMILY

10". Flowers ¾", pink or whitish, striped with dark pink, with 5 petals and 5 yellow stamens with pink anthers. Leaves dark green, linear, usu. 1 pair midway up stem. **BLOOMS** Apr.–May. **HABITAT** Moist woods. **RANGE** s N. Eng. and south.

BEACH HEATH
"False Heather"
Hudsonia tomentosa
ROCK-ROSE FAMILY

7". Semi-woody mats. Flowers tiny, sulphur yellow, 5-petaled, clustered atop short twigs. Leaves tiny, scale-like, gray, wooly, evergreen. **BLOOMS** May–July. **HABITAT** Seaside dunes, pondsides.

ROUGH-FRUITED CINQUEFOIL
Potentilla recta
ROSE FAMILY

20". Erect, hairy. Flowers pale yellow, ¾", with heart-shaped petals in sparse clusters atop branches. Leaves divided into 5–7 blunt-tipped, toothed leaflets. **BLOOMS** May–Aug. **HABITAT** Fields, roadsides.

WILD STRAWBERRY
Fragaria virginiana
ROSE FAMILY

6" (flower stalk). Creeper with leaves and flowers on separate stalks. Flowers 1", with 5 white roundish petals around yellow-green center, which matures into large, red, fleshy, edible cone—the strawberry. Leaves divided into 3 toothed leaflets on long, hairy stalks. **BLOOMS** May–June. **HABITAT** Fields, woodland edges.

MEADOWSWEET
Spiraea latifolia
ROSE FAMILY

4'. Thicket-forming woody shrub. Flowers tiny, white or pale pink, fuzzy, with many long stamens; clustered into feathery pyramidal spires atop reddish twigs. Leaves narrowly ovate, coarsely toothed, pale underneath. **BLOOMS** June–Sept. **HABITAT** Moist fields.

STEEPLEBUSH
Spiraea tomentosa
ROSE FAMILY

3'. Erect woody shrub with dense, steeple-shaped, branched flower clusters. Flowers tiny, pink, 5-petaled. Leaves 2", oblong, toothed; undersides pale brownish, wooly. Blooms (and then withers) from top downward. **BLOOMS** July–Sept. **HABITAT** Old fields, meadows.

COMMON ST.-JOHN'S-WORT
Hypericum perforatum
ST.-JOHN'S-WORT FAMILY
20″. Flowers 1″, bright yellow, have 5 petals with black-dotted edges and many stamens; in broad branched clusters. Leaves ovate, with translucent dots. **BLOOMS** June–Aug. **HABITAT** Roadsides, waste areas.

BLUE TOADFLAX
Linaria canadensis
SNAPDRAGON (FIGWORT) FAMILY
24″. Flowers ½″, light blue-violet, with 2 lobed lips, lower one white-centered, thin-spurred; along slender stem. Leaves linear; basal ones on trailing stems in rosette. **BLOOMS** May–Sept. **HABITAT** Sandy fields, rocky areas.

BUTTER-AND-EGGS
Linaria vulgaris
SNAPDRAGON (FIGWORT) FAMILY
24″. Flowers 1″, pale yellow, with 2 lobed lips, lower one with orange "yolk" and long spur; in terminal clusters. Leaves grayish, linear. **BLOOMS** June–Sept. **HABITAT** Fields, roadsides.

SQUARE-STEMMED MONKEYFLOWER
Mimulus ringens
SNAPDRAGON (FIGWORT) FAMILY
30″. Flowers 1″, blue-purple, with 2 lobed lips, lower one larger, yellow-based; paired on stalks. Stems square. Leaves oblong to lanceolate, toothed, paired, clasping. **BLOOMS** July–Aug. **HABITAT** Watersides, moist meadows.

COMMON MULLEIN
Verbascum thapsus
SNAPDRAGON (FIGWORT) FAMILY
7′. Stem and leaves wooly. Tightly packed, spike-like cluster of yellow, 5-petaled, 1″ flowers. Basal leaves very large, thick, oblong; form rosette **BLOOMS** June–Sept. **HABITAT** Roadsides.

COMMON SPEEDWELL
Veronica officinalis
SNAPDRAGON (FIGWORT) FAMILY
8″. Prostrate, mat-forming. Flowers tiny, pale lavender or blue, with 4–5 roundish petals; clustered in erect spikes from leaf axils. Leaves ovate, toothed, downy, paired. **BLOOMS** May–July. **HABITAT** Dry fields, lawns, open woods.

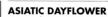

ASIATIC DAYFLOWER
Commelina communis
SPIDERWORT FAMILY

30″. Colony-forming creeper; reclining stems have upright leafy branches, each topped with 1 flower protruding from enfolding leaf. Flowers 1″, with 2 rounded, deep blue petals above 1 smaller white petal, and 6 long stamens with yellow anthers. Leaves fleshy, rounded, with sheathing bases. **BLOOMS** July–Sept. **HABITAT** Watersides, woods, waste areas.

ROUND-LEAVED SUNDEW
Drosera rotundifolia
SUNDEW FAMILY

8″. Leafless stalk bears elongated, 1-sided cluster of tiny white to pink-tinged flowers. Leaves round, reddish, in basal rosette; covered with sticky hairs that trap insects, which plant then digests. **BLOOMS** June–Aug. **HABITAT** Bogs.

WILD TEASEL
Dipsacus fullonum
TEASEL FAMILY

5′. Flowers tiny, lavender, in spiny, egg-shaped, thistle-like, 3″ clusters with long spiny bracts surrounding bases. Leaves lanceolate, toothed, paired, upper ones fused at bases around stems. **BLOOMS** July–Sept. **HABITAT** Meadows. **RANGE** w N. Eng.

ORANGE JEWELWEED
"Spotted Touch-me-not"
Impatiens capensis
TOUCH-ME-NOT FAMILY

6′. Flowers 1″, somewhat orchid-like, golden-orange splotched with reddish brown; extend backward into a spurred sac; dangle from succulent, translucent stems. Leaves thin, ovate, pale underneath. Fruit swollen capsules that burst at touch when ripe. **BLOOMS** July–Sept. **HABITAT** Shady marshes, moist woods.

BLUE VERVAIN
Verbena hastata
VERBENA FAMILY

6'. Square, branching stems bear candelabra-like groups of pointed spikes of tiny, blue-violet flowers. Leaves lanceolate, toothed. Flowers bloom a few at a time. **BLOOMS** July–Aug. **HABITAT** Watersides, moist fields.

SWEET WHITE VIOLET
Viola blanda
VIOLET FAMILY

4". Flowers ½", white, with 5 petals, upper 2 twisted, lower 1 purple-veined; fragrant; on separate, reddish stalks from heart-shaped, sharply pointed, shiny leaves. **BLOOMS** May. **HABITAT** Moist woods.

CANADA VIOLET
Viola canadensis
VIOLET FAMILY

12". Flowers 1", with 5 white petals with yellow bases; fragrant; on purplish hairy stems together with heart-shaped, toothed leaves. **BLOOMS** May–June; often again in fall. **HABITAT** Woods, esp. hilly country. **RANGE** w and n N. Eng.

COMMON BLUE VIOLET
Viola papilionacea
VIOLET FAMILY

8". Flowers ½", usu. blue or violet (sometimes white), lowest petal spurred; on separate stalks from heart-shaped, scalloped leaves. **BLOOMS** Apr.–June. **HABITAT** Moist woods, fields.

BIRD'S-FOOT VIOLET
Viola pedata
VIOLET FAMILY

8". Flowers 1½", deep lilac-violet, lowest petal veined, stamens have orange anthers; larger than most violets. Leaves finely cut. **BLOOMS** May–June. **HABITAT** Dry sandy fields, clearings.

DOWNY YELLOW VIOLET
Viola pubescens
VIOLET FAMILY

12". Softly hairy. Flowers ¾", yellow with 5 petals, lower 3 purple-veined; stalked together with heart-shaped, scalloped leaves. **BLOOMS** May–June. **HABITAT** Broadleaf woods. **RANGE** w and n N. Eng.

FRAGRANT WATER-LILY
"White Water-Lily"
Nymphaea odorata
WATER-LILY FAMILY

Floats on water. Flowers 5″, white or pink, with 20–30 long tapering petals that decrease in size toward center, and many yellow stamens. Leaves large, round, notched to center, often purple underneath, have soft, spongy, underwater stalks. One of the most common white water-lilies. **BLOOMS** June–Aug. **HABITAT** Ponds.

YELLOW POND-LILY
"Spatter Dock" "Cow-lily"
Nuphar lutea
WATER-LILY FAMILY

Flowers and leaves float on or emerge from water; stand high on long stalks when water level drops. Flowers 2″, yellow; tight balls open into cup shapes with several thick, waxy, petal-like sepals and numerous purplish stamens surrounding cylindrical pistil. Leaves large, heart-shaped, wrinkled. Fruit greenish to reddish, urn-shaped. **BLOOMS** May–Sept. **HABITAT** Ponds.

YELLOW WOOD SORREL
Oxalis stricta
WOOD-SORREL FAMILY

10″. Spreading. Flowers ½″, yellow, 5-petaled, in small clusters. Stems hairy, often much-branched. Leaves long-stalked, palmately compound, with 3 clover-like, heart-shaped leaflets. **BLOOMS** May–Sept. **HABITAT** Towns, open areas.

NORTHERN WOOD SORREL
Oxalis acetellosa (montana)
WOOD-SORREL FAMILY

5″. Low-growing. Flowers ¾″, with deep pink veins, 5 notched petals; 1 per stalk. Leaves clover-like, divided into 3 heart-shaped leaflets. **BLOOMS** June–July. **HABITAT** Hilly moist woods. **RANGE** n and c N. Eng.

Invertebrates

Biologists divide the animal kingdom into two broad groupings—vertebrates, animals with a backbone, and invertebrates, those without. While this distinction seems apt, perhaps because we are vertebrates ourselves, it is really one of mere convenience. Vertebrates are but a small subphylum of the animal kingdom, and invertebrates comprise the vast majority of animal life forms that inhabit water, air, and land. Invertebrates have thrived on earth for more than a billion years, with species evolving and disappearing through the eons; they include a fascinating spectrum of phyla with extraordinarily diverse life styles and evolutionary developments. This guide describes selected species from six phyla found in marine, freshwater, and terrestrial environments:

Phylum Cnidaria	Jellyfishes and sea anemones
Phylum Ctenophora	Comb jellies
Phylum Annelida	Marine worms, leeches, and earthworms
Phylum Mollusca	Chitons, gastropods, bivalves, and cephalopods
Phylum Arthropoda	Crustaceans, centipedes, millipedes, horseshoe crabs, arachnids, and insects
Phylum Echinodermata	Sea stars, sea urchins, and sea cucumbers

There are two basic invertebrate body structures. *Radially symmetrical* invertebrates, such as cnidarians and echinoderms, have a circular body plan with a central mouth cavity and a nervous system that encircles the mouth. *Bilateral* invertebrates have virtually identical left and right sides like vertebrates, with paired nerve cords that run along the belly, not the back, and a brain (in species with a head). All invertebrates are cold-blooded, and either become dormant or die when temperatures become too high or low.

In this guide, marine invertebrates are covered first, followed by freshwater and land invertebrates. Many of the groups covered below are described in more detail in separate introductions.

Plant or Animal?

Some marine invertebrates, such as sea anemones, are often mistaken for plants, but several key features place them in the animal kingdom. Plant cell walls, made of cellulose, are thick and strong, while those of animals are thin and weak. Plants have no nervous system, and therefore react slowly; almost all animals have a nervous system and can react quickly. Through the process called photosynthesis, most plants manufacture their own food from inorganic raw materials, while animals obtain energy by ingesting and metabolizing plants and/or other animals. Plants grow throughout their lives, while most animals stop growing at maturity (a few types, such as fish and snakes, keep growing but at a very slow rate). Finally, most plants are sedentary, while most animals move about. A sea anemone may be as immobile as a seaweed, but it qualifies as an animal on the basis of the above and other characteristics, such as the nature of its reproductive organs and its developmental pattern.

Marine Invertebrates

New England marine environments are home to a wide variety of clinging, digging, swimming, and scuttling invertebrates. This text covers representatives of classes from six invertebrate phyla. Members of other invertebrate marine phyla are generally small or difficult to see.

In the phylum Cnidaria are the gelatinous sea anemones and jellyfishes. All are radially symmetrical and many are quite beautiful, a trait that belies their fierce habits, as most possess tentacles armed with stinging cells that ensnare and paralyze animals within their reach. Most New England species are harmless to humans, although some, like the Lion's Mane, can be extremely dangerous. Comb jellies, of the phylum Ctenophora, are small to minute jellyfish-like animals without stinging organs; they are so transparent that they are almost invisible in the water. The phylum Annelida, or segmented worms, is divided into four classes. The most conspicuous annelids in New England waters are the bristle worms of the class Polychaeta. These worms have visible external segments covered with bundles of bristles that aid them in swimming, crawling, or digging; they are found in a wide range of habitats, from intertidal to abyssal depths. The phylum Mollusca, including many of the most familiar marine invertebrates, is discussed on page 183. Species of the phylum Arthropoda usually are identified by their rigid exoskeleton and jointed legs. Of the five marine arthropod classes, we cover two: horseshoe crabs (class Merostomata) and crustaceans (class Crustacea). The horseshoe crabs that ply our inshore waters are members of the ancient genus *Limulus,* which dates back 175 million years; they are crabs in name only, having more in common with spiders. Crustaceans, like barnacles, shrimps, crabs, and lobsters, live primarily in sunlit waters. Their forms are so diverse that their single common characteristic is paired antennae. Crabs and lobsters are discussed on page 189. Animals of the phylum Echinodermata, discussed on page 191, include sea stars, sea urchins, and sea cucumbers.

The following accounts give typical adult lengths or heights, unless otherwise noted. Many species can survive in a wide range of water depths, which are noted in the accounts; the term *intertidal zone* refers to the area between the high- and low-tide lines.

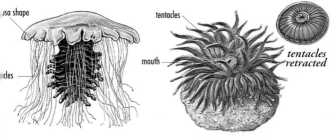

Jellyfish   Anemone, *tentacles out*

LION'S MANE
Cyanea capillata
JELLYFISH CLASS

W 15". Body a smooth, saucer-shaped, yellowish-orange to reddish-brown bell. 150 long, yellowish tentacles. World's largest jellyfish; can grow to 8' wide, with tentacles to 60' long, in Arctic. **CAUTION** Highly toxic; causes severe burns, blisters; can be fatal. **HABITAT** Ocean surface.

MOON JELLYFISH
Aurelia aurita
JELLYFISH CLASS

W 8". Body saucer-shaped, translucent. Many short, fringe-like, white tentacles. Round or horseshoe-shaped gonads near center: yellow, pink, or bluish in adults; white when imm. **CAUTION** Causes mild rash. **HABITAT** Inshore ocean surface; often washes ashore.

NORTHERN RED ANEMONE
Urticina felina (Tealia crassicornis)
CORAL AND SEA ANEMONE CLASS

3". Body columnar, smooth, red. 100 thick red, orange, and/or yellow retractable tentacles around mouth. Kills fish with stinging tentacles. **CAUTION** Stings. **HABITAT** Shallow ocean water; anchors to rocks. **RANGE** South to Cape Cod.

SEA GOOSEBERRY
Pleurobrachia pileus
COMB JELLY PHYLUM

W 1". Body spherical, transparent, with 8 iridescent comb plates. 2 whitish tentacles extend many times body length. Occurs in swarms. Catches small fish with sticky filaments on tentacles. **HABITAT** Ocean surface; in bays, shallow water.

CLAM WORM
Nereis virens
POLYCHAETE WORM CLASS

8". Body tapers toward rear. Iridescent bluish or greenish brown, with red, gold, or white spots; paler below. 200 segments; leaf-like side appendages. Swift; preys on invertebrates, carrion, algae. **HABITAT** Mud, sand, or vegetated ocean bottoms; estuaries.

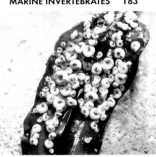

SLIME FEATHER DUSTER
Myxicola infundibulum
POLYCHAETE WORM CLASS

8″. Body pinkish to bluish; at head end, whorl of food-catching, feather-like, instantly retractable gills; tapers toward rear. Sedentary; lives in mass of slimy mucus. **HABITAT** Low-tide line to 170′ deep; rocks, gravel, pilings.

SINISTRAL SPIRAL TUBE WORM
Spirorbis borealis
POLYCHAETE WORM CLASS

⅛″. Shell tiny, calcified, white, snail-like. Whitish sedentary worm inside has 9 feathery gills. **HABITAT** Intertidal zone; anchors to shells, rocks, sea-weeds. **RANGE** South to Cape Cod.

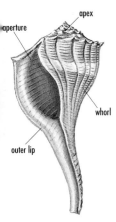

Gastropod Shell

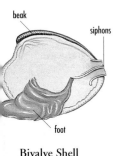

Bivalve Shell

Marine Mollusks

Mollusks, of the phylum Mollusca, are amazingly numerous and diverse, with New England species ranging in size from the microscopic Atom Snail to the 55-foot Giant Squid. Worldwide, seven classes of mollusks inhabit land, fresh-water, and marine environments; four are commonly found in inshore New England marine waters.

Chitons have eight-valved shells held together by a tough outer membrane; they crawl about on rocks and pilings, scraping up algae and microscopic ani-mals. Gastropods, including snails and their relatives, usually have a single calci-um carbonate shell, whorled to the right, although nudibranchs are shell-less; they feed on marine plants and animals, scraping food with their tiny teeth as they crawl or swim about. Bivalves, which include clams and oysters, have two separate shells called valves, from which protrude two siphons and a mus-cular foot; they filter-feed on microscop-ic plant and animal life. Normally, bivalves attach to a hard substrate or bur-row into sand, mud, clay, or wood, although some species, such as scallops, can also swim. Cephalopods, the most advanced mollusks, are shell-less, with highly developed eyes and long tentacled arms; they move by swimming and water propulsion and feed by grabbing and eating crabs, fish, and other mollusks.

Gastropods and bivalves can be easily observed at most coastal locations. Chitons are harder to find and must be specially searched for on or under rocks and inside dead whelk shells. Cephalopods are generally found only in subtidal waters. New England's inshore molluscan habitats include sand- and mudflats, peat banks, coastal rocks, tidepools, and wooden structures, like piers, pilings, and lobster traps. When exploring, remember to think small—many species measure less than an inch at maturity. Rocky tidepools are home to limpets, periwinkles, dogwinkles, and mussels; shallow flats support moon snails, whelks, scallops, and oysters; wooden pilings harbor colorful nudibranchs within their algae and hydroid colonies.

Shell-collecting, a popular hobby, has scarcely caught on in New England, and chances are you will have most of the shells on the beach to yourself. Very high tides and storm waves often bring up shells of deepwater species, so plan your trips accordingly. Recreational shellfishing is also popular but more tightly regulated—most towns in New England require a license. Environmental and seasonal conditions sometimes make local populations unsafe to eat, so always check with authorities before harvesting.

MOTTLED RED CHITON
Tonicella marmorea
CHITON CLASS

1½". Body oval; 8 smooth, slightly ridged shells with leathery surrounding girdle. Color variable: usu. mottled with red and brown, sometimes with green or blue. **HABITAT** Low-tide line to 300′ deep; on rocks. **RANGE** South to Cape Cod.

TORTOISE-SHELL LIMPET
"Atlantic Plate Limpet"
Notoacmaea (Acmaea) testudinalis
GASTROPOD CLASS

1". Shell low, smooth, cap-shaped, oval. Off-white, with brownish or bluish bands. 2 short tentacles; foot very large. Clings to exposed rocks at low tide. **HABITAT** Shallow ocean water; on rocks, algae.

COMMON PERIWINKLE
Littorina littorea
GASTROPOD CLASS

1". Shell bluntly conical; adult smooth, young finely ridged. Grayish to black, with thick, black outer lip, white inner lip. Feeds on seaweeds, algae. Most common snail in N. Eng. Edible. **HABITAT** Intertidal zone; rocks, sand.

COMMON SLIPPER SNAIL
Crepidula fornicata
GASTROPOD CLASS

1½″. Shell oval, curved to fit attachment site; apex turned to one side. Mottled white and brown. Flat white shelf partially covers opening. Rarely moves. **HABITAT** Intertidal zone to 40′ deep; attaches to hard objects.

Slipper snails on clam shell

NORTHERN MOON SNAIL
Lunatia heros
GASTROPOD CLASS

3″. Shell nearly round, with low spire. Whitish gray-brown. Tentacles yellow. Large foot leaves wide trail; when feeding, foot envelopes clam, while snail drills into it. **HABITAT** Low-tide line to 1,200′ deep; mud, sand bottoms.

ATLANTIC DOGWINKLE
Nucella (Thais) lapillus
GASTROPOD CLASS

1¼″. Shell rough, spindle-shaped, with spiral ridges. Variably colored pink, lavender, orange, brown, or black; some banded white or yellow. Outer lip thick, flaring. Feeds on mussels, barnacles. **HABITAT** Intertidal zone; rocks, crevices, seaweeds.

KNOBBED WHELK
Busycon carica
GASTROPOD CLASS

7″. Shell pear-shaped, with knobbed whorls; low conical spire; spout-like canal. Yellowish gray. Raids lobster and crab traps; foot pries open bivalves. Edible. **HABITAT** Intertidal zone to 15′ deep; sandy bottoms. **RANGE** Cape Cod and south.

RED-GILLED NUDIBRANCH
Coryphella verrucosa
GASTROPOD CLASS

1″. Shell-less, translucent white slug. 4 long antennae. Hundreds of long, red or orange, white-tipped projections on back. Feeds on hydroids. **CAUTION** Stings. **HABITAT** Low-tide line to deep water; among seaweeds, hydroids. **RANGE** South to Cape Cod.

RIBBED MUSSEL
Geukensia (Ischadium) demissa
BIVALVE CLASS
3″. Shell thin, elongated, fan-shaped, with radial ribs. Yellowish brown to brownish black. Burrows in mud or peat; fastens to pilings. **HABITAT** Intertidal salt marshes, bays.

EDIBLE MUSSEL
"Blue Mussel"
Mytilus edulis
BIVALVE CLASS
3″. Shell thin, shiny; front beaked; rear rounded or fan-shaped. Blue-black to black. Forms colonies; attaches to objects using strong, hair-like threads. Edible. **HABITAT** Intertidal zone; rocks, pilings.

ATLANTIC BAY SCALLOP
"Blue-eyed Scallop"
Argopecten (Aequipecten) irradians
BIVALVE CLASS
2½″. Shell nearly round, convex; 18 radiating ribs. Adult gray to brownish or reddish; imm. brightly colored. Dozens of blue eyes along mantle margin. Swims. Edible. **HABITAT** Shallow bays, eelgrass beds. **RANGE** Mainly Cape Cod and south.

ATLANTIC DEEP-SEA SCALLOP
Placopecten magellanicus
BIVALVE CLASS
6″. Shell nearly round, flattish, with fine lines and grooves. Yellowish, purplish gray, or whitish; lower shell white. Dozens of steely gray eyes. Swims. Edible. **HABITAT** 13–400′ deep; sand, gravel bottoms.

COMMON JINGLE SHELL
Anomia simplex
BIVALVE CLASS
1½″. Shell thin, roundish, smooth. Translucent gold, silver, or orange. Attachment muscle uses hole on lower valve. Several strung shells will jingle in breeze. **HABITAT** Low-tide line to 30′ deep; rocks, shells, wood.

EASTERN OYSTER
Crassostrea virginica
BIVALVE CLASS

7". Shell thick, irregularly oval to elongated, with coarse ridges; upper shell flattened, lower deeper. Grayish white. Free-swimming larvae settle on hard surfaces. Edible. **HABITAT** Intertidal zone to 40' deep; brackish bays, estuaries; attaches to solid objects.

NORTHERN QUAHOG
Mercenaria mercenaria
BIVALVE CLASS

5". Shell thick, almost round, raised, with concentric lines. Grayish or buffy. Edible; smallest are cherrystones, mid-size are littlenecks, largest used in chowder. **HABITAT** Intertidal zone to 50' deep; burrows in sand, mud.

COMMON RAZOR CLAM
Ensis directus
BIVALVE CLASS

7". Shell long, thin, flattish; sharp edges, square end; resembles straight-edged razor. Brown. Strong foot lets animal descend rapidly into oval burrow or sand. Edible. **HABITAT** Sandy intertidal flats, shallow waters.

ATLANTIC SURF CLAM
Spisula solidissima
BIVALVE CLASS

7". Shell thick, rounded triangular. Yellowish white, with dark brown "skin." Burrows into sand. Found broken on hard surfaces, dropped there by gulls to open. Edible. **HABITAT** Low-tide line to 100' deep; sand, mud, gravel.

SOFT-SHELLED CLAM
"Steamer Clam"
Mya arenaria
BIVALVE CLASS

4". Shell thin, oval, rounded in front; gap between valves. Whitish. Burrows in sand; siphons shoot up jets of water when disturbed. Edible. **HABITAT** Intertidal zone to 30' deep; brackish water; sand, mud.

ATLANTIC LONG-FINNED SQUID
Loligo pealei
CEPHALOPOD CLASS

20″. Shell-less; body cylindrical, tapers toward rear; milky white, with tiny reddish-purple spots. Head has 2 large eyes, 8 arms, 2 tentacles. Triangular fin on each side at rear. Edible. **HABITAT** Ocean surface to 600′ deep.

ATLANTIC HORSESHOE CRAB
Limulus polyphemus
HORSESHOE CRAB CLASS

Female 20″; male 15″. Carapace horseshoe-shaped, turtle-like, greenish brown; abdomen triangular; tail long, spiked; eyes bulbous, unstalked. Mouth surrounded by 5 pairs of walking legs; pincers in front. **HABITAT** Mud, sand bottoms to 75′ deep.

NORTHERN ROCK BARNACLE
Balanus balanoides
CRUSTACEAN CLASS

¾″. Shell mainly conical; elongated when crowded; flat at top; whitish. 4 shell-like plates protect retractable, feathery feeding appendages. **CAUTION** Plate edges are extremely sharp. **HABITAT** Shallow ocean water; attaches to hard objects.

SAND SHRIMP
Crangon septemspinosa
CRUSTACEAN CLASS

2″. Exoskeleton thin, transparent; pale green, gray, or buff, with blackish spots. Beak short; 1st pair of legs clawed, 2nd and 3rd slender; "tail fan" often blackish. **HABITAT** Eelgrass, tidepools, sand to 300′ deep. Other species of shrimp and related schooling krill live off N. Eng.'s coast.

Crabs and Lobsters

Crabs and lobsters, of the order Decapoda, fall into two categories: short-tailed decapods, or true crabs, and long-tailed decapods. As the name implies, all have ten legs. True crabs have a large cephalothorax, or fore-body, and a small abdomen tucked beneath their shells. They can move well in all directions, but usually walk sideways. Some, like Blue Crabs and Lady Crabs, have paddle-like hindlegs for swimming. Others, like male fiddler crabs, have a greatly enlarged pincer. Most species are scavengers, although some feed on living animals; fiddlers are generally plant-eaters. Long-tailed decapods, such as lobsters and hermit crabs, are named for their elongated abdomens, or "tails." Hermit crabs protect their soft abdomens by hiding in empty gastropod shells. They are fascinating to observe as they carry their homes about, switching shells as they grow or as their domestic tastes change. Take care when handling crabs and lobsters; some are aggressive, and all can pinch. Measurements in accounts refer to the carapace, the shell part that extends over the head and thorax, but not the abdomen.

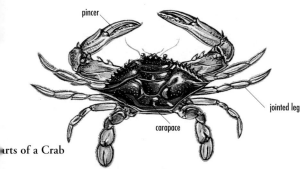

pincer

jointed leg

carapace

rts of a Crab

NORTHERN LOBSTER
"New England Lobster"
Homarus americanus
CRUSTACEAN CLASS

L 12–36". Head and thorax cylindrical, with large pincers; tail (abdomen) somewhat flattened. Greenish brown above, paler below; appendages and pointed beak red-tipped. One pair of antennae short, one very long; 2 eyes on short stalks. First 3 pairs of walking legs have pincers; 1st pair greatly enlarged, strong, not alike: one (often the left) heavier, blunt, with rounded teeth, used as crusher to open hard objects like snails or clams; other (usu. the right) less heavy, sharper, more pointed, used as cutter to tear apart carrion, vegetation, prey. Nocturnal scavenger and predator on sea stars, crabs, worms. Sheds exoskeleton yearly; a few individuals reach 100 years of age, weigh up to 45 lb.; avg. wt. 1–3 lb. Edible. **HABITAT** 10–2,000' deep; rocky, sandy bottoms; inshore in summer, deeper water in winter.

FLAT-CLAWED HERMIT CRAB
Pagurus pollicaris
CRUSTACEAN CLASS
L 1". Oblong; pinkish; eyestalks brown. Right pincer larger, broad, flat. 2 pairs of legs for scurrying, 3 smaller pairs for holding up body. **HABITAT** Estuaries, sand bottoms to 360' deep. **RANGE** Mainly Cape Cod and south.

LADY CRAB
Ovalipes ocellatus
CRUSTACEAN CLASS
W 2¼". Carapace fan-shaped, slightly wider than long; light gray with purple spots. Pincers large, sharp; 5th pair of legs paddle-like. Aggressive. **HABITAT** Sand, mud, rock bottoms to 150' deep. **RANGE** Cape Cod and south.

BLUE CRAB
Callinectes (Cancer) sapidus
CRUSTACEAN CLASS
W 6". Carapace wide, with long spine at each end. Bluish green, edged with red spines. Strong pincers blue (male) or red (female); legs blue. Fast swimmer. Edible. **HABITAT** Low-tide line to 120' deep; estuaries.

GREEN CRAB
Carcinus maenas
CRUSTACEAN CLASS
W 2". Carapace fan-shaped; above, green with blackish mottling; below, male yellow, female orange. Pincers large; 5th pair of legs pointed. N. Eng.'s most common crab. **HABITAT** Salt marshes, tidepools, rocks.

ATLANTIC ROCK CRAB
Cancer irroratus
CRUSTACEAN CLASS
W 4½". Carapace oval; yellow, heavily red-spotted; front edge has rounded teeth, grooves. Pincers short, stout; fingers bent downward. Legs short, hairy at edges. Edible. **HABITAT** Intertidal zone to 2,600' deep; rocks, gravel.

SAND FIDDLER
Uca pugilator
CRUSTACEAN CLASS
W ¾". Carapace squarish; male purplish with blackish markings; female darker, more subdued. 1 male pincer greatly enlarged. Eats detritus at low tide. **HABITAT** Salt marshes, mudflats, calm beaches. **RANGE** Cape Cod and south.

Echinoderms

In New England, the phylum Echinodermata is represented by sea stars, sea urchins, and sea cucumbers. *Echinoderm* means "spiny skin," and all species in this phylum are covered with spines or bumps of varying lengths. They are radially symmetrical and possess a unique water vascular system consisting of internal canals that pump fluids through the body. These canals end on the undersurface in tube feet, slender appendages that expand and contract to allow the animal to move and feed. Sea stars, named for their star-like shape, have varying numbers of arms radiating from a central disk; they feed mainly on mollusks and other echinoderms. Sea urchins, including sand dollars, feed on plankton, algae, and tiny organic particles in sand. The spines of the elongated sea cucumbers are actually embedded in the skin, which is outwardly smooth; these animals feed almost exclusively on plankton. Measurements in the accounts are of diameters, including arms and spines, unless otherwise noted.

tube feet

mouth

Underside of a Sea Star

SMOOTH SUN STAR
Solaster endeca
SEA STAR CLASS

12″. Disk medium-size; usu. 10 arms (can be 7–14), covered with small bumps. Orange, pink, red, or purple; arms edged with yellow. **HABITAT** Low-tide line to 900′ deep; rocky bottoms. **RANGE** South to Cape Cod.

SPINY SUN STAR
Crossaster papposus
SEA STAR CLASS

11″. Disk large, sunflower-like; usu. 12 arms (can be 8–14), covered with brush-like spines. Orange or red, with concentric bands of yellow, pink, or white. **HABITAT** Low-tide line to 1,000′ deep; rocky bottoms.

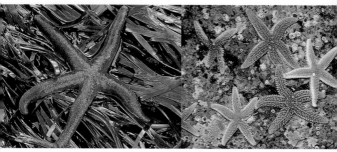

BLOOD SEA STAR
Henricia sanguinolenta
SEA STAR CLASS

4". Disk small; 5 long, slender, cylindrical arms, covered with short, blunt spines. Red or orange; arms tipped yellow. Absorbs nutrients through skin; also feeds directly on sponges. **HABITAT** Low-tide line to 15' deep; rocky bottoms.

NORTHERN SEA STAR
Asterias vulgaris
SEA STAR CLASS

11". Disk large; 5 long, flattened arms; soft, flabby, covered with short white spines that also form rows down centers of arms. Pink, orange, or purple. **HABITAT** Intertidal zone to 2,000' deep; rock, sand, gravel bottoms.

GREEN SEA URCHIN
Strongylocentrotus droebachiensis
SEA URCHIN CLASS

3". Body oval, cactus-like; with hundreds of 1" greenish spines. Spineless brownish-green bodies wash ashore. Roe edible. **CAUTION** Painful if stepped on. **HABITAT** Rocky shores, kelp beds, bays to 3,800' deep.

COMMON SAND DOLLAR
Echinarachnius parma
SEA URCHIN CLASS

3". Body round, flat, disk-like, with tiny dull spines. Purplish brown; white when washed ashore. 5 radial furrows branch from mouth on underside. **HABITAT** Low-tide line to 5,000' deep; sand, mud bottoms.

ORANGE-FOOTED SEA CUCUMBER
Cucumaria frondosa
SEA CUCUMBER CLASS

L 10". Long, cylindrical, tapered at rear; skin smooth, leathery; reddish brown. Head end has 10 branched, retractable orange tentacles. Edible. **HABITAT** Low-tide line to 1,200' deep; under rocky overhangs, in crevices. **RANGE** South to Cape Cod.

Freshwater and Land Invertebrates

Tens of thousands of invertebrate species thrive in New England's freshwater and terrestrial environments. Ponds and meadows are home to literally billions of invertebrates per acre, and even sheer rock faces and acidic bogs support a varied assortment. The most commonly seen New England invertebrates belong to three phyla.

Land and freshwater members of the phylum Mollusca are the generally small, drab species of slugs, snails, and clams. They are both aquatic, living amid vegetation or in bottom sediment, and terrestrial, found in leaf litter and under leaves, boards, and rocks. Some of these terrestrial species, like slugs, are our most annoying garden pests. The phylum Annelida includes leeches and earthworms. There are terrestrial leeches in parts of the world, but in New England leeches occur only in certain freshwater environments. They are so quick to sense the presence of a warm body that freshwater biologists need no sophisticated equipment to find them—the scientists merely wade into the water and wait! Earthworms can occur at an average of 1,000 pounds per acre; they help fertilize and oxygenate soil by pulling vegetation underground. The phylum Arthropoda comprises the largest number of freshwater and land invertebrates, with five classes covered here: crustaceans, millipedes, centipedes, arachnids, and insects. Crustaceans include the freshwater crayfish and the terrestrial pillbugs and sowbugs, commonly found under rocks and rotting logs. Terrestrial millipedes and centipedes look like worms with legs—two per segment for vegetarian millipedes and one per segment for predatory centipedes. Arachnids—spiders, daddy-long-legs (harvestmen), and ticks—are discussed on page 195. Insects, introduced on page 198, are comprised of many well-known invertebrate orders, including dragonflies, grasshoppers, beetles, flies, butterflies, and ants, wasps, and bees (see their separate introductions within the section).

FRESHWATER LEECH
Macrobdella decora
LEECH CLASS
L 2⅓". Body broad, flattened. Brownish green; black and red spots above. Good swimmer; undulates in water. Front and rear suckers attach to fish, frogs, turtles, mammals; front sucker draws blood. **HABITAT** Lakes, rivers.

EARTHWORMS
"Night Crawler"
Lumbricus species
EARTHWORM CLASS
L to 8". Body soft, cylindrical, with dozens of segments; purplish orange. Aerates damp soil; common on surface after heavy rains. **HABITAT** Woods, meadows, lawns.

LEOPARD SLUG
Limax maximus
GASTROPOD CLASS

L 5″. A shell-less mollusk. Head has 2 long, 2 short tentacles; body tapers to a point; gray with blackish spots. A garden pest; feeds on flowers, leaves. Chiefly nocturnal. **HABITAT** Gardens, woods. **RANGE** s N. Eng.

EASTERN CRAYFISH
Cambarus bartoni
CRUSTACEAN CLASS

L 4″. Similar to a lobster but smaller, with thinner pincers; grayish brown with dark speckles. 2 long antennae; 4 pairs of walking legs. Feeds on vegetation, small animals. Edible. **HABITAT** Small, clear streams, quiet ponds.

PILLBUGS/SOWBUGS
Armadillidium and *Porcellio* species
CRUSTACEAN CLASS

L ½″. Body convex, oval from above; with gray or brown shrimp-like plates, 7 pairs of short legs. Head has 2 short antennae. Feeds on decaying plant matter. Pillbugs roll into a ball when disturbed. **HABITAT** Under rocks, logs, leaves.

MILLIPEDES
Spirobolus species
MILLIPEDE CLASS

L 4″. All millipedes are slow-moving, with 30–200 legs, rounded anterior, short antennae; roll into spiral ball when threatened, releasing foul-smelling secretion to repel predators. This species: 55 reddish-ringed brown segments; 200 tiny legs. **HABITAT** Meadows, woods.

HOUSE CENTIPEDES
Scutigera species
CENTIPEDE CLASS

L 4″. All centipedes are fast-moving, with strong jaws, 2 long antennae, 1 pair long posterior legs. This species formidable-looking; light brown; 15 pairs of very long legs move in waves; nocturnal. **HABITAT** Leaf litter, dead trees, buildings.

Spiders and Kin

The class Arachnida includes spiders, ticks, mites, harvestmen, scorpions, and pseudoscorpions. These generally dreaded invertebrates are much maligned; in fact, most species are harmless to humans, many are beneficial to the environment, and all have habits worthy of the naturalist's attention.

Spiders have two body parts and eight legs. Most also have eight simple eyes, the arrangement of which differs from genus to genus. On jumping spiders, which hunt without benefit of a web, two eyes are tremendously enlarged, a trait that enables them to judge accurately distances to their prey. All spiders extrude three or four types of silk from spinnerets on their undersides: one to make cocoons for their eggs; another, much finer, for lowering themselves; sturdy strands to construct radial web lines; and finally, the sticky silk they use to entrap prey.

8 eyes

A spider's face

Spiders hunt by stalking, ambushing, or ensnaring their victims, then subduing or killing them with a poisonous bite. Their venom acts as a powerful digestive fluid, which liquifies their prey so they can suck it up. All spiders are venomous, but most are entirely harmless to humans, and indeed retreat quickly when we arrive on the scene. Spiders are not parasitic on humans or domesticated animals, nor do they transmit any diseases to humans. They can be incredibly abundant, especially in meadows, where hundreds of thousands can inhabit a single acre. Their hearty appetites help to control the insect population.

In addition to spiders, there are many other arachnids among us. Daddy-long-legs, also called harvestmen, are nonvenomous and have one body part and very long, fragile legs. They are normally solitary, but in winter they may huddle together in masses. Ticks are parasites with little foreclaws that grasp onto passing animals. To feed, they bury their heads under the skin and draw blood. Some species are carriers of serious diseases, including Lyme disease (see box, page 197).

The accounts below give typical lengths of females, not including legs; the rarely seen males are often much smaller.

BLACK-AND-YELLOW GARDEN SPIDER
Argiope aurantia
ARACHNID CLASS

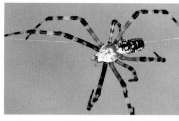

1″. Head/thorax has short silvery hair. Abdomen large, egg-shaped; black with bold yellow or orange markings. Legs long, hairy; banded yellow or reddish and black. Hangs head downward in center of web 12″ or more in diameter, with thick vertical zigzag pattern in center; placed among plants in sunny sheltered area. **HABITAT** Gardens, bushy meadows. **SEASON** Summer.

AMERICAN HOUSE SPIDER
Achaearanea tepidariorum
ARACHNID CLASS

¼″. Body pale brown; large abdomen mottled black and gray on sides. Male's legs orange; female's banded black and yellow. Builds irreg. web in corners of ceilings and windows. **HABITAT** Buildings. **SEASON** Year-round.

FUNNEL-WEB GRASS SPIDER
Agelenopsis naevia
ARACHNID CLASS

¾″. Funnel weavers: build massive fine webs over grass with horizontal funnel in corner; dash out after insects crossing web. This species: dark brown with pale yellow bands; legs hairy. **HABITAT** Lawns, shrubby meadows. **SEASON** May–Sept.

CAROLINA WOLF SPIDER
Lycosa carolinensis
ARACHNID CLASS

1¼″. Body as long as wide; gray-brown, sometimes with central abdominal stripe; well camouflaged. Legs hairy. 8 large eyes. Does not spin web; hunts at night in leaves, rocks, grass. **HABITAT** Meadows, woods. **SEASON** May–Sept.

GOLDENROD SPIDER
Misumena vatia
ARACHNID CLASS

⅜″. Female yellow or white, with red streaks on abdomen; legs thick, pale. Male abdomen white, with 2 red streaks. Hides in goldenrods and daisies, snatching insects. **HABITAT** Usu. white or yellow flowers in gardens, meadows. **SEASON** June–Oct.

DARING JUMPING SPIDER
Phidippus audax
ARACHNID CLASS

½″. Like a tiny tarantula. Black hairy; abdomen has whitish cross band, whitish spots. Legs short stout. Large eyes provide excellent vision. Makes spectacular leaps pouncing on prey. **HABITAT** Tree trunks, fallen limbs, leaf litter, windowsills. **SEASON** May–Oct.

DADDY-LONG-LEGS
Leiobunum species
ARACHNID CLASS

⅜″. Head/thorax and abdomen joined in single body; yellowish brown, with dark stripes. Legs long, arching; 2nd pair longest, used like antennae. Feeds on tiny spiders, insects, plant juices. **HABITAT** Tree trunks, buildings. **SEASON** Apr.–Nov.

WOOD TICKS
Dermacentor species
ARACHNID CLASS

⅛″. Body oval. Female reddish brown; silvery shield near small orange head. Male gray, with reddish-brown spots. **CAUTION** Remove tick head to prevent infection. **HABITAT** Brush, tall grass. **SEASON** Year-round. **RANGE** s and c N. Eng.

DEER TICK
Ixodes dammini
ARACHNID CLASS

¹⁄₁₆″. Body oval, minute; light brown (larvae, nymphs) to reddish brown (adults). **CAUTION** Can transmit Lyme disease, a serious illness (see box below). **HABITAT** Brushy fields, open woods. **SEASON** Year-round. **RANGE** s N. Eng.

Deer Ticks and Lyme Disease

Ticks of the genus *Ixodes* are carriers of Lyme disease, a dangerous illness that can be difficult to treat. In the Northeast, the Deer Tick carries the responsible spirochete (spiral-shaped bacterium), *Borrelia burgdorferi*. Both nymphs, active May through July, and adults, active on warm days from August through May, can be infectious. Deer Ticks are tiny and their nymphs are almost microscopic. They inhabit woods and fields, especially where deer are numerous. To avoid infection, it helps to wear light-colored pants tucked into socks, and carefully check clothing and skin after outings. Initial symptoms of Lyme disease vary, but about 75 to 80 percent of all victims develop a circular, expanding red rash around the tick bite, which can appear up to 35 days after the bite. Other symptoms include stiff neck, headache, dizziness, fever, sore throat, muscle aches, joint pain, and general weakness. Should these symptoms develop, consult a physician promptly, as antibiotics are most effective in early stages of infection. Untreated Lyme disease can be difficult to cure, and may cause chronic arthritis, memory loss, and severe headaches.

Insects

Insects (class Insecta) bring out special feelings: they fascinate children with their forms and colors; they bewilder naturalists with their ecological intricacies; they cause rational adults to cringe at their mere presence. Their vast repertory of environmental adaptations is overwhelming, as are their sheer numbers and staying power. Try as we might (and we have tried mightily), we have not succeeded in exterminating any New England insect pests. Perhaps instead we should spend more time observing their beauty and variety.

All insects have three main body parts—head, thorax, and abdomen—to which various other organs are attached. The head has a pair of antennae, which may be narrow, feathery, pointed, short, or long (sometimes much longer than the body). The eyes are compound and the mouthparts are adapted to chewing, biting, piercing, sucking, and/or licking. Insect wings (usually four) and legs (six) attach at the thorax. The abdomen, usually the largest section, houses the reproductive and other internal organs.

A remarkable aspect of invertebrate life is the transformation from egg to adult, known as metamorphosis. In complete metamorphosis, which includes a pupal stage and is unique to insects, the adults lay eggs from which the larvae are hatched. The larva feeds and grows, molting its skin several times, until it prepares for its immobile pupal state by hiding or camouflaging itself. Within the pupa, larval organs dissolve and adult organs develop. In incomplete metamorphosis, there is no pupal stage, and insects such as dragonflies, grasshoppers, and bugs gradually develop from hatched nymphs into adults.

It is impossible to overstate the importance of insects to the ecological health of the planet. In New England and other temperate regions, insects pollinate approximately 80 percent of the flowering plants. They are a vital link in every ecosystem.

This book introduces representative species or genera of insects from many orders in a sequence from primitive to more advanced. We have placed the large butterfly and moth section last, although traditionally they precede the ants, bees, and wasps. For many insects there is no commonly accepted English name at the species level. Descriptions and seasonal information refer to adult forms unless otherwise noted. Measurements are of typical adult body lengths, except in the butterfly accounts, in which wingspan measurements are given.

SNOW FLEA
"Snow Springtail"
Achorutes nivicola
SPRINGTAIL ORDER
1/16". Body dark blue; tapers toward tip. Wingless; organ below abdomen propels insect into air. Swarms appear as black mats on snowbanks on sunny days. A harbinger of spring. **HABITAT** Snow-covered forest, leaf litter. **SEASON** Feb.–Apr.

SILVERFISH
Lepisma saccharina
BRISTLETAIL ORDER

½". Body flattened, wingless, covered with silver scales; tapers to 3-pronged tail. Antennae thread-like; eyes small, compound. Fast runner. Feeds on glue, starch, dried cereal, paper. **HABITAT** Buildings. **SEASON** Year-round.

MAYFLIES
Ephemera species
MAYFLY ORDER

¾"; nymph to ½". Adult looks like a giant brownish mosquito with long forelegs, very long tail appendages, translucent veined wings with dark mottling. Adults rise from water in swarms, mate, lay eggs, die in day or two. Aquatic nymph (naiad) caterpillar-like, with biting mouth; favored by trout. **HABITAT** Rivers, streams, ponds. **SEASON** May–June.

Dragonflies

Dragonflies are large predatory insects many of which specialize in killing mosquitoes. The order is 300 million years old and comprises two major groups—dragonflies and damselflies. Both have movable heads and large compound eyes that in dragonflies nearly cover the head and in damselflies bulge out from the sides. Their legs are attached to the thorax just behind their heads, a feature that makes walking all but impossible but greatly facilitates their ability to grasp and hold prey while tearing into it with sharp mouthparts. They have four powerful wings that move independently, allowing for both forward and backward flight. At rest, the wings are held horizontally by

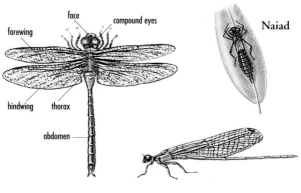

Naiad

Dragonfly

Damselfly

dragonflies, and together over the abdomen by damselflies. Nymphs, called naiads, live among the vegetation and muck in ponds and streams and feed on mosquito larvae, other insects, tadpoles, and small fish. Many of New England's 170 or so colorful species of dragonflies and damselflies have captured the interest of bird and butterfly enthusiasts. Some have been found to be migratory, gathering in swarms at many of the same coastal sites where migrating birds and Monarchs abound. In the accounts that follow, all species not noted as damselflies are dragonflies. The size given for dragonflies is the typical adult body length (not the wingspread).

EBONY JEWELWING
"Black-winged Damselfly"
Calopteryx maculata
DRAGONFLY ORDER
1¾". Damselfly. Male metallic green; wings black. Female duller brown; wings smoky with glistening white spot near tip. Naiad pale brown with darker markings. **HABITAT** Wooded streams, rivers. **SEASON** June–Aug.

SLENDER SPREADWING
Lestes rectangularis
DRAGONFLY ORDER
2". Damselfly. Wings short, clear; contrast with long, slender, dark abdomen. Eyes blue; blue shoulder stripe. Other N. Eng. spreadwings have blue tip on abdomen. **HABITAT** Ponds, marshes, bogs. **SEASON** Late June–Aug.

VARIABLE DANCER
"Violet Dancer"
Argia fumipennis violacea
DRAGONFLY ORDER
1¼". Damselfly. Male head black; thorax and abdomen violet; abdomen blue-tipped. Female dark brown to black. Wings clear. Common near outlets at lakes and dams. **HABITAT** Streams, rivers, ponds. **SEASON** Mid-June–early Sept.

NORTHERN BLUET
Enallagma cyathigerum
DRAGONFLY ORDER
1¼". Damselfly. Male body bright blue and black; abdomen blue-tipped. Female duller. Wings clear. **HABITAT** Vegetated ponds, bogs, swamps. **SEASON** Late May–July.

EASTERN FORKTAIL
Ischnura verticalis
DRAGONFLY ORDER

1″. Damselfly. Male thorax black with 2 lime-green stripes; abdomen black, blue-tipped. Female blue-gray or orange. Wings clear. N. Eng.'s most common damselfly. **HABITAT** Ponds, streams, rivers. **SEASON** Mid-May–Sept.

CANADA DARNER
Aeshna canadensis
DRAGONFLY ORDER

3″. Thorax brownish, with side stripes of blue above yellow; abdomen long, slender, with blue markings. Wings clear. N. Eng.'s most common blue darner. **HABITAT** Swamps, marshy pond edges. **SEASON** Aug.–Sept.

COMMON GREEN DARNER
Anax junius
DRAGONFLY ORDER

3″. Thorax green. Abdomen blue (male) or reddish brown (female). Wings clear, female's tinged with amber. Flies over fields in large numbers in late summer; seldom perches. **HABITAT** Ponds, streams, fields. **SEASON** May–Oct.; migrates in fall.

COMMON BASKETTAIL
Epitheca cynosura
DRAGONFLY ORDER

1½″. Body brown. Abdomen has yellow markings on sides; hindwing base often has dark markings. Large numbers hawk insects 10–20′ above ground. **HABITAT** Pond edges, fields, openings. **SEASON** Mid-May–mid-July.

CALICO PENNANT
"Elisa Pennant"
Celithemis elisa
DRAGONFLY ORDER

1¼″. Abdomen black with red (male) or yellow (female) markings on top. Wings spotted; hindwing base amber. **HABITAT** Marshy ponds, fields. **SEASON** Mid-June–late Aug.

HALLOWEEN PENNANT
Celithemis eponina
DRAGONFLY ORDER

1½″. Abdomen blackish with yellow or orange markings on top. Wings yellow-orange with large dark brown spots. Often perches atop prominent vegetation. **HABITAT** Fields, marshes. **SEASON** Mid-June–late Aug.

EASTERN PONDHAWK
"Green Jacket"
Erythemis simplicicollis
DRAGONFLY ORDER

1¾″. Female, called Green Jacket, and imm. bright green with dark markings on abdomen. Male face green; thorax and abdomen pale blue. Wings clear. Often rests on ground. **HABITAT** Ponds, nearby fields. **SEASON** Mid-June–early Sept.

WIDOW SKIMMER
Libellula luctuosa
DRAGONFLY ORDER

1¾″. Body dark brown, with yellowish markings on sides of abdomen. Inner half of wings black. **HABITAT** Ponds, marshes. **SEASON** Mid-June–early Sept. **RANGE** Most of N. Eng., ex. Cape Cod.

COMMON WHITETAIL
Libellula lydia
DRAGONFLY ORDER

1¾″. Body chunky. Male abdomen pale bluish white; wings have broad black band. Female brown with yellowish markings on sides of abdomen; 3 dark spots on wings. **HABITAT** Ponds, grassy swamps, pathways, gardens. **SEASON** June–early Sept.

TWELVE-SPOTTED SKIMMER
Libellula pulchella
DRAGONFLY ORDER

2″. Head/thorax chocolate to light brown; abdomen gray-brown to whitish. White and black spots on wings. Female and imm. differ from Common Whitetail in larger size, lack of obvious yellow on abdomen. **HABITAT** Ponds, marshes. **SEASON** Mid-June–Sept.

BLUE DASHER
Pachydiplax longipennis
DRAGONFLY ORDER

1½″. Male thorax striped black and yellow; abdomen blue with black tip. Female and imm. duller. Wings mostly clear. Common near quiet waters. **HABITAT** Ponds, marshes, sluggish streams. **SEASON** Late June–early Sept.

WANDERING GLIDER
"Globetrotter"
Pantala flavescens
DRAGONFLY ORDER

2″. Abdomen has golden-yellow sides; thorax light brown; eyes reddish. Wings clear. Flies almost constantly; widespread. Breeds in rain puddles. **HABITAT** Fields, open areas, sometimes ponds. **SEASON** Late June–Sept.

EASTERN AMBERWING
Perithemis tenera
DRAGONFLY ORDER

1″. Short, stocky. Body yellowish brown; 2 greenish stripes on thorax. Wings amber, female's with variable dark spots. Flies low over water or perches on vegetation. **HABITAT** Ponds. **SEASON** Late June–Aug. **RANGE** s N. Eng.

YELLOW-LEGGED MEADOWHAWK
Sympetrum vicinum
DRAGONFLY ORDER

1¼″. Thorax reddish brown; abdomen reddish orange. Wings clear; legs yellowish. Common late in season. **HABITAT** Fields, ponds. **SEASON** Late July–Oct.

AMERICAN COCKROACH
"Waterbug"
Periplaneta americana
COCKROACH ORDER

2″. Body reddish brown; large, pale yellow head shield; antennae longer than body. Yellow stripe on front margin of forewings. Legs dark. Largest cockroach in N. Eng. HABITAT Warm buildings. SEASON Year-round.

GERMAN COCKROACH
Blattella germanica
COCKROACH ORDER

⅝″. Body brown; 2 blackish stripes on pale yellow-brown shield behind head. With adhesive pads on pale legs, can climb vertical smooth surfaces. Introduced from Eurasia; pest in all N. Amer. cities. HABITAT Buildings. SEASON Year-round.

EUROPEAN EARWIG
Forficula auricularia
EARWIG ORDER

⅝″. Body slender; brownish to black; legs yellowish. Antennae bead-like. Pincers at abdomen tip curved (male) or straight (female). Eats flowers, fruit, garbage, mites, insect larvae and pupae. Female guards eggs, feeds young nymphs. HABITAT Decaying logs, leaf litter, trees, sheds. SEASON Apr.–Oct. RANGE s and c N. Eng.

NORTHERN WALKINGSTICK
Diapheromera femorata
WALKINGSTICK ORDER

3¾″. Body greatly elongated, almost cylindrical; stick-like; wingless. Head tiny; antennae thread-like, ⅔ body length. Legs thin, widely spaced. Male brown; female greenish brown. Superbly camouflaged. Remains motionless by day; eats leaves and plant juices at night. Nymph green. Eggs white with black stripe. HABITAT Broadleaf woods, esp. oaks. SEASON May–Oct.

PRAYING MANTIS
Mantis religiosa
MANTID ORDER

2½". Body elongated; head triangular; antennae thread-like. Male usu. brown; female green. 4 long thin legs grasp twigs; 2 forelegs held in "prayerful position" for quickly grasping insects. Wings long, extend beyond abdomen tip. Eyes large, brown, compound. Most flexible neck of any insect; able to look for prey or danger at most angles. Mouthparts strong; can tear apart hard exoskeleton of prey: flies, bees, wasps, butterflies, caterpillars. Female often eats male after mating; lays tannish egg masses up to 1½" long. Introduced from Europe. **HABITAT** Brushy fields, gardens. **SEASON** Aug.–Oct. **Chinese Mantis** *(Tenodera aridifolia; 3⅜")* of s N. Eng. has green margin on brown wings.

Grasshoppers and Kin

Members of the order Orthoptera are beloved for their musical abilities and despised for their voracious appetites. All species have mouthparts designed to bite and chew, and straight, membranous wings. Grasshoppers and crickets have greatly developed hindlegs for jumping. Females have long ovipositors, straight in most species but sickle-shaped in katydids; they lay eggs in soil or tree vegetation. While no insects have true voices, orthopterans manage to make themselves heard in a variety of distinctive ways; most melodies are produced by males trying to attract mates. Crickets and katydids raise their wings and rub together specialized parts to produce their well-known calls. Most crickets are "right-winged," rubbing their right wings over their left, while katydids are "left-winged." Grasshoppers rub their hindlegs and wings together, and also make rattling, in-flight sounds by vibrating their forewings against their hindwings.

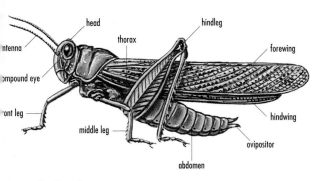

Parts of a Grasshopper

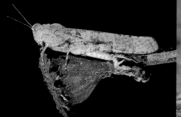

CAROLINA LOCUST
Dissosteira carolina
GRASSHOPPER ORDER

2″. Body cinnamon brown, incl. eyes. Hindwings black with broad, light yellow border (visible in flight). Flies with purring, fluttering sound. **HABITAT** Roadsides, meadows. **SEASON** June–Sept.

RED-LEGGED LOCUST
Melanoplus femur-rubrum
GRASSHOPPER ORDER

1″. Body dark brown, sometimes greenish. Hind femur herringbone-patterned; hind tibia red with black spines. Wings dusky; male's wings at rest project beyond abdomen tip. Eats grasses, weeds, field crops. **HABITAT** Fields. **SEASON** July–Oct.

TRUE KATYDID
"Northern Katydid"
Pterophylla camellifolia
GRASSHOPPER ORDER

2″. Body triangular in cross section with ridge on upperparts. Thorax shield and wings resemble yellowish-green, net-veined leaf. Both sexes make 2-part *katy-DID* and 3-part *katy-DIDN'T* calls from treetops to ground at night. **HABITAT** Broadleaf and mixed woods, esp. oaks. **SEASON** July–Sept. **RANGE** s N. Eng.

FIELD CRICKET
Gryllus pennsylvanicus
GRASSHOPPER ORDER

1″. Body black. Antennae as long as body; wings short, dusky. Hindlegs strong, spiny; spiky abdominal appendages. Gives series of ½-second triple chirps. **HABITAT** Fields, houses. **SEASON** June–Oct.

SNOWY TREE CRICKET
Oecanthus fultoni
GRASSHOPPER ORDER

⅝″. Body delicate, pale green; hindlegs and antennae long, thin. Wings clear; male's forewings paddle-shaped, held over back; female's narrow, curved around body. Many males together make series of rhythmic trills night or day. **HABITAT** Trees, shrubs. **SEASON** July–Sept.

PERIODICAL CICADAS
Magicicada species
CICADA ORDER

1". Body black, robust; eyes large, red; wings clear, orange-veined. Nymph feeds on sap in tree roots for 13–17 years; emergence years vary geographically. Adult lives about 1 month. Call a loud, rising and falling, staccato whine. **HABITAT** Broadleaf woods. **SEASON** July–Sept. **RANGE** s N. Eng.

DOGDAY HARVESTFLY
Tibicen canicularis
CICADA ORDER

1¼". Body black and green; eyes olive; wings veined, mostly clear, with green base. Adult gives a long, loud, buzz-saw sound on sunny summer days. Emerges annually, casting skin on tree trunks. **HABITAT** Mixed woods, esp. with pines. **SEASON** June–Sept.

MEADOW SPITTLEBUG
"Froghopper"
Philaenus spumarius
CICADA ORDER

⅜". Adults hop about on leaves like tiny frogs. This species: body long, pear-shaped; antennae and wings very short; varies from gray to green, yellow, or brown. Nymph oval, clear yellowish, scarcely pigmented; emits bubbly protective froth. **HABITAT** Brushy meadows, roadsides. **SEASON** May–Sept.

ANTLIONS
Myrmeleon species
NERVEWING ORDER

adult (left), larva (top right), funnel in sand (bottom right)

1½". Body soft, abdomen long; gray-green. Antennae knobbed. Wings clear, narrow; poor flier. Larva (⅝"), called "Doodlebug," builds funnel in sand, seizes sliding ants with powerful jaws. **HABITAT** Adult: woodland edges; larva: sandy areas. **SEASON** Summer.

EASTERN DOBSONFLY
Corydalus cornutus
NERVEWING ORDER

2″. Head large, round; body elongated. Wings long, rounded, translucent, grayish, veined. Male's mandibles forceps-like, ½ body length; female's shorter, but can bite strongly. Adult short-lived; probably does not eat. Larva (hellgrammite) an aquatic predator. **HABITAT** Nymph lives in streams; adult aerial over nearby woods; attracted to lights. **SEASON** June–July.

GREEN LACEWINGS
Chrysopa species
NERVEWING ORDER

⅝″. Body elongated, pale green; head narrow; eyes large, coppery; antennae long. Wings clear, veined; at least ¼ longer than body; fold together over back. Adult and larva eat destructive aphids. **HABITAT** Gardens, woodland edges. **SEASON** May–Sept.

WATER BOATMEN
Arctocorixa and *Corixa* species
TRUE BUG ORDER

½″. Body long, oval; gray-brown. Wings gray-brown, veined. Forelegs short, scoop-like; other legs paddle-shaped, used for rowing. Aquatic; can fly. Eats algae in birdbaths. **HABITAT** Ponds, rivers, small patches of water. **SEASON** May–Sept.

COMMON WATER STRIDER
Gerris remigis
TRUE BUG ORDER

⅝″. Body black, slender. Middle and hindlegs very long, slender. Skates over water using surface tension. Feeds on mosquito larvae and insects that fall in water. **HABITAT** Quiet fresh water. **SEASON** May–Oct.

SMALL MILKWEED BUG
Lygaeus kalmii
TRUE BUG ORDER

½″. Body oval, black; red band behind head. Forewings have large, bright red X. Toxic to predators. Lays eggs on milkweed; immune to plant's toxins. **HABITAT** Meadows with milkweeds. **SEASON** May–Oct.

GREEN STINK BUG
Acrosternum hilare
TRUE BUG ORDER

¾". Body shield-shaped, compact; green, with yellow-orange edges. Head small; antennae banded. Eats fruits, vegetables. Emits foul-smelling fluid when disturbed. **HABITAT** Orchards, gardens, field crops. **SEASON** Summer.

Beetles

There are more species of beetles (order Coleoptera) than any other animals on earth. Not all are called beetles: June bugs and fireflies are included in this order. Beetles' forewings are hardened dense sheaths known as *elytra,* which meet in a straight line down the back. Their hindwings underneath function as the organs of flight. Beetle legs and antennae vary from long and straight to stout and angled. Both adults and larvae, known as grubs, have mouthparts adapted for biting and chewing. They are vegetarians, predators, scavengers, and in a few instances parasites. Some, like lady beetles, are highly prized by gardeners because they eat aphids and other garden pests, while others, including the introduced Japanese Beetle, are nuisances at best. They range in size from microscopic organisms to some of the largest insects in the world.

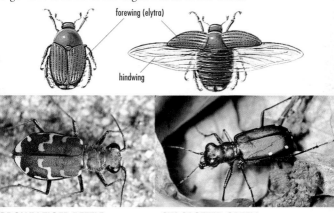

forewing (elytra)

hindwing

BROWN TIGER BEETLE
Cicindela repanda
BEETLE ORDER

½". Body elongated. Brownish bronze with creamy pattern above; metallic green below. Runs and flies fast; seizes prey insects with powerful jaws. Very alert; elusive. Bites. **HABITAT** Sand and gravel areas, often near water. **SEASON** Apr.–Oct.

SIX-SPOTTED GREEN TIGER BEETLE
Cicindela sexguttata
BEETLE ORDER

⅝". Body elongated; bright metallic green; antennae long, clubbed. Forewings have 6 or more large white spots along rear edge. Legs brilliant green, some with purplish sheen. Eats spiders, insects. Bites. **HABITAT** Open sandy areas in fields; woodland paths. **SEASON** Apr.–Oct.

EUROPEAN CATERPILLAR HUNTER
"Fiery Searcher"
Calosoma sycophanta
BEETLE ORDER

1⅛". Body robust; thorax shield circular, dark blue. Forewings iridescent golden-green, grooved. Ground beetle introduced from Eurasia to eat Gypsy Moth caterpillars; climbs trees to reach them. **HABITAT** Woods, gardens. **SEASON** May–Oct.

LARGE WHIRLIGIG BEETLES
Dineutus species
BEETLE ORDER

½". Body oval, flat; black with bronzy sheen. Forewings have shallow grooves. Hindlegs short, paddle-like. Gathers in groups that swim in circles. **HABITAT** Surface of ponds, streams. **SEASON** June–Oct.

ROSE CHAFER
Macrodactylus subspinosus
BEETLE ORDER

½". Body elongated; head has snout. Light brown. Eyes black; legs orange and black, spiny. Pest of grapes and ornamental roses, controlled by daily gloved removal from plants. **HABITAT** Gardens, watersides. **SEASON** May–Sept.

MAY BEETLES
"June Bugs"
Phyllophaga species
BEETLE ORDER

1⅜". Body bulky. Thorax shield chestnut. Forewings lighter brown, without grooves; hindwings well developed. Antennae end in right angle. Attracted by lights; slow, noisy, buzzing flight. **HABITAT** Broadleaf woods, fields. **SEASON** May–Aug.

JAPANESE BEETLE
Popilla japonica
BEETLE ORDER

½". Body rotund. Metallic green; forewings orange. Abdomen ringed with white hair tufts. Adult infests flowers, fruit; white grub eats lawn roots; can become serious garden pest. **HABITAT** Gardens, yards, open woods. **SEASON** May–Sept.

PENNSYLVANIA FIREFLY
"Lightning Bug"
Photuris pennsylvanicus
BEETLE ORDER

½". Body long, flattened. Head and thorax shield has black spot ringed with orange. Forewings brown or gray, edged with yellow. Flashes yellow-green light from abdomen every 2–3 seconds when courting. Eggs, larvae, pupae also luminous. **HABITAT** Fields, gardens, open woods. **SEASON** June–Aug.

TWO-SPOTTED LADY BEETLE
Adalia bipunctata
BEETLE ORDER

¼". Body oval, rounded. Forewings reddish orange with 1 black spot on each. Adult and larva feed on aphids. Overwinters in houses and under bark. **HABITAT** Fields, gardens. **SEASON** May–Oct.

CONVERGENT LADY BEETLE
Hippodamia convergens
BEETLE ORDER

¼". Body oval, rounded. White stripes behind head. Forewings reddish orange, usually with 13 black spots. Feeds on aphids. **HABITAT** Woods, meadows, gardens. **SEASON** May–Oct.

RED MILKWEED BEETLE
Tetraopes tetraopthalmus
BEETLE ORDER

½". Body long, cylindrical; bright red above with large black dots. Antennae gray-beaded. Makes grating sounds by rubbing thorax. Immune to milkweed poison; adult and larva poisonous to birds. **HABITAT** Meadows with milkweeds. **SEASON** Summer.

Flies and Mosquitoes

Flies and mosquitoes, some of humankind's least favorite insects, are nonetheless worthy of a second glance. All species have two wings and mouthparts formed for sucking, or for piercing and sucking. The legless and wingless larvae undergo complete metamorphosis, and can be either terrestrial (maggots) or aquatic (called by various names). Adults fly with a wingbeat frequency often of hundreds of beats per second. This incredible speed produces the familiar in-flight buzzing sounds. Flies feed on decomposing matter, nectar, and sometimes blood. Mosquitoes' lower lips form a proboscis with six knife-sharp organs, some smooth and some saw-toothed, that cut into skin. New England has more than 50 mosquito species.

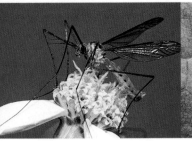

CRANE FLIES
Tipula species
FLY ORDER

2½". Body long, delicate, gray to gold; legs very long, slender. Wings clear, veined; held at 60-degree angle from body. Feeds on plants; does not bite humans. **HABITAT** Watersides; may enter houses. **SEASON** May–Sept.

PHANTOM CRANE FLY
Bittacomorpha clavipes
FLY ORDER

½". Body long, very thin, black. Legs long, delicate, with black and white bands. Wings clear, black veined. Drifts slowly in the air, with legs extended, seeming to appear and disappear. **HABITAT** Streamside woods. **SEASON** May–Sept.

GOLDEN SALTMARSH MOSQUITO
Aedes solicitans
FLY ORDER

¼". Body long, yellowish brown, female's with white stripes and golden bands. Wings clear. Male's antennae feathery; female's thread-like. Female has long proboscis for sucking blood; male drinks plant juices. Bites. **HABITAT** Salt marshes. **SEASON** June–Sept.

HOUSE MOSQUITO
Culex pipiens
FLY ORDER

¼". Body long. Thorax light brown, abdomen banded white and brown, often raised parallel to ground at rest. Wings dusky. Female sucks blood, male drinks plant juices. Common at night. Bites. **HABITAT** Watersides, woods, houses. **SEASON** May–Oct.

BLACK FLIES
Simulium species
FLY ORDER

⅛". Body humpbacked; head pointed down. Blackish. Antennae thick, wings clear. Larvae pupate in cocoons that coat rocks in streams. Female sucks bird and mammal blood. Abundant in north woods in early summer. **HABITAT** Woods, watersides. **SEASON** Late May–July.

GREENHEAD FLIES
Chrysops species
FLY ORDER

⅝". Body chunky, brownish. Wings spotted. Eyes large, green. Square boxes in salt marshes are traps for these sharp biters. **HABITAT** Salt marshes, nearby beaches. **SEASON** July–Aug. **RANGE** s ME and south.

AMERICAN HORSE FLY
Tabanus americanus
FLY ORDER

1". Body very large, wide, hairy; brown-black. Wings dusky. Eyes large, green; legs reddish. Anticoagulant in female's saliva causes bite wound to continue bleeding. **HABITAT** Watersides, farms. **SEASON** May–Sept.

DEER FLY
Chrysops callidus
FLY ORDER

½". Body flattish; head small. Thorax black; abdomen striped golden. Wings veined, with black patches. Circles targets silently, giving quick nasty bite on landing, often on head. **HABITAT** Woods and meadows near water. **SEASON** June–July.

BLUE BOTTLE FLY
Calliphora vomitoria
FLY ORDER

½". Body chunky; very hairy. Thorax dark gray; abdomen metallic blue. Wings clear. Eyes reddish. Eats flesh of dead or wounded animals. Very loud buzzing flight indoors. **HABITAT** Pastures, barnyards, buildings. **SEASON** May–Sept.

HOUSE FLY
Musca domestica
FLY ORDER

¼". Body rotund; gray with black stripes. Wings clear. Eyes large, red-brown; legs hairy. Egg hatches in 10–24 hours; matures to adult in 10 days; lives 15 (male) to 26 (female) days. Sucks liquid sugars from garbage; spreads disease. **HABITAT** Buildings, farms. **SEASON** May–Oct.

Ants, Wasps, and Bees

The insects of the order Hymenoptera include sawflies and narrow-waisted bees, wasps, and ants. Hymenopterans have two pairs of membranous, transparent wings, mouthparts modified to chew and lick, and, in adult females, an ovipositor. All species undergo complete metamorphosis.

Adult sawflies resemble typical wasps except for their rounded bodies. Sawflies are perhaps best known for their caterpillar-like larval state, when numbers of them, feeding communally on a piece of vegetation, will frantically wave about in unison if disturbed. The ovipositor of the adult sawfly is shaped like a saw, giving the group its common name.

The narrow-waists are divided into two broad groupings. The first, parasitic wasps, include the large and varied assemblage of nonstinging ichneumon wasps, who live as parasites during their larval stage. Some ichneumons are greatly feared by humans for their astonishingly long ovipositors, which are used not for stinging but to probe about in woody vegetation for suitable insects to lay eggs on. The second group of narrow-waists are the stinging insects, with ovipositors that have been modified into stinging organs. Included here are vespid wasps (such as hornets, yellow jackets, and potter wasps), bees, and many ants.

Carpenter ant colony

Paper wasp nest

Ants and some wasps and bees are highly social creatures, but some species in this order live solitary lives. The nests constructed by ants, wasps, and bees vary in complexity from the Eastern Sand Wasp's single-cell hole in the ground to the Honey Bee's elaborate comb structure. Many ant species excavate in soil or wood, building multi-chambered homes mostly hidden from sight. New England hosts hundreds of ant species. Bumble bees, yellow jackets, and some hornets build similar homes. Unlike ants, though, they build separate six-sided chambers for each of their young, made of a papery material that consists of wood or bark and adult saliva. Paper wasps and Bald-faced Hornets often construct their nests in open situations, while Honey Bees utilize man-made hives or hollow trees or logs. The Honey Bees' two-sided, vertically hanging beeswax combs can contain more than 50,000 cells.

Our bees and flowering plants have developed a great many interdependencies over the eons as they have evolved together. We would lose too many of our flowers and fruits were we to let our bees be poisoned out of existence. We would also lose some of the greatest known examples of animal industry.

NORTHEASTERN SAWFLY
Tenthredo originalis
ANT, WASP, AND BEE ORDER

⅜″. Body long; striped black and yellow. Wings smoky, red-veined; lower legs yellow; no stinger. Larva eats new willow leaves. **HABITAT** Watersides. **SEASON** Apr.–Sept.

PIGEON HORNTAIL
Tremex columba
ANT, WASP, AND BEE ORDER

1½″. Cylindrical. Head and body orange; abdomen long, with black and yellow bars; horny plate at end. Wings blackish to yellowish. Female has long ovipositor (not stinger) that deposits eggs deep into wood that larvae eat. **HABITAT** Woods. **SEASON** May–Sept.

BLACK CARPENTER ANT
Camponotus pennsylvanicus
ANT, WASP, AND BEE ORDER

½″. Queen large; workers smaller. Black; large part of abdomen has long brownish hairs. Antennae elbowed. Constructs intricate tunnel systems in wood, but does not eat it; can cause structural damage to buildings. **CAUTION** Bites. **HABITAT** Dying trees, logs, wooden structures. **SEASON** Mar.–Nov.

LITTLE BLACK ANT
Monomorium minimum
ANT, WASP, AND BEE ORDER

1/16″. Body slender, smooth, black or brown. Builds underground nest with cleared-off raised mound on surface; also nests in rotten wood. Carries off food particles from kitchens. **HABITAT** Fields, yards, buildings. **SEASON** Apr.–Oct.

RED MOUND ANT
Formica exsectoides
ANT, WASP, AND BEE ORDER

¼″. Head and thorax rusty red; abdomen and legs blackish brown. Builds dome-like nest mound. **CAUTION** Strong stinger. **HABITAT** Fields; behind beaches. **SEASON** May–Sept.

NORTHERN PAPER WASP
Polistes fuscatus
ANT, WASP, AND BEE ORDER
⅞". Body slender; waist narrow; head pointed; dark reddish brown, with thin yellow bands. Male's face pale, female's brown. Wings amber to reddish brown. Female builds round, hanging, paper-like nest. **CAUTION** Stings. **HABITAT** Fields, gardens, porches. **SEASON** May–Oct.

EASTERN YELLOW JACKET
Vespula maculifrons
ANT, WASP, AND BEE ORDER
⅝". Body stout; waist black; thin yellow bands on thorax and abdomen. Wings dusky. Nests under log or stone, or in crevice. Raids picnic food and trash cans. **CAUTION** Will sting repeatedly if bothered. **HABITAT** Fields, gardens, urban areas. **SEASON** May–Oct.

BALD-FACED HORNET
Vespula maculata
ANT, WASP, AND BEE ORDER
¾". Body rotund, black. Yellowish-white spots on short head, base of wings, waist, and abdomen tip. Builds football-size paper nest under branch or overhang. **CAUTION** Stings nest visitors. **HABITAT** Woodland edges. **SEASON** May–Sept.

EASTERN CARPENTER BEE
Xylocopa virginica
ANT, WASP, AND BEE ORDER
1". Body robust, metallic blue-black; less hairy than American Bumble Bee. Female burrows deep into wood of trees or houses, making egg chambers. **CAUTION** Stings, but rarely. **HABITAT** Woodland edges. **SEASON** May–Aug.

HONEY BEE
Apis mellifera
ANT, WASP, AND BEE ORDER
⅝". Body rounded. Thorax hairy, brown; abdomen banded black and golden. Wings dusky. Makes honey; pollinates crops; nests in tree holes. Introduced from Eurasia. **CAUTION** Stings, but is not aggressive; if stung, remove stinger immediately. **HABITAT** Fields, orchards. **SEASON** Apr.–Oct.

AMERICAN BUMBLE BEE
Bombus pennsylvanicus
ANT, WASP, AND BEE ORDER

⅞". Body robust, hairy, mainly yellow with black accents. Wings smoky. Busily pollinates flowers. Queen overwinters and nests underground. **CAUTION** Stings, but is not aggressive. **HABITAT** Fields. **SEASON** May–Sept.

Butterflies and Moths

The order Lepidoptera comprises the familiar groups of moths and butterflies. *Lepidoptera* means "scale-winged," and refers to the minute scales that cover the four wings of all butterfly and moth species. All lepidopterans share the same generalized life cycle—egg to larva to pupa to adult. Eggs are laid singly, or in rows, stacks, or masses, depending on the species. The emergent larva, usually referred to as a caterpillar, feeds on plant life, and grows through several stages, or instars, shedding its skin each time. When fully grown, the caterpillar prepares to pupate by spinning a silken cocoon (moth) or finding a secure hiding place (butterfly). Then the caterpillar sheds its last larval skin, revealing the pupa, an outer shell with no head or feet, within which the wings and other adult features fully develop. Finally, the pupal skin breaks open and the winged moth or butterfly emerges. The time required for this process is different for each species. Many have only one emergence of adults per year; others have two or three. Most New England lepidopterans live out their entire lives within the region, although a few species, like the world-famous Monarch, migrate south in the fall. The thousands of species that stay behind survive the winter as eggs, larvae, or pupae, although a few overwinter as adults.

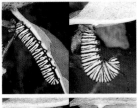

Metamorphosis of a Monarch

Several key differences distinguish moths and butterflies. Moths' antennae are either feather-like or wiry, and lack the clubbed tip of butterflies' antennae. Moths rest with their wings outstretched, folded, or at an angle above the body; butterflies rest with their wings outstretched or held together vertically, like a sail. Moths can fly day and night, while butterflies fly only by day. Color and size are poor general distinguishing features between the two groups.

When trying to identify a species, pay special attention to the wing colors, shape, and pattern. Most of the characteristic wing markings on moths are found on the uppersides. In butterflies, look for distinguishing markings on the uppersides of those species that rest with outstretched wings and on the undersides of those that rest with their wings folded up.

Butterflies drink nectar from many species of wildflowers and shrubs. Among the best wild nectar plants in New England are milkweeds, asters, Buttonbush, New Jersey Tea, and Joe-Pye-weed. Excellent garden flowers that attract butterflies and moths include Butterfly Bush, Gayfeather, Phlox, Bee Balm, and Coreopsis. Nocturnal moths are also drawn to lights.

Each larva, or caterpillar, species has its own select food plants, and the accounts that follow list many of these. Measurements are of typical wingspans for adult forms, from tip to tip.

BLACK SWALLOWTAIL
Papilio polyxenes
SWALLOWTAIL FAMILY

3¼″. Black above, with median yellow band (larger on male), yellow spots on rear edges; hindwings have tail, blue spots (larger on female). Below, hindwings have orange spots. Caterpillar pale green with black bands. **HABITAT** Fields, gardens. **FOOD PLANTS** Carrot family. **SEASON** May–Sept.

SPICEBUSH SWALLOWTAIL
Papilio troilus
SWALLOWTAIL FAMILY

4″. Forewings black above, with large light spots near trailing edge; hindwings widely washed greenish blue, with tail; orange spots where hindwings meet. Below, hindwings have rows of orange spots. Caterpillar dark green with eyespots. **HABITAT** Open woods. **FOOD PLANTS** Sassafras trees, Spicebush. **SEASON** May–Sept.

EASTERN TIGER SWALLOWTAIL
Papilio glaucus
SWALLOWTAIL FAMILY

4⅜″. Yellow above; forewings have 4 black stripes; yellow stripes on black trailing edge, mixed in hindwings with orange and blue spots. Below, yellow with narrow black lines; blue and orange spots along outer margins. Caterpillar green with black and orange eyespots. **HABITAT** Open woods, fields. **FOOD PLANTS** Cherry and poplar trees, lilacs. **SEASON** May–Aug. **RANGE** s N. Eng. **Canadian Tiger Swallowtail** (*P. canadensis*), virtually identical, occurs in n N. Eng.

MUSTARD WHITE
Pieris napi
WHITE AND SULPHUR FAMILY

1½". Mainly white above; unspotted. Below, strongly veined, often in gray. Black body contrasts with wings. **HABITAT** Woodland edges. **FOOD PLANTS** Cresses, Toothwort. **SEASON** Late Apr.–Sept. **RANGE** w and n N. Eng.

CABBAGE WHITE
Pieris rapae
WHITE AND SULPHUR FAMILY

1⅝". White above; forewing tips slaty, with 1 (male) or 2 (female) black spots. Below, yellowish white. Caterpillar green with yellow stripes. **HABITAT** Fields, gardens. **FOOD PLANTS** Mustard family. **SEASON** Late Apr.–early Oct.

CLOUDED SULPHUR
Colias philodice
WHITE AND SULPHUR FAMILY

1¾". Lemon yellow above; edges black (male) or dusky with yellow spots (female); forewings have 1 small black spot. White forms exist, almost exclusively of females. **HABITAT** Fields, roadsides. **FOOD PLANTS** White Clover. **SEASON** May–Oct.

ORANGE SULPHUR
Colias eurytheme
WHITE AND SULPHUR FAMILY

2". Orange-yellow to yellow-orange above; edges of wings solid black (male) or black with yellow spots (female). **HABITAT** Fields. **FOOD PLANTS** Alfalfa, clovers, vetches. **SEASON** May–Oct.

AMERICAN COPPER
Lycaena phlaeas
GOSSAMER WING FAMILY

1". Forewings orange above, with about 8 black dots, black outer edge; hindwings gray-brown with orange rear edge. Below, forewings have light gray edge; hindwings light gray, with fine black dots, narrow orange line. **HABITAT** Fields, openings. **FOOD PLANTS** Curly Dock, Sheep Sorrel. **SEASON** May–Sept.

CORAL HAIRSTREAK
Satyrium titus
GOSSAMER WING FAMILY

1⅛". Brown above; tail-less. Below, paler brown, with row of bright reddish-orange spots along rear border of hindwings. **HABITAT** Brushy fields. **FOOD PLANTS** Buds and young fruits of cherry and plum trees. **SEASON** July–Aug.

BANDED HAIRSTREAK
Satyrium calanus
GOSSAMER WING FAMILY

1⅛". Brown above; hindwings have small tails. Below, brown with bands of black and white; hindwings have large blue spot, row of orange spots. **HABITAT** Woodland edges, fields. **FOOD PLANTS** Oaks, hickories. **SEASON** Late June–July. **RANGE** s and c N. Eng.

STRIPED HAIRSTREAK
Satyrium liparops
GOSSAMER WING FAMILY

1⅛". Brown above; hindwings have small tails. Below, offset bands of brown and white; hindwings have large pale blue spot, row of orange spots. **HABITAT** Woodland edges, fields. **FOOD PLANTS** Rose and heath families. **SEASON** Late June–Aug. **RANGE** All N. Eng., ex. n ME.

BROWN ELFIN
Callophrys augustinus
GOSSAMER WING FAMILY

1". Brown above. Below, hindwings rich reddish brown, dark brown near body. Common early low flier. **HABITAT** Barrens, bogs. **FOOD PLANTS** Heath family, incl. blueberry bushes. **SEASON** Apr.–May.

EASTERN PINE ELFIN
Callophrys niphon
GOSSAMER WING FAMILY

1". Brown above. Below, pale brown and reddish brown, with variegated, striking mix of short, thin, black and white bands. **HABITAT** Pine and oak woods. **FOOD PLANTS** Pines. **SEASON** Late Apr.–June.

GRAY HAIRSTREAK
Strymon melinus
GOSSAMER WING FAMILY

1⅛″. Dark gray above; hindwings have orange spot, 2 black tails. Below, lighter gray, with distinct black and white line; orange patches near tail. Often rests with wings open. **HABITAT** Fields, gardens. **FOOD PLANTS** Varied. **SEASON** May–early Oct.

SPRING AZURE
Celastrina ladon
GOSSAMER WING FAMILY

1″. Male entirely pale blue above; female with black border. Below, grayish white with small dark spots. **HABITAT** Woodland openings. **FOOD PLANTS** Dogwoods, viburnums. **SEASON** Apr.–Aug.

EASTERN TAILED-BLUE
Everes comyntas
GOSSAMER WING FAMILY

⅞″. Blue (female) to bright blue (male) above, edged in slate and white; hindwings have orange spot near tiny tail. Below, pale gray (male) or pale brown (female), with tiny sparse black dots and large orange spots near tail. Flight low, weak. **HABITAT** Fields. **FOOD PLANTS** Pea family. **SEASON** May–Oct.

SILVERY BLUE
Glaucopsyche lygdamus
GOSSAMER WING FAMILY

1⅛″. Brilliant silvery blue above, with blackish border. Below, gray with white-fringed black dots along margins. **HABITAT** Fields, woodland edges. **FOOD PLANTS** Vetches. **SEASON** May–June. **RANGE** n and c N. Eng.

GREAT SPANGLED FRITILLARY
Speyeria cybele
GOSSAMER WING FAMILY

2½″. Orange above, brownish near body, with black marks. Below, shades of brown; forewings have black marks; hindwings have silvery-white spots, wide cream band. **HABITAT** Fields, gardens. **FOOD PLANTS** Violet family. **SEASON** Late June–early Sept.

SILVER-BORDERED FRITILLARY
Boloria selene
BRUSHFOOT FAMILY

1⅝". Orange above, peppered with black dots; black borders have small orange dots. Below, cream and orange-brown, with silver patches and row of black dots. **HABITAT** Moist meadows. **FOOD PLANTS** Violet family. **SEASON** Late May–Sept.

PEARL CRESCENT
Phyciodes tharos
BRUSHFOOT FAMILY

1¼". Orange above, with black borders and spots. Below, male brighter orange with black smudges; female pale brown with silvery areas. **HABITAT** Fields. **FOOD PLANTS** Aster family. **SEASON** May–Sept. **RANGE** s N. Eng. **Northern Crescent** *(P. selenis)*, virtually identical, occurs in n N. Eng.

BALTIMORE CHECKERSPOT
Euphydryas phaeton
BRUSHFOOT FAMILY

2". Black above, with tiny white spots, orange trailing edges. Below, black and white checkerboard pattern, with 2 orange bands. **HABITAT** Meadows. **FOOD PLANTS** Plantains, Turtlehead. **SEASON** June–July. **RANGE** All N. Eng., ex. n ME.

QUESTION MARK
Polygonia interrogationis
BRUSHFOOT FAMILY

2½". Forewings orange above, with large black spots, jagged tips; hindwings orange (fall) to very dark (summer), with pointed tail; violet edges. Below, silver "question mark" on hindwings. **HABITAT** Open woods. **FOOD PLANTS** Elms, nettles. **SEASON** Late May–Oct. **RANGE** All N. Eng., ex. n ME.

EASTERN COMMA
Polygonia comma
BRUSHFOOT FAMILY

2". Orange above, with large dark brown spots; edges jagged; tails rounded; hindwings orange (fall) to very dark (summer). Below, hooked silver "comma" on hindwings. **HABITAT** Woodland openings and edges. **FOOD PLANTS** Hop vines, elms, nettles. **SEASON** Late Mar.–Oct.; hibernates. **RANGE** All N. Eng., ex. n ME.

COMPTON TORTOISESHELL
Nymphalis vau-album
BRUSHFOOT FAMILY

2½". Orange above, with heavy black patches, 1 white spot on each wing; edges ragged. Below, mottled brown with gray band. **HABITAT** Broadleaf woods. **FOOD PLANTS** Birches, willows, aspens. **SEASON** Mar.–Oct.; hibernates.

MOURNING CLOAK
Nymphalis antiopa
BRUSHFOOT FAMILY

3⅛". Dark mahogany brown above, with creamy edges beyond blue-spotted black border. Below, blackish brown with pale border. Flies early through leafless woods. **HABITAT** Woods, fields. **FOOD PLANTS** Willows, elms. **SEASON** Mar.–Oct.; hibernates.

AMERICAN LADY
"American Painted Lady"
Vanessa virginiensis
BRUSHFOOT FAMILY

2". Orange above; outer forewings black with white line, white spots. Below, lacy brown, black, light gray, and pink; 2 large eyespots. Migratory. **HABITAT** Fields, gardens. **FOOD PLANTS** Everlastings. **SEASON** May–Oct.

RED ADMIRAL
Vanessa atalanta
BRUSHFOOT FAMILY

2". Brownish black above, with wide orange semicircle; forewings have large white spots near tip. Below, mottled brown and black; forewings have red, white, and blue spots. Migratory. **HABITAT** Meadows, woodland edges. **FOOD PLANTS** Nettles. **SEASON** May–Oct.

WHITE ADMIRAL
Limenitis arthemis arthemis
BRUSHFOOT FAMILY

3". Blackish above, with wide white semicircle; hindwings edged with blue spots. Below, white semicircle, plus many large orange spots. Common at puddles. **HABITAT** Woods, woodland edges. **FOOD PLANTS** Poplars, birches. **SEASON** June–Aug. **RANGE** w and n N. Eng.

RED-SPOTTED PURPLE
Limenitis arthemis astyanax
BRUSHFOOT FAMILY

3″. Iridescent dark blue above, edged with bands of light blue; forewings have red spots at tip. Below, slaty with large orange spots, pale blue spots on edges. **HABITAT** Woodland openings, meadows. **FOOD PLANTS** Cherry and aspen trees. **SEASON** June–early Sept. **RANGE** s and c N. Eng.

VICEROY
Limenitis archippus
BRUSHFOOT FAMILY

2¾″. Orange above, with blackish veins and blackish, white-spotted margins. Differs from larger Monarch in narrow black line crossing hindwings above and below; glides with wings horizontal. **HABITAT** Brushy meadows. **FOOD PLANTS** Willows, aspens. **SEASON** June–early Sept.

LITTLE WOOD SATYR
Megisto cymela
BRUSHFOOT FAMILY

1¾″. Pale dull brown above; each wing has 2 evenly spaced black spots, circled with yellow, visible above and below. **HABITAT** Woodland edges and meadows. **FOOD PLANTS** Grasses. **SEASON** Late May–mid-July.

COMMON RINGLET
Coenonympha tullia
BRUSHFOOT FAMILY

1½″. Pale orangy reddish above, with small eyespot on forewings. Below, hindwings have pale gray band. Flies slowly above grasses. Has recently spread south throughout N. Eng. **HABITAT** Fields. **FOOD PLANTS** Grasses. **SEASON** June, Aug.

COMMON WOOD NYMPH
Cercyonis pegala
BRUSHFOOT FAMILY

2⅜″. Dark brown above; forewings have prominent yellow patch, with 2 black eyespots above and below. Below, paler with fine, net-like, blackish lines. **HABITAT** Brushy fields, salt marshes. **FOOD PLANTS** Grasses. **SEASON** July–Sept.

MONARCH
Danaus plexippus
BRUSHFOOT FAMILY

3¾″. Orange above, with black veins, orange- and white-spotted blackish margins; male has black spot on vein of hindwing. Below, yellow-orange. Head and body black with white spots. Glides with wings held at an angle. Caterpillar banded black, white, and yellow. Adult and caterpillar are poisonous to predators. Eastern Monarchs migrate

adult (top left), pupa (top right),
caterpillar (bottom)

south in fall to overwinter in fir trees in mtns. of c Mexico. In spring, 1 or 2 generations pass as they fly back to N. Eng., and 1 or 2 more generations pass in N. Eng. before the next fall migration. **HABITAT** Fields. **FOOD PLANTS** Milkweed family. **SEASON** June–Oct.

SILVER-SPOTTED SKIPPER
Epargyreus clarus
SKIPPER FAMILY

2″. Chocolate brown above, with golden patches on forewings. Below, hindwings have large silver patch. Territorial; aggressively chases other butterflies away. **HABITAT** Fields, gardens. **FOOD PLANTS** Pea family, incl. locust trees. **SEASON** June–Aug. **RANGE** c and s N. Eng.

NORTHERN CLOUDYWING
Thorybes pylades
SKIPPER FAMILY

1½″. Patternless brown above; trailing edges buffy; forewings have few random white spots. Below, hindwings have darker brown mottling. **HABITAT** Fields. **FOOD PLANTS** Pea family. **SEASON** June–July. **RANGE** c and s N. Eng.

DREAMY DUSKYWING
Erynnis icelus
SKIPPER FAMILY
1⅛". Dark brown above; outer forewings have silvery patches, with dark bands; hindwings dotted with tiny yellow spots. Usu. seen with wings spread. **HABITAT** Trails, woodland openings. **FOOD PLANTS** Willows, poplars. **SEASON** May–June.

JUVENAL'S DUSKYWING
Erynnis juvenalis
SKIPPER FAMILY
1½". Dark brown above; male has 4 buffy-white spots in cluster on leading edge of forewings; female has many buffy spots. Usu. seen with wings spread. **HABITAT** Oak woods, edges. **FOOD PLANTS** Oaks. **SEASON** May–June.

LEAST SKIPPER
Ancyloxypha numitor
SKIPPER FAMILY
¾". Above, forewings dark brown (male) to blackish (female); hindwings orangish, with black margin. Below, hindwings yellow-orange. Notably tiny. **HABITAT** Marshes, pond edges. **FOOD PLANTS** Grasses. **SEASON** June–Sept. **RANGE** c and s N. Eng.

EUROPEAN SKIPPER
Thymelicus lineola
SKIPPER FAMILY
⅞". Orange above, with narrow dark borders and white fringes. Below, orange. Can be abundant. **HABITAT** Fields. **FOOD PLANTS** Timothy Grass. **SEASON** June–July. **RANGE** All N. Eng., ex. n and c ME.

PECK'S SKIPPER
Polites peckius
SKIPPER FAMILY
⅞". Forewings orange-brown above, with some black markings. Below, hindwings have large yellow patches. **HABITAT** Fields, yards. **FOOD PLANTS** Grasses. **SEASON** May–Sept.

LONG DASH
Polites mystic
SKIPPER FAMILY

1⅛". Forewings broadly orange above, divided by thick black line. Below, hindwings rusty gold with large yellow curved band. **HABITAT** Fields. **FOOD PLANTS** Grasses. **SEASON** June–July.

HOBOMOK SKIPPER
Poanes hobomok
SKIPPER FAMILY

1¼". Forewings orange above, broadly bordered in dark brown. Below, hindwings have broad yellow patch. **HABITAT** Fields. **FOOD PLANTS** Grasses. **SEASON** Late May–early July.

DUN SKIPPER
Euphyes vestris
SKIPPER FAMILY

1⅛". Uniformly brown above; male forewings have black line; female forewings have 3 tiny white spots in middle. Below, brown. **HABITAT** Fields, watersides. **FOOD PLANTS** Sedges. **SEASON** July–Aug.

TENT CATERPILLAR MOTHS
Malacosoma species
TENT CATERPILLAR MOTH FAMILY

1½". Wings brownish orange; forewings have 2 white bands. Body hairy. Caterpillar blue; orange lines along sides, white line above; in May, many construct communal tents in wild cherry, apple trees; can denude trees. **HABITAT** Young broadleaf trees. **FOOD PLANTS** Apple and cherry trees. **SEASON** June–Aug.

caterpillar (top left), caterpillars on tent (top right), adult (bottom)

LUNA MOTH
Actias luna
GIANT SILKWORM MOTH FAMILY

4″. Wings pale green, each with eye-spot; leading edge of forewings purple, all else edged white; hindwings have very long tail. Body pale green. Nocturnal. Caterpillar green with yellow side stripes, spiny points. **HABITAT** Broadleaf woods. **FOOD PLANTS** Many trees, incl. hickories, beeches. **SEASON** May–July.

POLYPHEMUS MOTH
Antheraea polyphemus
GIANT SILKWORM MOTH FAMILY

4½″. Wings pale orange-brown with eyespots: yellow on forewings yellow and black on hindwings; narrow black and white line near trailing edges. Body orange-brown. Nocturnal. Caterpillar green with yellow bands red bumps. **HABITAT** Broadleaf woods. **FOOD PLANTS** Many trees, incl. oaks. **SEASON** Mainly July.

CECROPIA MOTH
Hyalophora cecropia
GIANT SILKWORM
MOTH FAMILY

5¼″. Wings brown, with lighter margins, half-moon eyespots, wavy red and white bands. Body reddish, with white collar; abdomen ringed white. Nocturnal. Caterpillar bluish green with red,

yellow, and blue knobs. Largest moth north of Mexico. **HABITAT** Woods fields, towns. **FOOD PLANTS** Many trees, incl. Apple. **SEASON** May–July.

TOMATO HORNWORM MOTH
Manduca quinquemaculata
SPHINX MOTH FAMILY

4″. Wings narrow, pointed, gray brown. Body very large, tapered, with 5–6 pairs of yellow spots on abdomen Caterpillar bright green with wavy yellow lines; green and black horn at rear **HABITAT** Gardens. **FOOD PLANTS** Tomato, tobacco, and potato plants. **SEASON** June–Sept.

HUMMINGBIRD MOTH
Hemaris thysbe
SPHINX MOTH FAMILY

1¾". Wings red to brown (white below) with clear patches. Body spindle-shaped; orange and olive; long, flexible proboscis. Hovers by day at flowers like a hummingbird. Caterpillar yellowish green with darker lines, reddish-brown spots on abdomen; yellow tail horn. **HABITAT** Woodland edges, gardens. **FOOD PLANTS** Hawthorn and cherry trees, honeysuckles. **SEASON** May–Sept.

WOOLLY BEAR CATERPILLAR MOTH
Isia isabella
TIGER MOTH FAMILY

1¾". Forewings rusty orange, with rows of small black spots; hindwings lighter. Body rusty orange. Nocturnal. Caterpillar distinctive, hairy, reddish brown and black; often crosses roads, paths by day in Sept., Oct. **HABITAT** Shrubby fields, roadsides. **FOOD PLANTS** Dandelions, plantains, low-growing weeds. **SEASON** June–Aug.

FALL WEBWORM MOTH
Hyphantria cunea
TIGER MOTH FAMILY

1⅜". Wings ghostly white; forewings have black spots. Body white. Caterpillar variably colored, with long light hairs; in late summer makes large gray webs; conspicuous in fall. **HABITAT** Broadleaf and mixed woods. **FOOD PLANTS** Many broadleaf trees. **SEASON** June–July.

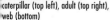

caterpillar (top left), adult (top right), web (bottom)

VIRGINIA CTENUCHID MOTH
Ctenucha virginica
CTENUCHID MOTH FAMILY

1⅝". Wings dull olive-brown, with narrow white trailing edges. Body metallic blue-green; head orange. Flies by day. Caterpillar brown, with clumps of blackish or creamy hairs; head red. **HABITAT** Moist meadows. **FOOD PLANTS** Grasses, sedges, irises. **SEASON** May–July.

larva hatching (left), caterpillar (center), adults (right)

GYPSY MOTH
Lymantria dispar
TUSSOCK MOTH FAMILY

Female 2", male ¾". Female wings and body creamy white with blackish wavy lines; flightless. Male pale brown, mottled; flies erratically. Female lays orange-brown egg masses on shady sides of trees, buildings. Caterpillar very hairy, so avoided by most predators; feeds up in trees by day, often on ground at night. Introduced inadvertently from Eurasia to MA in 1869; major pest and nuisance; defoliates vast forests, where you can hear the excrement drop from trees. Diseases and natural predators reduce numbers after several summers of infestation. **HABITAT** Woods, esp. oak. **FOOD PLANTS** Mainly broadleaf trees. **SEASON** July–Aug.

EIGHT-SPOTTED FORESTER
Alypia octomaculata
OWLET MOTH FAMILY

1⅛". Wings black; forewings have 2 yellow spots; hindwings have 2 white spots. Body hairy, black with yellow shoulders. Flies by day. Caterpillar banded black, white, and orange. **HABITAT** Woodland edges, brushy fields. **FOOD PLANTS** Grapes, Virginia Creeper. **SEASON** May–June.

ULTRONIA UNDERWING MOTH
Catocala ultronia
OWLET MOTH FAMILY

2½". Forewings brownish, with light gray central band. When flushed from daytime roost or flying at night, reveals shocking-pink hindwings, with 2 broad black bands and white trailing edge. Body brown. Nocturnal. Caterpillar twig-like; gray. **HABITAT** Broadleaf and mixed woods. **FOOD PLANTS** Apple and cherry trees. **SEASON** Aug.–Sept.

Vertebrates

There are approximately 43,000 vertebrate species on earth. The evolution of a variety of anatomical structures has made them extraordinarily successful for half a billion years. Today vertebrates are one of the most widespread groups of animals, inhabiting every corner of the globe, from ocean depths to mountaintops, deserts, and polar regions.

Vertebrata is one of three subphyla of the phylum Chordata. All members of Chordata possess an internal stiffening rod called a notochord during their embryonic development. The sac-like, marine sea squirts, salps, and their relatives (members of the subphylum Urochordata, the most primitive of the Chordata) lose their notochord completely as they develop, and in the file-shaped, marine lancelets (of the subphylum Cephalochordata) the notochord remains an unsegmented rod. In vertebrates the notochord is replaced during the animal's development by a series of cartilaginous or bony disks, known as vertebrae, that run along the back.

The evolution of the vertebrates stemmed from an invertebrate sea squirt-like animal, passed through a "missing link" invertebrate-to-vertebrate stage with the lancelets, and reached the beginnings of the vertebrate stage some 500 million years ago (mya) with the appearance of the first jawless fishes. During the following 350 million years, the various classes of vertebrates evolved. The ancestors of modern fishes developed from their jawless ancestors about 400 mya; 100 million years further into vertebrate development, amphibians evolved from fishes crawling about in search of water during the droughts of the Devonian period. Reptiles first appeared about 250 mya and flourished because of their ability to reproduce on land. Mammals and birds, warm-blooded and able to successfully live in places too cold for fishes, amphibians, and reptiles, spread across the world's environments, mammals beginning about 170 mya and birds about 150 mya.

Today's vertebrates share a number of characteristics that separate them from the estimated 50 million or so invertebrate species with which they share the earth. Virtually all vertebrates are bilaterally symmetrical; that is, their left and right sides are essentially mirror images of one another. Their strong but flexible backbone, composed of vertebrae, protects the spinal cord and serves as the main structural component of the internal skeletal frame and the segmented muscles that attach to it.

Vertebrates are well-coordinated runners, jumpers, swimmers, and/or fliers because of this unique combination of skeletal and muscular development. Other shared characteristics of nearly all vertebrates include one pair of bony jaws (with or without teeth), one or two pairs of appendages, a ventrally located heart (protected by a ribcage), and blood contained in vessels.

The subphylum Vertebrata includes several classes: three classes of living fishes, the amphibians, the reptiles, the birds, and the mammals.

Fishes

Living fishes fall into three major groups: the primitive hagfishes and lampreys, the cartilaginous fishes (sharks, skates, and rays), and the bony fishes. Aquatic, mostly cold-blooded vertebrates with fins and internal gills, fish are typically streamlined and have a muscular tail. Most move through the water by weaving movements of their bodies and tail fins, using their other fins to control their direction. The skin of a fish is coated with a slimy secretion that decreases friction with the water; this secretion, along with the scales that cover most fish, provides their bodies with a nearly waterproof covering. The gills are located in passages that lead from the throat usually to a pair of openings on the side, just behind the head. With rare exceptions, fish breathe by taking water in through the mouth and forcing it past the gills and out through the gill openings; the thin-walled gills capture oxygen from the water and emit carbon dioxide.

The body shapes of fishes vary from cylindrical eels and elongated, spindle-shaped mackerels (rounded in the middle, with tapered ends) to vertically compressed (flattened) sunfishes to horizontally compressed skates and rays. Body colors can vary within a species due to season, sex, age, individual variation, and water temperature, and the color normally fades or otherwise changes after death. Most fishes have one or more dorsal (back) fins that may be spiny or soft (a few fishes, such as trout and salmon, have an additional fleshy fin behind the dorsal fins, called an adipose fin); a tail (caudal) fin, usually with an upper and a lower lobe; and an anal fin, just in front of the tail along the edge of the ventral (belly) side. They also have a pair of pectoral fins, usually on the sides behind the head, and a pair of pelvic fins, generally under the middle of the body. Some fishes lack one or more of these fins.

The mouths and snouts of fishes may be disk-shaped, pointed, tubular, or sword-like; depending on the species, the upper jaw (the snout) projects beyond the lower, the two parts of the jaw are of equal length, or the lower jaw projects beyond the upper. Some species have sensory barbels, whisker-like projections of the skin, usually on the lower jaw, that detect objects, especially in muddy or murky water. Most fish are covered with scales, but some species lack scales altogether, and some lack scales on the head or other areas; in other species, scales have been modified into bony plates. Some fishes have a conspicuous lateral line, a sensory organ beneath the skin that responds to vibrations in the water and often looks like a thin stripe along the side; others have no lateral line, while a few have branching lateral lines.

Some fish species are solitary, some live in small groups, and others are found mainly in enormous schools, in which members respond as a unit to stimuli while feeding or migrating.

Lengths given (from the tip of the snout to the tip of the tail) are for typical adults, although, as fish continue to grow throughout their lives, larger individuals may be seen. The icon ⬛ denotes fishes that can be found in both salt and fresh water (see box, page 254).

Hagfishes and Lampreys

The primitive hagfishes and lampreys are jawless and eel-like in appearance; their skeleton is formed of cartilage. They lack scales and the paired pelvic and pectoral fins of the more advanced fishes. Hagfish (often called slime eels) are carrion-feeders that use their mouth, which contains teeth, for biting. Some lampreys are parasitic, using the mouth as a suction disk to hold on to prey, whose blood they suck as they are carried along by the host fish. Most lamprey species live in fresh water; all hagfishes live in salt water.

SEA LAMPREY Sea Lamprey (left) with prey
Petromyzon marinus
LAMPREY FAMILY

24–30". Eel-like, scaleless. Mottled brown above; yellowish on sides; white below. 2 dorsal fins wavy-edged; tail fin small, diamond-shaped. Row of 7 gill openings on each side. Mouth round, with many rasp-like teeth. Attaches to large fish, sucks blood, kills host over many days. **HABITAT** Streams; ocean to 1,640' deep.

ATLANTIC HAGFISH
Myxine glutinosa
HAGFISH FAMILY

18–24". Eel-like, scaleless, slimy, gray-brown. Tail fin elongated, flattened; anal fin runs into tail fin. Mouth has 2 rows of horny triangular teeth. Nearly blind; has well-developed sense of smell. Burrows most of body into muddy bottom, with only head exposed, waiting to locate dead or netted fish. **HABITAT** Ocean bottoms 100–3,150' deep.

Cartilaginous Fishes

The cartilaginous fishes have skeletons of somewhat flexible cartilage and several (usually five) pairs of conspicuous external gill slits. This group includes, in waters off New England, sharks, skates, and rays. Sharks typically have an elongated shape that tapers toward each end; one or two triangular dorsal fins, sometimes with a fin spine on the leading edge; two large pectoral fins; two smaller pelvic fins; a tail fin of which the upper lobe is usually larger than the lower; and sometimes an anal fin and a pair of horizontal keels at the base of the tail. The skates and rays have flattened bodies, usually round or diamond-shaped, with greatly enlarged pectoral fins attached to the side of the head, forming "wings" with which they "fly" through the water. The mouth is located on the underside of the head. Sharks have several rows of sharply pointed teeth; when a tooth breaks off or is worn down, a new tooth takes its place. The skin is rough and sandpapery, studded with tiny, tooth-like scales called denticles. Because cartilaginous fishes lack the swim bladder that keeps the bony fishes buoyant, and the efficient

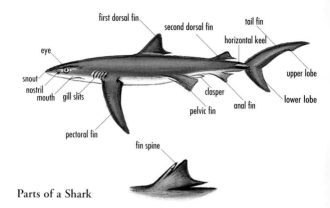

Parts of a Shark

"gill pump" of bony fishes that keeps water moving over their gills, many sharks must swim constantly. Most live in ocean waters, though a few may enter large rivers. The male has a pair of external copulatory organs called claspers, modifications of the pelvic fins that are used to internally fertilize the female. Depending on the species, the female lays eggs enclosed in a horny case, retains the eggs internally until they hatch, or gives birth to live young.

BASKING SHARK
Cetorhinus maximus
BASKING SHARK FAMILY

30–32′. Snout short, pointed, with rounded tip. Solid gray-brown, paler on belly. 1st dorsal fin very large, triangular, rounded at peak. Tail fin's upper lobe slightly larger than lower. Teeth very small, rounded. Very long gill slits almost encircle head. Swims on surface with mouth open; strains plankton from sea water with large combs of horny gill rakers. **HABITAT** Surface of open sea a few miles offshore and beyond. Basking is world's largest shark, along with warm-water, white-spotted **Whale Shark** *(Rhincodon typus),* which occurs rarely north to Gulf of Maine in summer.

WHITE SHARK
Carcharodon carcharias
MACKEREL SHARK FAMILY

10–12′. Snout bluntly pointed. Pale gray above, white below. 1st dorsal fin tall, thick, pointed; pectoral fins long; tail fin's upper lobe notched below tip. Teeth highly serrated, triangular. Young born alive, about 5′ long. Feeds on seals, porpoises, other small cetaceans, large fish, crabs. Rare off N. Eng. **CAUTION** Bites; will attack boats if nearby waters contain discarded fish parts. **HABITAT** Coastal and oceanic surface waters.

SHORTFIN MAKO
Isurus oxyrinchus
MACKEREL SHARK FAMILY

5–8′. Long, slender; snout pointed. Blue-gray to deep blue above, white below. 1st dorsal fin large, rounded. Teeth large, slender, smooth-edged, pointed backward. **CAUTION** Bites; has attacked boats. **HABITAT** Surface of open sea.

SMOOTH DOGFISH
Mustelus canis
REQUIEM SHARK FAMILY

3–4′. Snout long, pointed. Uniformly grayish brown. 2 dorsal fins large, rounded, equal in size; pectoral fins long, wide; tail fin's upper lobe notched, elongated; lower lobe very short, rounded. Eyes bulge at top of head. **HABITAT** Bottoms to 60′ deep or more; enters bays, river mouths to feed. **RANGE** Migratory. Summer: CT to MA. **Spiny Dogfish** *(Squalus acanthias),* 3′, elongated; gray-brown above, shading to dirty white below. 2 pointed dorsal fins equal in size; upper tail fin long, without notch.

BLUE SHARK
Prionace glauca
REQUIEM SHARK FAMILY

7–10′. Very slender; pointed snout longer than width of mouth. Dark blue above; sides light blue; white below. 1st dorsal fin relatively small, rounded; pectoral fins long, flexible, crescent-shaped; tail fin's upper lobe long, very swept-back. Teeth curved, triangular. Follows boats, waiting for offal. **CAUTION** Rarely bites beachgoers, but has attacked people swimming off boats at sea. **HABITAT** Usu. open sea; occ. near shore.

LITTLE SKATE
Raja erinacea
SKATE FAMILY

16–20″. Flattened body disk, square with rounded corners. Buffy brown, peppered with dark brown spots. Pectoral fins enlarged, wing-like; "flap" during movement; tail long, thin, upper lobe covered with short spines. Eyes on top of head; lower jaw shorter than snout. Empty egg case, black with 4 curled extensions, called mermaid's purse. **HABITAT** Sandy and gravelly shores to 300′ deep. Winter: inshore. Summer: offshore.

Bony Fishes

Bony fishes normally have harder, less flexible bony skeletons than cartilaginous fishes, as well as a gas- or fat-filled swim bladder that keeps them buoyant. Most bony fishes have overlapping scales embedded in flexible connective tissue, though some lack scales entirely. There is a single gill opening on each side protected by a hard gill cover.

More than 99 percent of all living fishes are ray-finned bony fishes; a few bony fishes (none of which occur in New England waters) are classified as lobe-finned fishes. The fins of ray-finned bony fishes consist of a web of skin supported by bony rays (either segmented soft rays or stiffer spines), each moved by a set of muscles, which makes the fins very flexible. The tail fin is typically symmetrical.

Most bony fishes reproduce by spawning: males directly fertilize eggs after the females release them from their bodies into the water. The eggs may float at mid-levels, rise to the surface, or sink to the bottom. A few fish species guard nests or incubate eggs in a pouch or the mouth. Newborn fish are called larvae; within a few weeks or months, a larva develops to resemble a miniature adult, and is called a juvenile or fry.

This section is presented as two categories—saltwater fishes (starting on page 238) and freshwater fishes (starting on page 255). Most fish species live strictly in either salt water or fresh water. Other species are frequently found in brackish water, where fresh and salt water mix, and some primarily saltwater species breed in fresh water, but return to spend most of their lives at sea. Species are placed in the category where they spend most of their time or are most likely to be seen The icon denotes those that live in both types of water (see box, page 254).

The lengths given for the bony fishes (from the tip of the snout to the tip of the tail) are for typical adults.

Parts of a Fish

ATLANTIC STURGEON
Acipenser oxyrhynchus
STURGEON FAMILY

6–8′. Enormous, elongated; snout long; 5 rows of bony plates on back, sides, belly. Bluish black above, shading to silvery below; plates white-tipped. 1 dorsal fin set far back; tail fin's upper lobe long, pointed. Fleshy, sensitive barbels hang from snout; mouth small, tubular, on underside below eye. Cruises slowly along bottom looking for small fish, crustaceans, mollusks; sucks in prey. Threatened. **HABITAT** Coasts, brackish estuaries. Spring: enters large rivers to spawn. **RANGE** ne MA, NH, ME.

Herrings

The herring family found in New England (family Clupeidae) also includes shads, sardines, and menhadens. These small silvery fishes are somewhat primitive, lacking fin spines and adipose fins. They mainly live in shallow coastal waters and tend to travel in schools. Most are marine, although some, such as the American Shad, travel up rivers to spawn and a few live exclusively in fresh water. Most herrings have a row of modified scales called scutes running lengthwise along the belly; some species have just one scute, located between the pelvic fins. Herrings are mainly filter feeders, straining plankton through small finger-like structures in their gills called gill rakers.

The spawning runs of the American Shad are a harbinger of spring in New England. They usually begin entering rivers in late April in Connecticut; farther north they run in May or June. The blooming of Downy Serviceberry shrubs, also known as "Shadbush" or "Shadblow," is said to coincide with the shad runs. Egg-laden females, known as shad roe, are particularly prized, as the roe are considered a delicacy.

ALEWIFE
Alosa pseudoharengus
HERRING FAMILY
10–11″. Herring family: smallish, silvery, schooling fish that filter plankton. This species: head scaleless; eyes large; lower jaw protrudes; mouth upward-slanting. Iridescent silvery green above; silvery below. 1 dorsal fin; large, triangular; tail fin deeply forked. **HABITAT** Most of year: bays, estuaries. Spring: spawning runs in rivers. Some landlocked in lakes.

AMERICAN SHAD
Alosa sapidissima
HERRING FAMILY
20–23″. Back rounded. Dark blue-green above; sides silvery with 6–10 small black spots, largest one above gills; belly whitish. 1 dorsal fin; small, triangular; tail fin deeply forked. Head scaleless; eyes yellow. **HABITAT** Most of year: bays, estuaries. Spring: spawning runs in rivers.

ATLANTIC MENHADEN
Brevoortia tyrannus
HERRING FAMILY
7–12″. Back rounded; midback has fatty ridge with modified scales. Heavy black spot near gills. Occurs in enormous schools. **HABITAT** All year: near surface of open ocean and estuary mouths. **Atlantic Herring**

(Clupea harengus) 6–12″; silvery with blue-green back, no dark spots; also occurs in large schools at sea.

CUSK
Brosme brosme
COD FAMILY

18–24". Elongated; cylindrical in front, compressed to rear. Slate brown above; sides yellowish; belly whitish. Long, continuous dorsal fin, rounded tail fin, and long anal fin all bordered with black stripe and white edge. Head laterally compressed; mouth upward-slanting. **HABITAT** Hard and rough bottoms 60–3,000' deep.

ATLANTIC COD
Gadus morhua
COD FAMILY

24–48". Front-heavy, tapering at both ends. Reddish brown or gray-green with many dark brown spots; lateral line pale. 3 dorsal fins wide-based; 2 anal fins; tail fin fan-shaped. Eyes large; upper jaw protrudes; 1 barbel on lower jaw. Eats mollusks. Can be very prolific: 9 million eggs recorded in one female. Smaller adults called scrod. **HABITAT** Shore to 1,500' deep, mainly on bottom of continental shelf. Near shore in cold weather.

Overfishing Georges Bank

Georges Bank, an extensive submarine plateau about 100 miles east of Cape Cod, was the focus of worldwide fishing efforts for more than 400 years. Early expeditions from Spain, England, and Portugal harvested holds full of fish, and tales of prodigious numbers of cod, haddock, and other species drew many ships of adventurous captains, crews, and their families to American shores. Fish populations held their own until after World War II, when factory ships from the U.S.S.R., Poland, Germany, France, and Spain came to these waters and went home with vast catches. In 1977 the United States imposed a 200-mile territorial boundary, and foreign fishing stopped. In short order, however, the U.S. fishing fleet's harvests more than equaled that of the Europeans. Efforts were made to regulate net mesh size and minimum fish size, but fishermen worked around the restrictions, and numbers of all species declined until in 1993, the last year before limits were set, the catch was only one-third its historical levels. In a recent further effort to protect fish populations, the Multi-species Fisheries Management Plan has been amended to limit the number of days boats can work the bank.

HADDOCK
Melanogrammus aeglefinus
COD FAMILY

14–23". Moderately elongated, tapering to narrow base of tail. Dark gray above, shading to white below; 1 square black patch below black lateral line and above pectoral fins. 3 dorsal fins wide-based, 1st ending in sharp point; tail fin notched; 2 anal fins. Mouth small; tiny barbel below short lower jaw. **HABITAT** Offshore banks to 600′ deep.

SILVER HAKE
"Whiting"
Merluccius bilinearis
COD FAMILY

14". Elongated; cylindrical in front, compressed and narrow toward back. Brownish, with silvery iridescence above; silvery below. 1st dorsal fin short, triangular; 2nd runs to tail with notch in middle; tail fin notched. Mouth ends below large eye; no chin barbel. **HABITAT** Bottom of continental shelf; common in Gulf of Maine.

ATLANTIC TOMCOD
Microgadus tomcod
COD FAMILY

6–12". Moderately elongated; rear half of body narrow; snout conical. Mottled dark brownish green and yellow-brown above and on sides; lateral line pale. 3 rounded dorsal fins; tail fin narrow, rounded; pelvic and anal fins large. Long barbel below short lower jaw. **HABITAT** Most of year: shallow bays, estuaries. Sept.–Jan.: spawns in estuaries, freshwater rivers.

POLLOCK
Pollachius virens
COD FAMILY

24–36″. Rather elongated, yet plump. Brownish green or dark gray above silvery below; lateral line white. 3 dorsal fins wide-based; tail fin notched pelvic and anal fins wide-based. Lower jaw protrudes beyond upper; tiny barbel below lower jaw. Runs in schools, young fish inshore, older fish in deep water. **HABITAT** Surface to 600′ deep.

GOOSEFISH
Lophius americanus
GOOSEFISH FAMILY

24″. Body horizontally flattened; head broad, large. Brown. 1st dorsal fin modified into "fishing pole" with dangling lure, 2nd and 3rd dorsal fins solitary, 4th with 3 spines, 5th with 10 spiny rays; pectoral fins wide, rounded; tail fin fan-shaped. Mouth wide, upward-pointed, lined

with many long sharp teeth. Lies on bottom ambushing large fish and seabirds attracted to waving lure. **HABITAT** Bottoms, muddy shallows to 1,200′ deep.

MUMMICHOG
"Mosquito Fish"
Fundulus heteroclitus
KILLIFISH FAMILY

3–4″. Stocky, with rounded back and wide base of tail; head blunt Dark green, with blackish and silvery bars on sides. 1 spineless dorsal fin set far back; tail fin large, rounded. Feeds at surface on small invertebrates and insect larvae. **HABITAT** Estuaries, tidal creeks, salt marshes, nearby fresh waters.

WHITE HAKE
Urophycis tenuis
PHYCID HAKE FAMILY

28″. Elongated; cylindrical in front, compressed toward back. Brown with irreg. white blotches. 1st dorsal

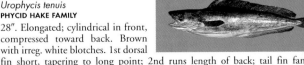

fin short, tapering to long point; 2nd runs length of back; tail fin fan shaped; anal fin runs along rear half of body; long, forked, white pelvic fin "feelers" hang below gills, in front of pectoral fins. Corner of mouth extends to below large eye; small barbel on chin. **HABITAT** Muddy or silty bottom from 40′ downward; breeds in estuaries.

THREESPINE STICKLEBACK

Gasterosteus aculeatus
STICKLEBACK FAMILY

2½″. Tapered at both ends; sides have bony plates. Olive-brown, silver below; when breeding, male red below. 3 stout, widely separated spines on back before dorsal fin; tail fin rounded. Lower jaw protrudes. Male territorial; builds cylindrical nest from water plants. **HABITAT** Grassy inshore shallows, estuaries; spawns in nearby freshwater streams Apr.–July. **RANGE** e MA, NH, ME.

ATLANTIC NEEDLEFISH

Strongylura marina
NEEDLEFISH FAMILY

12–20″. Very elongated, pencil-shaped; both jaws needle-like. Greenish blue above; lateral line blue. Single dorsal and anal fins both far back; tail fin forked. Teeth small. Actively chases small fish at night. **HABITAT** Coastal, brackish, and nearby fresh waters. Spawns in salt and fresh water; follows prey into rivers.

ATLANTIC SILVERSIDE
Menidia menidia
SILVERSIDE FAMILY

3½″. Silversides: small, elongated, schooling fish with large eyes, prominent silver side stripe. This species: gray-green above, whitish below. Head small. 2 dorsal fins, 1st small, with 4 spiny rays, often laid back. Tail fin forked; anal fin long-based, straight-edged. Important food fish for terns. **HABITAT** Off sandy beaches; shallow bays; estuaries.

NORTHERN PIPEFISH
Syngnathus fuscus
PIPEFISH FAMILY

4–8″. Pencil-like; horizontal; head narrow; snout tubular. Flexible body covered with rings of bony scales. Yellow-green. 1 rectangular dorsal fin; tail tiny, fan-like. Eyes red. Male has brood pouch on underside for female's eggs. **HABITAT** Eelgrass beds in bays and inlets; some occ. enter fresh water near coast.

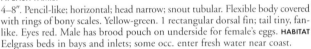

LINED SEAHORSE
Hippocampus erectus
PIPEFISH FAMILY

4″. Elongated; swims upright with head above body, tail dangling below; armored with lines and ridges. Head and tubular snout angle downward. Color varies with background: gray, brown, or dull red. Dorsal fin fan-shaped; tail prehensile, finless, curls around vegetation. Swims (weakly) by rapid vibration of dorsal fin. When mating, pair makes musical sounds; female lays eggs in male's pouch; young hatch and are expelled by male several weeks later. **HABITAT** Eelgrass beds in shallow water with tidal currents.

ACADIAN REDFISH
Sebastes fasciatus
SCORPIONFISH FAMILY

10″. Head large; forward body heavy, compressed. 2 dorsal fins orange-red, with sharp pointed spines; tail fin forked. Eyes large, yellow; lower jaw protrudes. A carnivorous bottom dweller. Most in this genus live on Pacific coast, where known as Rockfish. **CAUTION** Skin-piercing, venomous dorsal spines. **HABITAT** Shallow rocky ocean bottoms. **RANGE** Cape Ann to ME.

LUMPFISH
Cyclopterus lumpus
SNAILFISH FAMILY

14–16″. Body massive, almost round; triangular in frontal view. Skin rough, with 7 lateral knobby ridges, often black-tipped. Brown or olive; breeding male bright red below. Dorsal and anal fins square, adjacent to fan-shaped tail fin; pectoral fins almost meet at throat. Mouth small; jaws of equal length. Pelvic fins united to form a sucker; clings to rocks, debris. **HABITAT** Rocky shores, under mats of floating seaweed.

WHITE PERCH
Morone americana
TEMPERATE BASS FAMILY

8–10″. Oblong; very scaly; back rounded; head small. Blackish below dorsal fins; rest of body silvery, often with indistinct stripes. 1st dorsal fin has 8–10 indented strong spines; 2nd dorsal fin triangular; tail fin slightly forked. **HABITAT** Bays, brackish estuaries, freshwater rivers, lakes; spawns in fresh water. Some introduced populations landlocked.

STRIPED BASS
Morone saxatilis
TEMPERATE BASS FAMILY

25″. Elongated; moderately compressed; streamlined, with small fins. Pale; olive or slaty blue above; sides silvery, with 6–9 blackish side stripes; belly white. 2 dorsal fins triangular; tail fin notched. Lower jaw slightly protrudes. Numbers crashed due to pollution and overfishing, but are increasing. **HABITAT** Shallow coastal waters; rivers. **RANGE** Summer and early fall: entire coast; Connecticut River to Hartford.

SEA RAVEN
Hemitripterus americanus
SCULPIN FAMILY

16–18″. Elongated; forward body heavy; head and chin have fleshy tabs; skin has ridges of prickly scales. Brown to reddish. 3 dorsal fins rounded, 1st with ragged tips on spines; tail fin fan-shaped; exposed spines on all fins above and below. Inflates belly with air and water when captured; unable to submerge quickly if released. **CAUTION** Bites severely when caught; beware of spines. **HABITAT** Rocky bottoms, from shore to 350′ deep.

GRUBBY
Myoxocephalus aenaeus
SCULPIN FAMILY

4–5″. Head and forward body large; scaleless. Buffy brown, with 3 dark brown saddles on back. 2 dorsal fins rounded, with spiny rays; tail fin rounded. Eyes large, blue; short spines on forehead. **HABITAT** Estuaries and beaches to 420′ deep.

LONGHORN SCULPIN
Myoxocephalus octodecemspinosus
SCULPIN FAMILY

10″. Head large; rear body narrow; eyes large; long sharp spines on head and gill covers. Heavily mottled shades of brown; color varies darker to lighter with bottom color. Raised scales along lateral line. 2 dorsal fins; tail fin fan-shaped; pectoral fins all dark brown with buffy bands. **CAUTION** Beware of spines. **HABITAT** Harbors, estuaries, shallow coastal waters.

BLACK SEA BASS
Centropristis striata
SEA BASS FAMILY

15″. Elongated, moderately compressed; head large, unspotted, blackish. Male dark bluish black; female (pictured) brown; both have large whitish blotches on back and white centers on scales. Dorsal fin continuous, spiny, banded black and white; tail fin 3-lobed, upper lobe often with elongated ray. Lips thick; eyes yellow. **HABITAT** Harbors; over rough bottoms. **RANGE** Cape Cod and south, fewer north to ME.

BLUEFISH
Pomatomus saltatrix
BLUEFISH FAMILY

30″. Elongated, compressed schooling fish; head large; mouth wide. Blue-green above, shading to silvery below. 1st dorsal fin short, with 7 projecting spines; 2nd dorsal and anal fins similar, with long bases, lead rays longer; tail fin deeply forked. Teeth prominent and sharp. Sometimes called "piranha of the sea"; voraciously attacks and eats smaller fish and squid; when full, regurgitates and eats again, leaving trail of carnage. **CAUTION** When caught, will try to bite. When feeding, may bite swimmers. **HABITAT** Mainly June–Sept.: inshore and offshore surface waters.

TAUTOG
Tautoga onitis
WRASSE FAMILY

18″. Stout; head rounded, blunt; scales small. Blackish above; male mottled black and brown on sides. Female and young black and buff. Dorsal fin long, with rounded bump at rear; tail fin rounded. Cheeks scaleless; thick lips, powerful jaws, crushing teeth. **HABITAT** Summer: coastal waters to 600′ deep, rocky areas, docks in estuaries, musselbeds. Winter: deep waters.

CUNNER
Tautogolabrus adspersus
WRASSE FAMILY

6–10″. Somewhat elongated; back rounded; head pointed; scales large. Color varies greatly: plain reddish brown, greenish, or paler with red, blue, and brown spots. Dorsal fin long-based, with rounded bump at rear; tail fin rounded. Lips thick; teeth protruding. **HABITAT** Coastal waters to 600′ deep, estuaries; shallows near piers, rocks, eelgrass beds.

SCUP
"Porgy"
Stenotomus chrysops
PORGY FAMILY

12″. Oval schooling fish; head profile steep, slightly concave; scales large. Brownish above; sides silvery with indistinct thick bars and horizontal lines. Blue stripe under continuous, spiny dorsal fin; tail fin deeply forked. Jaws of equal length. Fine-toothed bottom feeder. **HABITAT** Mainly May–Oct.: inshore bottoms to continental shelf; estuaries.

OCEAN POUT
Macrozoarces americanus
EELPOUT FAMILY

16–28″. Long, tapered, eel-like; head massive. Color camouflaging: yellowish brown, with splotches of dark brown. Dorsal fin and anal fin low, appear continuous with tail fin; pectoral fins wide, rounded. Lips wide; teeth large. Skin smooth, covered with mucus. Ambushes organisms that fail to detect it. **CAUTION** Bites. **HABITAT** Bottoms from surf line to 600′ deep.

ATLANTIC WOLFFISH
Anarhichas lupus
WOLFFISH FAMILY

24″. Elongated; heaviest forward, tapering to tail. Head large, gray; eyes large; lips wide. Gray with vertical black bands. Dorsal and anal fins long, continuous; tail fin tiny, fan-shaped. Front teeth strong and sharp, rear teeth molar-like. **CAUTION** May be aggressive toward people. **HABITAT** Hard bottoms from near shore to 500′ deep. **RANGE** Mainly north of Cape Cod.

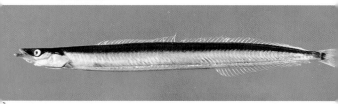

SAND LANCES
Ammodytes species
SAND LANCE FAMILY

6″. Eel-like, but body scaled, tail fin forked. Blue-green to brownish above; paler below. Dorsal fin long, low; lacks pelvic fin. Burrows in soft bottoms, and swims near surface in schools; undulates like a swimming snake. Over offshore banks, is major prey species for whales, seabirds, larger fish. **HABITAT** Surface to 120′ deep.

ATLANTIC BONITO
Sarda sarda
MACKEREL FAMILY

20″. Elongated, somewhat compressed; head large; snout pointed. Steel blue above; 7–11 slanted blackish stripes on sides; silvery below. Dorsal fins triangular: 1st long, with straight profile; 2nd short; 8 dorsal and 7 anal finlets; large median keel at base of tail; tail fin crescent-like. Lateral line wavy. Eyes large; jaws up-slanted, long, heavily toothed. Travels in large schools. **HABITAT** Mainly summer: near sea surface in warm waters, usu. well offshore.

ATLANTIC MACKEREL
Scomber scombrus
MACKEREL FAMILY

14–18″. Elongated, streamlined schooling fish; head large, pointed. Scales minute. Back blue-green, with about 30 black, wavy vertical bands down to lateral line; plain silvery below. 1st dorsal fin triangular; 2nd dorsal fin concave; 5 finlets above and 5 below on narrow tail before forked tail fin. **HABITAT** Open seas over continental shelf. Summer: some move inshore.

BLUEFIN TUNA
Thunnus thynnus
MACKEREL FAMILY

5–7'. Robust, deeper than mackerels; scales very small; head massive, pointed; mouth large. Dark blue-black above; yellowish stripe on side; silvery white below. 1st dorsal fin bluish, triangular; 2nd dorsal fin tall, brown, with short base; anal fin scythe-shaped. Base of tail has lateral keel, tooth-like finlets above and below; tail fin lobes narrow and pointed. Extremely fast swimmer; rips through schooling fishes. **HABITAT** Late summer: surface of open sea.

SWORDFISH
Xiphias gladius
SWORDFISH FAMILY

4–6'. Spindle-shaped; upper jaw very long, ⅓ body length, flattened and pointed. Blackish above; sides yellowish gray. Dorsal fin extremely large, swept-back, begins just behind head; lacks pelvic fins; tail fin shaped like crescent moon. Eyes large, above corner of mouth. Fast swimmer, reaches 60 mph; feeds on schooling fish. **HABITAT** Warm open seas from surface to 200' deep, usu. well offshore.

Flatfishes

Flatfish is the group name for three fish families (lefteye flounders, righteye flounders, and soles) with an unusual body form adapted to life on the seafloor. The larval fish starts life swimming normally, with an eye on each side. Soon one eye "migrates" to join the other on one side (right or left, depending on the species). The spineless, continuous dorsal fin and anal fins shift 90 degrees to become fringing horizontal fins, and for the rest of the fish's life it swims on one side. Flatfishes can change color and pattern, like chameleons, to match their backgrounds; their undersides are normally white. They usually lie partially buried in soft mud or sand bottoms, and dart quickly upward to seize passing small fish, crustaceans, and squid.

Parts of a Flatfish

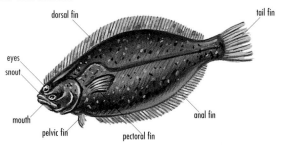

SUMMER FLOUNDER
Paralichthys dentatus
LEFTEYE FLOUNDER FAMILY

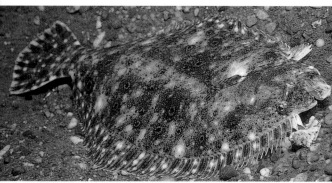

24". Flat, oval, with long, wedge-shaped tail fin. Gray, brown, or olive, with large variable dark or pale spots. Dorsal and anal fins fringe entire body edge except base of tail. Head pointed. Buries itself in sand, but fast swimmer in pursuit of prey. Called Fluke locally. **HABITAT** Sandy or muddy bottoms in bays, harbors, estuaries, and ocean to 650′ deep. **RANGE** Mainly Cape Cod and south.

WINDOWPANE
"Spotted Flounder"
"Sand Dab"
Scophthalmus aquosus
LEFTEYE FLOUNDER FAMILY

10–12". Flat; rounded or diamond-shaped, with long rounded tail fin; very thin body transmits light when held to sun. Gray, brown, or olive, with many small dark and pale spots. Continuous dorsal fin starts at snout, with first few rays free of membrane. Pelvic and anal fins fused to form a fringed crest. Mouth large. **HABITAT** Sandy bottoms, from shore to 150′ deep. Spawns in shallow estuaries.

WINTER FLOUNDER
Pleuronectes americanus
RIGHTEYE FLOUNDER FAMILY
12–15″. Body flat, oval, thick. Varies from pale olive green or reddish brown to blackish; often mottled with dark and light spots; lateral line straight. Head and mouth small; eyes bulbous. Continuous fringing dorsal and anal fins on sides of body; tail fin rounded. **HABITAT** Muddy and sandy bottoms to more than 100′ deep. **RANGE** In s N. Eng. mainly in winter; summers in deeper water.

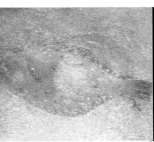

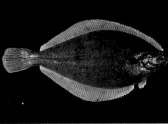

ATLANTIC HALIBUT
Hippoglossus hippoglossus
RIGHTEYE FLOUNDER FAMILY
5′; largest flatfish in N. Eng. Diamond-shaped; tail fairly long, with concave tail fin. Dark chocolate to grayish olive, with irreg. buffy blotches. Lateral line has distinct arch in front. Continuous fringing dorsal and anal fins on sides of body. Head pointed. Slow-growing; old ones huge. **HABITAT** Sandy and gravelly bottoms 200–3,000′ deep.

YELLOWTAIL FLOUNDER
Pleuronectes ferrugineus
RIGHTEYE FLOUNDER FAMILY
16–18″. Body flat, oval, thin; snout pointed. Olive green with large reddish-brown spots, small black spots; lateral line arched toward front. All fins yellow; continuous fringing dorsal and anal fins on sides of body; long rounded tail fin. Mouth small. **HABITAT** Sandy bottoms 100–300′ deep.

HOGCHOKER
Trinectes maculatus
SOLE FAMILY
5″. Body flat rounded rectangle; head blunt. Gray-brown. Adult has 7–8 thin black bars; scales small, spiny. Eyes small, close together, on right side; mouth small, wavy; few or no teeth. Continuous dorsal and anal fins fringe body edge; tail fin stubby, rounded; lacks pectoral fins. Imm. travels to 150 miles up major rivers to feed; spawns in salt water. **HABITAT** Muddy, silty, and sandy bottoms in shallow coastal bays, estuaries, rivers.

OCEAN SUNFISH
Mola mola
MOLA FAMILY

3–5′. Round, massive, compressed snout short; rear end has rounded flap-like tail fin that looks cut off scaleless. Back gray-blue; sides and belly silvery. Mirror-image single dorsal fin and anal fin huge, shark-like; placed far back on body; no pelvic fins. Eyes large, well back from mouth; mouth and gill openings small. Strong swimmer; lies on side at surface, siphoning in jellyfish, squid, fish larvae. This uncommon giant is not related to freshwater sunfish. **HABITAT** Warm ocean surface waters in late summer, early fall.

 Fishes That Live in Both Fresh and Salt Water

Scores of New England fish species spend occasional to great parts of their lives moving between salt and fresh water. Freshwater fishes such as Brook Trout, Chain Pickerel, and Largemouth Bass may visit brackish estuaries; marine fishes such as Scup and Summer Flounder may regularly move quite far up an estuary; and many other species occasionally cross the boundaries between salt and fresh waters.

Two categories of fishes notable for their mass journeys between marine and freshwater environments are the anadromous and catadromous species. An anadromous fish lives the greater part of its life in salt water but spawns in fresh water. Catadromous fishes reverse this process, spawning in salt water and living the greater part of their lives in fresh water. New England anadromous species include the Alewife, American Shad, Rainbow Smelt, Blueback Herring, and Atlantic Salmon. The American Eel is the sole catadromous fish in New England.

River pollution and especially river damming and overfishing have drastically reduced New England anadromous and catadromous species from the population levels of colonial days. However, there remain some excellent "herring runs"—shallows where great schools of migrating anadromous fishes may be seen in the spring. Fish-watchers gather at Cape Cod's Bourndale and Stony Brook runs in April and May to watch the "river herrings": large shoals of Alewives followed by smaller numbers of Blueback Herrings. Maine's Damariscotta River has a fine Alewife run, and the fish lift at Holyoke, Massachusetts, on the Connecticut River assists American Shad and occasionally Atlantic Sturgeon, Atlantic Salmon, and other species. The catadromous American Eels are more difficult to observe as they usually migrate at night.

AMERICAN EEL
Anguilla rostrata
FRESHWATER EEL FAMILY

24–42″. Long, snake-like; in cross section, round in front, flattened to rear; scales tiny, deeply embedded in skin. Gray-brown or yellowish brown above and on sides; paler below. Dorsal fin begins before anal fin; both low, continuous with tail fin; pectoral fins small. Mouth large; lower jaw protrudes slightly. Male prefers brackish waters; female swims far up rivers for 8–20 years before trip back to spawn and die. **HABITAT** Rivers, estuaries. Spawns in open ocean waters north of West Indies; larvae spend 1–3 years at sea becoming young eels (elvers), then enter rivers.

GOLDFISH
Carassius auratus
CARP AND MINNOW FAMILY

4½–8½″. Fairly deep, robust. Color varies: olive, gold, orange, or white. Single dorsal fin and anal fin each have heavy forward spine that tapers to rear; tail fin forked. Mouth small; no barbels on lower jaw. Native to China; common in home aquariums; often released. **HABITAT** Heavily vegetated artificial pools and natural ponds. **RANGE** s N. Eng.

COMMON CARP
Cyprinus carpio
CARP AND MINNOW FAMILY

24–30″. Oval; high rounded back. Dark olive above, shading to yellowish gray below. Dorsal fin long, begins at back's high point, has thick forward spine; tail fin forked, lobes round. 2 pairs of barbels on upper lip. Male thrashes about in surface waters in spawning frenzy. Native to Eurasia; destroys bottom plants needed by native fish as cover for eggs, young. **HABITAT** Clear or turbid rivers, lakes, reservoirs; sometimes brackish waters. **RANGE** s N. Eng., w VT.

FATHEAD MINNOW
Pimephales promelas
CARP AND MINNOW FAMILY

2¼". Stout, elongated; head blunt, rounded. Body tan or olive; head slaty. Single dorsal fin, anal fin, and paired pelvic fins rounded; tail fin forked, lobes rounded. Breeding male blackish, with swollen areas on top of head and back before dorsal fin. Introduced from Midwest. **HABITAT** Shallow ponds.

BLACKNOSE DACE
Rhinichthys atratulus
CARP AND MINNOW FAMILY

2". Elongated; snout long. Yellowish olive above with heavy black spots; sides brownish. Lateral line thick, black, extends from nose to tail. Single dorsal fin triangular; tail fin forked, lobes rounded. **HABITAT** Springs; cool, fast streams.

WHITE SUCKER
Catostomus commersoni
SUCKER FAMILY

18". Cylindrical. Back olive; sides silvery yellow; spawning male darker brown, with red fins. Single dorsal fin triangular; tail fin forked; ventral fins often yellow. Mouth protruding, toothless; adapted for sucking worms and insect larvae off bottom; no barbels. **HABITAT** Cool streams, lakes; sometimes brackish waters.

BROWN BULLHEAD
Ameiurus nebulosus
BULLHEAD CATFISH FAMILY

9″. Elongated, robust. Back and sides brown, heavily mottled, with darker brown blotches; belly whitish. Fins dusky; 1st dorsal fin narrow, high, rounded; adipose fin; anal fin long, low; tail fin square. 4 pairs of barbels flank mouth. Locally called Horned Pout, Catfish. **HABITAT** Ponds; vegetated pools in rivers and streams (common); brackish waters (rare).

RAINBOW SMELT
Osmerus mordax
SMELT FAMILY

4–8″. Elongated, slender, compressed. Back purple; sides violet; belly silvery. Single central dorsal fin large, triangular; adipose fin smaller, rounded; tail fin forked. Jaws and roof of mouth have canine teeth. **HABITAT** Inshore ocean waters, estuaries. Spring: spawns in gravelly streams. Some landlocked in lakes.

NORTHERN PIKE
Esox lucius
PIKE FAMILY

24″. Long, cylindrical; head large; snout long, wide, rounded. Olive green, camouflaged with numerous large yellow spots; whitish below. Single, rounded dorsal fin and anal fin set far back on body; tail fin forked; all fins pale, with dark mottling. Lower jaw protrudes; teeth fine. **HABITAT** Cold lakes, slow rivers with heavy vegetation. **RANGE** Mainly VT and NH.

CHAIN PICKEREL
Esox niger
PIKE FAMILY

15–18″. Elongated, moderately compressed; snout long, concave above. Olive to yellowish brown; sides covered with darker brown markings resembling interlocking chains. Single dorsal fin and anal fin both placed far back; tail fin deeply forked; all fins plain dusky. Mouth wide; dark vertical bar under yellow eye. **HABITAT** Lakes, swamps, vegetated stream pools, brackish waters (rare).

RAINBOW TROUT
Oncorhynchus mykiss
TROUT FAMILY

20″. Elongated; metallic blue or green above, silvery white below, with small black dots on body and tail fin. Freshwater fish have larger spots; long, rosy-red stripe on sides. Dorsal fin triangular; adipose fin small; tail fin slightly forked. Mouth white. Introduced from Pacific slope of N. Amer. **HABITAT** Inshore ocean waters, rivers; some landlocked in lakes. Some populations (steelheads) live in fresh water first 2–4 years, then migrate to ocean; adults return to fresh water each winter to spawn.

BROOK TROUT
Salvelinus fontinalis
TROUT FAMILY

8–16″. Elongated. Olive green above, with dark wavy lines; sides olive, with many large yellowish spots and few small red spots with blue halos; belly white (reddish in adult male). Dorsal fin spotted, triangular; tail fin squared off or slightly forked; ventral fins reddish, with white and black leading edges. Large jaws open well behind eye. Saltwater populations (from MA north) largest, body blue above, shading to silvery below; spots reddish. **HABITAT** Cold clear streams, cold lakes, tidal streams. Winter: some enter ocean to feed.

LAKE TROUT
Salvelinus namaycush
TROUT FAMILY

15–20″. Elongated, slightly compressed; head and mouth large. Dark green above, paler green on sides; heavily spotted with yellow. Triangular dorsal fin and deeply forked tail fin both spotted with yellow; ventral fins olive or reddish with white leading edge. Largest native North American trout. **HABITAT** Deep cold lakes. **RANGE** w and n N. Eng.

BROWN TROUT
Salmo trutta
TROUT FAMILY

18″. Elongated; head large. Brown above; sides olive with many or few dark brown and red spots haloed by white; belly silvery; head spotted. Dorsal fin rounded; tail fin squarish. Saltwater populations larger; silvery, with smaller spots. Tolerates higher water temperatures than other trout. Native to Eurasia; replaces Brook Trout in some areas. **HABITAT** Lakes, fast-flowing streams, estuaries, inshore salt water. Fall: sea-run populations enter rivers to spawn.

ATLANTIC SALMON
Salmo salar
TROUT FAMILY

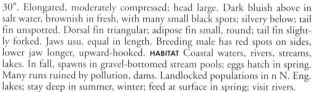

30″. Elongated, moderately compressed; head large. Dark bluish above in salt water, brownish in fresh, with many small black spots; silvery below; tail fin unspotted. Dorsal fin triangular; adipose fin small, round; tail fin slightly forked. Jaws usu. equal in length. Breeding male has red spots on sides, lower jaw longer, upward-hooked. **HABITAT** Coastal waters, rivers, streams, lakes. In fall, spawns in gravel-bottomed stream pools; eggs hatch in spring. Many runs ruined by pollution, dams. Landlocked populations in n N. Eng. lakes; stay deep in summer, winter; feed at surface in spring; visit rivers.

BURBOT
Lota lota
COD FAMILY

21″. Elongated, eel-like; in cross section, circular in front, compressed toward rear; head flattened. Dark brown, with mosaic of pale brown wavy lines and spots. 1st dorsal fin short; 2nd dorsal fin and anal fin long-based; tail fin rounded. Nostrils tubular; mouth wide; barbel on chin. **HABITAT** Deep cold lakes and rivers. Winter: spawns under ice. **RANGE** w and n N. Eng.

SLIMY SCULPIN
Cottus cognatus
SCULPIN FAMILY

2″. Elongated; cylindrical in cross section; head flattened. Dark brown, heavily mottled with black; yellowish below. 2 narrowly separated dorsal fins along most of back; fan-shaped tail fin yellowish, with black bands on rays. Mouth wide; 3 spines before bulging eyes. **HABITAT** Cold streams, springs, rocky areas and depths of lakes.

BANDED SUNFISH
Enneacanthus obesus
SUNFISH FAMILY

2¼". Sunfish are oval, vertically compressed; iridescent; large pointed flap covers gills. Male clears space on bottom for eggs, protects them until hatching. This species: olive-gray, with 6–8 wide, blackish, vertical bands, flanked by purplish or gold spots. Dorsal fin larger to rear; tail lobes rounded. Gill cover has black spot, size of eye. "Tear drop" below eye. **HABITAT** Lowland streams; swamps; lakes. **RANGE** se NH and south.

BLACK CRAPPIE
Pomoxis nigromaculatus
SUNFISH FAMILY

12–14". Oval, extremely compressed; forehead concave; lower jaw protrudes. Pale brown or sooty green, heavily mottled with dark brown spots. Single dorsal fin and anal fin large, rounded, begin with 6–8 spines; tail fin forked; most fins distinctly spotted. Native of VT, introduced to rest of N. Eng. **HABITAT** Ponds, warm streams, some in brackish waters.

BLUEGILL
Lepomis macrochirus
SUNFISH FAMILY

6–8". Oval, extremely compressed. Olive above, with 5–9 vertical dusky green bands; male orange below, with blue gills; female whitish below. Dark spot on rear of single dorsal fin; tail fin slightly forked. Gill cover deep blue, black-edged. Introduced from Midwest. **HABITAT** Shallow vegetated lakeshores, stream pools, some in brackish waters.

PUMPKINSEED
Lepomis gibbosus
SUNFISH FAMILY

6–8". Oval, compressed. Golden green above, shading to orangy yellow below, usu. speckled with darker pigment. Single dorsal fin (rounded at rear), notched tail fin, and anal fin all spotted; pectoral fins long, pointed, unspotted. Cheeks striped reddish and blue. Gill cover black and red, outlined in white. **HABITAT** Ponds, streams, marshes, some in brackish waters.

SMALLMOUTH BASS
Micropterus dolomieu
SUNFISH FAMILY

8–15". Elongated. Dark brown above; sides greenish yellow with diffuse vertical brownish bands; belly whitish. Lacks lateral band. 1st dorsal fin spiny; 2nd dorsal fin rounded; tail fin notched, lobes rounded. Mouth extends to point below front of eye. Introduced from Midwest. **HABITAT** Deep lakes; cool, clear streams over rocks.

LARGEMOUTH BASS
Micropterus salmoides
SUNFISH FAMILY

15–18″. Elongated; head large. Dark green above; sides olive green with brownish mottling; belly whitish. Dark mid-lateral band disappears with age. 1st dorsal fin spiny; 2nd dorsal fin rounded; tail fin slightly forked. Mouth extends to point below rear of eye. Introduced from South. **HABITAT** Warm shallow waters with vegetation, some in brackish waters.

YELLOW PERCH
Perca flavescens
PERCH FAMILY

10–12″. Oblong, moderately compressed; head small, pointed. Olive green or brownish, with 5–8 blackish vertical bars on back and sides. 2 separated dorsal fins dusky. 1st dorsal fin and first 2 rays of anal fin have sharp spines. **HABITAT** Clear streams, lakes with vegetation, some in brackish waters.

TESSELLATED DARTER
Etheostoma olmstedi
PERCH FAMILY

2¼″. Cylindrical; head small; eyes bulge on top of head. Olive-brown, with 6 dark saddles; sides have X and W markings. 2 dorsal fins large, rounded; tail fin fan-shaped; all fins strongly banded. **HABITAT** Stream pools, lakeshores. **RANGE** All N. Eng., ex. ME.

WALLEYE
Stizostedion vitreum
PERCH FAMILY

20″. Elongated. Head long; mouth large; teeth strong. Olive-brown to brassy greenish yellow; sides speckled with black dots. 2 separate dorsal fins; 1st dorsal fin spiny, with last 3 membranes black; tail fin forked, tip of lower lobe white. Native to n VT; introduced in reservoirs elsewhere. **HABITAT** Lakes, deep rivers.

Amphibians

The ancestors of today's amphibians began evolving from fish about 300 million years ago. Members of the class Amphibia typically start life in fresh water and later live on land. Most undergo metamorphosis (a series of developmental stages) from aquatic, water-breathing larvae to terrestrial or partly terrestrial, air-breathing adults. The most primitive of terrestrial vertebrates, amphibians lack claws and external ear openings. They have thin, moist, scaleless skin and are cold-blooded; their body temperature varies with that of their surroundings. In winter, they burrow deep into leaf litter, soft soils, and the mud of ponds, and maintain an inactive state. Unlike reptiles, amphibians can become dehydrated in dry environments and must live near water at least part of the year and for breeding. Their eggs lack shells, and most are laid in water.

Salamanders

Salamanders, members of the order Caudata, have blunt rounded heads, long slender bodies, short legs, and long tails. Most lay eggs in fresh water that hatch into four-legged larvae with tufted external gills; after several months or years, the larvae typically lose their gills and go ashore. Exceptions include the Mudpuppy *(Necturus maculosus),* introduced to some New England lakes, which retains its gills and is aquatic its entire life, and the Eastern Red-backed Salamander, which lays eggs on land and skips the gilled larval stage. Members of the newt family (Salamandridae) start out as aquatic larvae; most then transform into terrestrial subadults (the "eft" stage) and in one to three years change again into an aquatic life form. Adult lungless salamanders (Plethodontidae) lack lungs and breathe through their thin moist skin; mostly terrestrial, they live under bark, wood, or stones, sometimes near streams. Mole salamanders (Ambystomatidae), which breathe through lungs, burrow into soft soil. During all life stages, salamanders eat small animal life. They are generally voiceless and hard to see, as they feed under wet leaves and logs; they are easiest to see at night in early spring, when they congregate to mate and lay eggs at temporary pools of fresh water created by the spring thaw and rains. In winter, they become inactive, residing in decaying logs, between roots of trees, and in soil. Salamanders differ from lizards (reptiles not found in New England) in having thin moist skin (lizards have scales) and 4 toes on the front feet (lizards have 5), and in their lack of claws and external ear openings. There are several dozen salamander species in eastern North America, more than anywhere else in the world. However, like frogs, salamanders are fast declining in number worldwide, due to habitat destruction and perhaps acid rain, pesticides, and increasing ultraviolet light.

The size given for salamanders is the typical length from the tip of the nose to the end of the tail.

larval aquatic form

red eft

EASTERN NEWT
"Red-spotted Newt"
Notophthalmus viridescens
NEWT FAMILY

Eft 2½"; newt 3½". Newts have 3 forms: a larval aquatic form, followed by an immature land form called an "eft," and finally an aquatic adult form. This species: bodies of all forms have 10–12 red spots ringed in black, many small black dots. Land form, called "red eft," smaller, orange. In 1–3 years, becomes larger, aquatic newt: olive above, yellow below; paddle-shaped tail has high keel. **HABITAT** Woods (eft); ponds, streams (newt). **ACTIVITY** By day, Mar.–Oct.

DUSKY SALAMANDER
Desmognathus fuscus
LUNGLESS SALAMANDER FAMILY

3½". Body slender; head rounded. Distinct buffy "tear" line runs from below eye to base of mouth; back dark brown (finely black-spotted in imm.), bordered by slaty blotches; sides gray or buff; tail triangular in cross section. **HABITAT** Borders of rocky creeks, springs. **ACTIVITY** Day and night, Apr.–Oct.

EASTERN RED-BACKED SALAMANDER
Plethodon cinereus
LUNGLESS SALAMANDER FAMILY

3". Body slender; head rounded. Wide orange-red to brick red stripe on back, bordered by black; sides gray, with white flecks. Lead-backed form lacks orange back stripe. Local "red" form is reddish orange all over. Forages in leaf litter. **HABITAT** Under logs, rocks in mixed woods. **ACTIVITY** Nocturnal; may be active during winter thaws.

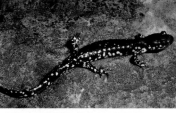

SPOTTED SALAMANDER
Ambystoma maculatum
MOLE SALAMANDER FAMILY

7″. Body stocky; snout broad. Body black or dark gray; 2 head-to-tail rows of large yellow (rarely orange) spots. Usu. in burrows or under logs, rocks. **HABITAT** Broadleaf woods. **ACTIVITY** Day and night, Mar.–Oct.

BLUE-SPOTTED SALAMANDER
Ambystoma laterale
MOLE SALAMANDER FAMILY

4½″. Body long, slender; head rounded; eyes bulbous. Glossy black, with hundreds of tiny, pale blue dots on body, tail, legs; pale gray below. Rarely seen; lives under logs and in burrows. **HABITAT** Broadleaf woods. **ACTIVITY** Day and night, Mar.–Oct. **RANGE** n and c N. Eng.

Frogs

Adult frogs and toads (order Anura) have large heads and eyes, and wide, usually toothless mouths; they appear neckless, and most lack tails. Many can rapidly extend a long tongue for capturing insects. They have two long muscular hindlegs and two smaller front legs. All must keep their skin moist and avoid drying out in the sun. All New England frogs pass the winter in a state of torpor, burying themselves in mud at the edge of a pond or crawling between the bark and trunk of a large tree. In the spring, the male vocalizes to attract the larger female, and clings to her while fertilizing eggs as she lays them, usually in water. The eggs hatch into round-bodied, long-tailed aquatic larvae called tadpoles or pollywogs, which begin life with external gills that are soon covered with skin. The tadpole later transforms into a tail-less ground, tree, or marsh dweller with air-breathing lungs. Toads are a family (Bufonidae) of frogs that have shorter legs for hopping and warty skin, which secretes poisons that cause irritations. In the treefrog family (Hylidae), tadpoles live in water and adults live in trees; treefrogs have disks on their toes for clinging. The true frogs (Ranidae) are large, with slim waists, long legs, pointed toes, and webs on their hindfeet; most live in or near water and are good jumpers. Like salamanders, frogs are declining in number worldwide, partly because of environmental pollutants.

Frogs and toads have excellent hearing and vocal capabilities. Their well-developed ears feature a conspicuous external eardrum, a round disk located behind the eye. In spring or summer, most male frogs and toads announce their presence with loud vocalizations that vary from species to species. When calling, the animals rapidly inflate and deflate balloon-like vocal sacs on the center or sides of the throat that amplify the sound. Calls are primarily used during the breeding season to attract mates; some species, like the Green Frog, give calls to defend feeding territories long after breeding.

With the first late-winter thaw, Wood Frogs and Spring Peepers open the breeding season by gathering in large, noisy groups that vocalize at dusk near water. Throughout the New England spring and summer, mainly at night, one can often hear a chorus of fascinating sounds made by several species of frogs. Bullfrogs, American Toads, and others also call in the daytime.

The size given for frogs is the typical length from the tip of the nose to the end of the body.

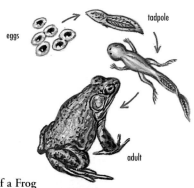

Life Cycle of a Frog

AMERICAN TOAD
Bufo americanus
TOAD FAMILY

2¾". Gray-brown; medium-size dark brown spots on back each have 1 or 2 rusty warts. **CAUTION** Contact may cause irritation to skin of humans and pets; esp. avoid eye and mouth contact. **VOICE** Long musical trill. **HABITAT** Yards, fields, woods. **ACTIVITY** Day and night, Apr.–Oct.

WOODHOUSE'S TOAD
Bufo woodhousii
TOAD FAMILY

2½". Fowler's Toad race gray-brown; large dark brown spots on back have 3 or more rusty warts each. Similar to American Toad: distinguished by voice, range, habitat. **CAUTION** Contact may irritate skin; avoid eye and mouth contact. **VOICE** Plaintive, descending *wraah,* like sheep bleat. **HABITAT** Sandy areas near water. **ACTIVITY** Mainly nocturnal, May–Oct. **RANGE** s N. Eng., esp. Cape Cod.

SPRING PEEPER
Hyla (Pseudacris) crucifer
TREEFROG FAMILY

1". Pale brown or rusty; darker X on back and bar between eyes. Very hard to see. Din of hundreds calling, usu. in evening, is one of earliest signs of spring; some males also call on warm autumn days. **VOICE** High, upwardly slurred *preep.* **HABITAT** Swamps, marshes. **ACTIVITY** Rarely seen by day; feeds at dusk and at night, Mar.–Nov.

GRAY TREEFROG
Hyla versicolor
TREEFROG FAMILY

1¾". Skin rough; to match surroundings, quickly changes color from green to brown to gray; dark-edged, whitish "teardrop" below eye. Nose broad; eyes protruding. Suction pads on toes. **VOICE** Fluttery, musical trill. **HABITAT** Lowland trees near water. **ACTIVITY** Rarely seen by day; feeds at night, May–Oct. **RANGE** c and s N. Eng.

BULLFROG
Rana catesbeiana
TRUE FROG FAMILY

4¾". Ridge from eye to large eardrum, but not along sides of back; midback bulge. Yellowish green above, with dark mottling; pale yellow below. Head large, rounded. Legs long, dark-banded; feet mainly webbed. Female lays up to 20,000 eggs; tadpoles develop into adults in 1–3 years. Largest frog in N. Eng. **VOICE** Deep, resonant *jug-o-rum,* day or night. **HABITAT** Marshes, ponds, slow rivers. **ACTIVITY** Day and night, feeds mainly at night, May–Oct. **RANGE** All N. Eng., ex. n ME.

GREEN FROG
Rana clamitans
TRUE FROG FAMILY

3″. Green above, with few dark spots on lower back and sides; blackish raised ridges on sides of back to mid back bulge; legs brown with blackish bands. Male has yellow throat and swollen thumbs. Mouth somewhat pointed. Not wary; if cornered, inflates itself and stands tall; gives high-pitched *eek* before leaping into water. **VOICE** Usu. 1 note, like plucked banjo string. **HABITAT** Swamps, brooks, pond shallows. **ACTIVITY** Day and night, Apr.–Oct.

PICKEREL FROG
Rana palustris
TRUE FROG FAMILY

2½″. Pale buffy brown; large, rectangular, dark brown spots on back and legs; sides and belly yellow; whitish on upper lip; nose pointed. **VOICE** Low steady "snore." **HABITAT** Vegetated streams, swamps. **ACTIVITY** Day and night, Apr.–Oct. **Northern Leopard Frog** *(R. pipiens)* green or brown with fewer, rounder spots; yellow ridges on sides of head.

WOOD FROG
Rana sylvatica
TRUE FROG FAMILY

2¼″. Unspotted dull brown; conspicuous blackish-brown mask from eye past eardrum; whitish on upper lip; nose somewhat pointed. Legs banded. Joins salamanders in breeding at fish-free vernal pools on early spring nights. **VOICE** Short raspy *quack.* **HABITAT** Moist woods. **ACTIVITY** Mainly by day, Mar.–Oct.

Reptiles

Members of the class Reptilia are cold-blooded, like amphibians. Their body temperature varies with that of their surroundings; reptilian activities come to a halt in cold weather, when they hibernate alone or in communal dens. Of the four orders of living reptiles, New England has two: turtles and scaled reptiles; the latter order includes both snakes and lizards (only a few stray lizards have been recorded in our region). The reptilian body is low-slung and has a long tail and, except for the snakes, four short legs. Unlike the thin-skinned amphibians, reptiles are covered with protective scales (some are modified into plates in turtles) that waterproof their bodies and help keep them from becoming dehydrated. They breathe via lungs. All breed on land and mate by internal fertilization. Their eggs have brittle or leathery shells; some give birth to live young.

Turtles

Members of the order Testudines, turtles are the oldest living group of reptiles, dating back to the time of the earliest dinosaurs. The upper part of their characteristic bony shell is the carapace, the lower part the plastron; both parts are covered with hard plates called scutes. Some species have ridges, called keels, on the carapace and tail. The exposed skin of turtles is scaly and dry. Most can withdraw the head and legs inside the shell for protection. Aquatic species have flipper-like legs. Turtles are the only toothless reptiles, but their horny beaks have sharp biting edges. Most spend hours basking in the sun. From October or November to March or April, turtles in New England hibernate. All turtles lay eggs; most dig a hollow, lay the eggs, cover them up, and leave them alone. When the eggs hatch, the young claw their way to the surface and fend for themselves. Lengths given are for the carapace of a typical adult.

Parts of a Turtle

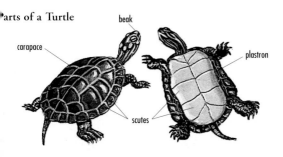

PAINTED TURTLE
Chrysemys picta
POND AND BOX TURTLE FAMILY

4¼". Carapace oval, fairly flat, smooth, keel-less; has 3 rows of smooth olive-brown to black scutes with pale yellow edges; fringing scutes at edge of carapace have fine red lines. Plastron yellow. Head, neck, and legs lined with yellow and red. Common. **HABITAT** Ponds, swamps, rivers. **ACTIVITY** Conspicuous; often basks in groups. **RANGE** All N. Eng., ex. mtns.

SPOTTED TURTLE
Clemmys guttata
POND AND BOX TURTLE FAMILY

4". Carapace oval, smooth-edged, somewhat flattened; black, smooth, keel-less; sparsely peppered with yellow dots: young has 1 dot per scute, adult several. Plastron yellow, with black center and border. Head, neck, limbs have yellow or orange spots. Uncommon. **HABITAT** Marshy meadows, moist woods. **ACTIVITY** Basks in spring. **RANGE** s ME and south.

COMMON BOX TURTLE
Terrapene carolina
POND AND BOX TURTLE FAMILY

5¼". Carapace oval, high-domed. Eastern race: dark brown, with intricate, variable, orange or yellow patterning. Plastron often yellowish; transverse hinge allows turtle to completely hide inside shell. Mainly terrestrial; will soak in mud or very shallow water. Scarce due to pet trade, automobiles. **HABITAT** Woods, meadows. **ACTIVITY** Does not bask. **RANGE** From s tip of ME south to w MA.

COMMON MUSK TURTLE
"Stinkpot"
Sternothaerus odoratus
MUSK AND MUD TURTLE FAMILY

4". Carapace highly domed, brown, with large scutes. Plastron small, buffy. Head large, pointed, black, with yellow stripes. Tail short, fat. Secretes foul fluid from musk glands under carapace. **HABITAT** Fresh waters with muddy bottoms. **ACTIVITY** Mainly by day; basks on logs and low trees. **RANGE** c and s N. Eng.

SNAPPING TURTLE
Chelydra serpentina
SNAPPING TURTLE FAMILY

15". Carapace oval, somewhat domed; smooth or with 3 rows of keels, with central keel heavier; trailing edge jagged; black or dark brown. Plastron cross-shaped, yellowish. Head massive, neck long. Tail as long as carapace, with saw-toothed keels. Female, mainly in June, searches riversides and open areas far from water for egg-laying site. Otherwise aquatic; fine swimmer. N. Eng.'s largest freshwater turtle. **CAUTION** Powerful jaws can give a serious bite. **HABITAT** Fresh waters with mucky bottoms. **ACTIVITY** Day and night.

Snakes

Snakes (suborder Serpentes of the scaled reptile order, Squamata) have elongated scaly bodies without limbs, eyelids, or external ear openings. They grow throughout their lives, shedding their skin, sometimes in one piece, from snout to tail several times each year. The discarded skins can sometimes be found. Snakes are carnivorous, and they swallow their prey whole. The flicking, forked tongue serves as an organ of smell, collecting information on potential prey and dangers. New England's snakes mate in the fall, before their winter hibernation, which usually begins in November and ends in April. Most species lay eggs in June that hatch in September; a few give birth to live young in September.

There are relatively few snakes in New England; the garter and water snakes of the colubrid snake family are the most familiar. The colubrids represent more than three quarters of the world's snake species. None of the colubrids in our range are harmful to people. They are generally active on hot days and warm nights, and are expert at avoiding humans.

New England snakes are nonpoisonous except for two localized species, the Copperhead and the Timber Rattlesnake (see their species accounts and the box on snakebite, below). They are members of the pit viper family, whose members are generally nocturnal and bear live young.

In the accounts that follow, the size given is the length of a typical adult.

RACER
Coluber constrictor
COLUBRID SNAKE FAMILY

4′. Medium girth; scales smooth. Northern Black Racer race almost all black, but chin and throat white. Alert, active; holds head high while moving forward. Climbs trees. Feeds on small rodents, frogs, snakes, birds; enters birdhouses. Bites prey and holds on; does not constrict. **CAUTION** Not poisonous, but aggressive—will bite if cornered. **HABITAT** Fields, open woods. **RANGE** c and s N. Eng.

MILK SNAKE
Lampropeltis triangulum
COLUBRID SNAKE FAMILY

30″. Medium girth. Ground color pale gray to yellowish; reddish-brown patches outlined in black along entire body, larger on back. Head equal to or slightly smaller than body, with Y- or V-shaped patch on nape. Scales smooth. Constricts rodents and other snakes. Similar, poisonous Copperhead has unmarked head and nape. **HABITAT** Barns, woods, fields. **RANGE** From s ME south.

BROWN SNAKE
"DeKay's Snake"
Storeria dekayi
COLUBRID SNAKE FAMILY
11". Medium girth. Dull brown, with pale gray dorsal stripe flanked by 2 rows of dark brown spots. Black cap on head, with black downward stripe behind eye. Belly pale brown or yellowish. Scales keeled. Secretive; common in rubble of vacant lots. Bears live young. **HABITAT** Woods, fresh and salt marshes, towns. **RANGE** c and s N. Eng.

SMOOTH GREEN SNAKE
Opheodrys vernalis
COLUBRID SNAKE FAMILY
17". Very slender; delicate. Bright grass-green; tail long, tapering; belly white with yellowish tinge. Scales smooth. Capable climber; move through tall grass and shrubs with ease, devouring insects and spiders. Few seen due to superb camouflage. **HABITAT** Meadows, woodland edges.

RING-NECKED SNAKE
Diadophis punctatus
COLUBRID SNAKE FAMILY
12½". Very slender. Slaty or blue-gray above; bright yellow-orange below; head black; collar golden-orange; smooth-scaled. Secretive; hides under rocks, logs, and stone walls. Rarely bites when handled but may void its cloaca. Constricts itself around prey (salamanders, frogs, earthworms). **HABITAT** Rocky woods with fallen trunks.

NORTHERN WATER SNAKE
Nerodia sipedon
COLUBRID SNAKE FAMILY
33". Robust. Gray-brown or yellow-brown; reddish-brown, black-edged bands are wider on back, narrower on sides. Head broad. Scales ridged. Older ones all dark brown or black. Adept swimmer; basks on shores and overhanging limbs. **CAUTION** Nonpoisonous, but bites when handled. **HABITAT** Ponds, rivers, swamps, salt marshes. **RANGE** From Lake Champlain and Bangor, ME, south.

EASTERN RIBBON SNAKE
Thamnophis sauritus
COLUBRID SNAKE FAMILY

22". Slender. Blackish brown, with 3 yellow stripes; scales keeled. Differs from Common Garter Snake in being slimmer, less spotted, and having dark stripe along margins of belly scales. Found in or near water, where it swims on surface; flees rapidly through shoreline grasses. Bears live young. **HABITAT** Swamps, freshwater marshes, shores. **RANGE** c and s N. Eng.

COMMON GARTER SNAKE
Thamnophis sirtalis
COLUBRID SNAKE FAMILY

22". Slender. Variable in color and pattern. Narrow yellowish stripe along entire mid-back; rest of back solid blackish or pale brown (some gray), with 2 rows of blackish spots; sides and belly pale buffy or gray. Molts several times a year. Bears live young. Hibernates in groups. N. Eng.'s most common snake. **HABITAT** Fields, scrub, gardens.

Poisonous Snakes and Snakebite

New England has two poisonous snake species—the Copperhead and the Timber Rattlesnake (see page 274)—both found in only a few specific areas; neither lives on Cape Cod and its offshore islands or in Maine. As snake populations have been decimated by automobiles, hunters, and loss of habitat, most people who hike frequently in New England's woods will never see a poisonous snake. Yet on very warm April days a local herpetologist could find dozens at favorite denning sites on southern and southwestern slopes of rocky hills in Massachusetts and Connecticut. Both New England species have retractable fangs that can deliver blood-destroying venom, but both will flee from footsteps. If you encounter one of these species, freeze to let it withdraw, then step away. For any poisonous snakebite the best course of action is to get to medical care as soon as possible, with the dead snake or positive identification of the species, so the proper antivenin can be administered. Meanwhile, the victim should avoid moving, as movement helps the venom spread through the system, and keep the injured body part motionless just below heart level. The victim should be kept warm, calm, and at rest while on the way to medical care. If you are alone and on foot, start walking slowly toward help, exerting the injured area as little as possible. If you run or if the bite has delivered a large amount of venom, you may collapse, but a snakebite seldom results in death.

TIMBER RATTLESNAKE
Crotalus horridus
PIT VIPER FAMILY

3′9″. Body thick. Head thick, triangular. Tail has silvery rattle. Dark phase has black head, dark gray body, black blotches edged in white, black tail. Pale phase yellowish brown, with dark brown blotches, black tail. **CAUTION** Poisonous; coils before striking. Retreat from rattled warning. **HABITAT** Wooded hills with rocky outcrops. **RANGE** From s NH and Lake Champlain south, and east to Blue Hills of e MA (very local).

COPPERHEAD
Agkistrodon contortrix
PIT VIPER FAMILY

30″. Body fairly thick; scales weakly keeled. Northern Copperhead race dull orange, with rich, brown, hourglass-shaped bands that are wide on sides, narrow on back. Head large, triangular, coppery red. Usu. lethargic; eats passing rodents. Hibernates in dens with rattlers, other snakes. **CAUTION** Poisonous—can strike vigorously. **HABITAT** Wooded hills with rocky outcrops. **RANGE** Blue Hills of e MA, sw MA, w CT (local).

Birds

Members of the class Aves, birds are the only animals that have feathers, and most are capable of flight. Like their reptile ancestors, they lay eggs; like mammals, they are warm-blooded. They generally have excellent sight and hearing, but few have a good sense of smell. The bird skeleton is adapted for flight: The bones are lightweight, with a sponge-like interior. The forelimbs have become wings, with strong pectoral muscles attached to a keeled breastbone, and the hindlimbs are modified for running, grasping, or perching. Wing shapes vary among types of birds, ranging, for example, from the long, broad wings of the soaring raptors to the narrow, fast-moving wings of hummingbirds.

While all Blue Jays look the same regardless of their gender or the time of year, this is not the case for most birds. Plumages may vary from immature to adult, from male to female, and from breeding to nonbreeding seasons (summer and winter, respectively). (If both sexes have a summer plumage distinct from nonbreeding plumage, we note this as "summer adult." If only the male has such a summer plumage, we note "summer male.") In some species, groups living in different geographic areas (subspecies, or races) have slightly or distinctly different plumages. Some birds within a given species have different colorations (called morphs or phases) that have nothing to do with where they live. Some birds have ornamental plumes, often developed in the breeding season. This guide describes the plumages most often seen in New England. The photograph shows the male or the adult (if adults look alike) unless otherwise noted.

Flight allows birds to migrate great distances, though some are resident year-round in one region. Many birds who spend the winter in warmer, southern climes migrate north to breed, taking advantage of the abundant animal life in summertime New England. Other birds breed to the north, in Canada, and pass through New England only in migration. Cold and snow rarely kill birds directly but may reduce the amounts of food (insects, animals, berries) they can obtain to maintain their ideal body temperature. Most of our breeding species winter in the southern United States or the tropics of Latin America. Most individuals return to the same breeding and wintering grounds throughout their lives.

Northbound migration occurs from March to early June, southbound from July to November. Migrants often wait until the wind is at their backs before beginning the journey. In spring, warm southwesterly winds help bring migrants back from southern regions to New England. In autumn, winds from the north aid southbound migrants on their journey south. A strong cold front with northwesterly winds at times floods our coastal points and islands with migrants returning to the nearest point of land after being blown out to sea, often in great numbers. For more about bird migration, see the essay on bird-watching on page 278.

In bird species that do not nest in colonies, a male who is ready to breed stakes out and defends a nesting territory from other males. The female chooses a male in part on the quality and size of his

territory, the presence of a secure nest site, and the quality of hi
plumage and song. The avian life cycle typically starts with th
female laying one or more eggs in a nest, which, depending o
the species, may be a scrape in the sand, a cup of rootlets and fibers
a woven basket, a stick platform, or another type of structure. Afte
an incubation period of roughly two to four weeks, the young ar
hatched and fed by their parents for a period varying from a fev
days (shorebirds) to a few weeks (most species) to many month
(raptors). Smaller birds tend to breed the year following their birth
while many larger birds remain immature for several years before
breeding. During the breeding season, many male birds exhibi
more colorful and elaborate plumages and courtship displays and

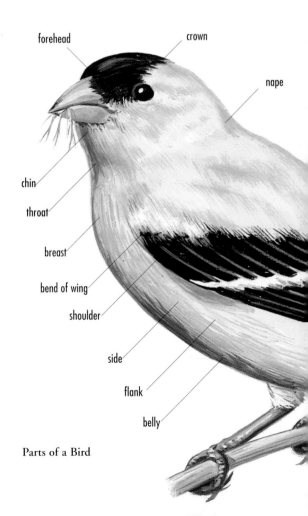

Parts of a Bird

rituals in order to attract a mate. Most species mate in solitary pairs, the males competing for breeding territories; other species nest colonially. In this section of the guide, assume a bird is a solitary nester unless the description notes that it nests in colonies. Space limitations prevent us from giving descriptions of nests.

Birds use their voices in many ways. In many species, contact and alarm call notes are given year-round by both sexes. The more musical songs, usually given only in spring and summer by the male, attract mates and define territory. Once the young are born, many birds stop singing; the New England woods are strangely silent in August as compared to June.

This section's descriptions give the length of the adult bird from the tip of the beak to the end of the tail. For some large species, both length (L) and wingspan (WS) are given.

For suggestions on attracting birds to your yard, see page 324. In this section, the icon 🕱 denotes species that will come into a yard to a feeder. The icon 🏠 indicates species that might use a nestbox in a yard.

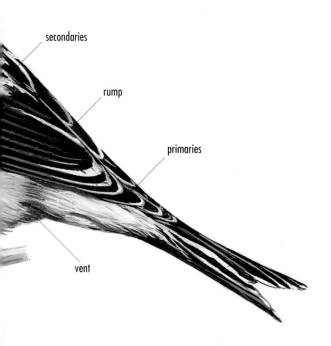

Bird-watching

Bird-watching, or birding, as it is often termed, can be a casual activity, develop into a hobby, or become a passion. It's possible to see 200 to 300 species a year in New England.

In breeding season, many birds tend to live in only one habitat and are active at certain times of day. Freshwater marsh birds (rails, bitterns, marsh songbirds) are most often calling and active at dawn and dusk. Until mid-morning on hot days, songbirds search woodlands, fields, and thickets for food; from mid-morning to late afternoon, they tend to be quiet, and forage again late in the day. Birds that live near beaches, lakes, and other aquatic habitats (herons, cormorants, ducks, sandpipers) may be active all day. Make an after-dark visit to a forest or swamp to find owls, which may respond to taped or imitated calls, and can be viewed with spotlights.

The greatest variety of birds can be seen during the migration seasons. In early spring (March–April), larger birds such as hawks and waterfowl return to New England, while many wintering birds move northward. Most songbirds migrate north to the region during the latter half of April and the month of May; males arrive a week or so before females in order to stake out territories. When the land bird migration tapers off in late May, sandpipers and plovers are still flying through. While larger birds migrate by day, most species, especially smaller, insect-eating ones, fly at night, resting and feeding during the day, tending to gather in quiet places where food is easy to find. In a light woodland along a stream, where there are newly opened leaves and plenty of small insects, it is possible to see a dozen or more species of warblers in a single spring morning. Migrating songbirds also concentrate in isolated groves of trees along the coast and in city parks.

Fall migration is under way by July, when the first southbound sandpipers and plovers reappear; adults in these groups migrate a week to a month before their offspring. From August into October, most of the songbirds pass through; if winds are strong from the northwest, large numbers will be blown toward the coast and islands. The migration of ducks, geese, and raptors starts in September and continues well into November.

For the serious birder, at least one good field guide is essential; many excellent ones are available, including the *National Audubon Society Field Guide to North American Birds (Eastern Region).* Binoculars (7-, 8-, 9-, or 10-power) are a must; a close-focusing pair is especially helpful. A 15-, 20-, or 30-power telescope with a wide field of view, mounted on a sturdy, collapsible tripod, is invaluable for viewing waterfowl, shorebirds, and raptors.

While many species are rather tame, others are shy or secretive. Learn to move slowly and quietly, and avoid wearing brightly colored or patterned clothing and making loud noises. Please respect local laws, do not unduly frighten birds, and take great care not to disrupt nesting or resting birds.

COMMON LOON
Gavia immer
LOON FAMILY

32″. Body stout, duck-like. Summer: back black, with large white spots; head, neck, and bill black; white bands on neck; eyes red. Winter: slaty above, white below; bill slaty. Bill heavy, pointed. In flight, legs extend beyond tail. **VOICE** Quavering laughter, yodeling; heard mainly on summer nights.

winter (top), summer (bottom)

HABITAT Summer and migration: lakes. Winter: coastal bays, ocean. **RANGE** Apr.–Oct.: VT, NH, ME. Sept.–Apr.: entire coast.

HORNED GREBE
Podiceps auritus
GREBE FAMILY

14″. Body duck-like. Winter: back and hindneck slaty; crown black; throat and foreneck white. Neck thin; bill slender; eyes red. Rarely seen flying; migrates at night. **VOICE** Silent in N. Eng. **HABITAT** Coastal waters, estuaries. **RANGE** Oct.–Apr.: entire coast.

PIED-BILLED GREBE
Podilymbus podiceps
GREBE FAMILY

13″. Body duck-like. Bill short, conical. Summer: body brown; chin black; black ring on silver bill. Winter: body brown; chin white; bill yellow or gray, lacks ring. Dives frequently for small fish. **VOICE** Series of 8 *cow* notes. **HABITAT** Summer: marshes with open water. Migration and winter: ponds, rivers. **RANGE** Apr.–Oct.: all N. Eng. (rare). Oct.–Apr.: s N. Eng. (uncommon).

GREATER SHEARWATER
Puffinus gravis
SHEARWATER FAMILY

19". Gull-like. Dark brown above; cap and tail black; throat, underparts, underwing, and rump white; bill narrow, hooked, black. Flies near surface with fast flaps and long glides on very stiff wings. **VOICE** Usu. silent in N. Eng. **HABITAT** Open sea; rarely seen from shore. **RANGE** June–Oct.: off RI to ME.

SOOTY SHEARWATER
Puffinus griseus
SHEARWATER FAMILY

17". Gull-like. Entirely sooty brown above and below; contrasting silvery-white underwing linings; bill narrow, black. Flies near surface, on very stiff wings, with fast flaps, long glides. **VOICE** Usu. silent in N. Eng. **HABITAT** Open sea; rarely seen from shore. **RANGE** May–Oct.: off RI to ME.

WILSON'S STORM-PETREL
Oceanites oceanicus
STORM-PETREL FAMILY

7". Swallow-like. Black, with white rump. Bill short, black. Long legs extend beyond tail in flight. Patters and hops over surface on fluttering wings. **VOICE** Silent in N. Eng. **HABITAT** Open sea. **RANGE** May–Sept.: off RI to ME.

NORTHERN GANNET
Morus bassanus
BOOBY AND GANNET FAMILY

3'2". Gull-like. Adult mostly white; primaries pointed, black; yellow wash on head. Bill silver, pointed; neck longish; tail wedge-shaped. 1st year bird brown, belly white. Makes spectacular feeding dives from on high; in migration, flies in lines low to water. **VOICE** Quiet at sea. **HABITAT** Open sea; migrates close to Cape Cod beaches. **RANGE** Apr.–May, Sept.–Nov.: off RI to ME.

immature (left), adult (right)

DOUBLE-CRESTED CORMORANT
Phalacrocorax auritus
CORMORANT FAMILY

33". Black with greenish cast; breeding crest (2 small tufts) hard to see. Bill narrow, hooked; orange skin on throat. Imm. brownish, whitish from throat to breast. Swims with bill angled upward; flocks often fly in V; spreads wings to dry while resting. Nests in colonies. Common summer cormorant in N. Eng. **VOICE** Usu. silent; croaks at nest. **HABITAT** Coasts; some on inland waters. **RANGE** Apr.–Nov.: entire coast, spreading to inland lakes.

GREAT CORMORANT
Phalacrocorax carbo
CORMORANT FAMILY

3'1". Winter adult glossy black; white patch at base of bill. Summer adult has white flank patch. Neck and tail long; bill narrow, hooked, silvery. Imm. blackish brown above; belly white. **VOICE** Grunts at nest. **HABITAT** Rocky coasts, nearby seas. **RANGE** May–Aug.: ME. Sept.–Apr.: all coasts.

GLOSSY IBIS
Plegadis falcinellus
IBIS FAMILY

23". Adult body rusty bronze; wings glossy green; appears black in poor light. Neck and legs long; bill extremely long and downcurved. Imm. dull brown. Nests in colonies, with herons. **VOICE** Guttural *ka-onk*. **HABITAT** Marshes. **RANGE** Apr.–Aug.: coast from s ME south.

Herons

Members of the heron family (Ardeidae)—herons, egrets, and bit terns—are large, long-legged, long-necked birds up to 4′ long. The wade in shallows and marshes, where they use their longish, dagger like bills to seize slippery fish and aquatic frogs, snakes, and inver tebrates. While storks, ibises, spoonbills, and cranes fly with out stretched necks, herons normally fold theirs in an S shape when air borne. During courtship (two to four weeks a year), adults of many of these species have ornamental plumes and bright facial colors Their nests are usually large platforms of sticks, often in large colonies that may include several species of herons and other large waders. Predominantly white heron species are called egrets Bitterns are shy denizens of marshes with distinct voices.

BLACK-CROWNED NIGHT-HERON
Nycticorax nycticorax
HERON FAMILY

adult (left), immature (right)

26″. Adult crown and back black; wings gray; lores (area btwn. eye and bill and underparts white; eyes red. Thick-necked; legs shortish, yellow. Imm brown, with heavy white streaks and spots. Nests in colonies, esp. on off shore islands. **VOICE** Low *kwock*. **HABITAT** Ponds, riversides, marshes. **RANG** Apr.–Oct.: entire coast; inland (local).

GREAT EGRET
Ardea alba
HERON FAMILY

L 3′3″; WS 4′3″. All white. Neck long, thin. Bill long, yellow; feet and long legs black. During courtship long, lacy, white plumes on back facial skin green. Nests in colonies with other species. **VOICE** Deep croak. **HABITAT** Marshes. **RANG** Apr.–Oct.: breeds along coast from ME south; disperses inland in c and s N. Eng.

GREAT BLUE HERON
Ardea herodias
HERON FAMILY

L 4′; WS 6′. Back and wings blue-gray; shoulder black; crown black with white center; short black plumes from back of head; face white; most of neck buffy gray; foreneck striped black and white. Belly blackish. Legs long, dark; bill yellow. Nests in colonies. **VOICE** Deep squawk. **HABITAT** Marshes, watersides. **RANGE** Apr.–Oct.: mainly inland south to MA; nests early, disperses widely by July. Oct.–Apr.: coast of s N. Eng.

SNOWY EGRET
Egretta thula
HERON FAMILY

24″. All white. Neck long. Bill slender, black; lores yellow. Legs long, black; feet yellow. During courtship, long, lacy, white plumes on back, chest, and crown. Imm. legs dark green. Nests in colonies. **VOICE** Harsh *aah*. **HABITAT** Marshes and ponds. **RANGE** Apr.–Oct.: coast from c ME south; disperses inland in late summer.

GREEN HERON
Butorides virescens
HERON FAMILY

19″. Adult back and wings slaty green; cap black; neck chestnut; legs orange. Legs shortish; bill dark. Imm. brownish; neck pale with heavy dark brown streaks; legs yellow-green. Often feeds by leaning over water from logs, rocks; also wades. **VOICE** Harsh *keyow*. **HABITAT** Ponds, streams, marshes. **RANGE** May–Sept.: all N. Eng.

AMERICAN BITTERN
Botaurus lentiginosus
HERON FAMILY

28″. Adult light brown, with thin white eyebrow and dark streaks on neck; black stripe partway down neck. Neck thick; legs greenish. Imm. lacks black neck stripe. Shy; points bill skyward if disturbed. **VOICE** Loud pumping *uunk-KA-lunk*. **HABITAT** Marshes. **RANGE** Apr.–Nov.: all N. Eng.

Waterfowl

The waterfowl family (Anatidae) contains the huge white swans, the medium-size geese, and a wide variety of smaller ducks. All have webbed feet, and thick bills designed for filtering small organisms in the water or for grasping underwater vegetation and invertebrates, often mollusks. Most waterfowl undergo lengthy migrations between northern or inland breeding areas and southern and/or coastal wintering waters. Ducks may be split into two main groups. Dabbling ducks upend on the surface of fresh and brackish waters, and can jump up and take flight straight out of the water. Diving ducks dive well under the surface of fresh and salt waters; in taking flight, they run and flap horizontally over the water's surface before gaining altitude. Swans and geese upend like dabbling ducks, rather than dive for food; most patter across the water to get airborne. Waterfowl males are in breeding plumage all winter and spring, and in late summer develop a drab nonbreeding plumage similar to that of females.

Mallard dabbling

Mallard taking off, straight up, from surface of water

Canada Goose taking off by running across water

MUTE SWAN
Cygnus olor
WATERFOWL FAMILY

L 5'; WS 8'. Adult all white; bill orange with black base; black knob over bill; black lores. Legs short, black. Neck held in S curve at rest. Wing feathers often fluffed up and arched over back while swimming. Imm. pale grayish brown; bill silvery. Flies with strong, steady, whistling wingbeats, neck outstretched. Introduced from Europe. Very aggressive toward humans and dogs near nest and young. **VOICE** Rarely heard hiss. **HABITAT** Coastal lagoons and coastal plain ponds. **RANGE** Resident in CT, RI, se MA.

CANADA GOOSE
Branta canadensis
WATERFOWL FAMILY

L 3'4"; WS 6'. Adult back and wings dark brown; head and long neck black; large white chinstrap; breast pale brown; vent and rump white; tail short, black. Imm. pale gray. Often flies in V. **VOICE** Honking *car-uunk.* **HABITAT** Marshes, ponds, fields, lawns with short grass. **RANGE** Once mainly migrant, with few wintering on Cape Cod; now common resident in s N. Eng. Some migrants Mar.–Apr., Oct.–Nov.

BRANT
Branta bernicla
WATERFOWL FAMILY

26". Head, neck, and chest black; patch of white lines on upper neck (absent in imm.); back and wings dark brown; belly pale brown; vent and large rump patch white. **VOICE** Throaty *cur-onk.* **HABITAT** Shallow saltwater bays, estuaries. **RANGE** Nov.–May: entire coast.

SNOW GOOSE
Chen caerulescens
WATERFOWL FAMILY

28". Adult all white, with black primaries; bill pink, with black "lips"; face often stained rusty; legs pink. Imm. pale brown above, white below; bill, legs, and primaries black. Flight reveals black wingtips; flies in V high overhead. Dark morph ("Blue Goose") has dark body, white head (rare). **VOICE** High nasal honks. **HABITAT** Marshes, fields. **RANGE** Mar.–Apr., Oct.–Nov.: all N. Eng.

AMERICAN BLACK DUCK
Anas rubripes
WATERFOWL FAMILY

23″. Dabbler. Male body and wings dark brown; head and upper neck distinctly paler brown; bill yellow. Female has dark saddle on bill. Legs red-orange. Flight reveals white underwing coverts, dark flight feathers, purple wing patch. **VOICE** Female: quack. **HABITAT** Ponds, rivers, marshes. **RANGE** Apr.–Nov.: all N. Eng. Oct.–Apr.: mainly coastal salt marshes.

GREEN-WINGED TEAL
Anas crecca
WATERFOWL FAMILY

14″. Dabbler. Male body gray, with vertical white stripe behind chest; head chestnut; bill small, black; green eye patch extends to fluffy nape; vent patch yellow. Female brown. Flight reveals green wing patch. N. Eng.'s smallest duck. **VOICE** Male: whistled *cricket*. **HABITAT** Marshes, ponds. **RANGE** Mar.–Apr., Sept.–Dec.: all N. Eng. A few breed in n N. Eng.; some winter along s N. Eng. coast.

NORTHERN PINTAIL
Anas acuta
WATERFOWL FAMILY

26″. Dabbler. Male back, wings, and sides gray; head and hindneck chestnut; foreneck and belly white; tail very long, black. Female smaller, pale brown. Neck thin; tail sharp, pointed. **VOICE** Male: wheezy *prip prip*. Female: quack. **HABITAT** Marshes, ponds. **RANGE** Mar.–Apr., Sept.–Nov.: all N. Eng. (local).

WOOD DUCK
Aix sponsa
WATERFOWL FAMILY

9″. Dabbler. Male iridescent; back dark purple; belly white; chest purple with white spots; sides buffy; head green with laid-back crest; throat and 2-pronged chinstrap white; eye ring and base of bill red. Female brown; long white eye ring. N. Eng.'s most colorful inland duck. **VOICE** Male gives high whistle when courting. Female: *oo-eek*. **HABITAT** Swamps, marshes. **RANGE** Apr.–Nov.: all N. Eng.

male

female

MALLARD
Anas platyrhynchos
WATERFOWL FAMILY

24″. Dabbler. Male body and wings gray; head and neck green; white ring above purplish chest; rump black; tail white; bill yellow. Female buffy brown; bill pale orange with dark saddle. Legs orange. Flight reveals purple wing patch, bordered with white. N. Eng.'s most widespread inland duck. **VOICE** Male: quiet; gives *reeb* call when fighting. Female: quack. **HABITAT** Ponds, rivers, marshes. **RANGE** Resident in N. Eng.

BLUE-WINGED TEAL
Anas discors
WATERFOWL FAMILY

15″. Dabbler. Male body brown, with black dots; head dull blue-gray; white crescent before eye; crown black. Female mottled brown. Flight reveals pale cerulean blue shoulders. Bill heavier, longer than Green-winged Teal's. **VOICE** Male: peep-like notes. Female: high quack. **HABITAT** Marshes, weedy ponds. **RANGE** Apr.–May, Aug.–Sept. (most common in Sept.): all N. Eng. Summer: rare breeder in n N. Eng.

AMERICAN WIGEON
Anas americana
WATERFOWL FAMILY

21″. Dabbler. Both sexes brownish; sides dull rusty orange; head speckled. Male forehead white; green patch behind eye; vent black and white. Flight reveals white shoulder patch. **VOICE** Male: whistled *whee whee whew.* Female: quack. **HABITAT** Shallow lakes, esp. near coast. **RANGE** Oct.–Mar.: coastal s N. Eng. Mar.–Apr., Sept.–Oct.: all N. Eng. (local).

GREATER SCAUP
Aythya marila
WATERFOWL FAMILY

18″. Diver. Male back gray; sides white; chest and tail area black; head dark green. Female dark brown with distinct white face. Bill plain gray; eyes yellow. Flight reveals long white stripe on trailing edge of wing. Often together in large rafts (flocks). **VOICE** Usu. silent. **HABITAT** Saltwater bays, estuaries; in migration, lakes. **RANGE** Oct.–Apr.: mainly along coast from CT to ME.

CANVASBACK
Aythya valisineria
WATERFOWL FAMILY

21″. Diver. Male back, wings, sides white; chest black; head reddish brown; eyes red; tail black. Female back, wings, sides gray; chest dark brown; head brown, with white eye ring; eyes dark; tail blackish. Sloping forehead forms straight line with sloping black bill. Flight reveals plain gray wings. **VOICE** Silent in N. Eng. **HABITAT** Lakes, estuaries. **RANGE** Nov.–Apr.: coastal s N. Eng. (local). Oct.–Nov., Mar.–Apr.: all N. Eng. (local).

COMMON GOLDENEYE
Bucephala clangula
WATERFOWL FAMILY

18″. Diver. Male striped black and white above; white below; head dark green, fluffed out at rear; large white spot near bill. Female head all dark brown, with white neck ring; body paler brown. Eyes golden. **VOICE** Quiet; wings whistle in flight. **HABITAT** Summer: lakes. Migration and winter: rivers, coastal bays. **RANGE** May–Oct.: far n N. Eng. Nov.–Apr.: c and s N. Eng.; entire coast, larger ice-free rivers.

WHITE-WINGED SCOTER
Melanitta fusca
WATERFOWL FAMILY

22″. Diver. Male black; white crescent around eye; bill orange with black knob. Female dark brown. White patch on secondaries. **VOICE** Usu. silent. **HABITAT** Ocean. **RANGE** Oct.–Apr.: off entire coast. **Surf Scoter** *(M. perspicillata)* male has white forehead and nape patch; no white on wings. **Black Scoter** *(M. nigra)* male lacks white; has orange knob on bill. All migrate in long low lines over water.

RING-NECKED DUCK
Aythya collaris
WATERFOWL FAMILY

17″. Diver. Male chest, back, and tail black; sides gray; shoulder stripe white; head dark purple; crown peaked. Female brown; pale buffy wash on face; pale eye ring. Flight reveals black shoulder, gray wing stripe. Bill patterned. **VOICE** Usu. silent. **HABITAT** Freshwater lakes, rivers, coastal bays. **RANGE** Mar.–Apr., Oct.–Nov.: all N. Eng. May–Sept.: some in n N. Eng. Dec.–Feb.: some in s N. Eng.

COMMON EIDER
Somateria mollissima
WATERFOWL FAMILY

25″. Diver. Adult male neck, back, shoulders white; flight feathers, belly, tail black; head white with black crown; hindcheeks and nape green; breast tinged pinkish. Female brown, barred. Forehead and long sloping bill merge. N. Amer.'s largest duck. **VOICE** Slurred and grating notes. **HABITAT** Ocean and bays; breeds on rocky islands. **RANGE** May–Sept.: ME coast. Oct.–Apr.: entire coast.

OLDSQUAW
Clangula hyemalis
WATERFOWL FAMILY

Male 22″; female 17″. Diver. Winter male mainly white; chest, wings, and long tail black; bill pink and black. Winter female chest and upperparts brown; head and sides buffy white. Usu. in rafts (flocks) of its own species. **VOICE** Male yodels. **HABITAT** River mouths, coastal waters. **RANGE** Oct.–May: entire coast.

BUFFLEHEAD
Bucephala albeola
WATERFOWL FAMILY

14″. Diver. Male back black; chest and underparts white; white wedge on rear half of head, which has greenish-purple gloss. Female brown, with large white spot behind eye. Bill short. Flight reveals extensive white secondaries. **VOICE** Usu. silent. **HABITAT** Coastal bays, estuaries; in migration, lakes. **RANGE** Oct.–Apr.: mainly along coast.

COMMON MERGANSER
Mergus merganser
WATERFOWL FAMILY

25″. Diver. Male back black; chest and underparts white; head green, with rounded nape. Female body gray; head and neck rusty; chin distinctly white. Bill red, slender but with thick base. **VOICE** Usu. silent. **HABITAT** Lakes, rivers; returns from coast to inland rivers with first thaw. **RANGE** May–Oct.: n N. Eng. Nov.–Apr.: s N. Eng.

RED-BREASTED MERGANSER
female (left), male (right)

Mergus serrator
WATERFOWL FAMILY

23″. Diver. Male back black; chest buffy; sides gray; neck and belly white; head dark green. Female gray; head rusty; throat and foreneck white. Bill long, slender, red; nape crest shaggy. **VOICE** Usu. silent. **HABITAT** Coastal waters. **RANGE** Oct.–Apr.: entire coast.

HOODED MERGANSER
Lophodytes (Mergus) cucullatus
WATERFOWL FAMILY

18". Diver. Adult male back, head, and neck black; sides rufous; head patch and chest white; eyes yellow. Female gray-brown, with fluffy brown nape. Crest expandable, fan-like; bill black. **VOICE** Low grunts, usu. silent. **HABITAT** Tree-fringed ponds, rivers. **RANGE** Mainly migrant (Mar.–Apr., Sept.–Nov.): all N. Eng. May–Aug.: all N. Eng. (local). Jan.–Feb.: a few in s N. Eng.

Raptors

The word "raptor" is usually used for birds of prey that are active in the daytime (some experts also use the term for the nocturnal owls, described starting on page 313). Families found in New England include the American vultures (Carthartidae), the hawks and eagles (Accipitridae), and the falcons (Falconidae). The bills of raptors are strong and sharp for tearing flesh, while the feet (usually yellow) are generally powerful (except in vultures), with curved talons for grasping prey. Many raptors migrate to warmer climes in winter.

The carrion-feeding vultures are black, with broad wings and bare heads. Members of the hawk and eagle family are the very large eagles, with feathered legs; the Osprey, an eagle-sized "fish hawk"; harriers, which fly low over open areas and use their superb hearing as an aid in hunting; and the hawks. There are two types of hawks: the accipiters, whose shorter wings allow them to achieve rapid twisting flight, and the broad-winged, soaring buteos. The pointed-winged falcons are fast fliers. Immature raptors, often striped below, take a year or more to reach adulthood. Females are 10 to 20 percent larger than males in most species. Raptors migrate during the day (unlike most songbirds). The broad-winged buteos and eagles ride rising thermals of air on sunny days. Acute vision allows them to spot unsuspecting prey from great heights. In the fall, impressive southbound hawk migrations can be viewed from many hilltops, such as Mount Tom and Wachusett Mountain in Massachusetts (buteos), and at such coastal sites as Monhegan Island, Maine; outer Cape Cod and its islands, in Massachusetts; Block Island, Rhode Island; and Lighthouse Point, at New Haven, Connecticut (falcons and accipiters).

Flight silhouettes of raptors *(illustrations not to relative scale)*

Turkey Vulture

Osprey

Bald Eagle

Northern Harrier

Sharp-shinned Hawk (Accipi

Red-tailed Hawk (Buteo)

American Kestrel (Falcon)

TURKEY VULTURE
Cathartes aura
AMERICAN VULTURE FAMILY

L 28"; WS 6'. Adult all black, brown-tinged above; head small, naked, red; bill yellow. Soars with wings held at 20 degrees above horizontal; seldom flaps wings. Long rounded tail and pale silver flight feathers can be seen from below. Finds carcasses by sight and smell. Gathers at nightly communal roosts in tall trees or towers. Has expanded rapidly from South into c N. Eng. in recent decades. **VOICE** Grunts and hisses, but usu. silent. **HABITAT** Woods, fields. **RANGE** Mar.–Nov.: north to White Mtns. Dec.–Feb.: s N. Eng. (local)

immatures adult

OSPREY
Pandion haliaetus
HAWK AND EAGLE FAMILY

L 23″; WS 5′6″. Adult brown above with white crown and dark line through eye; white below. Imm. has buffy crown, pale feather edges on wings and back. Feet gray; eyes yellow. Flies with wings bent at "wrist" like flattened M; flight feathers, tail finely banded. Hovers; often flies grasping fish in talons. Nest is mass of sticks topping dead tree or platform on Osprey pole. Devastated by DDT, it has rebounded since the pesticide was banned. **VOICE** Emphatic *kee-uk* and *cheep*. **HABITAT** Coastal estuaries, rivers, lakes. **RANGE** Apr.–Nov.: all coastal N. Eng. and n lakes.

adult immature

BALD EAGLE
Haliaeetus leucocephalus
HAWK AND EAGLE FAMILY

L 32″; WS 7′. Adult body, wings, and thighs dark chocolate brown (appears black); massive head white; bill yellow, strongly hooked; eyes, feet, massive legs yellow; tail white, somewhat rounded. Imm. all dark brown when perched; flight reveals diffuse whitish wing linings and base of tail. Flies with slow deliberate wingbeats, wings held flat, straight out, primaries spread. Perches on tall trees. Numbers increasing, with DDT ban and protection. **VOICE** Piercing scream. Call: Loud cackle. **HABITAT** Coastal bays, estuaries, rivers, lakes. **RANGE** Resident in N. Eng. (uncommon). Some migrants (esp. Sept.) and wintering birds (from Canada) in s N. Eng.

NORTHERN HARRIER
Circus cyaneus
HAWK AND EAGLE FAMILY

adult male (left), immature (right)

L 22″; WS 4′. Wings and tail long, narrow; rump white; head and bill small; owl-like facial disks. Adult male pearly gray; whiter below. Adult female brown above; dirty white with brown stripes below. Imm. brown above; solid rusty orange below. Flies low over open areas, wings raised at an angle, listening and watching for rodents, frogs, and baby birds; often hovers and drops. Generally perches near ground, not in trees. **VOICE** Weak *pee.* **HABITAT** Marshes, fields. **RANGE** May–Aug.: local, incl. se MA, c ME. Dec.–Feb.: s coastal N. Eng. (uncommon). Mar.–Apr., Sept.–Nov.: all N. Eng.

SHARP-SHINNED HAWK
Accipiter striatus
HAWK AND EAGLE FAMILY

adult (left), immature (right)

L 12″; WS 21″. Accipiters have slender bodies; short rounded wings; long narrow tails. This species: adult upperparts slate gray; underparts rusty barred; crown gray. Feet small, yellow. Imm. brown above, striped below. Flies with fast wingbeats followed by glides; tail square with notch in middle. Expert at capturing small birds. Soars during migration. **VOICE** High *kek* notes. **HABITAT** Woods. **RANGE** May–Aug.: all N. Eng. (local). Dec.–Mar.: near birdfeeders in c and s N. Eng. Apr., Sept.–Nov.: over ridges, along coast.

COOPER'S HAWK
Accipiter cooperii
HAWK AND EAGLE FAMILY

L 17"; WS 28". Plumages nearly identical to smaller Sharp-shinned Hawk's, but head larger and tail longer, distinctly rounded; adult has black cap. Imm. belly whiter, with fewer streaks than Sharp-shin. VOICE High *kek* notes. HABITAT Woods. RANGE Resident in N. Eng.; also spring and fall migrant.

NORTHERN GOSHAWK
Accipiter gentilis
HAWK AND EAGLE FAMILY

L 23"; WS 3'7". Adult dark gray above; fine gray barring below; black crown and stripe behind eye; wide white eyebrow. Imm. has heavy stripes below; wide white eyebrow. Flight reveals long rounded tail; fluffy white undertail feathers in adult. VOICE Harsh *kek* notes. HABITAT Mixed woods. RANGE Apr.–Nov.: n and c N. Eng. Oct.–Apr.: all N. Eng.

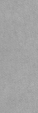

RED-SHOULDERED HAWK
Buteo lineatus
HAWK AND EAGLE FAMILY

L 20"; WS 3'4". Adult head and back brown; underparts barred orange on buff; wings barred black and white above; shoulder rufous; tail black, with 5 thin white bands. Imm. streaked below, like most buteos. Seen from below, white crescent at base of primaries. VOICE Screaming *kee yarr.* HABITAT Woods, swamps. RANGE In N. Eng. mainly Mar.–Nov. A few in s N. Eng. Nov.–Mar.

BROAD-WINGED HAWK
Buteo platypterus
HAWK AND EAGLE FAMILY

L 15"; WS 34". Adult head, back, and wings plain brown; underparts barred reddish brown on white. Imm. streaked. Flight reveals very white underwing, with narrow black borders; adult tail black with 2–3 wide white bands. Thousands pass hawk-watching sites on mountain ridges in Apr., Sept. VOICE High whistled *pee-teee.* HABITAT Broadleaf and mixed woods. RANGE Apr.–Sept.: all N. Eng.

immature (left), adult (right top and bottom)

RED-TAILED HAWK
Buteo jamaicensis
HAWK AND EAGLE FAMILY

L 22"; WS 4'2". Head, back, and wings dark brown; upper chest white; lower chest has band of heavy brown streaks contrasting with white thighs; tail pale orange below, dark rufous above. Imm. similar, but tail pale brown with many indistinct bands. Seen from below, underwings mainly white, with dark leading edge at shoulder and black crescent beyond wrist. Most frequently seen large hawk in N. Eng. year-round. Perches conspicuously in trees along highways. Often mobbed by crows, redwings, grackles, kingbirds. **VOICE** Down-slurred squeal: *keee-rrr.* **HABITAT** Woodland edges, isolated trees in fields. **RANGE** Resident in N. Eng., but leaves far northern areas in winter.

ROUGH-LEGGED HAWK
Buteo lagopus
HAWK AND EAGLE FAMILY

L 22"; WS 4'8". Adult head and upper chest striped black and white; back and wings dark brown; black patch across lower belly; tail white, with broad black terminal band. Adult dark morph black, with paler flight feathers. Flight reveals, from above, white patch at base of primaries; from below, black wrist patch at bend of wing. Often hovers. **VOICE** Usu. silent. **HABITAT** Open areas. **RANGE** Nov.–Mar.: all N. Eng. (uncommon).

adult (left), immature (right)

PEREGRINE FALCON
Falco peregrinus
FALCON FAMILY

L 18″; WS 3′4″. Adult upperparts and tail dark slaty gray; underparts and underwing finely gray-barred; head black above, white below. Feet heavy, powerful. 1 thick black sideburn. Imm. brown above, streaked below. Flight reveals pointed wings, broad at base; tail tapers to squared end. Flies low and high, often surveying bird flocks to spot slow-flying, injured individuals. Nests on ledges of cliffs, bridges, or tall buildings. Numbers plummeted with DDT; now in assisted recovery. **VOICE** Harsh *kak kak* at nest. **HABITAT** Coasts, marshes, cities. **RANGE** May–Aug.: a few breed on cliff faces of w and n N. Eng.; introduced pairs breed in cities. Nov.–Mar.: a few winter in cities and s N. Eng. Apr.–May, Sept.–Oct.: all N. Eng., mainly coastal.

MERLIN
Falco columbarius
FALCON FAMILY

L 12″; WS 25″. Adult male blue-gray above; buffy below, with heavy brown streaks; tail banded. Female and imm. dark brown above; heavily striped below; tail finely banded. 1 thin black sideburn. Flies fast and low when chasing small birds. **VOICE** High *ki ki ki ki.* **HABITAT** Coasts: marshes, open areas. **RANGE** Apr.–May, Sept.–Oct.: all N. Eng., mainly coastal.

AMERICAN KESTREL
Falco sparverius
FALCON FAMILY

L 11″; WS 23″. Male back rufous; wings blue-gray; chest pale buffy; tail rufous, with black terminal band. Female rufous above, with fine black bars. 2 thin black sideburns on white face. In flight, pointed wings obvious; often hovers. **VOICE** Shrill *killy killy.* **HABITAT** Fields, towns. **RANGE** Late May–mid-Sept.: all N. Eng. (local). Nov.–Mar.: s N. Eng. (uncommon). Apr.–early May, late Sept.–Oct.: all N. Eng.

RING-NECKED PHEASANT
Phasianus colchicus
PARTRIDGE FAMILY

Male 34″; female 22″. Male head and neck iridescent dark green; white necklace; rest of body rufous and bronze, with 1″ black and white chevrons above; red bare skin around eye. Female and imm. warm buffy, with black spots above. Tail feathers long, pointed. Flies with rapid wingbeats followed by glides.

male (top), female (bottom)

Introduced from Asia as a game bird; not holding its own in the wild. **VOICE** Male: loud *kaw kawk*. **HABITAT** Farms, meadows, large gardens. **RANGE** Resident in c and s N. Eng; coastal ME.

SPRUCE GROUSE
"Fool's Hen"
Dendragapus canadensis
PARTRIDGE FAMILY

16″. Male hindneck, back, wings gray-brown; face, foreneck, chest black; red wattle over eye; white line on sides of neck; tail black, tipped rusty. Female brown, heavily black-barred. Tail fairly short. Often foolishly tame along trails and back roads; does not fear humans. **VOICE** Male hisses. **HABITAT** Spruce woods. **RANGE** Resident in n VT, n NH, n ME, south to Acadia N.P. area.

RUFFED GROUSE
Bonasa umbellus
PARTRIDGE FAMILY

18″. Adult reddish brown or gray, speckled white and black (gray more common in N. Eng.); head small, slightly crested; neck patch and terminal tail band black. Tail longish. Male "drums" on low perch in spring by thumping wings against chest—slowly at first, then faster. **VOICE** Alarm call: *quit quit.* **HABITAT** Broadleaf and mixed woods. **RANGE** Resident in N. Eng., ex. islands.

WILD TURKEY
Meleagris gallopavo
PARTRIDGE FAMILY

Male 4′; female 3′. Male body dark brown; looks iridescent coppery green at close range; flight feathers black, banded white; tail rufous, with black bands; head bare, warty, red and/or blue; black "beard" hangs from chest. Legs red. Female similar, with smaller, duller head. Feeds on ground and visits rural bird feeders; roosts in trees at night. Once abundant, but extirpated as forests were cleared; with return of forests, has been reintroduced successfully. **VOICE** Male: repeated gobble. **HABITAT** Broadleaf woods; farms in winter. **RANGE** Resident in c and s N. Eng.

NORTHERN BOBWHITE
Colinus virginianus
PARTRIDGE FAMILY

10″. Male chest and upperparts rusty; belly speckled black and white; chestnut crown and face patch contrast with white eyebrow and throat. Tail short. Female similar, with buffy eyebrow and throat. Lives in family groups (coveys). **VOICE** Male: whistled *bob white.* **HABITAT** Brushy fields. **RANGE** Resident in s CT, RI, and se MA, incl. islands.

VIRGINIA RAIL
Rallus limicola
RAIL FAMILY

10″. Adult brown above; chest and wings rufous; sides barred black and white; cheeks gray; eyes red; bill long, thin, drooping, red with black tip; legs dull red. Toes long; tail short. Imm. has black chest. Usu. secretive. **VOICE** Repeated *kid ick;* grunting *oink* notes. **HABITAT** Freshwater marshes. **RANGE** Apr.–Oct.: all N. Eng. (local).

SORA
"Sora Crake"
Porzana carolina
RAIL FAMILY

9″. Adult blackish brown above; sides of neck and chest slaty; belly barred blackish; face and foreneck black; legs olive green. Bill short, thick, yellow. Imm. chest brown; throat white. Usu. secretive. **VOICE** Whistled *ker-wee;* descending whinny. **HABITAT** Freshwater marshes; saltwater marshes in migration. **RANGE** May–Oct.: all N. Eng. (local).

COMMON MOORHEN
"Common Gallinule"
Gallinula chloropus
RAIL FAMILY

14″. Summer adult brown-backed underparts, sides, neck dark slaty white stripe along sides and vent head black; frontal shield and bill bright red; bill yellow-tipped; legs red above knee, green below. Feet unwebbed. **VOICE** Variety of clucks, grating notes. **HABITAT** Cattail marshes with shallow open water. **RANGE** May–Oct.: VT, MA, RI, CT (very local).

AMERICAN COOT
Fulica americana
RAIL FAMILY

15″. Adult sooty gray; head and neck black; bill thick, white, black near tip; sides of undertail white. Feet not webbed, but toes lobed. Dives and skitters over surface to become airborne like a diving duck, swims like a duck—but not a duck. Often in rafts (flocks). **VOICE** Grating *kuk* notes. **HABITAT** Marshes, ponds. **RANGE** Mar.–Apr., late Sept.–Dec.: all N. Eng.; most common in fall. Some winter in s N. Eng.

Shorebirds

The term "shorebird" is used for certain members of the order Charadriiformes: plovers, oystercatchers, avocets and stilts, and sandpipers, including godwits, dowitchers, yellowlegs, curlews, and small sandpipers informally known as "peeps." Most shorebirds frequent open muddy, sandy, or rocky shores on the coast and around open inland wetlands. On the coast they tend to roost in moderate to enormous mixed-species flocks at high tide; at low tide they spread out to feed on small invertebrates. Most American shorebirds have a distinct breeding plumage in late spring and early summer.

Most seen in New England travel thousands of miles yearly between their breeding and wintering grounds. In our region shorebirds are most numerous in May and from July through September. In identifying shorebirds, proportion and shape, as well as behavior and voice, are frequently more useful than plumage color.

nonbreeding (left), breeding (right)

BLACK-BELLIED PLOVER
Pluvialis squatarola
PLOVER FAMILY

12″. Breeding: back and wings speckled black and white; crown, hindneck, sides of chest white; face, foreneck, chest black. Nonbreeding: grayish; back speckled; flight reveals black patch at base of underwings. Bill short, straight; eyes large, black; legs black. Usu. in flocks. **VOICE** Whistled *pee-a-wee.* **HABITAT** Beaches, mudflats. **RANGE** May, July–Oct.: common along entire coast; inland (rare).

SEMIPALMATED PLOVER
Charadrius semipalmatus
PLOVER FAMILY

7″. Upperparts dark brown; white below. Breeding: base of bill and legs yellow; black breast band. Nonbreeding and imm.: bill black; breast band brown. Appears neckless; bill short. **VOICE** Whistled *tu-wheet.* **HABITAT** Beaches, mudflats. **RANGE** May, July–Oct.: entire coast; inland (local).

PIPING PLOVER
Charadrius melodus
PLOVER FAMILY

7″. Upperparts very pale gray; white below; legs yellow. Breeding: partial black collar; base of bill yellow. Nonbreeding and imm.: bill black; lacks collar. Appears neck-less; bill short. Threatened species. **VOICE** Whistled *peep-lo.* **HABITAT** Barrier beaches. **RANGE** Apr.–Sept.: entire coast (local).

KILLDEER
Charadrius vociferus
PLOVER FAMILY

10″. Adult brown above; white below; 2 black chest bands; pied face with red eye ring; legs pale yellow, pink, or gray. Flight reveals wing stripe, unique orange rump. Common inland plover in open habitats. Parent feigns broken wing to attract intruders away from nest or chicks. **VOICE** Strident *kill-dee.* **HABITAT** Farms, fields. **RANGE** Mar.–Oct.: all N. Eng.

AMERICAN OYSTERCATCHER
Haematopus palliatus
OYSTERCATCHER FAMILY

19″. Adult back dark brown, with bold white wing stripe; underparts white; head, neck, and tail black; bill stout, long, straight, orange; legs pinkish. Imm. head and bill brown. Flight reveals white wing stripe. **VOICE** Loud *kleep.* **HABITAT** Beaches, mudflats. **RANGE** Apr.–Oct.: CT to Cape Cod, few northward.

GREATER YELLOWLEGS
Tringa melanoleuca
SANDPIPER FAMILY

14″. Breeding: back brown-black with white dots; head, neck, and sides speckled dark brown. Nonbreeding: paler; faint brown dots on chest. Neck long bill 1½ times longer than head, with relatively thick gray base and thin black, slightly upcurved tip. Legs long, bright yellow; rump white. Often nods head. **VOICE** Excited *tew tew tew.* **HABITAT** Marshes, mudflats, flooded fields. **RANGE** Apr.–May, July–Nov.: entire coast; inland (local).

LESSER YELLOWLEGS
Tringa flavipes
SANDPIPER FAMILY

11″. Smaller version of Greater Yellowlegs (see previous species): plumages similar; legs also bright yellow; bill shorter (equal to length of head), straight, all black. **VOICE** 1–2 mellow *tew* notes. **HABITAT** Mudflats; marsh pools. **RANGE** Late Apr.–May, July–Sept.: entire coast; inland (local).

SOLITARY SANDPIPER
Tringa solitaria
SANDPIPER FAMILY

9″. Dark brown, with white belly and eye ring; bill greenish at base, black at tip; legs dark. Flight reveals dark wings; outer tail banded white. **VOICE** Strident *peet weet.* **HABITAT** Wooded ponds, streamsides. **RANGE** May, July–Sept.: inland; rare on coast.

SPOTTED SANDPIPER
Actitis macularia
SANDPIPER FAMILY

8″. Breeding: brown above; large black spots on white underparts. Nonbreeding: unspotted; smudge on sides of chest. Often teeters rump. Flies on stiff bowed wings. **VOICE** *Pee-weet-weet.* **HABITAT** Riversides, ponds. **RANGE** Late Apr.–Oct.: all N. Eng.

WILLET
Catoptrophorus semipalmatus
SANDPIPER FAMILY

15″. Breeding: speckled brownish gray. Nonbreeding: plain gray. Bill thick-based, fairly long, straight; legs blue-gray; tail gray. Flight reveals startling black wings with broad white central stripe. **VOICE** Loud *pill-will-willet.* **HABITAT** Salt marshes, mudflats. **RANGE** May–Aug.: entire coast.

WHIMBREL
Numenius phaeopus
SANDPIPER FAMILY

18″. Adult and imm. neck, chest, and back speckled brown; belly dirty white; head with 4 dark brown stripes through eyes and bordering pale midcrown stripe; legs bluish. Neck thin; bill very long, thin, downcurved. In flight, appears uniformly brown. **VOICE** 5–7 whistled *ti* notes. **HABITAT** Salt marshes, mudflats. **RANGE** May, July–Sept.: entire coast.

RUDDY TURNSTONE
Arenaria interpres
SANDPIPER FAMILY

9". Breeding: back orange and black; head and chest black and white. Nonbreeding: duller; brown chest patch. Bill short, wedge-shaped; legs orange. Harlequin wing pattern. **VOICE** Rattling *tuk-e-tuk.* **HABITAT** Beaches, mudflats. **RANGE** May, July–Oct.: entire coast.

SEMIPALMATED SANDPIPER
Calidris pusilla
SANDPIPER FAMILY

6½". Breeding: spotted dark brown above and on chest; belly white. Nonbreeding: gray-brown above; faint streaking on sides of neck. Bill short, thick, straight, black; legs black. **VOICE** Low *jerk.* **HABITAT** Mudflats, marshes. **RANGE** May, July–Oct.: entire coast; inland (local).

DUNLIN
Calidris alpina
SANDPIPER FAMILY

8". Breeding: reddish brown above; white below, with fine black dots; black midbelly patch. Nonbreeding: gray; belly white. Bill long, drooping. **VOICE** Soft *krrit.* **HABITAT** Mudflats. **RANGE** May, Sept.–Nov.: entire coast.

PURPLE SANDPIPER
Calidris maritima
SANDPIPER FAMILY

9". Nonbreeding: head and chest plain gray; back scaly gray; belly white. Legs and base of slightly curved bill yellow. **VOICE** Low *weet-wit.* **HABITAT** Rocky shores, breakwaters. **RANGE** Nov.–May: entire coast.

SANDERLING
Calidris alba
SANDPIPER FAMILY

8". Breeding: head and upperparts rusty; belly white. Nonbreeding: gray above; white below; bend of wing black. Imm. crown and back heavily black-spotted. Bill short; legs black. Runs ahead of incoming waves. Usu. in parties of 10–20. **VOICE** Sharp *plic.* **HABITAT** Sandy beaches. **RANGE** May, July–Oct.: entire coast; rare in winter.

PECTORAL SANDPIPER
Calidris melanotos
SANDPIPER FAMILY

9". Scaly brown above; foreneck and chest buff, with fine black streaks, sharply demarcated from clear white belly. Bill slightly curved. **VOICE** *Krrip.* **HABITAT** Damp meadows, salt marshes. **RANGE** Migration: mainly southbound (Aug.–Oct.); very rare northbound (Apr.–May).

LEAST SANDPIPER
Calidris minutilla
SANDPIPER FAMILY

6". Breeding: reddish brown above; chest buffy brown, lightly spotted. Nonbreeding: browner than other small sandpipers. Bill short, thin, slightly drooping, black; legs yellow or green. **VOICE** High *kreet.* **HABITAT** Mudflats, marshes. **RANGE** May, July–Oct.: all N. Eng.

WHITE-RUMPED SANDPIPER
Calidris fuscicollis
SANDPIPER FAMILY

7½". Breeding: brown above; sides speckled black. Nonbreeding: gray above; sides speckled gray. Rump white; wings beyond tail at rest. **VOICE** High, thin *jeet.* **HABITAT** Mudflats, marshes. **RANGE** Late May (rare), Aug.-Oct.: entire coast.

HUDSONIAN GODWIT
Limosa haemastica
SANDPIPER FAMILY

16". Breeding: dark brown above; chestnut below, with fine black bars. Nonbreeding: plain gray above; paler below. Neck thin; bill very long, thin, upcurved, orange at base; legs long, dark. Flight reveals black underwing linings; white midwing stripe; white tail, with black terminal band. **VOICE** High *god-wit;* rarely calls. **HABITAT** Coastal mudflats. **RANGE** May, July–Oct.: se Cape Cod, ne MA, s ME.

SHORT-BILLED DOWITCHER
Limnodromus griseus
SANDPIPER FAMILY

12". Breeding: speckled brown above; neck, chest, and sides orange, dotted black; midbelly white. Nonbreeding: gray above, white below. Bill very long, straight. Flight reveals white rump extending up back in wedge. Feeds with rapid rapid, sewing-machine motion. **VOICE** Musical *tu tu tu.* **HABITAT** Mudflats, marshes. **RANGE** May, July–Sept.: entire coast; rare inland.

COMMON SNIPE
Gallinago gallinago
SANDPIPER FAMILY

11″. Adult and imm. dark brown above, with a few white stripes; sides barred; midbelly white; head has 4 bold blackish stripes; tail rusty. Legs short; bill very long, straight. Flies in erratic zigzag. **VOICE** Hoarse *skaip*. **HABITAT** Moist meadows, marshes. **RANGE** May–Aug.: local breeder in Berkshires, VT, NH, ME. Apr., Sept.–Oct.: all N. Eng.

RED KNOT
Calidris canutus
SANDPIPER FAMILY

11″. Breeding: back scaled with black; face and underparts orange. Nonbreeding: uniformly gray. Congregates in large flocks at a few sites. Legs short; bill straight, with thick base. Flight reveals thin white wing stripe, barred rump. **VOICE** Soft *knut*. **HABITAT** Seaside rocks; beaches, mudflats. **RANGE** May, July–Sept.: entire coast (local).

AMERICAN WOODCOCK
"Timberdoodle"
Scolopax minor
SANDPIPER FAMILY

11″. Mostly clear buff; back darker, speckled. Massive head with no apparent neck; crown has 3 rectangular black patches; eyes large; bill very long, straight, brownish yellow. Legs very short. Male noisy in high aerial courtship flights in early spring. **VOICE** Buzzy *peeent;* silent most of year. **HABITAT** Swampy areas in woods, thickets. **RANGE** Mar.–Nov.: all N. Eng. Dec.–Feb.: s N. Eng. (rare).

Gulls and Terns

All members of the gull family (Laridae)—gulls, jaegers, terns, and skimmers—have webbed feet and breed in the open, in colonies, on islands free of predators; their nests are usually mere depressions on the ground. Many people erroneously call gulls "seagulls." However, while gulls are common near the sea, few are found far at sea; in fact, many breed far inland near fresh water. Superb fliers, most gulls have wings with white trailing edges, and fairly long, strong bills that are slightly hooked at the tip. These generalist feeders and scavengers eat living and dead animal life, and many have adapted to feed on human refuse. Gulls go through a confusing array of plumages and molts until they reach adulthood in two years (small species), three years (medium), or four years (large). For many gull species, this guide describes selected life-stage categories, including juvenile (bird's birth summer), first winter, first summer (bird is 1 year old), second winter, summer adult, and winter adult.

Jaegers are quite large, dark brown seabirds that attack other seabirds and steal their fish. The small to medium-size terns, sleek and slender-billed, fly in a buoyant or hovering manner, diving headfirst for small fish; most have black caps (in summer) and elegant, forked tails. Skimmers are large and have extra-long lower bills that they use to skim fish from the water.

juvenile   summer adult

LAUGHING GULL
Larus atricilla
GULL AND TERN FAMILY

17″. Summer adult: back and wings slaty gray; head black; neck, underparts, and tail white; no white on wingtip; eye ring white; bill red. Bill droops downward. Juv.: upperparts and chest band unspotted gray-brown; bill black. Nests in colonies on islands. **VOICE** High *haah* notes. **HABITAT** Beaches, ocean. **RANGE** May–Oct.: coast from CT to c ME; breeds on islets off Cape Cod and ME.

PARASITIC JAEGER
Stercorarius parasiticus
GULL AND TERN FAMILY

L 18″; WS 3′6″. 2 morphs: typical adult dark brown above; white or light dusky sides and belly; yellowish-white collar; thin brown chestband; tail has 2 longer, pointed central tail feathers. Dark adult all brown. Both have whitish patch at base of primaries. Bill hooked at tip. Chases seabirds; forces them to drop food. **VOICE** Silent at sea. **HABITAT** Open ocean; beaches (rare). **RANGE** May, Aug.–Sept.: offshore RI to ME.

BONAPARTE'S GULL
Larus philadelphia
GULL AND TERN FAMILY

13″. Summer adult (migrant): back and wings silvery; neck, underparts, and tail white; head black; white leading edge of wing, black tips on primaries; legs red; bill short, black. Winter adult: head white; black spot behind eye. 1st winter: head white, tail black-tipped. Often hovers. **VOICE** Nasal *cher.* **HABITAT** Estuaries, bays. **RANGE** Dec.–Feb.: coast of s N. Eng. Mar.–May, Aug.–Nov.: entire coast.

RING-BILLED GULL
Larus delawarensis
GULL AND TERN FAMILY

L 19"; WS 4'. Summer adult: head and underparts white; back silvery; wings silvery; wingtips black with white spots; bill yellow with black ring near tip; legs greenish yellow. Winter adult: head flecked brown. 1st winter: back gray; wing coverts speckled brown; tail whitish, with black terminal band; bill pink with

summer adult (top), 1st winter (bottom)

black tip. Juv.: pale brown; speckled; bill black; legs gray. Nests in colonies on freshwater lakes. Population expanding. **VOICE** High-pitched *high-er*. **HABITAT** Estuaries, lakes, towns. **RANGE** May–Aug.: breeds on Lake Champlain, VT; nonbreeders in s N. Eng. Dec.–Feb.: entire coast, urban and suburban s N. Eng. Mar.–Apr., Sept.–Nov.: all N. Eng.

1st winter (left), summer adult (right)

HERRING GULL
Larus argentatus
GULL AND TERN FAMILY

L 25"; WS 4'10". Legs, feet pink in all ages. Summer adult: back and wings silvery; wingtips black with white spots; head and underparts white; bill yellow with red dot; legs pink. Winter adult: head and chest flecked with brown. 1st winter: brown, with speckled back; bill black. 2nd winter: pale brown with brown spots; flight feathers and tail black; bill pink with black tip. N. Eng.'s most common large seaside gull. Eats bivalves, fish, baby tern, garbage; drops clams on rocks or pavement. Nests in colonies on coastal islands. **VOICE** Varied, incl. series of loud *kee-yow* and *gah* notes. **HABITAT** Coasts, ocean, lakes, rivers, towns, dumps. **RANGE** Resident along entire coast, over major inland waters, in cities; inland mainly in winter.

ICELAND GULL
Larus glaucoides
GULL AND TERN FAMILY

25″. Winter adult white, with pale silver mantle; head and chest flecked with brown; wingtips often have a few dark gray spots; bill yellow; legs pink. Arctic version of Herring Gull; no black on wingtips; bill smallish. 1st winter: pale buff or white; bill black. Joins more common gulls. VOICE Quiet in winter. HABITAT Coasts, harbors. RANGE Nov.–Apr.: mainly coastal (uncommon).

GLAUCOUS GULL
Larus hyperboreus
GULL AND TERN FAMILY

28″. Winter adult white, with pale silver mantle; head and chest flecked brown; bill yellow; legs pink. Arctic version of Great Black-backed; no black on wings; bill large. 1st winter: pale buff or white; bill pink with black tip. Joins more common gulls. VOICE Quiet in winter. HABITAT Coasts, harbors. RANGE Dec.–Apr.: mainly coastal (uncommon).

adult (left), 2nd winter (right)

GREAT BLACK-BACKED GULL
Larus marinus
GULL AND TERN FAMILY

L 30″; WS 5′5″. Adult (summer and winter): back and wings black; head and underparts white; bill yellow with red dot. Legs and feet pink; bill heavy. 1st winter: back and wings speckled blackish brown; head white; bill black. 2nd winter: back black; wings dark brown; bill pink with black tip. Feeds on fish, offal; also kills ducks, terns, and other seabirds. Nests in colonies on coastal islands. N. Amer.'s largest gull. VOICE Loud, low, repeated *coo-up*. HABITAT Coastal waters and shores; inland dumps and lakes. RANGE Resident along entire coast, over major inland waters, in cities; inland mainly in winter.

ROSEATE TERN
Sterna dougallii
GULL AND TERN FAMILY

15″. Summer adult: back and wings silvery; cap black; bill slender, black; tail forked, all-white, extends past wingtips at rest. Flight shows primaries white above. Nests in colonies. N. Eng. is main home in U.S. **VOICE** Musical *chee-week;* raspy *kaa-a-aak.* **HABITAT** Coastal islands, beaches. **RANGE** May–Sept.: entire coast (local). Breeds along coastal CT, Cape Cod, and ME; after breeding, disperses along s N. Eng. coast.

ARCTIC TERN
Sterna paradisaea
GULL AND TERN FAMILY

16″. Summer: silver above; light gray below; cap black; bill red. Flight reveals primaries gray above, thin black trailing edge below. Shorter bill and shorter legs than Common Tern. Nests in colonies. Dives at and strikes heads of intruders into nesting colonies. **VOICE** High *keer-keer,* drawn-out *kee-arr.* **HABITAT** Coastal waters, islands. **RANGE** May–Aug.: ME coast, se MA (local).

COMMON TERN
Sterna hirundo
GULL AND TERN FAMILY

15″. Summer adult: back and wings silvery, with blackish primaries; white below; cap and hindneck black; bill reddish orange with black tip; legs short, reddish orange; tail deeply forked, outer streamers dusky. Winter adult: forehead white; nape black; black shoulder bar. Juv. has scaly brown back. Flight shows primaries blackish above, with wide black trailing edge below. Terns dive headfirst for fish; return to nest with fish in bill. Suitable nesting sites squeezed by gull overpopulation. Nests in colonies. N. Eng.'s most widespread tern. **VOICE** Short *kip;* drawn-out *kee-arr.* **HABITAT** Beaches, coastal waters. **RANGE** May–Sept.: entire coast; islands.

LEAST TERN
Sterna antillarum
GULL AND TERN FAMILY

9″. Summer: back and wings silvery; neck and underparts white; crown black, with white forehead; bill yellow with black tip; legs yellow; tail forked. Juv. pale scaly brown above. N. Eng.'s smallest tern. Nests in small colonies; do not disturb at nests (scrapes in sand). **VOICE** Repeated *kip;* harsh *chee-eek.* **HABITAT** Ocean beaches, coastal waters. **RANGE** May–Aug.: CT to c ME.

BLACK TERN
Chlidonias niger
GULL AND TERN FAMILY

10″. Summer: back, wings, and tail uniformly gray; head and underparts black; bill and legs black; vent white. Winter: dark gray above; face and underparts white; nape and earspot black. Tail short, notched. Nests in small colonies. **VOICE** Sharp *kreek.* **HABITAT** Reedy lakes; seacoast. **RANGE** May–Aug.: n VT, inland ME. May, Aug.–Sept.: entire coast; uncommon inland.

BLACK SKIMMER
Rynchops niger
GULL AND TERN FAMILY

18″. Adult black above; forehead and underparts white; legs red, short; tail mainly white, short, notched. Bill long, black-tipped, red, lower mandible much longer. Imm. brown above, with white scaly feather edges. Creates ripple in calm waters with lower bill; circles back for fish. **VOICE** Short barks. **HABITAT** Barrier islands. **RANGE** May–Sept.: CT to Cape Cod (local).

BLACK GUILLEMOT
Cepphus grylle
PUFFIN FAMILY

13″. Summer: all black ex. for large, oval, white wing patch. Winter: back scaly gray; upperwings black, with large white patch; head and underparts white. Bill shortish, thin; legs red. Fast, low, whirring flight. **VOICE** High *peeee.* **HABITAT** Rocky shores; nearby seas. **RANGE** Apr.–Oct.: ME coast. Nov.–Mar.: CT to ME coast, mainly from Cape Ann north.

RAZORBILL
Alca torda
PUFFIN FAMILY

17″. Summer: black head, neck, and upperparts; white below; white line from eye to top of black bill; bill grooved, flattened vertically, with 1 white stripe; legs black. Winter: similar, but throat white. Nests in colonies, with puffins. **VOICE** Deep growl. **HABITAT** Islands, open ocean. **RANGE** May–Oct.: e ME islands. Nov.–Apr.: off coast from RI to ME. **Common Murre** *(Uria aalge)* similar, but has thin, pointed bill; breeds on ME islands.

ATLANTIC PUFFIN
Fratercula arctica
PUFFIN FAMILY

13″. Black above; white below, with white face (darker in winter), thick black collar; tail short; legs and webbed feet orange. Bill massive, vertically flattened; in summer, red, black, and yellow; duller in winter. **VOICE** Low *aar* at nest. **HABITAT** Islands, seas. **RANGE** May–Aug.: e ME islands. Sept.–Apr.: seas well offshore.

ROCK DOVE
Columba livia
PIGEON AND DOVE FAMILY

13″. Typical: head dark gray; coppery iridescence on neck; body and tail pale gray; white on upper rump; 2 black bars on secondaries; tail tipped black. Variations range from black to pale brown and white. Bill short, black; legs short, red. Powerful flier; flight reveals pointed wings. Common city pigeon, introduced from Europe. **VOICE** Gurgling *coo-cuk-crooo*. **HABITAT** Towns, parks, farms. **RANGE** Resident in N. Eng.

MOURNING DOVE
Zenaida macroura
PIGEON AND DOVE FAMILY

12″. Back, wings, tail dull brown; head and underparts pale buffy; bill short, black; black spot below eye; legs short, red; black and white edges on long, wedge-shaped, pointed tail. Wings whistle when taking flight. **VOICE** Mournful coo *Who-o coo, coo, coo.* **HABITAT** Fields, towns, sandy scrub. **RANGE** Apr.–Sept.: all N. Eng. Oct.–Mar.: c and s N. Eng.

BLACK-BILLED CUCKOO
Coccyzus erythropthalmus
CUCKOO FAMILY

12″. Upperparts, crown, cheeks soft brown; underparts clear white; bill black, thin, slightly downcurved; eye ring red; tail long and narrow, with thin white crescents below. **VOICE** Series of *cucucu* notes. **HABITAT** Broadleaf woodland edges, thickets. **RANGE** May–Sept.: all N. Eng. **Yellow-billed Cuckoo** (*C. americanus*) has rufous primaries, large white spots under tail, yellow bill.

Owls

Owls are nocturnal birds of prey that range in size in New England from 8 to 23 inches long. They have large heads, with large, forward-facing eyes (yellow in most species). Their eyesight and hearing are both acute. Distinct facial disks conceal large ear openings that provide them with keen hearing, which can pinpoint a squeak or a rustle in the grass in total darkness. The ears are asymmetrically placed on either side of the head, providing greater range of sound and better triangulation for pinpointing sources of sounds. Some owls have ornamental tufts of feathers at the corners of the head that look like ears or horns and are called ear tufts. Their fluffy-looking bodies are cryptically colored and patterned to blend with the background of their daytime nest or roost. Owls are most readily seen in winter in open areas and leafless woodlands. Their bills are short but strongly hooked. The legs are also typically short, and the feet have sharp curved talons. Owls fly silently; their feathers are delicately fringed and very soft. Imitations and tapes of their distinctive voices, given or played at night, bring a response from an owl, which may call, or fly in close to the source of the call, or both; in daytime, the same sound may bring crows, jays, and song-birds, which usually mob roosting owls they discover.

ear tufts

facial disk

Parts of an Owl

EASTERN SCREECH-OWL
Otus asio
OWL FAMILY

9″. 2 color morphs: gray and rufous. Facial disk pale gray or orange, ringed in black; dark streaks on breast; row of white spots on shoulder. Tail short; eyes yellow; fluffy ear tufts. **VOICE** Mournful whinny, rising then falling in pitch; also fast, even-pitch series of *hu* notes. **HABITAT** Woods, swamps, cemeteries, towns. **RANGE** Resident from s ME and c NH south.

NORTHERN SAW-WHET OWL
Aegolius acadicus
OWL FAMILY

8″. Adult dark brown above; thick rusty stripes below; large white spots on shoulders; fine white stripes on crown; facial disk striped brown. Head large; eyes yellow; lacks ear tufts. Very tame when roosting in winter evergreens. Rarely seen. **VOICE** In late winter and spring, mechanical *too* repeated 100 times a minute. **HABITAT** Dense conifer stands. **RANGE** Resident in N. Eng.

SNOWY OWL
Nyctea scandiaca
OWL FAMILY

24″. Face, chest, leg feathers snow white. Old male pure white; female and younger male crown, upperparts, belly laced with black dots and scales. Head rounded; no ear tufts; eyes yellow. Feeds by day or night in winter; sits on exposed perches. **VOICE** Quiet in winter. **HABITAT** Marshes, dunes, farms, airports. **RANGE** Nov.–Mar., but not every winter: entire coast in salt marshes; inland (rarer).

GREAT HORNED OWL
Bubo virginianus
OWL FAMILY

L 23″; WS 4′7″. Dark brown with black spots above; underparts pale brown, with heavy dark brown bars; dark streaks on upper chest; facial disk rich rusty brown, ringed in black. Head large; eyes yellow; fluffy ear tufts. **VOICE** 3–8 deep hoots, 2nd and 3rd rapid and doubled. **HABITAT** Woods. **RANGE** Resident in N. Eng.

SHORT-EARED OWL
Asio flammeus
OWL FAMILY

16″. Brown above, with darker and paler brown spots; buffy below, with brown stripes; facial disk buffy, with blackish "eye shadow" around yellow eyes. Flight reveals brown wings above, buffy patch near bend of wing. Head small for owl; tiny ear tufts. **VOICE** Barking *wow* near nest. **HABITAT** Open grasslands; marshes. **RANGE** May–Sept.: few breed on islands off Cape Cod. Oct.–Apr.: entire coast; inland valleys (rare).

BARRED OWL
Strix varia
OWL FAMILY

L 21″; WS 3′8″. Dark brownish gray with black spots above; heavily striped underparts; dark bars on upper chest; facial disk gray, ringed in black. Eyes brown; no ear tufts. Many males spend winter in urban areas, return to home territories in early spring. Feeds at night; some sit on tree limbs by day. **VOICE** 2 sets of *hoo* notes: *Who cooks for you? Who cooks for you-all?* Caterwauling calls in spring. **HABITAT** Swamps, woods. **RANGE** Resident in N. Eng.

COMMON NIGHTHAWK
Chordeiles minor
NIGHTJAR FAMILY

10″. Dark brown, heavily gray-spotted; throat white; legs very short. Flight reveals long, pointed, black primaries with prominent white bar; long notched tail. Flies high, erratically. Hunts at night for insects. Late-summer flocks, esp. along Conn. River Valley, are N. Eng. migrating spectacle. **VOICE** Nasal *peeent*. **HABITAT** Fields, towns. **RANGE** May–Sept.: all N. Eng.

WHIP-POOR-WILL
Caprimulgus vociferus
NIGHTJAR FAMILY

10″. Dark gray-brown above and below, with fine black spots; throat black above, partial white collar below. Corners of tail white in male, buffy in female. Flight reveals rounded, reddish-brown wings; tail long, rounded. Nocturnal; rarely seen. **VOICE** Weak *whip*, followed by louder, slurred *poor-weell;* heard at night. **HABITAT** Open mixed woods. **RANGE** May–Sept.: all N. Eng.

CHIMNEY SWIFT
Chaetura pelagica
SWIFT FAMILY

5½″. Sooty gray; bill tiny; wings extend past tail. Flight reveals pale gray throat; wings long, pointed; tail squared-off. Clings upright with very small feet. Flies fast, fairly high, in arcs. For nest, cements sticks with saliva to vertical spaces in buildings, tree hollows. Does not perch on wires and branches. **VOICE** Rapid *chitter* and *chip* notes, given often in flight. **HABITAT** Towns, fields. **RANGE** May–Sept.: all N. Eng.

RUBY-THROATED HUMMINGBIRD
Archilochus colubris
HUMMINGBIRD FAMILY

female (left), male (right)

3½". Male upperparts and crown iridescent green; chest and vent white; sides green; black line below eye; iridescent red throat often appears black; tail black, forked. Female green above; white below; tail corners tipped black and white. Bill long, needle-like, black; small white spot behind eye. Immatures of both sexes resemble adult female. Hovers at hummingbird feeders and flowers, preferring red or orange tubular ones. Beats wings dozens of times a second; male's wings can make humming sound. Hummingbirds are the only birds that can fly backward. **VOICE** High *chips,* squeaks. **HABITAT** Woodland edges, fields, gardens. **RANGE** May–Sept.: all N. Eng.; urban areas during migration.

BELTED KINGFISHER
Ceryle alcyon
KINGFISHER FAMILY

female (left), male (right)

13". Male blue above, with tiny white spots; head blue; throat, neck, and belly white; blue belt on chest. Female similar; belly has 2nd (rufous) belt extending onto sides. Head large, with ragged fore and rear crests; bill very long, thick, pointed, black; white spot before eye. Active, calls often; dives headfirst to seize small fish. As nest, excavates tunnel 1–2′ into earthen bank, sometimes far from water. **VOICE** Loud woody rattle. **HABITAT** Rivers, lakes, coasts. **RANGE** Apr.–Oct.: all N. Eng. Nov.–Mar.: a few in s N. Eng.

Woodpeckers

Woodpeckers, which range in size from small to mid-size birds, cling to the trunks and large branches of trees with their sharp claws (on short legs) and stiff, spine-tipped tails that help support them in the vertical position. Their long pointed bills are like chisels, able to bore into wood. Curled inside the woodpecker head is a narrow tongue twice the length of the bill, tipped with spear-like barbs that impale wood-boring insects. Members of this family laboriously dig out nest holes in living or dead tree trunks and limbs. The sexes are very much alike, but the red (or yellow) patches on the heads of the males are reduced or lacking in females of many species. In spring, males rapidly bang their bills against resonant wood on trees and buildings in a territorial drumming that is louder and more rapid than the tapping made while feeding. Most New England woodpeckers are year-round residents, but most flickers and all sapsuckers migrate.

RED-BELLIED WOODPECKER
Melanerpes carolinus
WOODPECKER FAMILY

9″. Back and wings barred black and white; face and underparts clear pale gray; virtually no red on belly. Male forehead, crown, hindneck red. Female crown gray; forehead spot and nape red. Flight reveals large white spot in black primaries, white rump. **VOICE** Rolling *chuurr;* double *chiv chiv;* drum is brief. **HABITAT** Open woods. **RANGE** Resident in CT, RI, MA; spreading north.

YELLOW-BELLIED SAPSUCKER
Sphyrapicus varius
WOODPECKER FAMILY

8″. Adult back and wings speckled; upper chest black; belly pale yellow; forecrown red; head boldly pied; throat red in male, white in female. Long white shoulder patch. Drills rows of holes in thin bark; sucks sap; eats insects drawn to sap. **VOICE** Nasal downward *cheerrr;* drum rapid, then slow. **HABITAT** Broadleaf woods. **RANGE** June–Aug.: Berkshires, VT, NH, ME. Apr.–May, Sept.–Oct.: all N. Eng.

DOWNY WOODPECKER
Picoides pubescens
WOODPECKER FAMILY

6½″. Like Hairy Woodpecker, head boldly pied; back white; wings black, white-spotted; underparts white; male has red nape patch. Downy is smaller than Hairy, with much shorter bill and black spots on white outer tail feathers. **VOICE** Rapid descending whinny; flat *pick;* long drum. **HABITAT** Woods, suburbs. **RANGE** Resident in N. Eng.

HAIRY WOODPECKER
Picoides villosus
WOODPECKER FAMILY

9″. Like more common Downy Woodpecker, head boldly pied; back white; wings black, white-spotted; underparts white; male has red nape patch. Hairy is larger, with much longer bill and clear, white, unspotted outer tail feathers. **VOICE** Loud rattle; sharp *peek;* long drum. **HABITAT** Woods, suburbs. **RANGE** Resident in N. Eng.

PILEATED WOODPECKER
Dryocopus pileatus
WOODPECKER FAMILY

18″. Black; crest pointed, red; white and black stripes on face and down sides of neck. Male forehead and "mustache" red; female forehead and "mustache" black. Neck thin; bill heavy, silver. Flight reveals white underwing linings, black flight feathers. A special treat when seen or heard. **VOICE** Rapid irregular series of *cuk* and flicker-like *wucka* notes. **HABITAT** Woods. **RANGE** Resident in most of N. Eng; rare in se N. Eng.

NORTHERN FLICKER
Colaptes auratus
WOODPECKER FAMILY

13″. Yellow-shafted race: male back brown, with blackish bars; belly pale buff, with heavy black spots; crown gray; red crescent on nape; face buffy, with black "mustache"; black crescent on chest. Female lacks "mustache." White rump; yellow under wings and tail. Often feeds on ground. **VOICE** Rapid series of *wic* and *woika* (or *flicker*) notes; loud *klee-err;* drums softly. **HABITAT** Woods, farms. **RANGE** Apr.–Oct.: all N. Eng. Nov.–Mar.: some in s N. Eng.

Songbirds (Passerines)

The birds described from here to the end of the birds section belong to a single order called Passeriformes. Known as passerines or, more commonly, perching birds or songbirds, they are the most recently evolved of the 25 bird orders; members of this order comprise more than half the world's birds. Their sizes range from 3½″ kinglets to 24″ ravens, but they are generally small land birds with pleasing songs; among the finest songsters are the wrens, mockingbirds, and thrushes. Songbirds give call notes year-round, while most give their songs only during the breeding season (spring and early summer). In some species, the male has a particularly colorful summer breeding plumage that is changed in winter to drabber, female-like coloration. In the spring, migrant males generally arrive in New England seven to ten days before the females and stake out breeding territories, which they defend against neighboring males. After a male shows a female around his territory, she may be satisfied (especially if the vegetation and insect life are plentiful) and stay with him, or search for another singing male whose territory is more to her liking. Most songbirds build open-topped, rounded nests of grasses, sticks, vegetable fibers, and rootlets in a fork of a tree, in a shrub, or tucked under tall grass. Some eat insects year-round, while others focus on seeds, grains, or fruit; all feed insects to their hatchlings. In the fall, the sexes may migrate south together, the adults often several weeks or more before the young born that year.

EASTERN WOOD-PEWEE
Contopus virens
TYRANT FLYCATCHER FAMILY

6″. Dark grayish brown above; dingy white below; sides of chest gray; 2 narrow white wing bars; head often appears pointed; lower mandible dull orange; lacks eye ring. Late-returning migrant. Hard to see; stays high in trees. **VOICE** Slurred *pee-ah-weee*. **HABITAT** Broadleaf and mixed woods. **RANGE** Mid-May to Sept.: all N. Eng.

LEAST FLYCATCHER
Empidonax minimus
TYRANT FLYCATCHER FAMILY

5″. Grayish olive-brown above; dirty white below, sometimes with light yellow wash on belly; 2 white wing bars; bold white eye ring. Head fairly large; tail short. Hunts from lower open branches. **VOICE** Emphatic *che-BECK*. **HABITAT** Open woods. **RANGE** May–Sept.: all N. Eng.

EASTERN PHOEBE
Sayornis phoebe
TYRANT FLYCATCHER FAMILY

7″. Back gray-brown; dingy white below; wings and tail dark brown. Some fall birds show yellowish wash on belly. Bill black; lacks eye ring and wing bars. Wags tail often. Early-returning migrant. Easy to see; perches low. Nests under bridges, building overhangs. **VOICE** Hoarse *fee-bree*. **HABITAT** Watersides, woods, suburbs. **RANGE** Mar.–Oct.: all N. Eng.

GREAT CRESTED FLYCATCHER
Myiarchus crinitus
TYRANT FLYCATCHER FAMILY

8″. Upperparts and crown dull brown; throat and chest grayish white; belly bright yellow; primaries and tail edged rufous; 2 thin white wing bars. Head a bit fluffy, but no true crest; bill heavy, pointed; tail fairly long. More often heard than seen; stays fairly high in trees. **VOICE** Loud rising *wheeep*. **HABITAT** Broadleaf woods. **RANGE** May–Sept.: all N. Eng.

EASTERN KINGBIRD
Tyrannus tyrannus
TYRANT FLYCATCHER FAMILY

8″. Back and wings slaty; throat and underparts white; head black; tail black, with white terminal band. Often flies slowly, with quivering wings. Flies fast when attacking crows and hawks that come near its territory. Perches on tips of trees and on wires. **VOICE** Rapid agitated *kit-kit-kittery;* nasal *tzeer*. **HABITAT** Trees near fields, waterways, roads. **RANGE** May–Sept.: all N. Eng.

HORNED LARK
Eremophila alpestris
LARK FAMILY

7½″. Brown above, with light streaks; belly white; black crown stripe; male has 2 tiny "horns"; black, yellow, and white patches on head and foreneck. Legs short; bill slender, black. Flight reveals white underwings; tail black; outer tail feathers white. **VOICE** Song: high tinkling. Call: *tsee-titi*. **HABITAT** Large fields, airports, dunes. **RANGE** Resident locally; most common in se MA; more widespread in winter.

PURPLE MARTIN
Progne subis
SWALLOW FAMILY

8″. Male mainly dark iridescent blue-purple; flight feathers black. Female upperparts and head dull purplish; throat and chest dusky gray, with darker fine scales and streaks; belly and vent white. Tail forked. Glides more than other swallows; often circles with short flaps, then a glide. **VOICE** Song: low gurgling series. Call: throaty *chew chew*. **HABITAT** Fields, marshes, towns. **RANGE** Apr.–Aug.: mainly se N. Eng. (local).

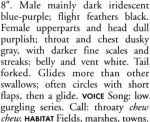

TREE SWALLOW
Tachycineta bicolor
SWALLOW FAMILY

6″. Adult dark iridescent green-blue above; entirely snowy white below. Imm. uniformly brown above. Tail notched. Slow flier; short flapping circles and a climb. Massive flocks in late summer over coastal salt marshes. **VOICE** Song: *weet-trit-weet.* Call: *cheat cheat.* **HABITAT** Fields, marshes, waterways. **RANGE** Mar.–Oct.: all N. Eng.

NORTHERN ROUGH-WINGED SWALLOW
Stelgidopteryx serripennis
SWALLOW FAMILY

5½″. Dull brown above; throat and chest pale brown; breast and vent dull white. Tail notched. Flies with slow deep wingbeats. Often in solitary pairs. **VOICE** Raspy *brit.* **HABITAT** Ponds, rivers, fields. **RANGE** Apr.–Sept.: c ME and south. **Bank Swallow** has sharp dark neck band and whiter underparts. **Tree Swallow** imm. brown above, all snowy white below.

BANK SWALLOW
Riparia riparia
SWALLOW FAMILY

5″. Dull brown above; white below, crossed by distinct brown neck band. Flies with rapid wingbeats. Often in flocks, very social. **VOICE** Low flat *chert chert*; buzzy chatter. **HABITAT** Waterways, fields, banks. **RANGE** May–Aug.: all N. Eng. **Northern Rough-winged Swallow** has pale brown throat; lacks neck band. **Tree Swallow** imm. brown above, all snowy white below.

CLIFF SWALLOW
Hirundo pyrrhonota
SWALLOW FAMILY

6″. Adult back and wings blue; underparts grayish white; forehead yellow; crown blue; neck gray; tail black, short, square; rump buffy, distinct. Nests in colonies; declining as House Sparrows usurp nests. **VOICE** Song: harsh creaking. Call: grating *syrup.* **HABITAT** Farms, fields, waterways. **RANGE** May–Sept.: all N. Eng. (local).

BARN SWALLOW
Hirundo rustica
SWALLOW FAMILY

7". Streamlined. Adult glossy blue above; forehead chestnut; throat dark orange; thin blue necklace; rest of underparts buffy orange; outer tail streamers very long. Fast flier. Nest is open cup of mud pellets and grass inside or under overhang of barn or bridge. **VOICE** Song: long twittering. Calls: soft *vit vit* and *zee-zay*. **HABITAT** Fields, farms, waterways. **RANGE** Late Apr.–Sept.: all N. Eng.

GRAY JAY
Perisoreus canadensis
CROW AND JAY FAMILY

11½". Adult back, wings, and tail dull, dark gray; crown, cheeks, and underparts white; nape black. Bill black; tail long, rounded. Imm. all slaty; white "mustache." Bold food robber at human campsites. Northern Mockingbird similar, but has white wing patch, outer tail feathers.. **VOICE** Low *chuck*. **HABITAT** Spruce, fir woods. **RANGE** Resident in n VT, n NH, n and c ME.

BLUE JAY
Cyanocitta cristata
CROW AND JAY FAMILY

12". Crest and back blue; dingy white below; face whitish; black necklace; wings and long, rounded tail bright blue, banded black, edged in white. Brash; conspicuous. Roaming flocks in autumn. **VOICE** Noisy; harsh *jaay*; liquid *queedle*; imitates hawks. **HABITAT** Woods, towns. **RANGE** Present year-round; N. Eng. breeders winter in mid-Atlantic states; most N. Eng. winterers breed in Canada.

AMERICAN CROW
Corvus brachyrhynchos
CROW AND JAY FAMILY

18″. All glossy black; bill heavy, black. Flight reveals rounded wings, "fingered" wingtips; squarish tail with rounded corners. Bold, noisy. Huge night roosts in winter. **VOICE** Loud descending *caw.* **HABITAT** Farms, fields, shores, roadsides, urban areas. **RANGE** Resident in N. Eng.; many shift southward or toward cities in winter. **Fish Crow** (*C. ossifragus*) slightly smaller; gives high nasal *cah;* occurs from Boston south.

COMMON RAVEN
"Northern Raven"
Corvus corax
CROW AND JAY FAMILY

24″. All glossy black; bill black, very heavy; throat has long shaggy feathers. Flight reveals pointed wings; "fingered" wingtips; wedge-shaped, long tail. Soars frequently. Shy but conspicuous. **VOICE** Very low *croonk.*

HABITAT Mtns., woods, fields. **RANGE** Resident in n VT, n NH, ME; expanding south; a few breed or winter south to w and c MA.

Attracting Birds to Your Yard

Many people enjoy attracting birds into their yards, and supplemental feeding helps birds in winter, when naturally occurring foods are covered by snow. Once started, winter feeding should be continued into spring. In the birds section, species that will come into a yard to feed are indicated by the icon 🐦.

Birdfeeders come in many designs. Hanging, clear seed feeders with short perch sticks are popular with goldfinches, siskins, and other finches. Window boxes and platforms on a pole are best for such medium-size birds as Evening Grosbeaks, Northern Cardinals, and Blue Jays, while Dark-eyed Juncos, Mourning Doves, and many sparrows prefer to feed on the ground. Mounting a birdfeeder inevitably means an ongoing struggle with squirrels, who are endlessly resourceful at defeating devices intended to keep them out of the feeders.

Grains and seeds are the best all-purpose fare for feeders. Many species like sunflower seeds, but your local birds may have particular preferences. Thistle seed is popular with goldfinches, white millet seed is a good choice for small species, and cracked corn is appreciated by large, ground-feeding birds. Many seed mixes are available at supermarkets and garden supply stores.

Birds also like fruit. In summer, you can lay out orange slices for Baltimore Orioles; apples, oranges, and grapes can also be put out on a platform or lawn or mounted on feeders. The fat and protein

BLACK-CAPPED CHICKADEE
Parus atricapillus
CHICKADEE FAMILY
5½". Back, wings, and long narrow tail gray; white below, with light buffy sides; wings edged white; cap and throat black; face white. Friendly, inquisitive; often in family groups. Acrobatic when feeding. **VOICE** Song: clear *fee-bee*. Call: *chick-a-dee-dee-dee*. **HABITAT** Woods, scrub, gardens. **RANGE** Resident in N. Eng.; some years migrates in fall.

TUFTED TITMOUSE
Parus bicolor
CHICKADEE FAMILY
6". Adult upperparts, pointed crest, and tail gray; underparts dull white; sides washed rusty; forehead black; white area around beady black eye. Imm. forehead gray. Cheerful, active. Immigrant from South. **VOICE** Song: whistled *peter-peter-peter*. Call: nasal scolding. **HABITAT** Woods, towns. **RANGE** Resident south from c VT, s ME, ex. islands off Cape Cod.

in nuts makes them disappear quickly. Suet, in a mesh holder hung from a branch or mounted on a tree trunk, attracts birds such as nuthatches and woodpeckers that feed on insects in tree bark and bushes; it should be discontinued in summer, when it spoils quickly and mats feathers. Hummingbirds will come to specially designed red plastic dispensers of sugar water.

Water is important, especially during periods when natural water sources dry up or freeze over. Many species are attracted to a bird bath, which should be regularly scrubbed with a brush to rid it of algae and prevent diseases from spreading.

You might want to make or purchase a nest box to attract breeding birds. The most popular—inviting to Tree Swallows, chickadees, nuthatches, wrens, and bluebirds—is an enclosed box with a square floor area 4–7" wide and long, and about twice as high as it is wide (8–12"). Specifications vary depending on the species, and include floor area, the size of the entrance hole, height from the base of the box to the hole, and proper siting of the box. Larger boxes of particular dimensions attract Screech-Owls and Wood Ducks. Other birds will nest in open-fronted shelves or martin houses. Information on building and siting nest boxes and feeders is available from your local Audubon Society or nature center. In the birds section, the icon denotes species that have used nest boxes in the right habitat.

RED-BREASTED NUTHATCH
Sitta canadensis
NUTHATCH FAMILY

4½″. Male back steel blue; chin white; underparts rufous; cap black; face white; black line through eye. Female similar, but crown gray; buffy below. Tail short. Often seen on conifer cones. VOICE High nasal *enk* series. HABITAT Coniferous woods. RANGE Resident in N. Eng. Erratic in numbers; some years, many migrate south (Sept.–Oct.).

WHITE-BREASTED NUTHATCH
Sitta carolinensis
NUTHATCH FAMILY

6″. Male back steel blue; wings edged white; face and breast white; narrow black crown; vent and sides washed rusty. Female crown and back grayer. Creeps headfirst in all directions on tree trunks. VOICE Song: rapid *wer* notes. Call: loud *yank.* HABITAT Broadleaf and mixed woods. RANGE Resident in N. Eng.

BROWN CREEPER
Certhia americana
CREEPER FAMILY

5½″. Brown with buff stripes above; white below; wing stripe buffy; rump rufous; eye line white; tail tips spiny. Looks like a wren; sings like a warbler; climbs trees like a woodpecker: starts at bottom of trunk, probes bark with slender bill. VOICE Song: high *see see see tu wee.* Call: 1 high *tsee.* HABITAT Woods. RANGE Resident in N. Eng.

CAROLINA WREN
Thryothorus ludovicianus
WREN FAMILY

6″. Upperparts and crown dark rufous-brown; light orange below; fine black bars on wings and tail; long white eyebrow bordered in black; throat white. Head large; tail long. VOICE Song: rollicking repeated *tea-kettle.* Call: harsh *jeer.* HABITAT Shrubs, towns. RANGE Resident in CT, RI, s MA; spreading north.

WINTER WREN
Troglodytes troglodytes
WREN FAMILY

4″. Dark brown above and below; sides, wings, and tail finely black-barred; indistinct eyebrow and throat buffy. Often cocks very short tail over back. N. Eng.'s smallest wren. **VOICE** Song: beautiful long series of warbles and trills. Call: hard *kip kip*. **HABITAT** Woodland ravines, brush piles. **RANGE** May–Aug.: mainly w and n N. Eng. Nov.–Mar.: s N. Eng. (rare). Apr., Sept.–Oct.: all N. Eng.

HOUSE WREN
Troglodytes aedon
WREN FAMILY

5″. Head and back plain dull brown; wings and tail lightly dotted or barred black; mainly clear brownish white below; sides finely barred. Tail cocked. Aggressive to other nearby hole-nesters; destroys their eggs. **VOICE** Song: long, pleasing, descending gurgle. Call: *chuurr*. **HABITAT** Shrubs, vines, towns. **RANGE** May–Oct.: all N. Eng.

MARSH WREN
Cistothorus palustris
WREN FAMILY

5″. Back black, with bold white stripes; white below; wings, rump, and tail rufous; sides buffy; white eyebrow under dark brownish crown. Tail cocked. **VOICE** Song: gurgling rattle. Call: loud *check*. **HABITAT** Large cattail marshes. **RANGE** Apr.–Oct.: all N. Eng. (local).

BLUE-GRAY GNATCATCHER
Polioptila caerulea
OLD WORLD WARBLER SUBFAMILY

4½″. Blue-gray above; white below; tail black, with white outer tail feathers; eye ring white. Male has black line over eye in summer. Often wags tail sideways. **VOICE** Song: thin wheezy warble. Call: inquiring *pweee*. **HABITAT** Open woods, waterside trees. **RANGE** Apr.–Sept.: c and s N. Eng.; expanding north.

GOLDEN-CROWNED KINGLET
Regulus satrapa
OLD WORLD WARBLER SUBFAMILY

3½″. Back olive; dingy olive below; wings have yellowish edging and wing bars; crown black, with center orange and yellow (male) or yellow (female); eyebrow white; black line through eye. Tail short, notched. **VOICE** Call: 3 high *tsee* notes. Song: same, then chatter. **HABITAT** Spruce and mixed woods. **RANGE** May–Aug.: w and n N. Eng. Nov.–Apr.: all N. Eng. Sept.–Oct.: all N. Eng.

RUBY-CROWNED KINGLET
Regulus calendula
OLD WORLD WARBLER SUBFAMILY

4". Drab olive all over, but paler below; 2 white wing bars; large white eye ring. Male raises red midcrown patch when displaying. Tail has short notch. Quickly flicks its wings when perched. **VOICE** Song: high warbles ending with 3 *look-at-me's*. Call: scolding *je-dit*. **HABITAT** Summer: conifers. Migration: mixed woods, shrubs. **RANGE** June–Aug.: n N. Eng. Nov.–Mar.: s N. Eng. (rare). Apr.–May, Sept.–Oct.: all N. Eng.

EASTERN BLUEBIRD
Sialia sialis
THRUSH SUBFAMILY

7". Male brilliant deep blue above; throat, chest, and sides rusty orange; midbelly and vent white. Female similar but with blue-gray head and back. Imm. scaled dark brown. Sits upright on snags and wires. **VOICE** Song: pleasing, down-slurred *cheer cheery charley*. Call: musical *chur-lee*. **HABITAT** Fields and woodland edges. **RANGE** Mar.–Nov.: all N. Eng. Oct.–Apr.: a few in s N. Eng.

BICKNELL'S THRUSH
Catharus bicknelli
THRUSH SUBFAMILY

7½". Back, head, wings grayish brown; dark brown spots on pale buffy throat and chest; belly white; tail rusty gray; cheeks gray; very thin, pale eye ring. Forages on forest floor. Once considered race of **Gray-cheeked Thrush** *(C. minimus)*. **VOICE** Song: nasal, rising at end: *whee-wheeoo-ti-ti-whee*. Call: down-slurred *whee-ah*. **HABITAT** Summer: krummholz, near tree line. **RANGE** June–Aug.: mountaintops in n N. Eng. May, Sept.–Oct.: all N. Eng.

VEERY
Catharus fuscescens
THRUSH SUBFAMILY

7". Uniformly dull rufous brown above; throat and upper chest buffy, with tiny, diffuse, rufous spots; sides gray; midbelly and vent white; very thin, pale eye ring. **VOICE** Song: descending spiral of flute-like notes. Call: low *pheeuw*. **HABITAT** Swamps, riverside broadleaf woods. **RANGE** May–Sept.: all N. Eng.

SWAINSON'S THRUSH
Catharus ustulatus
THRUSH SUBFAMILY

7″. Back, head, wings, and tail olive-brown; dark brown spots on buffy throat and chest; belly white; lores and wide eye ring buffy. **VOICE** Song: beautiful, breezy, up-slurred whistles. Calls: *whit* and *heep.* **HABITAT** Mixed woods, thickets. **RANGE** June–Aug.: Berkshires and n N. Eng. May, Sept.–Oct.: all N. Eng.

HERMIT THRUSH
Catharus guttatus
THRUSH SUBFAMILY

7″. Head, back, wings brown; sides grayish buff; dark brown spots on throat and upper chest; center of chest and belly whitish; rump and tail bright rufous brown; very thin, pale eye ring. **VOICE** Song: clear, flute-like; similar phrases repeated at different pitches. Call: low *chuck.* **HABITAT** Mixed and coniferous woods; thickets. **RANGE** Apr.–Nov.: all N. Eng. Dec.–Mar.: a few in s N. Eng.

WOOD THRUSH
Hylocichla mustelina
THRUSH SUBFAMILY

8″. Crown and upper back rich reddish brown; snowy white below, with heavy black spots; wings, lower back, and tail brown; thin white eye ring. Tail fairly short. **VOICE** Song: flute-like *ee-oo-lay?* Call: *wit-wit-wit.* **HABITAT** Broadleaf woods. **RANGE** May–Sept.: all N. Eng.

adult   immature

AMERICAN ROBIN
Turdus migratorius
THRUSH SUBFAMILY

10″. Male breast and sides rufous-orange; back and wings gray-brown; head blackish, with broken white eye ring; throat striped; bill yellow; tail black, with tiny white corners; vent white. Female head and back duller brown. Tail fairly long. Imm. buffy white below with heavy blackish spots; pale buffy scaling on back. In spring and summer, an earthworm specialist. In fall and winter, roams in berry-searching flocks, forms large communal roosts. **VOICE** Song: prolonged, rising and falling *cheery-up cheery-me.* Calls: *tut tut tut* and *tseep.* **HABITAT** Woods, shrubs, towns. **RANGE** Mar.–Nov.: all N. Eng. Dec.–Mar.: some in s N. Eng.

NORTHERN MOCKINGBIRD
Mimus polyglottos
MOCKINGBIRD FAMILY

10″. Back, head, shoulder rump gray; paler grayish white below; 2 slender wing bars and large wing patch white; tail blackish with white outer tail feathers. Bill short, thin. Sings conspicuously by day and often at night. Bold brash newcomer from South since 1950s. **VOICE** Song: mimics other birds, repeats songs 3–6 times. Calls: loud *chack,* softer *chair.* **HABITAT** Shrubs, fields, towns **RANGE** Resident in c and s N. Eng.; spreading north.

GRAY CATBIRD
Dumetella carolinensis
MOCKINGBIRD FAMILY

9″. Entirely slaty gray ex. for black crown and rusty vent. A skulker; often cocks or swings tail. **VOICE** Song: mimics other birds; doesn't repeat songs. Calls: cat-like *meeow;* sharp *check.* **HABITAT** Dense shrubs, woodland edges, gardens. **RANGE** May–Oct.: all N. Eng., ex. mtns. Nov.–Apr.: a few in s N. Eng.

BROWN THRASHER
Toxostoma rufum
MOCKINGBIRD FAMILY

11½″. Bright rufous-brown above buffy white below, with dark brown stripes; white wing bars; gray cheeks around yellow-orange eyes. Bill sturdy, downcurved; tail very long, rounded. **VOICE** Song: mimics other birds, repeating each song twice. Call: loud *chack.* **HABITAT** Thickets; oak woods. **RANGE** Apr.–Oct.: all N. Eng.

CEDAR WAXWING
Bombycilla cedrorum
WAXWING FAMILY

7″. Adult back and laid-back crest brown; soft brown chest grades to yellow belly; wings gray, with waxy red tips on secondaries; black eye mask, edged in white. Tail gray, with yellow band at tip. Imm. striped brown; with white eye line. Often in flocks. **VOICE** Call: high thin *zeee.* **HABITAT** Woodland edges, shrubs, gardens. **RANGE** May–Nov.: all N. Eng. Nov.–Apr.: c and s N. Eng.

NORTHERN SHRIKE
Lanius excubitor
SHRIKE FAMILY

10″. Back and crown gray; white below, with fine gray bars; wings black with large white spot; black eyemask; long, rounded, white-edged black tail. Head large; bill heavy, hooked. Preys on small birds and rodents; impales surplus on thorns. **VOICE** Call: loud *chek-chek.* **HABITAT** Trees in fields. **RANGE** Nov.–Mar.: all N. Eng., but scarce most winters.

EUROPEAN STARLING
summer   winter
Sturnus vulgaris
STARLING FAMILY

8″. Summer adult glossy green-purple; bill yellow. Winter adult blackish, heavily speckled with white; bill dark. Wings short, pointed, rusty-edged; bill sturdy, pointed; legs dull red; tail short, square. Imm. uniform gray-brown. Usu. in flocks. Very successful species introduced from Europe, but very detrimental to native birds. Boldly takes over most nest holes and bird-houses, occupied or not. Aggressively depletes wild and garden fruit stock and feeder suet. **VOICE** Song: mix of whistles, squeals, and chuckles; will mimic other birds. Calls: rising, then falling, *hoooeee,* harsh *jeer.* **HABITAT** Towns, farms, fields. **RANGE** Resident in N. Eng.

YELLOW-THROATED VIREO
Vireo flavifrons
VIREO FAMILY

5½″. Vireos have thicker hooked bills and move more slowly than warblers (see below). This species: upperparts grayish olive; belly and wing bars white; throat, chest, and "spectacles" yellow. Bill hooked. **VOICE** Song: *burry tweoo toowee three-eight.* Longer pauses between songs than Red-eyed and Solitary Vireos. **HABITAT** Broadleaf woodland canopies. **RANGE** May–Sept.: all N. Eng., ex. n and c ME.

SOLITARY VIREO
Vireo solitarius
VIREO FAMILY

5½″. Back olive; sides washed yellow; underparts and wing bars white; head slaty; white "spectacles." **VOICE** Song: slow, sweet whistled phrases; higher and sweeter than Red-eyed Vireo. Call: harsh *churr.* **HABITAT** Mixed woods. **RANGE** Late Apr.–Oct.: all N. Eng.

RED-EYED VIREO
Vireo olivaceus
VIREO FAMILY

6″. Olive green above; white below; yellow wash on belly in fall; no wing bars; crown gray, bordered by black; eyes red; black line through eye; white eyebrow. **VOICE** Song: monotonous *cher-eep cher-oop,* repeated up to 40 times a minute, all day long until end of July. Call: scolding *meew.* **HABITAT** Broadleaf woodland canopies. **RANGE** May–Oct.: all N. Eng.

WARBLING VIREO
Vireo gilvus
VIREO FAMILY

5″. Pale gray above, with slight olive cast; dusky white below; no wing bars; eyebrow white, not outlined in black. Imm. sides washed yellow-green. **VOICE** Song: melodious warbling; like that of Purple Finch, but slower. Call: wheezy *twee.* **HABITAT** Broadleaf woods, esp. on riversides. **RANGE** May–Sept.: all N. Eng.

Wood Warblers

As there is a bird subfamily called Old World warblers, those in the New World are often called wood warblers or just warblers; they are the subfamily Parulinae, part of the warbler, grosbeak, and sparrow (Emberizidae) family. In May, some 30 species of warblers can flood New England with color and song in "warbler waves" when overnight winds are from the southwest. Many adult males have the same plumage year-round, but some have breeding (summer) and nonbreeding (winter) plumages. Females, fall males, and immature birds often have a trace of the summer male pattern. Each species has a distinct song, while the warbler call tends to be a simple *chip.* During the summer, these birds breed in a variety of woodland and scrub habitats. Most nests are cups on small forks of branches or hidden under bushes. Warblers glean insects from leaves with their thin unhooked bills. In early autumn, most return to tropical forests of Central and South America.

BLUE-WINGED WARBLER
Vermivora pinus
WOOD WARBLER SUBFAMILY

4¾″. Back and nape olive; yellow unstriped head and underparts; wings blue-gray, with white wing bars; black line through eye. Replacing and interbreeds with Golden-winged Warbler. **VOICE** Song: lazy "inhale/exhale" *beee buzz.* **HABITAT** Young broadleaf woods, shrubs. **RANGE** May–Sept.: c ME and south.

NORTHERN PARULA
Parula americana
WOOD WARBLER SUBFAMILY

4½". Male upperparts and head dull blue; olive patch on back; belly white; yellow throat and upper breast crossed by blue and orange band; white wing bars; incomplete white eye ring. Female lacks breast band. Tail short. **VOICE** Song: rising trill, with sudden lower ending: *zeeeeeeee-up.* **HABITAT** Coniferous and broadleaf woods, often near water. **RANGE** May–Sept.: Cape Cod, n N. Eng. May, Sept.–Oct.: all N. Eng.

GOLDEN-WINGED WARBLER
Vermivora chrysoptera
WOOD WARBLER SUBFAMILY

4¾". Gray above and on sides; white below; golden crown and wing patch; mask and throat black in male, gray in female; white eyebrow and "mustache." Threatened in N. Eng. **VOICE** Song: *buzzy zee bee bee bee,* 1st note high. **HABITAT** Shrubby fields with saplings. **RANGE** May–Sept.: c and s N. Eng. (very local).

NASHVILLE WARBLER
Vermivora ruficapilla
WOOD WARBLER SUBFAMILY

4¾". Back, wings, and tail olive green; no wing bars; throat and underparts clear, unstriped yellow; gray head with white eye ring. **VOICE** Song: 2-part *see-it see-it see-it titititi-ti.* **HABITAT** Young broadleaf woods, woodland edges. **RANGE** May–Oct.: all N. Eng.

YELLOW WARBLER
Dendroica petechia
WOOD WARBLER SUBFAMILY

5". Male olive-yellow above; head, underparts, and wing and tail edging bright yellow; chestnut stripes on chest and sides. Female lacks stripes. **VOICE** Song: cheerful rapid *sweet sweet sweet I'm so sweet.* **HABITAT** Shrubby areas, esp. watersides, gardens. **RANGE** May–Sept.: all N. Eng.

CHESTNUT-SIDED WARBLER
Dendroica pensylvanica
WOOD WARBLER SUBFAMILY

5". Summer: olive above, with heavy black stripes; gleaming white below; sides chestnut; yellow crown; black "mustache" and line through eye; white cheek and wing bars. **VOICE** Song: cheerful slow *please please pleased to meet chyou.* **HABITAT** Woodland undergrowth; shrubs. **RANGE** May–Sept.: all N. Eng.

MAGNOLIA WARBLER
Dendroica magnolia
WOOD WARBLER SUBFAMILY

5″. Summer male black above, with yellow rump; yellow below, with heavy black streaks; white wing and tail patches; gray crown; white line over black mask. Female duller gray above; fainter streaking below. **VOICE** Song: musical *weetee weetee weeteo*. **HABITAT** Mixed and young coniferous woods. **RANGE** May–Aug.: w and n N. Eng. May, Sept.–Oct.: all N. Eng.

CAPE MAY WARBLER
Dendroica tigrina
WOOD WARBLER SUBFAMILY

5″. Summer male olive above, with black stripes; white wing patch; yellow rump; yellow below, with many black stripes; chestnut cheek on yellow face. Female greenish brown above; pale yellow neck patch and rump. **VOICE** Song: high *seet seet seet seet*. **HABITAT** Summer: spruces. **RANGE** May–Aug.: n N. Eng. May, Sept.–Oct.: all N. Eng., esp. coastal areas.

BLACK-THROATED BLUE WARBLER
Dendroica caerulescens
WOOD WARBLER SUBFAMILY

5″. Male dark blue above; white square on primaries; face, throat, and sides black; midbelly and vent white. Female plain brownish olive above, buff below, with pale wing spot. **VOICE** Song: lazy *sir sir sir please?* **HABITAT** Shrubs in mixed woods. **RANGE** May–Aug.: w and n N. Eng. May, Sept.–Oct.: all N. Eng.

BLACK-THROATED GREEN WARBLER
Dendroica virens
WOOD WARBLER SUBFAMILY

5″. Male crown and back olive green; belly white; throat and chest black, sides white with black streaks; white wing bars; face yellow. Female similar, but throat yellow; appears yellow-headed. **VOICE** Song: unmusical *see see see suz-ee*. **HABITAT** Coniferous and mixed woods. **RANGE** May–Oct.: all N. Eng.

PRAIRIE WARBLER
Dendroica discolor
WOOD WARBLER SUBFAMILY

4¾″. Male olive green above; red stripes on back; underparts and face yellow; black lines on face and sides; pale yellow wing bars. Female duller; lacks red back stripes. Wags tail. **VOICE** Song: 8–10 buzzy *zee* notes, each one higher. **HABITAT** Brushy fields. **RANGE** May–Sept.: c and s N. Eng.

BLACKBURNIAN WARBLER
Dendroica fusca
WOOD WARBLER SUBFAMILY

5″. Summer male black above; whitish below; black side stripes; large white shoulder patch; bright orange head, throat; mask and crown stripes black. Female striped brown above and on sides; throat orange-yellow. **VOICE** Song: high thin *sip sip sip titi zeeee*. **HABITAT** Conifers, esp. hemlocks; mixed woods. **RANGE** May–Sept.: w and n N. Eng. May, Sept.: all N. Eng.

PINE WARBLER
Dendroica pinus
WOOD WARBLER SUBFAMILY

5½″. Adult upperparts and cheeks plain olive green; belly and wing bars white; throat and chest yellow; faint olive stripes on sides. Imm. plain brown above; dingy white below; 2 white wing bars. **VOICE** Song: slow musical trill on one pitch. **HABITAT** Pines. **RANGE** Apr.–Oct.: c and s N. Eng. Nov.–Mar.: a few in se N. Eng.

YELLOW-RUMPED WARBLER
"Myrtle Warbler"
Dendroica coronata
WOOD WARBLER SUBFAMILY

5½″. Summer male gray above, with black streaks on back and white wing bars; white below; chest patch and side streaks black; yellow patches on crown and sides of chest; black mask. Female mask and upperparts brown. Rump strikingly yellow. Common early arrival in spring. **VOICE** Song: musical trill. Call: loud *check*. **HABITAT** Summer and migration: coniferous and mixed woods. Winter: coastal bayberry thickets. **RANGE** May–Sept.: w and n N. Eng. Oct.–Apr.: coastal se N. Eng. Apr.–May, Sept.–Oct.: all N. Eng.

PALM WARBLER
Dendroica palmarum
WOOD WARBLER SUBFAMILY

5½″. Summer: olive above; crown rufous; underparts and eyebrow yellow; rusty stripes on sides. Winter: faintly brown-striped; vent yellow. Wags tail more or less constantly. **VOICE** Song: slow buzzy trill. **HABITAT** Summer: bogs, waterside shrubbery. Migration: brushy fields. **RANGE** June–Aug.: n and e ME. Apr.–May, Sept.–Oct.: all N. Eng.

summer male (left), fall immature (right)

BLACKPOLL WARBLER
Dendroica striata
WOOD WARBLER SUBFAMILY
5½". Summer male brownish gray above; white below; black stripes on back and sides; white wing bars; crown black; cheek and throat white; black "mustache." Summer female grayish with weak stripes. Autumn adults olive-brown above; black stripes on back; white wing bars; yellow throat and chest, with faint dusky streaks; belly and vent white. Imm. streaked greenish. **VOICE** Song: high, thin, on one pitch (louder in middle): *ze ze ze ze ZEE ZEE ZEE ze ze*. **HABITAT** Summer: spruce-fir woods. Migration: mixed woods. **RANGE** June–Aug.: w and n N. Eng. May, Sept.–Oct.: all N. Eng.

BLACK-AND-WHITE WARBLER
Mniotilta varia
WOOD WARBLER SUBFAMILY
5¼". Male body striped black and white; cheeks and throat black; crown black, with median white stripe; white eyebrow and "mustache." Female cheeks gray; throat white. Creeps along branches and tree trunks. **VOICE** Song: 6–12 high, double *wee-zy* notes. **HABITAT** Mixed woods. **RANGE** Apr.–Oct.: all N. Eng.

male (left), female (right)

AMERICAN REDSTART
Setophaga ruticilla
WOOD WARBLER SUBFAMILY
5". Adult male mainly black; midbelly white; large orange patches on wings, sides of chest, basal corners of tail. Female olive-brown above; white below; yellow or yellow-orange patches on wings, sides of chest, basal corners of tail; head gray; narrow white "spectacles." Often fans tail. **VOICE** Songs: variable; 4 double *teet-sa*'s, ending with *teet,* and 4 single *zee*'s, ending with rising or falling note. **HABITAT** Broadleaf woods, shrubs. **RANGE** May–Sept.: all N. Eng.

OVENBIRD
"Teacherbird"
Seiurus aurocapillus
WOOD WARBLER SUBFAMILY

6". Upperparts and sides of head brownish olive; white below, with black stripes; crown stripe orange, bordered by black; eye ring white; legs pink. Walks on forest floor. **VOICE** Song: *TEACH-er*, repeated 6–8 times, ever louder; commonly heard. **HABITAT** Mixed broadleaf woods. **RANGE** May–Sept.: all N. Eng.

NORTHERN WATERTHRUSH
Seiurus noveboracensis
WOOD WARBLER SUBFAMILY

6". Upperparts and head plain brown; underparts and eyebrow (tapers to rear) yellowish white; throat dotted; breast striped brown; legs pink. Bill short, thin compared to sparrow look-alikes. Often bobs tail. **VOICE** Song: rapid *wit wit wit sweet sweet sweet chew chew chew*. **HABITAT** Swamps, moist woods, watersides. **RANGE** May–Sept.: all N. Eng.

LOUISIANA WATERTHRUSH
Seiurus motacilla
WOOD WARBLER SUBFAMILY

6". Upperparts and head plain brown; underparts and eyebrow (wider at rear) pure white; throat unspotted; breast striped brown; legs pink. Bill medium-thin. Often bobs tail. **VOICE** Song: 4 slow, upslurred notes, then a fast jumble of high and low notes. **HABITAT** Woodlands with flowing streams. **RANGE** Apr.–Aug.: c and s N. Eng.

MOURNING WARBLER
Oporornis philadelphia
WOOD WARBLER SUBFAMILY

5¼". Male dark olive green above; bright yellow below; solid gray hood blending into black chest patch. Female similar, but lacks black on chest. **VOICE** Song: *cheery cheery chorry chorry*. **HABITAT** Shrubs in woods; bogs. **RANGE** June–Aug.: w and n N. Eng. (uncommon). Late May, Sept.: scarce migrant in all N. Eng.

COMMON YELLOWTHROAT
Geothlypis trichas
WOOD WARBLER SUBFAMILY
5″. Male upperparts and sides uniformly olive green; throat and chest yellow; midbelly white; black mask over forehead and cheeks; broad white line above mask. Female olive-brown above; pale eye ring; throat yellow. Feeds low; often raises tail at angle. **VOICE** Song: rollicking *witchity-witchity-witchity-witch*. Call: flat *chep*. **HABITAT** Wooded swamps, marshes, shrubs. **RANGE** May–Oct.: all N. Eng.

HOODED WARBLER
Wilsonia citrina
WOOD WARBLER SUBFAMILY
5½″. Male olive green above; clea[r] yellow below; black hood encircle[s] yellow face and beady black eye[;] white stripes in fanned tail. Fema[le] olive above, yellow below, show[s] trace of hood. **VOICE** Loud *wee-[?]* *wee-ta wee-tee-oo*. **HABITAT** Shrubs [in] broadleaf woods. **RANGE** May–Sept[.:] CT, RI; strays to e MA.

WILSON'S WARBLER
Wilsonia pusilla
WOOD WARBLER SUBFAMILY
4¾″. Male olive green above; underparts, forehead, and eyebrow yellow; round black cap. Female has trace only of cap. Beady black eye on clear yellow face. **VOICE** Song: rapid, thin *chi chi chi chi jet jet*. **HABITAT** Woodland edges, waterside thickets. **RANGE** June–Aug.: ne VT, n NH, n and c ME. May, Sept.–Oct.: all N. Eng.

CANADA WARBLER
Wilsonia canadensis
WOOD WARBLER SUBFAMILY
5½″. Male upperparts and crow[n] slaty gray; yellow below, with neck[?] lace of black stripes on chest; yello[w] "spectacles"; lores and area belo[w] eyes black. Female gray above; ye[l]low below; faint gray necklace. **VOI[CE]** Song: musical *CHIP chupedy-swe[?]* *ditchety*. **HABITAT** Mixed wood[s,] waterside shrubs. **RANGE** May–Sep[t.:] all N. Eng.

female (left), male (right)

SCARLET TANAGER
Piranga olivacea
TANAGER SUBFAMILY

7". Summer male body and head brilliant scarlet red; wings, tail, and legs black; no crest or black on face like cardinal. Female and imm. olive green above; yellow below; wings and tail dusky olive. Bill thick, ivory, conical. Treetop dweller; often hard to see without binoculars and patience. **VOICE** Song: *sweet, burry shureet shureer shurooo*, like a hoarse robin. Call: *chip-burr*, 2nd note much lower. **HABITAT** Tall broadleaf woods, esp. oaks. **RANGE** May–early Oct.: all N. Eng.

male (left), female (right)

NORTHERN CARDINAL
Cardinalis cardinalis
GROSBEAK SUBFAMILY

9". Male grayish red above; underparts, crest, and cheeks bright red; black face encircles swollen, pointed, red bill. Female buffy brown; top of crest red; face black; bill red; wings and tail dusky red. Imm. like female, but bill black. Sought-after feeder bird that likes sunflower and safflower seeds, cracked corn. Virtually unknown 50 years ago in N. Eng; invaded from South due to winter bird-feeding. **VOICE** Song: pleasing clear whistles; variations on *wait wait wait cheer cheer cheer*. Call: short *chip*. **HABITAT** Woodland edges, shrubs, yards, gardens. **RANGE** Resident in all but higher mtns. and n ME.

male (left), female (right)

ROSE-BREASTED GROSBEAK
Pheucticus ludovicianus
GROSBEAK SUBFAMILY

8". Male back, head, wings, and tail black; large white patches on wings; rosy triangular patch on chest; sides, belly, and rump white. Female and imm. look like giant female Purple Finch: dark brown above; buffy white below with dark streaks; wing bars white; most of head solid brown; eyebrow and median crown stripe white. Bill thick, pale gray. **VOICE** Song: melodious deep warbling; robin-like, but faster. Call: sharp *squeak* or *chink*. **HABITAT** Broadleaf woods and woodland edges. **RANGE** May–Oct.: all N. Eng.

female (left), male (right)

INDIGO BUNTING
Passerina cyanea
GROSBEAK SUBFAMILY

5½". Summer male rich deep blue all over; wings and tail partly black; often appears all dark, ex. in very good light. Female uniformly dark brown above; pale dusky brown below; trace of blue on primaries. Bill medium-size, conical; slaty. Male sings conspicuously from exposed perch. **VOICE** Song: sweet paired *sweet sweet chew chew sweet sweet*. Call: sharp *spit*. **HABITAT** Woodland edges, shrubby fields. **RANGE** May–Oct.: all N. Eng.

EASTERN TOWHEE
"Rufous-sided Towhee"
Pipilo erythrophthalmus
AMERICAN SPARROW SUBFAMILY

8″. Male back, head, throat, and wings black; sides rufous; midbelly white. Female head, throat, and upperparts brown; sides rufous; breast and belly white. Eyes red; bill conical; white patches on wings; tail fairly long, outer tail feathers and terminal half of undertail white. Kicks around for insects in dead leaves. **VOICE** Song: 2 whistles, followed by high trill: *DRINK your teeeeee.* Call: loud *che-wink* or *tow-whee.* **HABITAT** Brushy areas, oak woods, open woods. **RANGE** Apr.–Oct.: c and s N. Eng. Nov.–Mar.: a few in se N. Eng.

AMERICAN TREE SPARROW
"Winter Sparrow"
Spizella arborea
AMERICAN SPARROW SUBFAMILY

6″. Rufous brown above; black stripes on back; unstreaked grayish white below; white wing bars; rufous eyeline and cap, not outlined; pale gray eyebrow, throat, and chest; black ace on chest. Usu. in flocks. **VOICE** Call: weak musical *twee-dle eet.* **HABITAT** Weedy fields, shrubs. **RANGE** Oct.–Apr.: all N. Eng.

CHIPPING SPARROW
Spizella passerina
AMERICAN SPARROW SUBFAMILY

5½″. Summer: brown above, with black streaks; clear pale gray below; white wing bars; rufous cap; white eyebrow; black eye line; narrow notched tail. Winter: striped brown crown. **VOICE** Song: long, run-together series of about 20 dry *chip* notes. **HABITAT** Open woods, fields, towns. **RANGE** Apr.–Oct.: all N. Eng. Nov.–Mar.: se N. Eng. (rare).

FIELD SPARROW
Spizella pusilla
AMERICAN SPARROW SUBFAMILY

5½". Upperparts, crown, and thin eye stripe rufous; black back stripes; white wing bars; breast clear grayish white; bill pink; eye ring white. **VOICE** Song: pleasing series of *teeuw* notes, each one higher in scale. **HABITAT** Fields with shrubs. **RANGE** Apr.–Sept.: c ME and south. Oct.–Mar.: some in s N. Eng.

SAVANNAH SPARROW
Passerculus sandwichensis
AMERICAN SPARROW SUBFAMILY

5½". Brown-and-white striped above and below; front of and often entire eyebrow yellow; bill and legs pink. Tail short, notched. Ipswich Sparrow race larger, paler; winters in small numbers alongside dark form in coastal dunes. **VOICE** Song: buzzy *zit zit zit zeeee zaaay*. **HABITAT** Grasslands, marshes, sandy areas. **RANGE** Apr.–Oct.: all N. Eng. Nov.–Mar.; some in coastal areas.

FOX SPARROW
Passerella iliaca
AMERICAN SPARROW SUBFAMILY

7". Upperparts and long tail bright rufous, with gray wash on back; white below, with heavy rufous stripes; gray eyebrow. Rustles in dead leaves. **VOICE** Song: rising, clear notes, followed by melodious, descending whistles. **HABITAT** Mixed woods, brush. **RANGE** Dec.–Feb.: some in s N. Eng. Mar.–Apr., late Oct.–Nov.: all N. Eng.

SONG SPARROW
Melospiza melodia
AMERICAN SPARROW SUBFAMILY

6¼". Dark brown stripes on warm brown back and on white underparts; grayish-brown eyebrow; large, central, dark brown spot on chest; tail fairly long, unpatterned, rounded. **VOICE** Song: *sweet sweet sweet towhee tritritritri*. **HABITAT** Shrubs, marshes, fields, watersides. **RANGE** Apr.–Oct.: all N. Eng. Oct.–Apr.: entire coast, lower-elevation valleys.

SWAMP SPARROW
Melospiza georgiana
AMERICAN SPARROW SUBFAMILY

5½". Summer: brown above, striped black on back; breast clear gray; with thin stripes on sides; belly whitish; much of wings and crown rufous; eyebrow gray; thin black "mustache"; throat white. **VOICE** Song: slow musical trill on one pitch. **HABITAT** Freshwater cattail marshes; shrubs. **RANGE** Apr.–Oct.: all N. Eng. Nov.–Mar.: s N. Eng. (local).

WHITE-THROATED SPARROW
Zonotrichia albicollis
AMERICAN SPARROW SUBFAMILY

6¾". Brown-striped above; white below; cheeks and chest gray; black and white (or dark brown and buff) crown stripes; yellow spot before eye; throat white; tail long, notched. **VOICE** Song: whistled *old Sam Peabody, Peabody, Peabody.* **HABITAT** Mixed woods, brush. **RANGE** June–Sept.: n and c N. Eng. Dec.–Mar.: s N. Eng. Apr.–May, Oct.–Nov.: all N. Eng.

DARK-EYED JUNCO
Junco hyemalis
AMERICAN SPARROW SUBFAMILY

6". Adult mainly slaty gray; midbelly white; bill white or pale pink, conical. Outer tail feathers white. Imm. gray areas are browner. Juv. has brown striped chest and back. Travels in flocks. **VOICE** Song: loose musical trill. Call: light *snack.* **HABITAT** Woods, summits, brush. **RANGE** May–Sept.: n and c N. Eng. Oct.–Apr.: c and s N. Eng.

BOBOLINK
Dolichonyx oryzivorus
BLACKBIRD SUBFAMILY

7″. Summer male black with large golden yellow nape patch; rump and base of wings white. Male from Aug. on, female, and imm.: buffy; sparrow-like; brown stripes on head, back, and sides. In spring, male flies in slow circles, with rapidly beating wings. In late summer, birds gather in marshes at dusk to roost. **VOICE** Song: rollicking repeated *bob-bob-o-lincoln*, often given in flight. Call: clear *pink*. **HABITAT** Hayfields and grasslands; perches on nearby fences, shrubs, trees. **RANGE** May–Sept.: all N. Eng.

EASTERN MEADOWLARK
Sturnella magna
BLACKBIRD SUBFAMILY

9″. Speckled brown above and on sides; yellow throat and breast, with black V on chest; dark brown and whitish head stripes. Flight reveals white outer tail feathers. Bill long, pointed, gray. Flies with flaps and glides. **VOICE** Song: slurred whistles *tee-you tee-yerr*. Call: harsh *serrt*. **HABITAT** Grasslands. **RANGE** Apr.–Oct.: all N. Eng. Nov.–Mar.: a few in se N. Eng.

RUSTY BLACKBIRD
Euphagus carolinus
BLACKBIRD SUBFAMILY

9″. Summer male dull purplish black; wings and tail glossed green. Summer female dull dark gray. Winter: both sexes blackish or brown with rusty scaling. Tail flat; bill long, thin; eyes yellow; no red on shoulder. **VOICE** Song: creaky *cush-a-lee cush-lay*. Call: harsh *shaq*. **HABITAT** Bogs, wooded and grassy watersides. **RANGE** Apr.–Sept.: n N. Eng. Mar.–Apr., late Sept.–Oct.: all N. Eng.

male   female

RED-WINGED BLACKBIRD
Agelaius phoeniceus
BLACKBIRD SUBFAMILY

9". Male all glossy black, with red shoulder epaulets bordered by yellow; yellow and much of red less visible in late summer and fall. Female heavily streaked brown: crown and eye line dark brown; eyebrow buffy. Bill fairly long, pointed; eyes black; tail fairly long and rounded. This species, robins, and grackles are earliest returning birds in spring. Frequently in flocks outside breeding season. **VOICE** Song: gurgling *conk-a-ree*. Calls: harsh *check*, high *tee-eek*. Calls from trees, shrubs, tall reeds. **HABITAT** Marshes, swamps, fields. **RANGE** Late Feb.–Nov.: all N. Eng. Dec.–mid-Feb.: some in s N. Eng.

COMMON GRACKLE
Quiscalus quiscula
BLACKBIRD SUBFAMILY

13". Male often appears black; actually has iridescent blue-green head, dark purple wings, bronzy green back and breast; long, wedge-shaped tail is held flat, or carried in V in courtship. Female very dark gray. Bill heavy, long, pointed; eyes yellow. Usu. in small to very large flocks outside breeding season. **VOICE** Song: short high *gurgle-eek*. Call: loud *shack*. **HABITAT** Farms, watersides, gardens, fields. **RANGE** Mar.–Nov.: all N. Eng. Dec.–Feb.: some in s N. Eng.

BROWN-HEADED COWBIRD
Molothrus ater
BLACKBIRD SUBFAMILY

7″. Adult male dark, shiny, greenish black with brown head. Adult female uniformly dull gray or dark brown. Imm. changes from drab brown-striped to slate gray. Bill medium-size, conical, gray. Flaps wings out and back to body quickly in flight. Travels in tight flocks outside nesting season. Brood parasite that is causing great losses in numbers of

male (left), female (top right), nestling (bottom right)

native songbirds; female lays single eggs in several nests of native songbirds; baby cowbird pushes out other eggs and babies, and is raised by foster parents. **VOICE** Song: bubbly, creaking *bubble-lee come seee*. Flight call: high *weee teetee*. **HABITAT** Open fields, farms, lawns. **RANGE** Apr.–Nov.: all N. Eng. Dec.–Mar.: some in s N. Eng.

BALTIMORE ORIOLE
"Northern Oriole"
Icterus galbula
BLACKBIRD SUBFAMILY

male (left), female (right)

8½″. Male back, head, throat, wings, and tail black; underparts and shoulder bright orange; white patches on wing; yellow tail corners. Female brownish or olive-gray above; face, underparts, and rump yellowish. Bill fairly thin, pointed. Stays quite high in trees; will visit feeders for fruit and sugar water. Builds woven, hanging, sock-like grass and fiber pouch that stays on tree through most winters. **VOICE** Song: 4–8 pleasing whistles. Call: low whistled *tee-tew*. Call of young: plaintive *tee dit-it* from treetops. **HABITAT** Broadleaf woods, shade trees. **RANGE** May–Sept.: all N. Eng.

PINE GROSBEAK
Pinicola enucleator
FINCH FAMILY

9". Male back black-striped; underparts, head, and rump pink; wings black, with white wing bars; tail black, long, notched. Female body gray; head rusty. Bill rather small, stubby. **VOICE** Song: musical warble. Call: whistled *tee wee tee.* **HABITAT** Summer: coniferous woods. Winter: broadleaf trees with fruit. **RANGE** Resident in far n N. Eng. Some winters (Nov.–Mar.): all N. Eng.

AMERICAN GOLDFINCH
Carduelis tristis
FINCH FAMILY

5". Summer male brilliant yellow; cap, wings, and notched tail black; rump white. Summer female olive green above; throat and chest yellow. Winter male brown above; face and shoulder yellow. Winter female grayish with or without trace of yellow on throat. All have white wing bars on black wings. Slow, undulating flight. **VOICE** Song: canary-like; long, pleasing, rising and falling twittering. Call: rising *sweee-eat.* Flight call: *per chicory.* **HABITAT** Fields, woodland edges, farms, yards. **RANGE** Resident in N. Eng.

male (left), female (right)

PURPLE FINCH
Carpodacus purpureus
FINCH FAMILY

6". Male back and wings mixed brown and rose; head, throat, chest sides, and rump rosy; dull brownish-red cheek and "mustache." Female darker brown and more heavily striped than House Finch; head has white eyebrow, dark brown cheek patch, and wide brown "mustache." Tail deeply forked. **VOICE** Song: lively complex warbling. Calls: musical *pur-lee* and sharp *chink.* **HABITAT** Coniferous and mixed woods, woodland edges, yards. **RANGE** Apr.–Nov.: all N. Eng. Dec.–Mar.: some in s N. Eng.

female

male

HOUSE FINCH
Carpodacus mexicanus
FINCH FAMILY

5½". Male back, midcrown, wings, and tail brown; sides and belly whitish, streaked brown; 2 pale wing bars; wide eyebrow, throat, and chest rosy red. Female upperparts and head plain dull brown; dusky below, with brown streaks. Recent introduction from w U.S. and Mexico; now far more common than related Purple Finch, esp. in cities, suburbs, and at feeders. Sings and initiates courtship in early Feb. **VOICE** Song: musical warbling ending with a downslurred *jeer*. **HABITAT** Cities, residential areas, garden trees. **RANGE** Resident in c and s N. Eng.

COMMON REDPOLL
Carduelis flammea
FINCH FAMILY

5". Male whitish, with brown stripes; red cap; pink wash on chest; white wing bars; stubby yellow bill; black chin; tail black, deeply notched. Female similar; has white chest. Tail forked. **VOICE** Call: rising *swee-eet*. **HABITAT** Brushy and weedy areas. **RANGE** Dec.–Mar.: all N. Eng.; very common every few winters.

PINE SISKIN
Carduelis pinus
FINCH FAMILY

5". Very heavily striped brown above and below; yellow stripe on wing; yellow on basal sides of notched tail. Bill thin, pointed. **VOICE** Song: wheezy trills and warbles mixed with its calls. Calls: loud *clee-up* and rising *shreee*. **HABITAT** Coniferous and mixed woods, yards. **RANGE** May–Sept.: w and n N. Eng. Oct.–Apr.: all N. Eng.

male   female

EVENING GROSBEAK
Coccothraustes vespertinus
FINCH FAMILY

8″. Male back brown; rump yellow; breast brown; belly yellow; head dark brown; eyebrow and forehead yellow; wings black, with white secondaries. Female plain gray-brown; wings black, with large white spots. Bill massive, ivory; head large; tail black, fairly short. **VOICE** Song: short warble. Call: ringing *cleeer*. **HABITAT** Mixed woods; trees in residential areas. **RANGE** Resident in w and n N. Eng. Nov.–Apr.: c and s N. Eng. Common in some winters.

male   female

HOUSE SPARROW
Passer domesticus
OLD WORLD SPARROW FAMILY

6″. Male back and wings rufous; underparts, crown, cheeks, and rump gray; 1 white wing bar; throat and upper chest black (only chin black in winter); wide chestnut stripe behind eye. Female plain brown above, ex. for blackish back streaks; pale dusky below. Abundant European import and follower of human activities. Takes bulk of seed at most feeders; kills nestlings and removes eggs of other birds at birdhouses. **VOICE** Song: frequently given *chireep* and *chereep* notes. Call: *chir-rup*. **HABITAT** Cities, malls, parks, farms. **RANGE** Resident in N. Eng.

Mammals

All members of the vertebrate class Mammalia are warm-blooded and able to maintain a near-constant body temperature. Males generally have an external penis for direct internal fertilization of the female's eggs. Almost all mammals are born live rather than hatching from eggs (exceptions are the platypus and the echidnas of Australia). Mammary glands, unique to mammals, produce milk that is high in nutrients and fat and promotes rapid growth in the young. Mammals have abundant skin glands, used for temperature regulation (sweating), coat maintenance, territory-marking, sex and species recognition, breeding cycle signals, and even defense, as in skunks and others that can repel predators with their powerful secretions.

Nine mammalian orders are represented in New England, including humans (members of the primates order). Opossums (order Didelphimorphia) give birth to young in an embryonic state; they then develop in a separate fur-lined pouch on the mother's belly. The tiny energetic shrews and moles (Insectivora), which eat insects and other invertebrates, have long snouts, short dense fur, and five toes on each foot. Bats (Chiroptera), with their enlarged, membrane-covered forelimbs, are the only mammals that truly fly.

Hares and rabbits (Lagomorpha) resemble large rodents but have four upper incisor teeth—a large front pair and a small pair directly behind them—that grow continuously, and five toes on their front feet and five in back; digits on all feet are very small. Rodents (Rodentia—including chipmunks, marmots, squirrels, mice, rats, muskrats, voles, porcupines, and beavers) have two upper incisor teeth that grow continuously, and most have four toes on their front feet and five in back.

Carnivores (Carnivora)—bears, coyotes, wolves, foxes, weasels, raccoons, cats, and seals—have long canine teeth for stabbing prey, and most have sharp cheek teeth for slicing meat. The even-toed hoofed mammals (Artiodactyla), in New England represented by the deer family, have two or four toes that form a cloven hoof. The whales, dolphins, and porpoises (Cetacea) are hairless; in both seals and cetaceans, the legs have evolved into flippers.

Most mammals have an insulating layer of fur that allows them to maintain a fairly constant body temperature independent of their surroundings, making them among the most successful animals in cold climates. Many molt twice a year and have a noticeably thicker coat in winter. Some, such as certain weasels and hares, change colors, developing a concealing white coat in winter. In whales, porpoises, and dolphins, thick layers of insulating blubber, rather than hair, retain body heat. The ability to maintain a high body temperature allows many mammals to prosper in below-freezing temperatures.

The body parts and appendages of mammals exhibit a wide and adaptive variety of sizes, shapes, and functions. Most mammals have well-developed eyes, ears, and noses that provide good night vision, hearing, and sense of smell. Mammalian teeth range from fine points for capturing insects (bats and insectivores) to chisel-like gnawing teeth (rabbits, rodents, and hoofed mammals), wide plant-crushers (rodents and hoofed mammals), and heavy pointed instruments for flesh-ripping (carnivores and seals). The whales' huge brushes, called baleen, for straining plankton, are not actually teeth but are composed of fingernail-like keratin.

Mammals generally have four limbs. In many rodents, in some carnivores, and in primates, the ends of the forelimbs are modified into complex, manipulative hands. Solid hooves support the heavy weight of moose and deer.

In the species accounts, the typical adult length given is from the tip of the nose to the end of the tail, followed by the tail length; for larger mammals, shoulder height is also given. Wingspan is given for bats, when known.

Mammal Sign and Tracks

The evidence that a particular animal is or has been in a certain area is called its "sign." The sign can be scat (fecal matter), burrow openings, nutshells, tracks, or other evidence. Tracks are a useful aid in confirming the presence of mammal species. Impressions vary depending on the substrate and whether the animal was walking or running. Animals can leave clear tracks in mud, dirt, snow, and sand, usually larger ones in wet mud and snow. Because animals come to ponds or streams to drink or feed, tracks are likely to be found on their shores; damp mud often records tracks in fine detail, sometimes showing claws or webbing. Prints in snow may leave a less clear impression but can often be followed for a long distance, and may show the pattern of the animal's stride. The track drawings below, of selected mammals that live in New England, are not to relative scale.

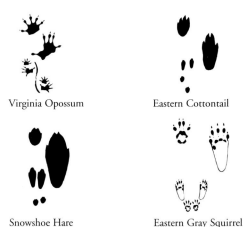

Virginia Opossum

Eastern Cottontail

Snowshoe Hare

Eastern Gray Squirrel

American Beaver

Common Muskrat

Common Porcupine

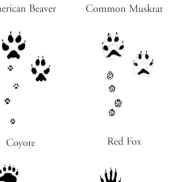

Coyote

Red Fox

Common Gray Fox

Black Bear

Common Raccoon

Long-tailed Weasel

Mink

Striped Skunk

Northern River Otter

Bobcat

White-tailed Deer

Moose

VIRGINIA OPOSSUM
Didelphis virginiana
OPOSSUM FAMILY

L 28″; T 11″. Grizzled gray, with mix of black underfur and longer white guard hairs. Head pointed; nose long; face white, with long whiskers; ears small, round, black with white tip. Legs short, black; feet have 5 digits; hind-feet have opposable, grasping inner thumbs. Tail long, tapered, naked, pink with black base. Eats fruit, nuts, bird eggs, large insects, carrion. Hangs from branches using wraparound, prehensile tail. If surprised at close range, may play possum" (play dead). **BREEDING** 1–14 (avg. 8) pea-size young attach themselves to nipples in mother's pouch for 2 months; 2–3 litters per year. **SIGN** Tracks: hindprint 2″ wide, 3 middle toes close, outer toes well spread; foreprint slightly smaller, star-like. **HABITAT** Broadleaf woods, watersides, farms. **ACTIVITY** Nocturnal; much less active in winter. **RANGE** c and s N. Eng.; from White Mtns. and s ME south.

NORTHERN SHORT-TAILED SHREW
Blarina brevicauda
SHREW FAMILY

L 4¾″; T 1″. Body and head grayish black. Nose conical; jaws long, open wide, exposing many fine teeth. Eyes tiny; ears tiny, hidden in fur. Legs short; 5 toes on each foot. Tail nearly hairless, short for a shrew. Heart can beat up to 700 times a minute. Eats its weight daily; attacks worms, snails, insects, and mice, paralyzing them with poisonous saliva. Builds underground tunnels where it caches food. **CAUTION** Poisonous, but not fatal to humans; bites result in intense painful swelling. **BREEDING** 3–10 (avg. 5–7) young; several litters per year. **HABITAT** Woods, meadows, watersides, brush. **ACTIVITY** Intensely active day and night; year-round.

HAIRY-TAILED MOLE
Parascalops breweri
MOLE FAMILY

L 6"; T 1¼". Slate-colored. Snout pointed, naked, flexible; eyes and ears tiny, hidden. Legs very short; feet short, wide, long-clawed, turned outward. Tail short, hairy. Eats earthworms, other invertebrates. Builds winter foraging tunnels up to 20" below ground. **BREEDING** 4–5 blind, naked young Apr.–May. **SIGN** Low, rounded ridges in soil. **HABITAT** Well-drained woods, lawns. **ACTIVITY** Day and night; year-round.

STAR-NOSED MOLE
Condylura cristata
MOLE FAMILY

L 7"; T 3". Slate-colored, with star-like snout fan of 22 pink tentacles (may be prey-sensing device). Eyes and ears tiny, hidden. Legs very short; feet short, wide, long-clawed, turned outward. Tail long, hairy, wider in middle. Often aboveground. **BREEDING** 3–7 young May–June. **SIGN** Piles of dirt outside 2" burrow openings. **HABITAT** Waterside woods, fields, lawns. **ACTIVITY** Day and night; year-round.

Bats

Bats are the only mammals that truly fly (the flying squirrels glide). The bones and muscles in the forelimbs of bats are elongated; thin, usually black wing membranes are attached to four extremely long fingers. When bats are at rest, the wings are folded along the forearm; they use their short, claw-like thumbs for crawling about. Small insectivorous bats beat their wings six to eight times a second.

Bats are mainly nocturnal, though some species are occasionally active in the early morning and late afternoon. Their slender, mouse-like bodies are well furred, and their eyesight, while not excellent, is quite adequate to detect predators and general landscape features. Most use echolocation (sonar) to locate flying insects and avoid obstacles. In flight, they emit 30–60 high-frequency calls per second that bounce off objects and return to their large ears. Bats interpret these reflected sounds as they close in on prey or evade an obstacle. Echolocation sounds are mainly inaudible to humans, but bats also give shrill squeaks most humans can hear. By day, most bats hang upside-down from the ceilings of caves, tree hollows, and attics, using one or both feet. Members of solitary species may roost alone under a branch or among the foliage of a tall tree. In other species, large colonies gather in caves and under natural and man-made overhangs.

All New England bats are insect-eaters. By night, they pursue larger individual insects through the air or glean them from trees, and skim open-mouthed through swarms of midges. A bat will trap a large flying insect in the membrane between its hindlegs, then seize it with its teeth. Because of the lack of insects in winter, New England bats either hibernate here or migrate south to hibernate or feed in winter. Sheltered hibernation roosts provide protection from extreme cold.

Watch for bats overhead on warm summer evenings, especially around water, where insects are abundant and where bats may skim the water surface to drink.

Parts of a Bat

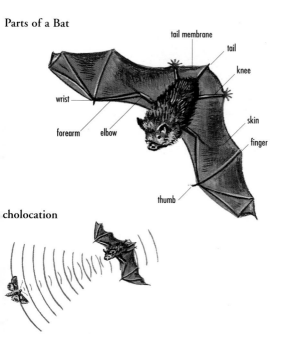

tail membrane · tail · knee · wrist · skin · forearm · elbow · finger · thumb

cholocation

LITTLE BROWN MYOTIS
"Little Brown Bat"
Myotis lucifugus
VESPERTILIONID BAT FAMILY

L 3½"; WS 9". Rich glossy brown above; buffy below. Ears short for a bat, rounded, black; face broad, blunt, black. Often flies before dusk; flight erratic. Squeaks are audible. Most common bat in N. Eng. **BREEDING** Mates in fall; female stores sperm until spring; 1 young born in June in attics, barns, caves. **HABITAT** Streams, lakes, trees, fields, attics; roosts in trees, caves, mines, dark places. **ACTIVITY** Summer: active. Winter: hibernates in caves.

EASTERN RED BAT
Lasiurus borealis
VESPERTILIONID BAT FAMILY

L 4½"; WS 12". Body white below. Male head and upperparts rich reddish orange. Female buffy, frosted white, above; head pale buffy-orange. Ears short, rounded. Wings long, pointed. Tail pointed. Flight strong, fast; gives sharp audible chirp. **BREEDING** 1–4 young in June. **HABITAT** Woods, woodland edges; roosts in tree foliage. **ACTIVITY** Summer: active. Winter: most migrate south, some by day along coast and over ocean.

BIG BROWN BAT
Eptesicus fuscus
VESPERTILIONID BAT FAMILY

L 4½"; WS 12". Dark brown above; pale brown below. Wing and tail membranes furless. Face and ears broad, black. Flight straight, fast. Flies later in autumn, earlier in spring than others. **BREEDING** 2 young in June. **HABITAT** All habitats; roosts and breeds in attics, barns, tree hollows, behind shutters, under bridges. **ACTIVITY** Summer: active. Winter: hibernates in N. Eng.

EASTERN COTTONTAIL
Sylvilagus floridanus
HARE AND RABBIT FAMILY

L 17″; T 1½″. Grayish brown, mixed with black hairs; belly white. White eye ring; many have white spot on forehead. Ears to 2½″ long, with thin black stripe on upper edges. Rusty wash on nape. Legs buffy; hindlegs heavily muscled. Raises fluffy tail when bounding away, displaying white underside ("cottontail"). **BREEDING** 4–5 young Apr.–May; several litters each year. **SIGN** Clean-cut woody sprigs; stripped bark on young trees above deep snow. Tracks: 3″ oblong hindprints in front of smaller, round foreprints. Scat: piles of dark brown, pea-size pellets. **HABITAT** Fields, woodland edges, thickets, gardens. **ACTIVITY** Late afternoon, night, early morning; spends midday in nest-like "form" in grass, thickets; year-round, ex. in deep snows. **RANGE** s and w N. Eng. **New England Cottontail** *(S. transitionalis)* has black patch between ears, usu. lacks rusty nape.

SNOWSHOE HARE
"Varying Hare"
Lepus americanus
HARE AND RABBIT FAMILY

L 19″; T 2″. Summer: brown, with reddish or yellowish wash; somewhat blackish toward rear; short tail dusky white below. Winter: pure white (sometimes mottled with brown), ex. for black ear tips; thick fur on hind-feet creates "snowshoes." Larger than a cottontail, with longer (4″) black-tipped ears, larger hindfeet. If surprised, may thump hindfeet, then run off at up to 30 mph. **BREEDING** 3 young per litter; alert, furred, able to hop in hours. 1st litter April; 2 more follow. **SIGN** Packed-down trails in snow. Scat: piles of brown, lima bean–size pellets. Hindprint 4–5″, toes widely spread. **HABITAT** Coniferous and mixed woods. **ACTIVITY** Nocturnal; rests by day in nest-like "form" or hollow log. **RANGE** w, n, and c N. Eng.

Rodents

Rodentia is the world's largest mammalian order; more than half of all mammal species and many more than half of all mammal individuals on earth are rodents. In addition to the mice and rats (a family that also includes the mouse-like but chubbier voles and the muskrats), other rodent families in New England are the squirrels (including chipmunks and the Woodchuck), jumping mice, porcupines, and beavers. New England species range from mice weighing roughly an ounce to the American Beaver, which may weigh up to 66 pounds, but most rodents are relatively small. They are distinguished by having only two pairs of incisors—one upper and one lower—and no canines, leaving a wide gap between incisors and molars. Rodent incisors are enameled on the front only; the working of the upper teeth against the lower ones wears away the softer inner surfaces, producing a short, chisel-like, beveled edge ideal for gnawing. The incisors grow throughout an animal's life (if they did not, they shortly would be worn away), and rodents must gnaw enough to keep the incisors from growing too long. The eyes are bulbous and placed high on the side of the head, enabling the animals to detect danger over a wide arc.

EASTERN CHIPMUNK
Tamias striatus
SQUIRREL FAMILY

L 9″; T 4″. Reddish brown above; gray stripe from crown to back; sides have whitish-buff stripe edged with black; belly white. Pale buffy lines above and below eye; ears short, buffy. Tail long, fluffy, grizzled blackish. Calls include bird-like *chip* and soft *cuck-cuck.* Gathers nuts, seeds; usu. forages on ground. **BREEDING** 3–5 young in May. **SIGN** Burrow entrances 2″ wide, without dirt piles, on wooded slope. Tracks: hindprint 1⅞″; foreprint much smaller. **HABITAT** Mixed woods, brush. **ACTIVITY** Summer: active. Winter: hibernates.

WOODCHUCK
"Groundhog" "Eastern Marmot"
Marmota monax
SQUIRREL FAMILY

L 21″; T 5″. Grizzled brown above, some with blackish or rufous tones; buffy below. Ears short, rounded; face has pale buffy patches. Legs short, powerful. Tail bushy. Gives shrill whistle, followed by *chuck, chuck.* Vegetarian; eats heavily in summer, early fall; does not store food. Climbs trees; digs burrows. **BREEDING** 4–5 young Apr.–May. **SIGN** 8–12″ burrow entrance, with dirt piles on sides. **HABITAT** Fields, woodland edges, farms, gardens. **ACTIVITY** Summer: feeds by day. Winter: hibernates early, deeply.

RED SQUIRREL
Tamiasciurus hudsonicus
SQUIRREL FAMILY

L 13″; T 5″. Underparts white; tail long, bushy, reddish. Summer: dark reddish gray above, with black side stripe; ears rounded. Winter: paler above; no side stripe; ears tufted. Mainly arboreal. Stores seeds, nuts in large caches. Noisy; gives angry chattering *chick-r-r-r-r*. **BREEDING** 4–5 young Apr.–May and/or Aug.–Sept. in tree cavity or leaf-and-stick nest in treetop. **SIGN** Cones, nuts with ragged hole at one end. Tracks: hindprint 1½″; 5 toes print. **HABITAT** Mixed woods. **ACTIVITY** Mainly by day, year-round.

SOUTHERN FLYING SQUIRREL
Glaucomys volans
SQUIRREL FAMILY

L 9″; T 3″. Brown above: darker, redder in summer, paler fawn in winter; white below. Eyes huge; ears rounded. Tail flat, bushy, narrow-based. Folds of furred skin connect fore- and hindlimbs, allowing glides up to 200′. Visits birdfeeders at night; mainly eats insects. **BREEDING** 3–4 blind, naked young in spring, late summer. Nests in tree cavities, attics, birdhouses. **HABITAT** Broadleaf and mixed woods. **ACTIVITY** Nocturnal. Winter: enters state of torpor in cold spells; active during thaws. **RANGE** c and s N. Eng. **Northern Flying Squirrel** *(G. sabrinus)* larger (11″), richer brown; n and c N. Eng.

EASTERN GRAY SQUIRREL
Sciurus carolinensis
SQUIRREL FAMILY

L 19″; T 9″. Gray above, white below; in summer head, legs, and sides tawny brown. Eye ring and edge of snout buffy; tail long, bushy, grizzled blackish and white. All-black individuals occur locally. Vocal; gives variety of chattering and clucking calls. Eats nuts, buds, inner bark, fruit on ground and in trees. N. Eng.'s most commonly seen mammal. **BREEDING** 2 litters of usu. 2–3 young Apr.–May in nest in tree cavity. **SIGN** Summer: stick platform in tree; gnawed nutshells and corncobs. Winter: spherical leaf nest in tree; holes in snow above nut caches. Tracks longer hindprints in front of smaller foreprints. **HABITAT** Broadleaf and mixed woods; towns. **ACTIVITY** By day, year-round.

AMERICAN BEAVER
Castor canadensis
BEAVER FAMILY

lodge

gnawed tree

L 3′4″; T 16″. Rich dark brown. Back high, rounded. Eyes and ears small. Legs short; feet webbed; claws small. Paddle-shaped tail black, scaly, rounded, flattened horizontally. Eats bark, twigs of broadleaf trees; stashes branches underwater for winter use. Swims with only head above water. Slaps tail on water loudly to warn family of danger. Fells trees by gnawing trunk down to a "waist" that finally cannot support the tree. Dams small streams with sticks, reeds, saplings caulked with mud. In middle of new pond, builds dome-like lodge up to 6′ high and 20′ wide; underwater tunnels reach up to dry chambers, hidden from view, above water level. Ponds formed by dams promote growth of habitat (broadleaf trees) favored by beavers; dams also help form marshes for other wildlife. N. Amer.'s largest rodent. **BREEDING** Usu. 3–5 young May–July, inside lodge. **SIGN** Dams, lodges, cone-shaped tree stumps. 12″ territorial scent mounds of mud and grass. Tracks: 4–6″, 5-toed hindprint covers smaller foreprint. **HABITAT** Ponds, rivers, adjacent woods. **ACTIVITY** Mainly at dusk and night, year-round.

WHITE-FOOTED MOUSE
Peromyscus leucopus
MOUSE AND RAT FAMILY

L 7″; T 3″. Reddish brown; middle of back blackish. Ears and eyes large. Tail long, finely haired. Host, with White-tailed Deer, of Lyme disease tick and bacterium. **BREEDING** Many litters of usu. 5 young Apr.–Nov. in tree nest. **SIGN** Piles of nuts, each with 2–3 small openings. Hindprint ⅝″; narrow heel, 5 splayed toes. **HABITAT** Dry pine-oak woods. **ACTIVITY** Nocturnal, year-round, ex. in extreme weather. **RANGE** All N. Eng., ex. n ME.

BROWN RAT
"Norway Rat"
Rattus norvegicus
MOUSE AND RAT FAMILY

L 15″; T 7″. Grayish brown above; belly gray; ears partly hidden in fur; tail long, scaly. Digs network of tunnels 2–3″ wide in ground. Eats insects, stored grain, garbage. **BREEDING** 6 litters of 6–8 young a year. **SIGN** Holes in walls, paths to food supplies. Tracks: long, 5-toed hindprint in front of rounder foreprint. **HABITAT** Cities, farms. **ACTIVITY** Mostly nocturnal, year-round.

MEADOW VOLE
Microtus pennsylvanicus
MOUSE AND RAT FAMILY

L 7″; T 2″. Buffy brown in summer; grayish brown in winter. Ears small. Tail much shorter than body. Major prey of foxes, owls, hawks. **BREEDING** 6–17 litters of 1–9 young per year. **SIGN** Summer: piles of grass cuttings along runways. Winter: runways in snow and underground. Nests under boards, grass clumps. Hindprint ⅝″; 5 widely splayed toes. **HABITAT** Marshes, fields, woods, farms. **ACTIVITY** Day and night, year-round.

SOUTHERN RED-BACKED VOLE
Clethrionomys gapperi
MOUSE AND RAT FAMILY

L 5″; T 1½″. Reddish brown; chestnut stripe above, from nose to lower back; grayish below. Ears small. Tail shorter than body. Its color makes this one of the most easily identifiable small mammals. **BREEDING** Several litters of 2–8 young Mar.–Dec. **SIGN** Runways and burrows on forest floor. **HABITAT** Coniferous and mixed woods. **ACTIVITY** Mainly nocturnal, year-round.

MEADOW JUMPING MOUSE
Zapus hudsonius
JUMPING MOUSE FAMILY

L 9″; T 5″. Dark brown on back; orange-brown on sides; white below. Head small, rounded. Large hind thighs allow hops of up to 3′. Tail thin, much longer than body. **BREEDING** 2 litters of 2–8 young June–Oct. **SIGN** Match-length cuttings of grass. **HABITAT** Meadows, marshes, brush. **ACTIVITY** Summer: day and (esp.) night. Winter: hibernates for long period.

COMMON MUSKRAT
Ondatra zibethicus
MOUSE AND RAT FAMILY

L 23″; T 10″. Fur rich brown, dense, glossy; belly silver. Tail long, scaly, blackish, vertically flattened, tapering to a point. Hindfeet partially webbed, larger than forefeet. Eyes and ears small. Excellent, steady swimmer, with head, back, and sculling tail visible. Mainly eats aquatic vegetation. **BREEDING** 2–3 litters of usu. 6–7 young a year Apr.–Sept. **SIGN** Conspicuous "lodge" of cattails, roots, and mud floats in marsh or other body of water; rises up to 3′ above surface of water. Burrows in stream banks. Tracks: 2–3″ narrow hindprint (5 toes print); smaller round foreprint; often with tail drag mark. **HABITAT** Fresh and salt marshes, ponds, rivers, canals. **ACTIVITY** Day and night; lodge-bound on coldest days.

COMMON PORCUPINE
Erethizon dorsatum
NEW WORLD PORCUPINE FAMILY

L 33″; T 8″. Blackish. Long wiry guard hairs on front half of body; up to 30,000 shorter, heavier quills (hairs modified into sharp, mostly hollow spines) on front of body but mainly on rump and longish, rounded tail; underfur long, soft, wooly. Back high-arching; legs short. Soles of feet knobbed; claws long, curved; walks pigeon-toed on ground. Voice: squeals and grunts. Eats green plants, and twigs, buds, and bark of trees; sometimes damages wooden buildings and poles. **BREEDING** 1 young Apr.–June. **SIGN** Tooth marks on bark; irreg. patches of bark stripped from tree trunks and limbs. Tracks: inward-facing, up to 3″ long; claw tips well forward. Scat: piles of variable-shaped pellets near crevice or base of feeding tree. **HABITAT** Woods. **ACTIVITY** Mainly nocturnal, year-round.

Carnivores

Members of the order Carnivora mainly eat meat, though many also eat a variety of fruit, berries, and vegetation. Carnivores vary greatly in size, from tiny weasels to massive bears. They have long canine teeth for stabbing prey, and most have sharp cheek teeth for slicing meat. None truly hibernates, but several den up in well-insulated logs and burrows, and sleep soundly during colder parts of the winter. Most live on land, although otters spend most of their time in water, and seals (covered on page 372 with other marine mammals) haul out on land mainly for mating and giving birth. Most carnivores have a single yearly litter of offspring, which are born blind and receive many months, sometimes even a year or more, of parental care. New England carnivore families include the bears, dogs (coyote and foxes), weasels (fisher, mink, skunk, otter), raccoons, cats, and seals.

COYOTE
Canis latrans
DOG FAMILY

H 25″; L 4′; T 13″. Coat long, coarse; grizzled gray, buffy, and black. Muzzle long, narrow, brownish; ears rufous; tail bushy, black-tipped. Voice: bark; flat howl; series of *yip* notes followed by wavering howl. Runs up to 40 mph. Eats small mammals, birds, frogs, snakes. 20th-century invader from w U.S. **BREEDING** 4–8 pups Apr. **SIGN** Den mouths 2′ wide, on slopes. Tracks: in nearly straight line; foreprint larger, 2⅜″ long. Scat: dog-like, usu. full of hair. **HABITAT** Woods, brushy fields, towns. **ACTIVITY** Mainly nocturnal, year-round.

RED FOX
Vulpes vulpes
DOG FAMILY

H 15″; L 3′2″; T 14″. Rusty orange above; whitish below; legs reddish above, black below. Muzzle narrow; ears pointed, black. Tail bushy, white-tipped. Eats rodents, rabbits, birds, insects, berries, fruit. Has strong scent. Gives short *yap*, long howls. Native and introduced English stock now intermixed. **BREEDING** 1–10 young Mar.–Apr. **SIGN** Den often a woodchuck burrow on a rise, entrance enlarged to 3′. Tracks: slightly larger foreprint 2⅛″ long; shows 4 toe pads. **HABITAT** Brushy and open areas. **ACTIVITY** Mainly nocturnal, year-round.

COMMON GRAY FOX
Urocyon cinereoargenteus
DOG FAMILY

H 15″; L 3′2″; T 13″. Grizzled silvery gray above; throat, midbelly white; collar, lower sides, legs, sides of tail rusty; top and tip of tail black. Eats rabbits, rodents, birds, grasshoppers, fruit, berries. Climbs trees. **BREEDING** 2–7 young in summer. **SIGN** Den hidden in natural crevice in woods; often has snagged hair, bone scraps near entrance. Tracks: foreprint 1½″ long; hindprint slightly narrower. **HABITAT** Wooded and brushy areas. **ACTIVITY** Day or night, but secretive; year-round. **RANGE** c and s N. Eng.; more common in se MA.

BLACK BEAR
Ursus americanus
BEAR FAMILY

H 40″; L 5′; T 4″; male much larger than female. Black, long-haired; often has white patch on chest. Head round; muzzle long, brownish; ears short, rounded. Legs long. More vegetarian than most carnivores; eats inner layer of tree bark, berries, fruit, plants, fish, honeycombs, insects in rotten logs, and vertebrates, incl. small mammals. Powerful swimmer and climber; runs up to 30 mph. N. Eng.'s largest carnivore. **CAUTION** Do not feed, approach, or get between one and its food or cubs; will usu. flee, but can cause serious injury. Campers must firmly seal up food. **BREEDING** Usu. 2 cubs, about ½ lb. at birth, born in den Jan.–Feb. **SIGN** Torn-apart stumps; turned-over boulders; torn-up burrows; hair on shaggy-barked trees. Tracks: foreprints 5″ wide; hindprints to 9″ long. Scat: dog-like. **HABITAT** Woods, swamps, dumps; spreading closer to suburbs. **ACTIVITY** Mainly nocturnal, but often out in day-time; does not hibernate. **RANGE** nw CT; w MA; VT; c and n NH; ME.

COMMON RACCOON
Procyon lotor
RACCOON FAMILY

L 32″; T 9″. Coat long and thick, grizzled grayish brown. Black mask below white eyebrow; white sides on narrow muzzle. Legs medium-length; paws buffy; flexible toes used for climbing trees and washing food. Tail ⅓ body length; thick; banded pale yellow-brown and black. Swims well; can run up to 15 mph. Omnivorous; feeds in upland and aquatic habitats; raids trash bins. **BREEDING** Usu. 4 young Apr.–May. **SIGN** Den in hollow tree or crevice. Tracks: flat-footed; hindprint much longer than wide, 4″; foreprint round-ed, 3″; claws show on all 5 toes. **HABITAT** Woods and scrub near water; towns. **ACTIVITY** Mainly nocturnal, but sometimes seen in daytime. Winter: dens up; active in milder periods.

SHORT-TAILED WEASEL
"Ermine"
Mustela erminea
WEASEL FAMILY

L 11"; T 2"; female smaller. Summer: brown above; underparts, insides of legs, feet white; tail has brown base, black tip. Winter: white, with black tail tip. Tail thin, furred. Expert mouser; also takes rabbits, birds, frogs, insects. Tireless, active hunter. **BREEDING** 4–9 young in Apr. **SIGN** Spiral scat along trails. Tracks: similar to Long-tailed Weasel's, but slightly smaller. **HABITAT** Brush, fields, wetlands. **ACTIVITY** Day and night, year-round.

FISHER
Martes pennanti
WEASEL FAMILY

L 3'2"; T 15"; female smaller. Dark brown above and below; white-tipped hair gives frosted appearance. Head broad; neck heavy; snout pointed; ears small; tail bushy. Usu. solitary. Hunts porcupines; attacks head, then eats through unprotected underside; rarely eats fish. **BREEDING** 1–4 young born in Mar. **SIGN** Porcupine remains. Tracks: 2½" wide in snow; wider than long. Scat: 4–6"; dark, cylindrical, often with porcupine quills. **HABITAT** Coniferous and mixed woods. **ACTIVITY** Day and night, in trees and on ground; year-round. **RANGE** w and n N. Eng., expanding into e MA.

Rabies

Rabies is a serious viral disease that is carried and can be transmitted by bats, foxes, raccoons, and skunks, as well as domestic animals; it can make humans deathly ill. Infected animals may be agitated and aggressive, or fearless and lethargic; noctural animals who are diseased may roam about fearlessly in daytime. As the disease drives infected individuals to try to bite others, rabid animals must be avoided. Stay away from any animal that is acting strangely, and report it to animal-control officers. The disease, which attacks the central nervous system, has an incubation period of 10 days to a year. If you are bitten by a possibly rabid animal, you must immediately consult a doctor for a series of injections that will save your life. There is no cure once symptoms emerge.

winter coat

LONG-TAILED WEASEL
Mustela frenata
WEASEL FAMILY

L 16″; T 5″; female smaller. Brown above; white below; feet and outside of legs brown. Tail thin, furred, with brown base, black tip. Many, but not all, develop white winter coat Nov.–Mar., but retain black tail tip. Wraps sinewy body around prey; kills by biting base of skull. Good swimmer, climber. **BREEDING** 6–8 young Apr.–May. **SIGN** Cache of dead rodents under log; drag marks in snow. Tracks: hindprint ¾″ wide, 1″ long; foreprint a bit wider, half as long. **HABITAT** Woods, brush, fields. **ACTIVITY** Day and night, year-round.

MINK
Mustela vison
WEASEL FAMILY

L 21″; T 7″; female smaller. Lustrous blackish brown above and below; chin white. Muzzle pointed; ears tiny; tail bushy. (Weasels are white below; have thinner tails.) Swims often; eats fish, birds, rodents, frogs; often travels far in search of food. **BREEDING** 3–4 young Apr.–May. **SIGN** Holes in snow (where mink has pounced on vole). 4″ burrow entrance in stream bank. Tracks: round, 2″, in snow. **HABITAT** Freshwater shores. **ACTIVITY** Late afternoon to early morning, year-round; dens up in coldest, stormiest periods.

STRIPED SKUNK
Mephitis mephitis
WEASEL FAMILY

L 24"; T 9". Coat thick, fluffy, mainly black; large white nape patch continues as 2 stripes along sides of back, usu. reaching tail; narrow white forehead stripe. Head pointed; ears and eyes small. Legs short; rear large; tail long, bushy. In some individuals, most of upper back and tail white. If threatened, raises tail, backs up, may stomp ground; may emit foul-smelling, sulphurous spray that travels to 15', stings eyes of predators, pets, humans. Eats insects, rodents, bird and turtle eggs, fruit, roadkills, garbage. **CAUTION** Can turn and spray in an instant. **BREEDING** 6–7 young in May. **SIGN** Foul odor if one has sprayed or been run over recently. Scratched-up lawns and garbage bags. Tracks: round foreprint 1" long; hindprint broader at front, flat-footed, 1½" long. **HABITAT** Woods, fields, towns. **ACTIVITY** Dusk to dawn; dens up and sleeps much of winter.

NORTHERN RIVER OTTER
Lutra canadensis
WEASEL FAMILY

L 3'7"; T 16". Fur dense, dark brown, often silvery on chin and chest. Ears and eyes small. Legs short; feet webbed. Tail long, thick-based, tapering to a point. Swims rapidly, stops with head raised out of water. Eats fish, frogs, turtles, muskrats. Runs well on land; loves to exercise and play; wanders widely. **BREEDING** Mates in water; 2–3 young born blind but furred in Apr. **SIGN** 12"-wide slides on sloping, muddy riverbanks, in flat areas. Vegetation flattened in large patch for rolling, feeding, defecating. Trails between bodies of water. Tracks: 3¼" wide, toes fanned. **HABITAT** Clean rivers, wood-edged ponds, lakes. **ACTIVITY** Day and night, year-round.

BOBCAT
Lynx rufus
CAT FAMILY

20″; L 3′; T 5″. Orange-brown in summer; paler grayish in winter; black spots and bars on legs and ear. Face wide and flat; black lines radiate onto facial ruff; ears slightly tufted, backsides black. Underparts and insides of long legs white; many black spots on legs. Gives yowls and screams, though mostly silent. Stalks and ambushes mammals and birds at night. **BREEDING** Usu. 2 young in May. **SIGN** Tracks in snow, scent posts and scratching trees. Tracks: like domestic cat, but 2″ wide vs. 1″. **HABITAT** Woods, scrub, swamps. **ACTIVITY** Mainly nocturnal, year-round. **RANGE** Mainly w and n N. Eng.

Hoofed Mammals

Most hoofed mammals worldwide are in the order Artiodactyla, the even-toed ungulates. (Ungulates are mammals that instead of claws have hooves, an adaptation for running. The order Perissodactyla—the odd-toed ungulates: horses, zebras, rhinos, and tapirs—has no extant native species in North America.) Even-toed ungulates have a split, two-part hoof (actually two modified toes) and two small dewclaws (vestigial toes) above the hoof on the rear of the leg. Their lower incisors are adapted for nipping or tearing off vegetation, their molars for grinding it. Most hastily swallow their food, which is stored temporarily in the first, largest compartment of their four-chambered stomachs; the food then passes to the second stomach, where it is shaped into small pellets of partly digested plant fiber (the cud). While the animal is at rest, the cud is returned to the mouth, slowly chewed to pulp, and swallowed; it then passes through all four chambers of the stomach. This process allows an animal to feed quickly, reducing its exposure to predators, and afterward chew its cud in a concealed spot.

The deer family (Cervidae) is the only family of wild hoofed mammals extant in New England. Members of the cattle family (Bovidae), which includes domestic cows, goats, and sheep, have permanent horns that stay on and grow continuously. Those in the deer family have paired bony antlers that grow, usually only on males, during the summer, at which time they are soft and tender, and covered with a fine-haired skin ("velvet") containing a network of blood vessels that nourishes the growing bone beneath. By late summer, the antlers reach full size, and the velvety skin dries up, loosens, and peels off. The bare antlers then serve as sexual ornaments; rival males may use them as weapons in courtship battles in fall. As winter nears, the antlers fall off; the animal grows a new pair the next summer. As long as an individual has an adequate diet, its antlers become larger and have more points each year until it reaches maturity.

WHITE-TAILED DEER
Odocoileus virginianus
DEER FAMILY

H 3′3″; L 6′; T 12″; male ⅓ heavier than female. Rich reddish brown in summer, grayish brown in winter. Ears large; nose and hooves black. Ring around nose, eye ring, throat, midbelly, and underside of tail white. Summer male develops antlers with main beam curving out and up, points issuing from it. Fawn reddish orange with many white spots. Communicates danger by loud whistling snort; flees with white undertail prominently erected. Can run 35 mph, clear 8′ tall obstacles, leap 30′. Host, with White-footed Mouse, of Lyme disease tick and bacterium. Wipes out many valuable plants when allowed to overpopulate in areas free of predators and hunting. **BREEDING** Mates Oct.–Nov.; bucks with swollen necks wander widely to find receptive does. Usu. 1–2 fawns in late spring; nibble greens at 2–3 weeks; weaned at 4 months. **SIGN** Raggedly browsed vegetation along well-worn trails. "Buck rubs" occur where male rubs bark off trees with antlers. Flattened beds in grass or snow. Tracks: "split hearts," with narrow, pointed end forward, 2–3″ long; dots of dewclaws behind. Scat: ¾″ cylindrical dark pellets. **HABITAT** Broadleaf and mixed woods and edges, fields, watersides. **ACTIVITY** Day and night, year-round.

male shedding "velvet"

female and c[alf]

MOOSE
Alces alces
DEER FAMILY

H 7′; L 9′; T 7″; male ⅓ larger than female. Coat long, dark brown; legs long, silvery. Muzzle long, with overhanging snout; ears large; large bear (dewlap) on throat. High shoulder hump. Tail very short. Summer and fall male sports massive, flattened, palmate antlers with many points; usu. 5′ wide. Female lacks antlers. Calf paler brown. Voice: in breeding season, both sexes give a cow-like moo, male's shorter, ending with upward inflection. Often eats water plants in ponds in summer; at other seasons, browses on twigs, leaves of many broadleaf and coniferous trees. **BREEDING** Mates Oct.; 1–2 calves late May. **SIGN** Raggedly torn shrub branches; stripped tree bark. Bed of flattened vegetation; muddy wallows smelling of urine. Scat oblong, 1¾″ long. Tracks: 5–6″ cloven hoofprints, with dewclaw prints behind. **HABITAT** Spruce woods, broadleaf thickets, swamps, ponds. **ACTIVITY** Day and night, mainly dawn and dusk, year-round; gather together during deep snow. **RANGE** VT, n NH, c and n ME; wandering south to MA and CT.

Marine Mammals

Marine mammals—the seals, sea lions, and Walrus of the order Carnivora, and the whales and dolphins of the order Cetacea—mainly live in ocean waters, though a few enter estuaries.

Seals are covered with fine, dense fur and insulating layers of fat; their legs have been modified into front and rear flippers. New England's seals belong to the hair seal family (Phocidae), whose members have no external ear flaps, only small orifices, and rear flippers that are permanently turned backward; their fore and rear flippers have "fingernails." Fast swimmers, they move in a slow, clumsy fashion on land, propelled solely by muscular contractions of the body and dragging their rear flippers; whenever possible, they roll or slide on ice. Seals spend weeks at sea, but haul out when near shore or when tending young. New England's seals mate in the water; young are born on beaches and seaside rocks. Lengths given are from the tip of the snout to the tip of the tail.

Cetaceans (dolphins, porpoises, and whales) have thick, hairless skin and insulating layers of blubber. Their front legs have been modified into flippers. The tail ends in wide, horizontally flattened flukes for propulsion. They breathe through one or two nostrils (blowholes) on the top of the head; the cloud of vapor exhaled is called a spout or a blow. Cetaceans can dive deep and swim fast; larger species can remain submerged for lengthy periods—sperm whales can stay under for more than an hour. Most smaller species prey on large fish, while many of the larger whales instead use broom-like structures called baleen to strain the water for schools of smaller fish and shrimp-like krill. The baleen whales have throat grooves (pleats) that expand when the animal takes in a vast amount of water and prey, and contract as water strains out. Cetaceans never haul out on land; young are born live in the water. Lengths given are from the tip of the snout to the end of the tail flukes.

Most cetacean species occur in waters off New England erratically; their presence depends on the availability of food. In spring, summer, and fall, the region's offshore waters are an important whale sanctuary. Some Humpback, Fin, and Minke Whale individuals summer here, while the majority of individuals of these species, plus right whales, pass through these waters in April and May and between October and December as they migrate between their Arctic feeding grounds and tropical calving waters.

Ports from Rhode Island to Maine offer part- and full-day whale-watching boat trips from May to October. From Point Judith and Newport, Rhode Island, boats typically travel to Cox's Ledge; from Gloucester, Boston, Barnstable, and Provincetown, Massachusetts, they head for Stellwagen Bank; from Newburyport, Massachusetts, and Portsmouth, New Hampshire, they go to Jeffrey's Ledge; from Maine ports, destinations vary. Boats may encounter one or more species of whales and seabirds (gannets, shearwaters, storm-petrels, jaegers), plus dolphins and other surface marine life, such as sharks, Ocean Sunfish, and, rarely, marine turtles.

HARBOR SEAL
Phoca vitulina
HAIR SEAL FAMILY

5′. Heavy; appears neck-less. Yellowish gray, mottled with dark spots and whitish rings; pale silvery when dry; enormous individual color variation. Short, dog-like muzzle on wide face; V-shaped nostrils; large, round, black eyes; no external ear flaps. When in water, can be noisy (snorts, growls, barks, grunts), playful, shy but curious. Hauls out at low tide; feeds in incoming and high tides on fishes, crustaceans, mollusks; may follow fish runs up to 10 miles inland on major rivers. **BREEDING** Mates in water in August; 1 pup born Apr.–May, fully furred, alert, able to swim at birth; nurses for 3–4 weeks. **SIGN** Haul-out slides in mud. **HABITAT** Coastal waters, rivers near sea. Hauls out on rocks, jetties, beaches, mudflats, ice. **RANGE** Summer: common off ME; spotty south to se MA. Winter: entire coastline.

GRAY SEAL
Halichoerus grypus
HAIR SEAL FAMILY

8′; female ¼ smaller than male. Male blackish slate, with lighter splotches. Female lighter, with darker splotches. Both paler below, paler when dry. Heavy; massive hump at shoulder; head enormous, rectangular, horse-shaped; nostrils form W shape; no external ear flaps. Social; groups of several dozen may bob, play, vocalize (grunts and barks), and inspect small boats. Eats bottom-dwelling fish and invertebrates; dives to 475′. **BREEDING** Male fights to keep harem of up to 6 females; 1 pup born in winter, weaned for 2–3 weeks ashore. **SIGN** Haul-out pathways in sand. **HABITAT** Inshore ocean waters. Hauls out and breeds on remote protected islands. **RANGE** Resident in ME and MA off se Cape Cod (e.g., Monomoy N.W.R.) and islands west of Nantucket (local). Disperses widely outside breeding season.

MINKE WHALE
Balaenoptera acutorostrata
RORQUAL FAMILY

25′. Streamlined, slender; head fairly small; snout pointed. Dark blue-gray above; white below. Baleen plates yellowish white; has about 50 throat grooves. Flippers pointed, fairly small; white central band above; white below. Dorsal fin located ⅔ of way back on body; broad-based; swept-back, with pointed, curved tip. Tail dark above, white below. Follows and swims under boats and ships, lifting head to look around. **BREEDING** Breeds and gives birth in winter. 1 young 9′ at birth; nurses for 6 months. **SIGN** Spout single, short, with rounded vapor cloud. **HABITAT** Inshore and deep sea waters. **RANGE** Mainly Apr.–Dec.: off RI to ME.

FIN WHALE
"Finback Whale"
Balaenoptera physalus
RORQUAL FAMILY

70′. Relatively slender; head flat. Brownish black above; white below. Dorsal fin small, swept-back; located ⅘ of way back on body. Lower jaw white on right, blackish on left. Baleen unusually colored: all left and rear of right dark, front of right yellowish white. Has 50–80 throat grooves. Flippers fairly small. Tail fluke dark above, white below; rarely seen. Swims on side when feeding. Fast swimmer. Does not breach like a Humpback. 2nd largest mammal on earth. **BREEDING** May mate for life. Gestation 1 year. 1 young 20′ at birth; nurses for 6 months. **SIGN** Spout rises as a 20′ column; expands into an ellipse. **HABITAT** Ocean. **RANGE** Mainly Mar.–Nov.: off RI to ME.

HUMPBACK WHALE
Megaptera novaeangliae
RORQUAL FAMILY

40'. Blackish above; white below. Head adorned with fleshy bumps and barnacles; throat has about 25 massive grooves. Small hump just in front of leading edge of rounded dorsal fin; when diving, back angles down sharply after dorsal fin. Extremely long, white flippers: 15', with fleshy knobs along leading edge. Tail variously patterned, with white below; variations help researchers identify individuals (hundreds have been catalogued). Sometimes playful and active. Only large whale that regularly breaches (jumps clear out of the water), rolls, then comes crashing down. Also rolls on surface from side to side, slapping long flippers, and performs head-down "lobtail," slapping flukes down. Creates cylindrical "net" of rising air bubbles deep down that confuses and walls in schools of small fish; whale then rises up with mouth open inside the "net." Most popular target of whale-watching boats. **BREEDING** Gestation 1 year; 1 young, 16' at birth, born in tropics; stays with mother 1 year. **SIGN** Spout is expanding column up to 20' high. **HABITAT** Ocean. **RANGE** Apr.–Nov.: off RI to ME, esp. MA.

BLACK RIGHT WHALE
"Northern Right Whale"
Balaena glacialis
RIGHT WHALE FAMILY

40'. Body, baleen plates of mouth, flippers, and flukes black; some whitish splotches on belly. Head is ⅓ of total length; many barnacles grow on it; mouth highly curved. Small eye located above base of lips and in front of short rectangular flippers. Only N. Eng. baleen whale that lacks a dorsal fin. Slow swimmer when skimming krill at surface; will dive for up to 20 minutes. Named in 1600s, when it was the "right" whale to harpoon, as it floated when dead; now endangered. **BREEDING** Mates Feb.–Apr.; gestation 1 year; 1 young every 2 years; young about 20' at birth, nurses for a year. **SIGN** Spout diverges in 10–15' V-shape. **HABITAT** Ocean. **RANGE** June–Sept.: mainly off far e ME in Bay of Fundy. Apr.–June, Sept.–Nov.: off MA, where it has been named the state marine mammal.

LONG-FINNED PILOT WHALE
"Blackfish" "Common Pilot Whale"
Globicephala melas
OCEAN DOLPHIN FAMILY

20′; male much larger than female. Elongated. All black, with white chest patch. High bulging forehead above short protruding beak. Prominent, swept-back dorsal fin forward of body center. Flippers long, narrow, pointed. Tail fluke black, narrow. Strong herd instinct; often touches other individuals. Occasionally entire pod (group) follows leader blindly onto shallow beaches, with dozens or more becoming stranded and dying as tide goes out. Migrates north and south with seasons, feeding mainly on squid. **BREEDING** Mates May–Nov.; gestation 16 months; 1 young 6′ at birth; nurses for 22 months. **HABITAT** Ocean. **RANGE** Apr.–June and Sept.–Nov.: off RI to ME ; strandings mainly on n shore of Cape Cod.

BOTTLE-NOSED DOLPHIN
Tursiops truncatus
OCEAN DOLPHIN FAMILY

10′. Slaty bluish gray above; paler gray on sides; whitish gray on throat; belly white or pinkish. Beak fairly long and broad. Dorsal fin large, swept-back, pointed. Travels in small parties; will ride ship's bow waves. **BREEDING** 1 young every 2–3 years. **HABITAT** Warm offshore ocean waters. **RANGE** Chiefly south and east of Cape Cod June–Oct. Other dolphins sometimes seen off N. Eng. include **Saddle-backed (Common) Dolphin** *(Delphinus delphis),* 7′, black above, gray or yellowish on sides (hourglass pattern), white below; narrow beak and flippers black; **Atlantic White-sided Dolphin** *(Lagenorhynchus acutus),* 8′, black above, with long white patch, enclosed by black, on rear half of sides, white below; **White-beaked Dolphin** *(L. albirostris),* 9′, all black, ex. white snout and chest. **Harbor Porpoise** *(Phocoena phocoena),* 5′, blackish above, white below; back fin low, triangular; fluke small; feeds near surface of inshore waters; year-round.

Parks and Preserves

Introduction

For the plant lover, New England has Bartholomew's Cobble with its 55 species of ferns, West Quoddy Head with its marvelous raised coastal bog, Cape Cod National Seashore with its resilient dune vegetation, and thousands of other choice botanizing locales. For the birdwatcher, there are Peregrine Falcons over the cliffs at Gay Head, Hooded Warblers at Devil's Hopyard, secretive bitterns at Dead Creek, and

Devil's Hopyard State Park, Connecticut

countless ibises, grouse, and swallows in other intriguing settings. Whether your interest is weather, geology, insects, mushrooms, wildflowers, trees, marine life, reptiles, or just about any other subject, some place in New England has what you seek.

Parker River National Wildlife Refuge, Massachusetts

Ascutney State Park, Vermont

Within its 66,608 square miles New England has 20 national wildlife refuges, two national forests, a national park, a national seashore, and hundreds of state parks, forests, beaches, and wildlife management areas. It also has thousands of small parcels, managed by municipalities and nonprofit groups, that have been set aside as conservation properties. The sum is a vast mosaic of plant and wildlife habitats for visitors to explore and cherish.

This section provides introductions to 50 of the most important natural sites in New England, plus annotated listings of dozens of others. Mailing addresseses and telephone numbers are given for all sites (most will send brochures and other information), and driving directions are given for the 50 featured sites. Since fees and exact hours of operation change frequently, they are not included in the listings, though seasonal access is noted.

This guide highlights some of the predominant plants and animals you may see as you visit sites, but always ask if local lists of flora and fauna are available, as these can help pin down identifications.

Beavertail State Park, Rhode Island

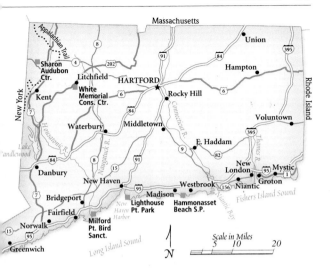

Connecticut

Like most of the New England states, Connecticut is fairly small (5,009 square miles) but comprises an enviable diversity of natural features, plant life, and wildlife. Roughly rectangular in outline, the state is bisected by the broad, north-south trending Connecticut Valley, which extends from just south of the Vermont–Massachusetts border to Long Island Sound and is one of New England's most distinctive geological formations. The mighty Connecticut River flows through the valley until Middletown, where it turns southeast before emptying into Long Island Sound. The state's three other principal rivers are the Housatonic and the Naugatuck in the west and the Thames in the east.

On either side of the Connecticut Valley rise the uplands that are such a distinctive part of the state's landscape. Elevations increase from south to north in the west until one reaches the extreme northwestern corner of the state, where the peak of Mount Frissell, at 2,380 feet, is the highest point. A tiny tongue of northern broadleaf forest that dips south into northwestern Connecticut is surrounded by a slightly larger region of transition woodlands; this, in turn, gives way to the oak-hickory and other woods that cover the remainder of the state. The eastern highlands are less dramatic but no less scenic.

Along the coast, numerous little bays, rocky promontories, sandy beaches, and salt marshes compete with urban and suburban sprawl. Most of the islands are clusters of inshore rocky islets.

Connecticut has a national wildlife refuge, 91 state parks, and 30 state forests. The Connecticut Forest and Park Association's privately maintained 700-mile-long Blue-blazed Hiking Trail is one of the longest and finest marked trails in the nation; for information call 860-346-TREE.

HAMMONASSET BEACH STATE PARK   Madison

Less than an hour's drive from many of Connecticut's major urban areas, 919-acre Hammonasset Beach State Park is a magnet for the summer beach crowd. During other seasons, the park offers uncrowded walks in a variety of settings.

Salt marsh

Long Island Sound

At the park rotary, the first turnoff leads to a large parking and picnic area. Many species of gulls flock here, and the sometimes flooded fields attract many shorebirds, including Sanderlings, when there is standing water. Chase Pool is home to a resident pair of Mute Swans, summering Purple Martins, and herons and waterfowl in season.

Beginning at Meigs' Point Nature Center, a secondary loop road has parking areas and trails that lead to two fascinating upland "islands" in the coastal marshland. In the fall Willard's Island and Cedar Island, their stunted woodlands and varied shrubs rising from the surrounding wetlands, are feeding and resting oases for migrant songbirds. The bayberry thickets often hold impressive numbers of

Sanderlings

vireos, thrushes, and warblers from August through September, and hordes of sparrows invariably appear later in the season. Watch skyward for opportunistic Merlins, Peregrine Falcons, and Sharp-shinned Hawks.

At Meigs' Point proper, Bluefish may be schooling (and striking), and flounder and Striped Bass are also often caught from the jetty. Shell collectors can expect to find scallops, Common Jingle Shells, and numerous gastropods, including variously patterned Atlantic Dogwinkles. Flocks of migrating and wintering scoters may be seen from October to April.

Before leaving the park, take a walk in the cedar groves on both sides of the road between the rotary and the park gate. Five species of owls have been found roosting here; take care not to upset the resting birds.

CONTACT Hammonasset Beach S.P., P.O. Box 271, Madison, CT 06443; 203-245-2785 (park office); 203-245-1817 (camp office). **HOW TO GET THERE** From I-95, take exit 62 and drive south about 1 mile to the park entrance. **SEASONAL ACCESS** Year-round. Lifeguards and naturalists on duty in summer. Camping avail. mid-May–Oct. **VISITOR CENTER** Meigs' Point Nature Ctr. (closed in winter) at park's eastern end.

MILFORD POINT BIRD SANCTUARY   Milford

Milford Point Bird Sanctuary, covering just 10 acres, is perhaps the best year-round shorebird and waterfowl viewing site in Connecticut. Beginning at the boat ramp, scan the marsh for herons and dabbling ducks. In migration season, peer into the many shrubby thickets for flycatchers, kinglets, warblers, orioles, finches, and sparrows. On the beach just beyond the sanctuary's parking lot (south of the boat ramp) is a summer colony of Least Terns, along with a few pairs of Piping Plovers. The beaches and mudflats of the point stretch out for about a mile, offering excellent opportunities to spot Black-bellied and Semipalmated Plovers, Ruddy Turnstones, and rarer Black Terns and American Oystercatchers. Much of the adjoining land here is private; only responsible behavior will ensure continued access.

CONTACT Conn. Audubon Coastal Ctr., 1 Milford Pt. Rd., Milford, CT 06460; 203-878-7440. **HOW TO GET THERE** From I-95, take exit 35, drive south to U.S. 1, turn right, proceed to the first stoplight and turn left on Lansdale Ave. At the next light, turn right on Milford Pt. Rd., bear right on Seaview Ave. and follow it to the parking lot. **SEASONAL ACCESS** Year-round. **VISITOR CENTER** Connecticut Audubon Coastal Ctr., on-site.

LIGHTHOUSE POINT PARK   New Haven

Botanists, beachcombers, and anglers are at home here all year, but fall is the season of greatest activity at 84-acre Lighthouse Point Park. The air is filled with Monarchs and other migrant butterflies on their autumn flights, and myriad dazzling dragonflies. The park's woods and thickets fill with cuckoos, flycatchers, thrushes, and other songbirds, and the skies swarm with Northern Flickers, swallows, Blue Jays, blackbirds, and American Goldfinches. From September to November, 20,000 to 30,000 Broad-winged and Sharp-shinned Hawks, Ospreys, Northern Harriers, American Kestrels, Merlins, and Peregrine Falcons, as well as other raptors, head south over Lighthouse Point in one of North America's greatest hawk flights. The main parking area is the best vantage point.

CONTACT Lighthouse Pt. Park, New Haven Parks Dept., 720 Edgewood Ave., New Haven, CT 06515; 203-946-8005. **HOW TO GET THERE** From I-95, take exit 50 (Woodward Ave.). At second stoplight, turn right on Townsend Ave., then right on Lighthouse Rd. **SEASONAL ACCESS** Year-round. Lifeguards on duty in summer. **VISITOR CENTER** East Shore Ranger Sta. (203-946-8790) is near the lighthouse.

SHARON AUDUBON CENTER   **Sharon**

The rural northwestern corner of Connecticut is a pleasing mix of old farms, pretty towns, rivers, and wooded hills. The National Audubon Society's educational facilities for its northeast region are located here at the Sharon Audubon Center, which houses displays, offices, and a tribute to New England nature writer Hal Borland.

Springtime hikers along the 754-acre sanctuary's woodland trails may see such wildflowers as Yellow Lady's Slippers and Jack-in-the-pulpits and perhaps hear the drumming of male Ruffed Grouse and Pileated Woodpeckers. Eastern White Pines, Tamaracks, Eastern Hemlocks, Northern Red and Chestnut Oaks, and Cinnamon and Christmas Ferns share woodland recesses with breeding Veeries, American Redstarts, and Scarlet Tanagers. Mammal sightings along the 11 miles of trails might include Woodchucks, American Beavers, Red and Eastern Gray Squirrels, Northern River Otters, Red Foxes, and White-tailed Deer.

CONTACT Sharon Audubon Ctr., National Audubon Society, 325 Cornwall Bridge Rd., Sharon, CT 06069; 860-364-0520. **HOW TO GET THERE** Exit U.S. 7 at Cornwall Bridge; the center is about 7 miles west on Rte. 4 in Sharon. **SEASONAL ACCESS** Year-round. **VISITOR CENTER** Adjacent to parking area.

WHITE MEMORIAL FOUNDATION AND CONSERVATION CENTER   **Litchfield**

Located in a lovely town in the Berkshire foothills, White Memorial's 4,000 acres of woodland, meadow, and waterfront are home to a museum, an outstanding natural history library, day-use facilities for groups large and small, four camping areas, and 35 miles of maintained trails and roads.

After viewing the museum's dioramas or touring the Holbrook Bird Observatory, head off to the wilds. **LAUREL HILL** is well named, for it is covered with dense stands of Mountain Laurel. It's the place to be during the May bird migration. Look for Spring Azure butterflies here and throughout the woodlands. **LITTLE POND** has a raised boardwalk that offers access to the breeding areas of secretive rails and bitterns, as well as fine opportunities for studying wetland plants and invertebrates. **CAITLIN WOODS** has majestic stands of old-growth Eastern Hemlock and Eastern White Pine. Look and listen for Barred and Great Horned Owls.

CONTACT White Memorial Foundation and Conserv. Ctr., P.O. Box 368, 71 Whitehall Rd., Litchfield, CT 06759; 860-567-0857. **HOW TO GET THERE** From Litchfield, drive west about 2 miles on U.S. 202. Entrance is on left. **SEASONAL ACCESS** Year-round. **VISITOR CENTER** Next to museum and library.

BIGELOW HOLLOW STATE PARK   Union

Bigelow Pond and Lake Mashapaug, whose clear waters offer outstanding trout fishing, also serve as beautiful backdrops for a day trip to this 513-acre park. **CONTACT** Bigelow Hollow S.P., c/o Quaddick S.P., 818 Quaddick Town Farm Rd., Thompson, CT 06277; 860-928-9200.

BLUFF POINT STATE PARK   Groton

The last remaining large piece of undeveloped land on the Connecticut coast, this 778-acre park is accessible by foot travel only and has fine salt-marsh and upland habitats. **CONTACT** Bluff Point S.P., c/o Ft. Griswold Battlefield S.P., 57 Fort St., Groton, CT 06340; 860-424-3200.

CONNECTICUT AUDUBON CENTER AT FAIRFIELD   Fairfield

Together with the adjoining 152-acre Larsen Sanctuary, the center has trails, scheduled events, and a compound for rehabilitating raptors. **CONTACT** Conn. Audubon Ctr., 2325 Burr St., Fairfield, CT 06423; 203-259-6305.

DEVIL'S HOPYARD STATE PARK   East Haddam

Scenic Chapman Falls and an impressive variety of wood warblers make this 860-acre site a rewarding venue for photographers and birders. **CONTACT** Devil's Hopyard S.P., c/o Cockaponset S.F., 18 Ranger Rd., Haddam, CT 06438; 860-345-8521.

DINOSAUR STATE PARK   Rocky Hill

This 63-acre Jurassic park displays approximately 500 dinosaur tracks along with interpretive exhibits. **CONTACT** Dinosaur S.P., 400 West St., Rocky Hill, CT 06067; 860-529-5816.

AUDUBON CENTER IN GREENWICH   Greenwich

Hike along 8 miles of woodland trails or set yourself up at the Quaker Ridge Hawk Watch Site to do a little fall raptor-watching. **CONTACT** Audubon Ctr., 613 Riversville Rd., Greenwich, CT 06831; 203-869-5272.

MACEDONIA BROOK STATE PARK   Kent

Stream-fishing and hiking are popular activities in this 2,300-acre park. The trail crossing Cobble Mountain offers sweeping views of the Catskill and Taconic Mountains. **CONTACT** Macedonia Brook S.P., 159 Macedonia Brook Rd., Kent, CT 06757; 860-927-3238.

Macedonia Brook State Park

STUART B. MCKINNEY NATIONAL WILDLIFE REFUGE   Westbrook

Connecticut's first national wildlife refuge provides year-round access, via 2½ miles of trails, to fields, upland woods, and a restored tidal salt marsh. **CONTACT** Stuart B. McKinney N.W.R., Salt Meadow Unit, P.O. Box 1030, Westbrook, CT 06498; 860-399-2513.

PACHAUG STATE FOREST   Voluntown

This forest's 22,938 acres feature rhododendrons and Atlantic White Cedars for botanists and miles of trails for equestrians, cyclists, and hikers. **CONTACT** Pachaug S.F., P.O. Box 5, Voluntown, CT 06384; 860-376-2920.

TRAIL WOOD   Hampton

This property was the home and private nature sanctuary of Edwin Way Teale, one of America's most gifted nature writers. Birds and insects abound in the 156-acre upland reserve. **CONTACT** Trail Wood, Edwin Way Teale Memorial Sanct., c/o Conn. Audubon Society, 118 Oak St., Hartford, CT 06106-1514; 860-455-0759.

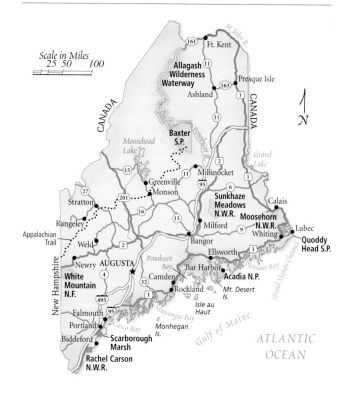

Scale in Miles
25 50   100

Maine

With an area of 33,215 square miles, Maine is almost exactly the same size as the other five New England states combined. "Rugged" is a good defining word for the Maine outdoors: rugged mountains, rugged forests, rugged coastlines, and rugged weather. Of the mountains, the most rugged must be the Mahoosucs in western Maine. Hikers say the boulder-strewn path through these mountains is the toughest of any of the 276 miles of Appalachian Trail in Maine and perhaps the single most difficult stretch of the entire trail. Isolated Mount Katahdin, northeast of the Mahoosuc Range, is the backbone of Baxter State Park and the state's loftiest peak, at 5,268 feet. Also of interest are coastal Mount Agamenticus, Mount Megunticook, and Cadillac Mountain, the three tallest mountains on the eastern U.S. seaboard.

Scarborough Marsh

Sandy Stream Pond, Baxter State Park

Maine is blanketed with forests: both northern broadleaf (birch, beech, and maple) and coniferous (spruce, hemlock, fir, and pine). To get around in them, you will need waterproof boots, because these woods can be wet indeed. Maine's cool, moist climate is perfect for the formation of peatlands; 750,000 acres of these bogs are scattered all over the state. Around 6,000 lakes and ponds, some of them very large, dot the Maine map. The largest, Moosehead Lake, feeds the Kennebec River, which joins the Androscoggin and drains much of western Maine. The Penobscot River, Maine's largest, flows southeast from the Katahdin area. Other major river systems are the St. John–Allagash, flowing northward through the wilderness of northwest Maine, and the Saco in the south.

Quoddy Head State Park

There are three ways to measure the coastline of Maine. From point to point, from Calais to the New Hampshire border, it is 230 miles long. But a tally of the actual distance covered by the sometimes crenulated, sometimes fjord-like mainland shoreline of peninsulas, bays, and inlets yields about 3,500 miles, and adding in Maine's island coastlines pushes the total to more than 7,000 miles. Only in the very southernmost stretches does the magnificent, raw, spruce-backed, rocky Maine coastline give way to short, sandy strands. Some of the state's more than 2,000 maritime islands are a stone's throw from the mainland; others are miles out at sea.

Moosehorn National Wildlife Refuge

Monhegan Island

Maine is home to 27 state parks, four national wildlife refuges, a national forest (a small portion of the White Mountain National Forest, most of which is in New Hampshire), and one superb national park. Some locations of sites along the Maine coast are shown on the back endpaper map.

ACADIA NATIONAL PARK   Bar Harbor

View from Cadillac Mountain

It is during July and August that most of each year's 2½ million visitors descend upon Acadia National Park, the main portion of
which covers some 35,000 acres on Mount Desert Island (Desert is
pronounced "dessert," as in the French *mont desert*, or "bare mountain"). Be sure to take in some of the more than 120 miles of hiking trails and 57 miles of woodland carriage trails. Take time to
savor the dramatic scenery, diverse floral displays, fabulous bird life,
and unparalleled inshore marine life. Innumerable superb natural
areas await you at Acadia. A few of the best are mentioned here.

HULLS COVE VISITOR CENTER Stop here to pick up a bird checklist, a
general island map and trail maps, and a schedule of programs for
visitors. In the summer, the park offers a wide range of natural history programs for adults and children in botany, geology, marine bi-
ology, and other subjects.

SIEUR DE MONTS SPRING It is a curious fact that the northeastern part
of Mount Desert Island has trees and breeding birds of more
southerly affinities, while the southwestern section of the island is
inhabited by boreal (northern) species, mainly conifers. The great
fire of 1947 was the culprit that transformed what had been a uniformly coniferous woodland. More than 10,000 acres in Acadia's
northeast were devastated by the inferno, which burned for weeks.
In the wake of the fire, latent seeds of broadleaf tree species (more
common in southern New England than in Maine) sprang to life
from the ashy ground. What had once been a spruce-fir forest was
transformed into woodlands of birches, aspens, and Pin Cherries,
with a spectacular understory of Lowbush Blueberries and Fire-
weeds. In the newly sprouted broadleaf woodlands, seen to full advantage at Sieur de Monts Spring, nesting birds now include
Broad-winged Hawks, Black-billed Cuckoos, Great Crested Flycatchers, Baltimore Orioles, and Rose-breasted Grosbeaks. While
here, visit the Acadia Wild Garden. The garden, which has approximately 300 species of labeled native plants in natural settings, will
help you sort out the park's varied plant life.

CADILLAC MOUNTAIN One of 17 peaks on Mount Desert Island, Cadillac Mountain, at 1,530 feet, is the highest point along the U.S. Atlantic seaboard. Almost every park visitor stops here, but do not let the crowds deter you. The views of Bar Harbor, Eagle Lake, Frenchman Bay, and indeed the whole island are spectacular.

JORDAN POND This stop on the 20-mile park loop road is another nice place to admire and learn about local flora. A ½-mile self-guided trail here identifies trees and some intriguing lichens, such as the ubiquitous Old Man's Beard.

Jordan Pond

BIG HEATH OR SEAWALL BOG Located at the southern end of the western lobe of Mount Desert Island, along Rte. 102A, this area and the two woodlands in the next entry are three highlights of any naturalist's sojourn at Acadia. In the 420-acre Big Heath, Palm Warblers and Common Yellowthroats nest among Swamp Pink orchids, Bog-laurel, Bog-rosemary, and Labrador Tea. Carnivorous pitcher-plants and sundews are common on the spreading mats of Peat Moss. In order to minimize disturbance to the fragile plant life, please keep to the paths.

WONDERLAND AND SHIP HARBOR Here are two of the loveliest warbler-laden woodlands anywhere. Trails wind through mixed broadleaf and coniferous habitats, and the trees ring with the songs of Blackburnian, Wilson's, Magnolia, Yellow-rumped, and many other northern warblers. At the water's edge, look for Black Guillemots, Harbor Seals, and occasional Bald Eagles and Harbor Porpoises.

SCHOODIC PENINSULA Across Frenchman Bay, to the east of Mount Desert Island, lies Schoodic Peninsula, the mainland section of Acadia National Park. Heavily wooded and highly scenic, it offers good land birding in the vicinity of Schoodic Head, and excellent tidepool exploring and marine bird-watching at Schoodic Point.

Schoodic Peninsula

CONTACT Acadia N.P., P.O. Box 177, Bar Harbor, ME 04609; 207-288-3338. **HOW TO GET THERE** From Ellsworth, drive 20 miles southeast on Rte. 3 to reach Mt. Desert Is. or go 19 miles east on U.S. 1 to Rte. 186 to get to Schoodic Peninsula. The small piece of Acadia located on Isle au Haut is accessible year-round by ferry from Stonington, on Deer Isle. **SEASONAL ACCESS** Year-round. Back-country, group, and RV camping sites are available on Mt. Desert Island, and there are many restaurants and motels in Bar Harbor and nearby. Motel reservations are necessary in summer. **VISITOR CENTER** Hulls Cove V.C., located on Rte. 3 on northeast Mt. Desert Is., is open May–Oct. At other seasons, stop at park hdqtrs. on Rte. 233, west of Bar Harbor.

BAXTER STATE PARK   **Millinocket**

A visit to Baxter State Park is a glorious step back in time. There are no paved roads, no water, sewer, or electric hook-ups, no pets, no lifeguards, no gas, no groceries, no radios or cellular phones (these are not allowed)—just an awesome mountain surrounded by 200,000 acres of undisturbed habitat for Moose, Common Porcupines, Peregrine Falcons, Spruce Grouse, and hardy human visitors. The park is one of the most popular natural destinations in the East, so available campsites disappear far in advance of the

Nesowadnehunk Tote Road

summer season. Reservations, with advance payment, may be made starting January 1, through the mail or in person.

The six peaks of massive Mount Katahdin loom over the south-central part of Baxter. The park tote road, narrow, curving, and 41 miles in length, arcs around the western and northern sections of the park and offers easy access to numerous ponds, lakes, and woodlands. Most of the park's bird and mammal life can be spotted along this road, especially in early morning and late afternoon. Nesowadnehunk Lake, a little over halfway out on the road, has excellent Brook Trout fishing.

Every trail in Baxter has great potential, but two places are high on many visitors' lists:

Sandy Stream Pond

SANDY STREAM POND Located near the Roaring Brook Campground, this is a prime area for watching Moose and American Beavers.

MOUNT KATAHDIN Many trails lead to the tableland, the square mile of summit lands. The climbs are strenuous but the views are magical. Take extra clothing and food and enjoy the tranquility. American Pipits and the Mount Katahdin race of the Polixenes Arctic butterfly, along with dozens of glacial relict wildflowers, live only in the alpine region.

CONTACT Baxter S.P., 64 Balsam Dr., Millinocket, ME 04462; 207-723-5140. **HOW TO GET THERE** From I-95, take exit 56 and drive west on Rte. 157/11. Watch for state park signs in Millinocket; Baxter is 18 miles north on Golden Rd. **SEASONAL ACCESS** Open for general use May 15–Oct. 15; other times call ahead. **VISITOR CENTER** Togue Pond V.C. is located near the park's south gate. Park hdqrs. are in Millinocket, at the corner of Central and Sycamore Sts.

MONHEGAN ISLAND

Envision a picturesque island off the Maine coast. Make it home to a spruce-fir forest inhabited by invisible woodland gnomes (their houses, built out of sticks and pine cones, are everywhere), towering seaside cliffs, an artists' colony, and bewildering numbers of common, unusual, and sometimes rare migrant birds, and you have the beginnings of a description of Monhegan. At any time of year, it is a treasure. Most visitors travel to Monhegan between May and September. Leaving cars and even bikes behind, they are ferried the 11 miles to the island from Port Clyde, Boothbay Harbor, or New Harbor. Along the way, look for shearwaters, eiders, Bald Eagles, Black Guillemots, Harbor Seals and Harbor Porpoises.

Because of its isolation, Monhegan is a magnet for tired, disoriented, and hungry migrant birds that find themselves flying out over the Gulf of Maine. During May and again from late August to mid-October, the island may be flooded with sapsuckers, flickers, flycatchers, thrushes, vireos, warblers, and sparrows; look for them as they lurk in thickets around the Ice Pond or in the wet meadow in the center of the village. Peregrine Falcons, Merlins, and Sharp-shinned Hawks scour the island looking for inattentive songbirds. Rarer species such as Red-headed Woodpeckers, Dickcissels, and Blue Grosbeaks are regularly seen.

In summer or fall, wander the 17 miles of trails, watch for deer around the village, climb up to the lighthouse (where Fringed Gentians bloom in late summer), make the pilgrimage to Cathedral Woods, and savor as many of the locally caught lobsters as you can.

You may want to spend a few leisurely days on Monhegan. It is necessary to make advance reservations at the island's inns and guest houses. The boat lines can provide information.

Fringed Gentian

FROM PORT CLYDE Monhegan-Thomaston Boat Line, P.O. Box 238, Port Clyde, ME 04855; 207-372-8848. From Brunswick, drive north on U.S. 1 through Thomaston, turn right onto Rte. 131, and follow it south to the dock at Port Clyde. Service year-round. **FROM BOOTHBAY HARBOR** Balmy Days Cruises, P.O. Box 535, Boothbay Harbor, ME 04538; 800-298-2284. Take U.S. 1 to Rte. 27 and drive south to dock on left in Boothbay Harbor. Trips June–mid-Oct. **FROM NEW HARBOR** Hardy Boat Cruises, P.O. Box 326, New Harbor, ME 04554; 207-677-2026. From Rockland, take U.S. 1 south to Rte. 32 and drive about 19 miles to dock on left in New Harbor. Service mid-May–mid-Oct.

RACHEL CARSON
NATIONAL WILDLIFE REFUGE   Wells

A series of small units in the national wildlife refuge system are named for Rachel Carson, the U.S. Fish and Wildlife Service biologist who wrote so eloquently about marine life and who shocked the public into caring about the wanton misuse of pesticides. Rachel Carson National Wildlife Refuge stretches intermittently from Kittery to Portland, and in Wells there are two units, at Webhannet Marsh and—a few miles farther north—at the headquarters. Both areas protect fine salt marshes. Laudholm Farm, just to the south of headquarters, is the delightful 1,600-acre home of the Wells National Estuarine Research Reserve (207-646-1555), where marine-life educational programs for naturalists of all ages are offered from spring through fall.

CONTACT Rachel Carson N.W.R., R.R. 2 Box 751, Rte. 9 East, Wells, ME 04090; 207-646-9226. **HOW TO GET THERE** From Wells, drive .7 mile east on Rte. 9 to the refuge headquarters at the Upper Wells Division. Webhannet Marsh is reached from three consecutive roads running east off U.S. 1: Mile Rd., Harbor Rd., and Drakes Island Rd. **SEASONAL ACCESS** Year-round. **VISITOR CENTER** Hdqrs. and information desk at Upper Wells Division.

BIDDEFORD POOL/EAST POINT
SANCTUARY   Biddeford

For year-round birding, the mile-wide basin known as Biddeford Pool is one of Maine's most productive spots. A great many species of shorebirds utilize the pool as a migratory staging (resting and feeding) area. Greater and Lesser Yellowlegs, Semipalmated Sandpipers, Dunlins, dowitchers, Willets, Whimbrels, and others stop here on their north-

and southbound journeys, and startling rarities show up on occasion. Because the pool is so wide, it is best to visit during a rising tide, when the flats are gradually covered, and the shorebirds are pushed into close range for easy viewing. Hattie's Deli, on the southeast side of the pool, is the locals' favorite sandwich stop and parking lot. Several species of herons nest on nearby Wood Island and feed in the vicinity. At the north end of the pool is 30-acre East Point Sanctuary, with thickets for migrant land birds and a shoreline attractive to shorebirds and waterfowl in season.

CONTACT East Pt. Sanct., c/o Maine Audubon Society, P.O. Box 6009, Falmouth, ME 04105; 207-781-2330. **HOW TO GET THERE** From Biddeford, drive southeast on Rte. 9/208 approximately 5 miles, then turn left on Rte. 208. Biddeford Pool is .5 mile on the left. **SEASONAL ACCESS** Year-round.

SCARBOROUGH MARSH

Scarborough

Scarborough Marsh is an incomparable 3,000-acre marsh community that can be explored on its own or combined with a trip to Biddeford Pool for a total coastal wildlife experience. The marshlands are accessible by car, foot, or boat. Rent a canoe at Scarborough Marsh Nature Center to come into intimate contact with the marsh's invertebrates and skulking birds such as the Sharp-tailed Sparrow. Bisecting the upper reaches of Scarborough Marsh, Eastern Road passes salt pans that attract hordes of shorebirds in season. Watch for migrant Canada and Snow Geese in spring.

CONTACT Scarborough Marsh, c/o Maine Audubon Society, P.O. Box 6009, Falmouth, ME 04105; 207-781-2330. **HOW TO GET THERE** Both sections of the marsh are accessible from U.S. 1 in Scarborough. The nature center is on Rte. 9 (Pine Pt. Rd.), south of U.S. 1. To reach Eastern Rd., turn south on Rte. 207 (Black Pt. Rd.) and drive .4 mile. **SEASONAL ACCESS** Year-round. **VISITOR CENTER** Scarborough Marsh Nature Ctr. is open in summer (207-883-5100).

GILSLAND FARM

Falmouth

Gilsland Farm, headquarters of the Maine Audubon Society, incorporates in its 60 acres an array of natural environments and educational opportunities. The site has 2½ miles of trails over and through upland meadows and Northern Red Oak and Eastern White Pine woodlands. The gentle meadow trails pass nesting grounds of Eastern Meadowlarks and Bobolinks and provide splendid views of the Presumpscot River and its extensive marshlands, where migrant shorebirds and waterfowl are a feature. The Pond Meadow Trail may be the shortest, but it includes the greatest habitat diversity, with woodlands, a pond, and an apple orchard—and, of course, their attendant wildlife, including songbirds such as thrushes and warblers. In addition to the walking trails, there is the native species Goduti Wildlife Garden, the organic Community Gardens, and the Teacher's Resource Center, which lends curriculum materials to educators. Natural history and environmental programs are offered throughout the year for adults and children.

CONTACT Gilsland Farm Environmental Center and Sanctuary, c/o Maine Audubon Society, P.O. Box 6009, Falmouth, ME 04105; 207-781-2330. **HOW TO GET THERE** From Portland, take I-295 north to exit 9. Drive 1.9 miles north on U.S. 1 and turn left on to Old Rte. 1 at the Maine Audubon sign. **SEASONAL ACCESS** Year-round.

MATINICUS ISLAND AND MATINICUS ROCK

Matinicus Island, well offshore and never burdened by tourist crowds, has varied natural habitats, including coniferous woods, shrubland, fields, and a marsh. Especially during spring and fall migration periods, the 2-mile-long and 1-mile-wide island can be a refuge for large numbers of land birds, including many of the same species found on Monhegan Island.

Matinicus Rock, a 30-acre islet 5 miles south of Matinicus Island, has a thriving summer seabird colony. Landing on the island is not possible, but your boat captain can get you close enough to see and photograph Atlantic Puffins, Razorbills, Black Guillemots, Common Murres, Common Eiders, terns, gulls, and cormorants.

CONTACT Matinicus Chamber of Commerce, P.O. Box 212, Matinicus, ME 04851; 207-366-3868. **HOW TO GET THERE** By boat from Rockland, contact Capt. Richard Moody (207-366-3700), Atlantic Expeditions (207-372-8621), or Maine State Ferry service (207-596-2202); from New Harbor, contact Hardy Boat Cruises (207-677-2026). **SEASONAL ACCESS** Boats run most frequently in summer.

MACHIAS SEAL ISLAND

Administered by the Canadian Wildlife Service, 25-acre Machias Seal Island is a naturalist's paradise, at its best in June and July. If the Gulf of Maine is clear of fog, the 1½-hour boat ride to the island can feature views of seals, occasional whales, and many seabirds, including jaegers, gannets, guillemots, shearwaters, storm-petrels, and cormorants. But as the boat nears the island, everyone tries to spot the first Atlantic Puffin, with its oversized, colorful bill the most striking seabird in the North Atlantic.

If weather and seas are favorable, your captain will anchor offshore and transport you by dory to the edge of the island. Once on land, prepare to run a gauntlet of highly perturbed Arctic Terns, which dive at your head as you pass their nests. In the shelter of one of the two observation blinds, you will be enchanted by the puffins (the deep whirring noises emanating from the rocks around and beneath you are puffins calling from their hidden lairs) and penguin-like Razorbills. It is impossible to have too much film here.

HOW TO GET THERE All visits to Machias Seal Is. are by boat. **CONTACT** Norton of Jonesport, R.R. 1 Box 990, Jonesport, ME 04649-9704; 207-497-5933. Lubec Marine Services, 9 High St., Lubec, ME 04652; 207-733-5584. Bold Coast Charter Company, P.O. Box 364, Cutler, ME 04626; 207-259-4484. **SEASONAL ACCESS** Boat service available May–Aug.

QUODDY HEAD STATE PARK   Lubec

For sheer drama, the scenery at 481-acre Quoddy Head State Park is unbeatable— 200-foot cliffs, wind-sculptured evergreens, pounding surf, and Maine's only red-and-white striped lighthouse perched on a bluff at the easternmost point in the United States. Scan seaward and you have a fair chance of seeing Fin or Minke Whales. Overhead, a flock of Evening Grosbeaks or a raven or two may appear. An elusive Spruce Grouse may suddenly stroll out from the cover of the spruce-fir woodlands, perhaps accompanied by a flock of tiny cheepers. A brown-capped Boreal Chickadee may give its burry call from a nearby thicket.

Do not miss the West Quoddy Head Bog Trail. A boardwalk rambles through a 7-acre bog, where the various specialized peat-land plants, such as sundews and pitcher plants, are well labeled and can be studied at point blank range with dry feet.

CONTACT Quoddy Head S.P., R.R. 2 Box 1490, Lubec, ME 04652; 207-733-0911. **HOW TO GET THERE** From Lubec, turn south off Rte. 189 onto South Lubec Rd. (watch for state park sign); after about 3 miles, turn left on West Quoddy Head Rd., and follow it to the park. **SEASONAL ACCESS** Open May 15–Oct. 15. At other seasons, park outside the gate (do not block the road) and walk a few hundred yards into the park.

MOOSEHORN NATIONAL WILDLIFE REFUGE (BARING UNIT)   Calais

The American Woodcock, or Timberdoodle, is one of North America's most endearing birds. With its plump silhouette, long bill, comical voice, and spectacular aerial courtship displays, it is a sight to see. Here at Moosehorn National Wildlife Refuge, a summer population of approximately 1,800 birds lives in habitats specially managed and groomed for the species. Spring and early summer are the best seasons for viewing the birds' twilight aerial displays, and park biologists allow visitors to assist in banding programs.

Moosehorn has much to offer besides American Woodcocks. Bald Eagles often nest alongside U.S. 1, some 300 American Beavers live here, and more than 16,000 acres of mixed forest and wetlands shelter a wealth of mammals and at least 125 species of breeding birds.

CONTACT Moosehorn N.W.R. (Baring Unit), R.R. 1 Box 202, Suite 1, Baring, ME 04694-9703; 207-454-7161. **HOW TO GET THERE** From Calais, drive about 3 miles southwest on U.S. 1 and watch for refuge signs. **SEASONAL ACCESS** Year-round. **VISITOR CENTER** Refuge hdqrs. located off Charlotte Rd. about 2 miles inside the refuge.

SUNKHAZE MEADOWS
NATIONAL WILDLIFE REFUGE   **Milford**

Many of the wildlife areas featured in this guide are easily accessible: You merely have to drive up to the beach or lake or woodland path that is your destination. Sunkhaze Meadows National Wildlife Refuge is different. You have to work a lot harder for your rewards. The 9,337 acres of boglands, streams, and marshes here are home to American Beavers, Common Muskrats, Northern River Otters, Moose, and Mink. Wonderful nesting birds such as American Bitterns and the Common Snipe share this refuge with Blue-winged Teals and Hooded Mergansers, among other waterfowl species. While beaver dams can sometimes make for tough paddling, canoeing is the best way to get around at Sunkhaze. Be sure to ask at headquarters for information on the best access routes.

CONTACT Sunkhaze Meadows N.W.R., 1033 S. Main St., Old Town, ME 04468; 207-827-6138. **HOW TO GET THERE** Refuge hdqrs. on east side of Rte. 2, approx. 1.5 miles after crossing Stillwater Rd. in Orono. **SEASONAL ACCESS** Accessible throughout the year by foot or canoe or, in winter, by skis. **VISITOR CENTER** Refuge hdqrs.

ALLAGASH WILDERNESS WATERWAY

Established in 1966 and added to the National Wild and Scenic River System in 1970, the Allagash Wilderness Waterway is for the adventurer who has some time to enjoy a true North Woods experience. The Allagash is buggiest in June, busiest in

July and August. Sixty-six campsites dot the 92-mile-long corridor. Canoeists take 7 to 10 days to complete the river trip; along the way, they run a few sections of Class II white water, share a lake or two with Moose, and fall asleep to the sound of yipping Coyotes and whooping Barred Owls. This trip is not for beginners, except in the company of a qualified guide.

CONTACT Allagash Wilderness Waterway, c/o Northern Region, Maine Bureau of Parks and Lands, Maine Dept. of Conserv., 106 Hogan Rd., Bangor, ME 04401; 207-941-4014. **HOW TO GET THERE** Access to most of the area is by private roads; for information, contact the organization of private owners: North Maine Woods, Inc., P.O. Box 421, Ashland, ME 04732; 207-435-6213. **SEASONAL ACCESS** Year-round, but in winter plan extremely well and cautiously as the weather is often bitter and little help is available should difficulties arise.

AROOSTOOK STATE PARK · Presque Isle
Hike picturesque Quaggy Jo Mountain or rent a canoe and paddle out among the Common Loons and Ospreys in this 600-acre park. **CONTACT** Aroostook S.P., 87 State Park Rd., Presque Isle, ME 04769; 207-768-8341 (summer); 207-764-2040 (winter).

BACK COVE · Portland
A 3½-mile pedestrian pathway encircles this downtown birders' paradise, best visited late summer through winter. 215 species of birds have been identified here. **CONTACT** Convention and Visitors Bureau, 305 Commercial St., Portland, ME 04101; 207-772-4994.

BIGELOW PRESERVE
Stratton

Bigelow Preserve

This 35,000-acre public preserve comprises the entire Bigelow Range, 30 miles of the Appalachian Trail, and 21 miles of lake frontage. **CONTACT** Bigelow Preserve, Maine Bureau of Public Lands, P.O. Box 327, Farmington, ME 04938; 207-778-4111.

BORESTONE MOUNTAIN
WILDLIFE SANCTUARY · Monson
At almost 2,000 feet, the mountain towers above this 1,600-acre Audubon sanctuary and offers unparalled views of the surrounding central Maine landscape. **CONTACT** Borestone Mtn. W.S., National Audubon Society, Maine State Office, P.O. Box 524, Dover-Foxcroft, ME 04426; 207-564-7946.

CAMDEN HILLS STATE PARK · Camden
One of the finest fall hawk-watching sites in New England, the park also has 25 miles of outstanding woodland trails and plenty of breathtaking views. **CONTACT** Camden Hills S.P., HCR 60 Box 3110, Camden, ME 04843; 207-236-3109 (May 1–Oct. 15); 207-236-0849 (Oct. 16–Apr. 30).

COBSCOOK BAY STATE PARK · Dennysville
Cobscook derives from an Indian word meaning "boiling tides"—the tide averages 24 feet here. Tide-watching and eagle-watching are equally exciting in this 888-acre park. **CONTACT** Cobscook Bay S.P., R.R. 1, Box 127, Dennysville, ME 04628; 207-726-4412.

GRAFTON NOTCH STATE PARK · Newry
Shrublands, alpine wildflowers, and spectacular gorges, cliffs, and geology highlight this 3,112-acre backpackers' paradise near the Maine–New Hampshire border. **CONTACT** Grafton Notch S.P., HC 61 Box 330, Newry, ME 04261; 207-824-2912.

GREAT WASS ISLAND PRESERVE · Beals
Here among the exposed headlands and coastal raised bogs, 3½ miles of preserve trails wander through areas of outstanding beauty, habitat for a variety of plants, including several rarities. **CONTACT** Great Wass Is. Preserve, c/o Maine Chapter, The Nature Conservancy, P.O. Box 338, Topsham, ME 04086; 207-729-5181.

INDIAN POINT–BLAGDEN PRESERVE · Bar Harbor
Located on a part of Mount Desert Island that escaped the ravaging fire of 1947, the 110-acre preserve protects mature spruce-fir-cedar woodlands, as well as 1,000 feet of coastline. **CONTACT** Indian Point–Blagden Preserve, c/o Maine Chapter, The Nature Conservancy, 14 Maine St., Suite 401, Brunswick, ME 04011; 207-729-5181.

LILY BAY STATE PARK
Greenville

The 925-acre park is an excellent base for discovering the natural wonders of Maine's largest lake, Moosehead. Gamefish including Brook Trout and "Landlocked" Salmon await. **CONTACT** Lily Bay S.P., HC 76 Box 425, Greenville, ME 04441; 207-695-2700.

MOUNT BLUE STATE PARK
Weld

Bicknell's Thrush, the Northeast's only endemic bird species, and a fine variety of other breeding birds may be glimpsed during summer in this sprawling 4,398-acre park. **CONTACT** Mt. Blue S.P., R.R. 1 Box 610, Weld, ME 04285; 207-585-2347 (summer); 207-585-2261 (winter).

PETIT MANAN NATIONAL WILDLIFE REFUGE
Milbridge

Petit Manan Point, the mainland section of this 3,335-acre refuge, offers blueberry barrens, woodlands, freshwater and salt marshes, and cobble beaches. **CONTACT** Petit Manan N.W.R., P.O. Box 279, Milbridge, ME 04658; 207-546-2124.

RACHEL CARSON SALT POND PRESERVE
New Harbor

Littoral marine life, such as seaweeds, crabs, sea urchins, and limpets, may be quietly appreciated at this 70-acre sanctuary. **CONTACT** Rachel Carson Salt Pond Preserve, c/o Maine Chapter, The Nature Conservancy, 14 Maine St., Suite 401, Brunswick, ME 04011; 207-729-5181.

RANGELEY LAKE STATE PARK
Rangeley

Wood warblers, an amazingly colorful and fascinating subfamily of birds, appear in abundance from May through August in this 730-acre park. Hikers and anglers should pack their bird guides. **CONTACT** Rangeley Lake S.P., HC 32 Box 5000, Rangeley, ME 04970-5000; 207-864-3858.

REID STATE PARK
Georgetown

Naturalists and day-trippers alike can appreciate the 766 acres of sandy beach, tide pools, lagoon, and mixed woodlands throughout the year. **CONTACT** Reid S.P., HC 33 Box 286, Georgetown, ME 04548; 207-371-1303.

ROQUE BLUFFS STATE PARK
Roque Bluffs

This 271-acre park has an intriguing combination of salt- and freshwater habitats that are easily viewed from the roadside parking area. **CONTACT** Roque Bluffs S.P., RFD Box 202, Machias, ME 04654; 207-255-3475.

Reid State Park

WELLS NATIONAL ESTUARINE RESEARCH RESERVE
Wells

Tours beginning at the visitor center introduce the natural history of this 1,600-acre estuarine habitat, where the Merriland, Webhannet, and Little Rivers meet the ocean tides. **CONTACT** Wells National Estuarine Research Reserve, R.R. 2 Box 806, Wells, ME 04090; 207-646-1555.

WOLFE'S NECK WOODS STATE PARK
Freeport

More than 200 acres of forested shoreland are just a few minutes from town. Five miles of hiking trails are maintained here. **CONTACT** Wolfe's Neck Woods S.P., 106 Wolfe's Neck Rd., Freeport, ME 04032; 207-865-4465 (Apr.–Oct.); 207-624-6080 (Nov.–Mar.).

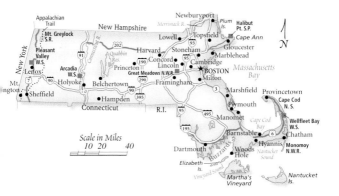

Massachusetts

In general terms, elevations in the Commonwealth of Massachusetts (total area 8,257 square miles) are highest in the western part of the state and gradually diminish to sea level on the coastal plain. Mount Greylock, in the northwest corner, is the tallest peak (3,491 feet) and one of few above 2,500 feet. Westernmost Massachusetts is dominated by two upland ridges, the Taconics and the Berkshires, where broadleaf forests mix at the highest elevations with northern spruce and fir. To the east lies the wide Connecticut Valley, with its rich, deep farmland soils. Farther east are the Worcester County hill country and the huge Quabbin and Wachusett Reservoirs. The state's eastern lowlands give way to the coastal regions, granite and muscular on Cape Ann, sandy and marshy in the southeast. Cape Cod and its offshore islands are the state's celebrated easternmost extensions.

There are 28 river basins in the Bay State. Some of the most significant are the Housatonic, home to a number of rare plants and animals, including Bog Turtles; the Deerfield, with the greatest average annual precipitation (50 inches) in the state; the Connecticut, which has been called New England's principal inland highway of bird migration; the Chicopee, the Commonwealth's largest river basin; the Nashua, a great environmental success story; the Sudbury, Assabet, and Concord system (made famous by Thoreau), northwest of Boston; and the Charles, which twists and turns for 80 miles from Hopkinton to Boston.

Massachusetts has 2,700 species of plants, 1,750 of which are native, and impressive numbers of vertebrates, including a remarkable 460 bird species sighted within its boundaries. Many of the state's reptiles are locally rare or threatened.

Massachusetts has 39 state parks, nine state forests, three state reservations, six national wildlife refuges, and one incomparable national seashore.

CAPE COD NATIONAL SEASHORE

Encompassing almost 45,000 acres, Cape Cod National Seashore protects the outer Cape's treasured beaches, coastal tidal marshes, upland pine-oak woodlands, glacial ponds, and spectacular dunes. From Orleans' Nauset Beach at the Cape's "elbow" to Race Point at terra firma's farthest reach into the Atlantic, the National Seashore lands stretch along the entire eastern edge of Cape Cod. There are hundreds of starting points from which to explore this area; here we will travel from south to north and describe some of the major sites.

NAUSET BEACH For the walker who wants Cape Cod beach the way Thoreau experienced it, Nauset Beach offers miles of crashing waves and sand, and solitude most of the year. About a mile's walk south of the parking area, privately owned Pochet Island is a birder's paradise, with fine trails and thickets. Residents normally welcome considerate naturalists.

Nauset Beach

FORT HILL Overlooking vast Nauset Marsh, Fort Hill's superb setting makes it a "must" at any time of year. Peregrine Falcons hunt the marshlands in fall and are likelier here than at any other spot on the Cape. Great Blue Herons and Common Terns are common. A nature trail winds around the open meadows and through a Red Maple swamp. The fields attract many butterflies. While studying the skippers and hairstreaks feeding at the milkweed blossoms, look for handsomely striped land snails on the milkweed stalks and leaves.

SALT POND VISITOR CENTER AND VICINITY The road to the visitor center also leads to two fine outer strands—Coast Guard Beach and Nauset Light Beach. Away from the parking areas, these beaches are relatively uncrowded, and the botanizing and birding potential is great. The Buttonbush Trail for the Blind is near the visitor center.

MARCONI STATION SITE Location of the first U.S. wireless station and present headquarters of the national seashore, Marconi is a fascinating area for nature lovers. Horned Larks breed here, as do some of the Cape's last remaining Vesper Sparrows. The vegetation is a mixture of pines, bayberry, and moorland plants, including Bearberry and the local Broom Crowberry. The boardwalk along the Atlantic White Cedar Swamp Trail traverses a beautiful cedar stand, home to the endangered Hessel's Hairstreak butterflies and nesting Eastern Screech- and Northern Saw-whet Owls.

GRIFFIN ISLAND and **GREAT ISLAND** Detour about 12 miles north and west of Marconi, through the town of Wellfleet, and take in the shoreline of Cape Cod Bay on Griffin and Great Islands, now part of the mainland. Picnicking and beachcombing are popular pursuits, but watch the tides carefully, as parts of the area are impassable at higher tides.

PILGRIM HEIGHTS The perfect spot for the migration watcher, Pilgrim Heights offers fabulous views of the North Truro–Provincetown dunelands. Dragonflies, butterflies, and hawks of all kinds stream by Pilgrim Heights in both directions on favorable spring and fall winds.

Atlantic White Cedar Swamp Trail

BEECH FOREST The Beech Forest, along Race Point Road in Provincetown, is a remnant of the varied woodlands that once covered large areas of Cape Cod. American Beech and numerous species of pines and oaks dominate the vegetation and surround a series of fine freshwater ponds. Cape Cod birdwatchers consider the Beech Forest to be the region's single most productive spot for migrant songbirds in spring. The woods also shelter acrobatic but harmless Eastern Hognose Snakes.

RACE POINT BEACH Although the panoramic views here are inspiring even to the unaided eye, a telescope or binoculars may reveal a great deal more of the activities a short way out to sea. Several hundred yards offshore, the water changes color from light to deep blue, marking a drop-off to deep water. Huge baleen whales, especially Humpback and Fin, which require deep water for feeding, can navigate surprisingly close to land at Race Point and may readily be seen by the careful observer. Seabirds, too, may concentrate off Race Point, sometimes in incredible abundance.

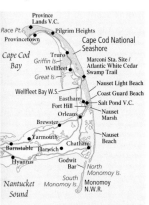

CONTACT Cape Cod N.S., 99 Marconi Site Rd., Wellfleet, MA 02667; 508-255-3421. **HOW TO GET THERE** Most of the seashore is located adjacent to U.S. 6, along the outer Cape. The 25-mile-long Cape Cod Rail Trail, used by cyclists, equestrians, walkers, and joggers, runs from Dennis north to Wellfleet and passes close to many seashore sites. **SEASONAL ACCESS** Visitor centers and trails are open year-round. Lifeguards generally on duty only in summer. **VISITOR CENTERS** Salt Pond V.C. is located east of U.S. 6 in Eastham. Province Lands V.C. is located at the end of Race Pt. Rd. in Provincetown.

CAPE ANN: GLOUCESTER AND ROCKPORT

Cape Ann includes four towns: Essex, Manchester-by-the-Sea, Gloucester, and Rockport. Here we concentrate on easternmost Gloucester and Rockport, the heart of Cape Ann. Everywhere the visitor, whether Massachusetts native or first-time out-of-stater, is struck by the beauty of the place. Artist colonies, fishing boats, and magnificent rocky headlands draw crowds during warm-weather months, though the quaint, narrow, winding streets can be uninviting during the height of the summer tourist season. Fortunately for the nature enthusiast, Cape Ann wildlife-watching is at its peak outside the summer months.

Rocky shore, Gloucester, Massachusetts

The compact Eastern Point Wildlife Sanctuary in Gloucester is Massachusetts' premier Monarch stopover in fall—2,000 or more may be seen on favorable days in September and early October. The nearby breakwater is a good spot for wintering Glaucous and Iceland Gulls and Black Guillemots. Niles Pond, along the causeway road, sometimes shelters unusual waterfowl and gulls.

In Rockport, Halibut and Andrew's Points are centers of avian interest from fall through spring. Jutting into the North Atlantic, they thrust the observer out into the migrating swarms of cormorants, scoters, and eiders, and during a nor'easter offer sometimes spectacular opportunities for viewing windblown pelagic seabirds such as jaegers, phalaropes, shearwaters, and Dovekies. Andrew's Point, easily reached by road, has excellent views of the ocean. Halibut Point State Park's dramatic 54-acre grounds are accessible by walking paths. The area has a historic granite quarry and winter-resident scoters and eiders. Guided tours to observe birds, wildflowers, and tidepools are offered on a regular basis throughout much of the year. Whale-watching trips leave from Gloucester during the warmer months.

CONTACT Halibut Point S.P., Gott Ave., Rockport, MA 01966; 978-546-2997; or Eastern Point W.S., c/o Mass. Audubon Society, 208 S. Great Rd., Lincoln, MA 01773; 781-259-9500. HOW TO GET THERE Cape Ann is reached via Rte. 128, off I-95 or U.S. 1. Numerous rotaries and winding roads make a good road map indispensable. SEASONAL ACCESS Year-round.

PARKER RIVER NATIONAL WILDLIFE
REFUGE/PLUM ISLAND   Newburyport

Plum Island, comprising parts of the towns of Newburyport, Newbury, and Rowley, is home to the Parker River National Wildlife Refuge. With its 6½-mile road, the refuge offers drive-by access to dunes, tidal marshes, and freshwater impoundments specially managed for migratory birds. From the extensive tidal flats of the Merrimack River to the barrier dunes of Plum Island, the refuge's 4,662 acres fairly swarm with fascinating bird life in all seasons.

Near the north end of the refuge, the salt pans on the right side of the main road attract Hudsonian Godwits, dowitchers, dunlins, and other shorebirds (the refuge has recorded an amazing 43 species) from May to October. New Pines, a pine grove a mile ahead on the left, may hold wintering finches or a Northern Saw-whet Owl. About a half mile farther on the right is Hellcat Swamp. In spring, the swamp and woods trail may be swarming with kinglets, thrushes, and warblers. In late summer, the evening flight of herons and egrets coming to roost in the Hellcat marshes can be phenomenal, and tens of thousands of Tree Swallows swirl above the tall marsh grasses, snapping up mosquitoes; White-tailed Deer, Common Muskrats, and Red Foxes are also often seen. Snowy Owls may be spotted atop the dikes at Hellcat in winter.

Plum Island sand dunes

Sandy Point State Reservation, at the southern tip of Plum Island, has nesting Piping Plovers and access to good beach areas. Shell collecting can be very good along any of the island beaches, especially after a storm: the world's largest mollusk, the Giant Squid, has even been washed up here.

CONTACT Parker River N.W.R., Northern Blvd., Plum Is., Newburyport, MA 01950; 978-465-5753. **HOW TO GET THERE** From I-95, take exit 57 and go east on Rte. 113 for about 3.5 miles. At the traffic light adjacent to the Newbury town common, turn left on Rolfe's Lane and drive to its end. The Merrimack River is in front of you. Turn right onto Plum Is. Tpke. and drive about 2 miles, over the bridge and onto Plum Is. The first right goes to the refuge. **SEASONAL ACCESS** Year-round. The refuge's beach is closed Apr.–Aug. to protect breeding Piping Plovers. **VISITOR CENTER** Mass. Audubon Society is developing one on the Merrimack River side of the Plum Is. Tpke.

WELLFLEET BAY WILDLIFE SANCTUARY

South Wellfleet

Wellfleet Bay Wildlife Sanctuary is a serene landscape of 1,000 acres of pine woods, salt marshes, moorlands, estuaries, and freshwater ponds, where one can stroll past gaudy Orange Milkweed, carpets of heathland Bearberries, and little batallions of fiddler crabs scurrying across the mudflats. At any season, it is possible to find a quiet corner here. Wellfleet Bay is also a beehive of activity, the center of nature study on the outer Cape. The sanctuary offers an extraordinary array of programs, including walks, canoe trips, wildlife tours, even a fall natural history weekend. A telephone hotline (508-349-WING) keeps callers up to date on sightings and happenings.

CONTACT Wellfleet Bay W.S., Mass. Audubon Society, P.O Box 236, S. Wellfleet, MA 02663; 508-349-2615. **HOW TO GET THERE** Follow U.S. 6 along the outer Cape to S. Wellfleet and watch for distinctive signs for the sanctuary located on the west side of the road. **SEASONAL ACCESS** Year-round. **VISITOR CENTER** Nature Ctr. located adjacent to main parking area.

MONOMOY NATIONAL WILDLIFE REFUGE

Chatham

The venerable Ludlow Griscom, dean of New England birdwatching, used to drive down the long sandy beaches of Monomoy Point, and routinely make fantastic ornithological discoveries. A series of winter storms turned Monomoy Point into North and South

Monomoy Islands by 1978, and Mr. Griscom and his beach wagon are no longer with us, but the abundant bird life remains. Although getting to Monomoy requires a bit of planning, a trip to this 2,750-acre refuge is a splendid natural history adventure.

North Monomoy is famous for its shorebirds. Godwit Bar on the island's west side has hosted all four of the world's species of godwits, as well as great numbers of other sandpipers, curlews, plovers, oystercatchers, yellowlegs, and dowitchers. South Monomoy, the larger island, has coastal shrublands, magnificent dunes, and freshwater ponds. Remember to bring food, plenty of water, and sunscreen, and be aware that South Monomoy in particular has a lot of Poison Ivy, so dress appropriately.

CONTACT Monomoy N.W.R., Wiki Way, Chatham, MA 02633; 508-945-0594. **HOW TO GET THERE** Tours of North and South Monomoy Islands are available through the Mass. Audubon Society (508-349-2615) or the Cape Cod Museum of Natural History (508-896-3867). Limited ferry service is available in Chatham.

GREAT MEADOWS NATIONAL WILDLIFE REFUGE

Sudbury and Concord

Refuge at Sudbury

Great Meadows National Wildlife Refuge, consisting of 3,400 acres in two units along 12 miles of the Concord and Sudbury Rivers, was established and is managed for migratory birds. Visit both of the reserve units to get a feeling for the true magnitude of the refuge. The site in Sudbury has the visitor center and headquarters, as well as a 1-mile trail skirting a pond, a Red Maple swamp, a marsh, and upland woods. The Concord unit has extensive dikes, which enclose freshwater impoundments bursting with American Lotus and other diverse plant life. An observation tower at the main parking area and a few photographers' blinds offer different perspectives on the marsh and pond life.

More than 220 species of birds have been seen here, from soaring, tilting Turkey Vultures to skulking, bobbing Northern Waterthrushes. The refuge waters teem with Canada Geese, Mallards, American Black Ducks, Blue-winged Teals, and Wood Ducks, all of which can be seen trailing lines of youngsters in late spring and early summer. The woodlands shelter some of the most colorful New England songbirds, including Baltimore Orioles, Rose-breasted Grosbeaks, and Scarlet Tanagers, while the skies are liberally sprinkled from spring to fall with dashing swallows of many species. Raptors such as Red-tailed and Broad-winged Hawks and Great Horned Owls are also common, though usually much less obvious.

Rose-breasted Grosbeak

If you visit during the warm-weather months, take some time to identify, photograph, sketch, and just enjoy some of the myriad damselflies and dragonflies that reside here. They belong to a marvelously varied order of insects, with such euphonious English names as skimmer, glider, dancer, bluet, and jewelwing. Their manner is dashing, their colors are bedazzling. There is no better place to become acquainted with these glorious creatures than at the marshes, ponds, and riversides of Great Meadows.

CONTACT Great Meadows N.W.R., Weir Hill Rd., Sudbury, MA 01776; 978-443-4661 **HOW TO GET THERE** To reach the refuge hdqrs. from Wayland, drive northwest 1.7 miles on Rte. 27, turn right on Water Row Rd., continue to the end of the road, turn right on Lincoln Hill Rd., travel .5 mile, turn left on Weir Hill Rd. To reach the Concord Unit from Concord Center, drive northeast on Rte. 62 for 1.3 miles and turn left on Monson Rd. The entrance road is on the left. **SEASONAL ACCESS** Year-round. **VISITOR CENTER** Weir Hill V.C., at the hdqrs. building.

MARTHA'S VINEYARD

The island of Martha's Vineyard is 108 square miles of exceptional summer vacationland and year-round nature exploration. Its highlights are many, including the following areas: **GAY HEAD** Visit the towering, multicolored cliffs at Gay Head during fall migration and you may be inundated with birds too numerous to count. **FELIX NECK WILDLIFE SANCTUARY** Wild Turkeys, Barn Owls, and Ospreys can be seen along 6 miles of trails across grasslands, heaths, woodlands, and marsh. A nighttime moth program may offer a glimpse of the magnificent Imperial Moth. **KATAMA PLAINS** Open-country raptors such as Short-eared Owls and Rough-legged Hawks prowl these open spaces (not a protected preserve). Watch for sparrows in fall and masses of sulphurs, whites, and other butterflies in summer.

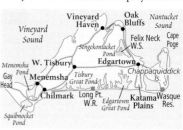

CONTACT Felix Neck W.S., Mass. Audubon Society, P.O. Box 494, Vineyard Haven, MA 02568; 508-627-4850. Martha's Vineyard Chamber of Commerce, P.O. Box 1698V, Vineyard Haven, MA 02568; 508-693-0085. **HOW TO GET THERE** Ferries run from Falmouth, Hyannis, and New Bedford May–Sept., and from Woods Hole year-round. **SEASONAL ACCESS** Year-round. **VISITOR CENTER** The Barn at Felix Neck.

NANTUCKET ISLAND

Smaller (about 35,000 acres), quieter, wilder, and farther from the mainland than Martha's Vineyard, Nantucket is a delightful place to enjoy nature in all seasons. Keep watch from the ferry over for such pelagic birds as jaegers, shearwaters, and storm-petrels well away from land, and gulls, terns, and sea ducks in abundance closer to shore. Once on the island, stop at the headquarters of the Maria Mitchell Association, a few blocks up Main Street from the wharfs. Maria Mitchell was an astronomer, and the association's astronomical observatory is frequently open to the public. The staff can point you toward the island's natural attractions. The association offers programs in saltmarsh ecology, botany, birds, and other topics.

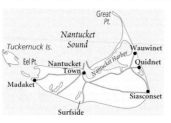

CONTACT Maria Mitchell Assoc., 2 Vestal St., Nantucket, MA 02554; 508-228-9198. Nantucket Is. Chamber of Commerce, 48 Maine St., Nantucket, MA 02554; 508-228-1700. **HOW TO GET THERE** Ferries run from Hyannis year-round and Martha's Vineyard in summer. **SEASONAL ACCESS** Year-round. **VISITOR CENTER** Hinchman House, hdqrs. of the Maria Mitchell Assoc., 7 Milk St.

QUABBIN RESERVOIR PARK AND RESERVATION

Belchertown

Construction of the Quabbin Reservoir began in 1926 to provide a major new water source for the state's burgeoning population. The towns of Dana, Enfield, Greenwich, and Prescott were flooded when the reservoir was filled to its 412-billion-gallon capacity. Today the 120-square-mile reservation is the most significant wild area in the state, home to Coyotes, Bobcats, American Beavers, Northern River Otters, Fishers, and Common Porcupines.

During the winter months especially, Quabbin is a prime Bald Eagle–watching area. From Enfield Lookout, a few miles beyond the visitor center, scan across to Prescott Peninsula and beyond and you may be rewarded with views of a dozen or more eagles. Quabbin's 55 access roads (called "gates" and all numbered) provide great hiking opportunities year-round. Dress for cold in winter, insects in summer. A map of the region is available at the visitor center.

CONTACT Quabbin Reservoir Park and Res., Metropolitan District Commission, 485 Ware Rd., Belchertown, MA 01007; 413-323-7221. **HOW TO GET THERE** From I-90 (Mass. Tpke.), take exit 7 to Rte. 21, and follow it north to Rte. 9. Drive east 2 miles to Quabbin Reservoir–Winsor Dam sign. Turn left and drive .25 mile to brick administration building. **SEASONAL ACCESS** Year-round. **VISITOR CENTER** In Quabbin administration building.

ARCADIA WILDLIFE SANCTUARY

Easthampton

Massachusetts is blessed with many woodlands of varied make-up, age, and extent. One of the least common forest types is the so-called floodplain forest, dominated by American Sycamores, Eastern Cottonwoods, and Silver Maples. The delightful Arcadia Wildlife Sanctuary protects a significant and handsome floodplain forest on its 550 acres. A number of rare freshwater mussels, snails, turtles, and plants reside in the aquatic and riparian habitats. An observation tower, from which you may spot some of the 215 birds on the sanctuary's checklist, overlooks a marsh. Rap gently on a hollow tree and a flying squirrel or two may appear. There are hiking trails, guided tours on land and by canoe, and a scenic Connecticut River oxbow, formed by the meandering course of the river.

CONTACT Arcadia W.S., Mass. Audubon Society, 127 Combs Rd., Easthampton, MA 01027; 413-584-3009. **HOW TO GET THERE** From I-91, take exit 18 and head south on U.S. 5. In 1.5 miles, turn right on East St., drive about 1 mile, turn right on Fort Hill Rd., and continue 1 mile to sanctuary. **SEASONAL ACCESS** Year-round. **VISITOR CENTER** At main parking area.

MOUNT GREYLOCK STATE RESERVATION

Lanesborough

An isolated mountain 3,491 feet high, Mount Greylock harbors many plants and animals usually found farther north. It has Purple and Painted Trilliums, Trout Lilies, Mountain Maples, Red Spruces, American Beeches, Hobblebush Viburnums, and the only

Showy Mountain Ash in the state. Sperry Road, which runs through the camping area, is lined with Eastern Hemlocks where flame-throated Blackburnian Warblers breed. The 11,000-acre reservation is also home to the Early Hairstreak, one of the most difficult butterflies to find in the wild, as well as Canadian Tiger Swallowtails and both the banded and unbanded forms of the Red-spotted Purple.

A stay at Bascom Lodge, perched atop Mount Greylock, is an ideal way to enjoy the area (for reservations, call 413-443-0011). Naturalists provide workshops on many subjects at the lodge.

CONTACT Mt. Greylock S.R., P.O. Box 138, Lanesborough, MA 01237; 413-499-4262/3. **HOW TO GET THERE** From I-90 (Mass. Tpke.), take exit 2, drive north on U.S. 20 to U.S. 7 and continue north 2 miles past Lanesborough. Watch for signs on the right. **SEASONAL ACCESS** Year-round. In winter access limited to snowmobile or foot. **VISITOR CENTER** On right just outside gate.

PLEASANT VALLEY WILDLIFE SANCTUARY

Lenox

Yellow-bellied Sapsuckers, Pileated Woodpeckers, and Winter Wrens are but three of the 89 bird species that nest at this appropriately named sanctuary. Wander some of the 1,400 acres of meadow, swamp, upland broadleaf woodlands, and rocky, hemlock-covered slopes; admire some of the 700 or so plant species that grow in this rich, calcareous soil; discover some of the American Beavers that populate Yokun Brook. Seven miles of trails pass through elevations ranging from 1,161 to 1,980 feet. If your time is short, try Pike's Pond Trail, which covers a good cross section of habitats in a short distance. Should your visit coincide with a warm early spring rain, come back in the evening and watch the Spotted and Jefferson's Salamanders migrate across the sanctuary road to the pond that is their breeding habitat.

CONTACT Pleasant Valley W.S., Mass. Audubon Society, 472 W. Mountain Rd., Lenox, MA 01240; 413-637-0320. **HOW TO GET THERE** From the intersection of U.S. 7 and 20 in Lenox, drive 3 miles north on the combined routes to West Dugway Rd. Turn left and follow signs for 1.6 miles to sanctuary entrance. **SEASONAL ACCESS** Year-round. **VISITOR CENTER**. Trailside Museum, open May–Oct., is at sanctuary entrance.

BASH BISH FALLS · Mount Washington

You may admire 200-foot-high Bash Bish Falls and its dramatic gorge from viewing areas at either the top or the bottom of the falls. Rare Ferns and wildflowers are a highlight. **CONTACT** Bash Bish Falls, Mt. Washington S.F., East St., Mt. Washington, MA 01258; 413-528-0330.

BARTHOLOMEW'S COBBLE · Sheffield

The limestone and marble outcrops (cobbles) in the 277-acre reservation generate an alkaline soil that nurtures a spectacular variety of ferns and wildflowers, drawing botanists from across the region. **CONTACT** Bartholomew's Cobble, The Trustees of Reservations, P.O. Box 128, Ashley Falls, MA 01222; 413-229-8600.

BLUE HILLS RESERVATION · Milton

Twenty hills to climb, 125 miles of trails to hike, and fine wildlife exhibits to view—all within sight of Boston—make this an outstanding 5,800-acre metropolitan reserve. **CONTACT** Blue Hills Res., 695 Hillside St., Milton, MA 02186; 617-698-1802.

DANIEL WEBSTER WILDLIFE SANCTUARY · Marshfield

As a 476-acre sanctuary for threatened grassland species, this former dairy farm is home to Pearl Crescent butterflies, Bobolinks, and Rough-legged Hawks at various seasons. **CONTACT** Daniel Webster W.S., Mass. Audubon Society, Winslow Cemetery Rd., Marshfield, MA 02050; 781-837-9400.

DEMEREST LLOYD STATE PARK · Dartmouth

Nearby Horseneck Beach draws the crowds away from this jewel of a park. Its seemingly endless tidal sandbars abound with marine life. **CONTACT** Demerest Lloyd S.P., c/o Horseneck Beach State Recreation Area, Rte. 88, Westport, MA 02790; 508-636-3298.

DRUMLIN FARM EDUCATION CENTER AND WILDLIFE SANCTUARY · Lincoln

New England farm life and birds of prey are two of the many ongoing exhibits at this small sanctuary, where special family events are held throughout the year. **CONTACT** Drumlin Farm Education Ctr. and W.S., South Great Rd., Lincoln, MA 01773; 781-259-9807.

GARDEN IN THE WOODS · Framingham

Specially designed habitats showcase more than 1,600 varieties of plants in this 45-acre garden devoted to temperate North American species. **CONTACT** Garden in the Woods, New England Wildflower Society, 180 Hemenway Rd., Framingham, MA 01701; 508-877-6574

IPSWICH RIVER WILDLIFE SANCTUARY · Topsfield

River exploration is one of the highlights of a visit to this 2,217-acre sanctuary, the Massachusetts Audubon Society's largest. Waterfowl and even an occasional Mink or Northern River Otter may be observed. **CONTACT** Ipswich River W.S., 87 Perkins Row, Topsfield, MA 01983; 978-887-9264.

LAUGHING BROOK EDUCATION CENTER AND WILDLIFE SANCTUARY · Hampden

This 354-acre sanctuary is home to more than 60 percent of the state's reptile species, as well as fine hemlock, hickory, and beech woods. **CONTACT** Laughing Brook Education Ctr. and W.S., 789 Main St., Hampden, MA 01036; 413-566-8034.

MANOMET OBSERVATORY FOR CONSERVATION SCIENCES · Manomet

The observatory staff conducts biological research throughout New England and the entire Western Hemisphere. Volunteer and intern opportunities are available. **CONTACT** Manomet Observatory for Conserv. Sciences, P.O. Box 1770, Manomet, MA 02345; 508-224-6521.

MARBLEHEAD NECK WILDLIFE SANCTUARY   Marblehead

During spring and fall migration periods, this compact coastal wooded headland is often one of the hottest places on the map for flycatchers, warblers, and vireos. **CONTACT** Marblehead Neck W.S., c/o Ipswich River W.S., 87 Perkins Row, Topsfield, MA 01983; 978-887-9264.

MIDDLESEX FELLS RESERVATION
Stoneham

The 2,060-acre reservation covers parts of five towns and features fine hiking and cross-country skiing trails over varying terrains. **CONTACT** Middlesex Fells Res., c/o Metropolitan District Commission, Public Information Office, 20 Somerset St., Boston, MA 02108; 617-727-5215.

Middlesex Fells Reservation

MOUNT AUBURN CEMETERY   Cambridge

Depending on your interests, a stroll through this 174-acre garden cemetery can reveal a blaze of migrant songbirds in May or a wonderland of tree and shrubs year-round. **CONTACT** Mt. Auburn Cemetery, 580 Mt. Auburn St., Cambridge, MA 02138; 617-547-7105.

MOUNT TOM STATE RESERVATION   Easthampton and Holyoke

Famous as a hawk-watching site in spring and fall, this 1,800-acre park has more than 20 miles of recreational trails and fine views of the Connecticut Valley. **CONTACT** Mt. Tom S.R., P.O. Box 985, Northampton, MA 01061; 413-527-4805.

NEW ENGLAND AQUARIUM   Boston

From the mesmerizing giant ocean tank to the hands-on tidepool exhibit, the New England Aquarium is a visual and educational treat. **CONTACT** New England Aquarium, Central Wharf, Boston, MA 02110-3399; 617-973-5200.

OXBOW NATIONAL WILDLIFE REFUGE   Harvard

The wet woodlands of this 711-acre refuge harbor Blanding's Turtles, Blue-spotted Salamanders, and a nice assortment of breeding birds. **CONTACT** Oxbow N.W.R., c/o Great Meadows N.W.R., Weir Hill Rd., Sudbury, MA 01776-1427; 978-443-4661.

PLYMOUTH BEACH   Plymouth

Plymouth Beach is one of the region's premier migrant shorebird spots, a wonderful place to study nesting terns of four species, and home to thousands of waterfowl in season. It's about 5 miles to the end of the beach and back. **CONTACT** Plymouth Beach, c/o Destination Plymouth, 225 Water St., Suite 202, Plymouth, MA 02360; 800-872-1620.

WACHUSETT MEADOW WILDLIFE SANCTUARY   Princeton

Upland meadows, a vast Red Maple swamp, and abundant bird and insect life, as well as one of America's most majestic Sugar Maples, make these 1,000 acres special. **CONTACT** Wachusett Meadow W.S., Mass. Audubon Society, 113 Goodnow Rd., Princeton, MA 01541; 978-464-2712.

WACHUSETT MOUNTAIN STATE RESERVATION   Princeton

A popular 2,000-acre winter ski resort, the 2,006-foot-high mountain is one of the country's premier fall hawk-watching spots—as many as 20,000 raptors have been seen in a single September day. **CONTACT** Wachusett Mtn. S.R., Mountain Rd., P.O. Box 248, Princeton, MA 01541; 978-464-2987.

WALDEN POND STATE RESERVATION   Concord

Thoreau wrote *Walden* while living in a cabin here. Miles of trails penetrate woodlands and skirt the shores of the 411-acre lake. **CONTACT** Walden Pond S.R., Rte. 126, Concord, MA 01742; 978-369-3254.

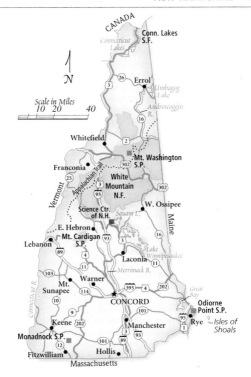

New Hampshire

The Granite State (9,304 square miles) is 85 percent forested, with 1,300 natural lakes and ponds and some outstanding mountainous areas. It has an enormous national forest, three national wildlife refuges, 27 state parks, and two state beaches.

In the southwest, a series of long ridges make up New Hampshire's western hills (average elevation 2,000 feet). Isolated Mount Monadnock is in this region, a favorite of day-hikers. In the southeast, between the Merrimack Valley and the coast, are the New Hampshire lowlands, home to most of the state's residents. The seacoast, only 18 miles long but an important natural and cultural region, has some fine estuarine habitats.

To the north lies the lakes region, centered on massive Lake Winnipesaukee, which has a 280-mile shoreline and 300-foot depths. Sugar Maple, American Beech, and Yellow Birch are dominant trees in the forests, and summering Common Loons are frequently heard on the lakes. Above the lakes, in north-central New Hampshire, spread the jagged and glorious peaks of the White Mountains, whose year-round splendor is legendary. Finally, where the state's eastern and western boundaries begin to converge, the North Woods begin. Lake Umbagog and the Connecticut Lakes, with their dual appeal of Moose and spruce, are for really adventurous lovers of wilderness.

WHITE MOUNTAIN NATIONAL FOREST

Autumn on Swift River, off Kancamagus Highway

The White Mountain National Forest is a sprawling, exquisite natural region in central and northern New Hampshire (with a small portion extending into western Maine). Numbers cannot adequately measure its significance, but here are a few statistics: nearly 800,000 acres in area; 48 mountain peaks above 4,000 feet; 1,167 miles of hiking trails; 100 miles of cross-country ski trails; more than 800 campsites; 650 miles of streams and rivers; and the highest, most breathtaking mountain in the Northeast. The White Mountains draw skiers, rock climbers, hikers, kayakers, painters, flower lovers, birders, and just about everyone in New England at one time or another (most often during fall foliage season). Temperatures average 78 degrees in midsummer and 26 degrees in winter; snowfall averages 100 inches annually.

Because of the enormous size of the forest, visitors need a good map just to get oriented. If you plan to hike, the *Appalachian Mountain Club White Mountain Guide* is indispensable; it guides you along the main highways and back roads, details trail conditions, and provides invaluable information on safety, weather patterns, availability of water, and the club's eight spartan "huts." The huts are actually large cabins, spread out along 56 trail miles, where lodging and camaraderie are offered at the end of a day's hike. Six of the sites serve meals. Huts accomodate between 18 and 80 people and must be booked well in advance (603-466-2727).

The various roads take hiker and nonhiker alike through marvelously picturesque mountain ravines, such as Franconia Notch and Pinkham Notch, and even to the summit of Mount Washington. The world-famous 34½-mile Kancamagus Highway has some of the most memorable scenery in New England. Moose and White-tailed Deer are seen throughout the region, and Peregrine Falcons, though not readily observed, are breeding on the White Mountain cliffs again after a long absence. Blue Jays and Gray Jays, Wood Thrushes and Bicknell's Thrushes, Downy Woodpeckers and Black-backed Woodpeckers share the same mountainsides—the first of each pair at the trail bases, the second in the heights.

Mount Washington, at 6,288 feet the highest point in New England, peaks well above other mountains of the Presidential Range. Judging by the number of cars emblazoned with "This car climbed Mount Washington" bumper stickers, a lot of visitors make the trek. The 8-mile auto road on the east flank, open from mid-May to late October, carries "climbers" to the apex of the largest alpine area in the East; bicyclists, auto racers, and runners all have yearly races to the top. Another dramatic method of reaching the top is to ride the 3-mile cog railway on the west flank, billed as the second-steepest railway in the world; one section climbs a 37-percent grade. Both the auto road and railway are private enterprises.

Mount Washington

For the purist, there are many exceptional hiking trails to the summit. Most are long and quite strenuous, so start early and be prepared for cold wet conditions. The glacial cirques of Tuckerman's Ravine and Great Gulf are favorites of hikers, as are the Alpine Gardens, which bloom with glacial relict alpine flowers in June and July. The White Mountain race of the Melissa Arctic butterfly, which inhabits many of the high Presidential peaks, flies mostly in July and can be looked for among the heaths and rock outcrops above 5,000 feet. Bird life may include the Spruce Grouse and Gray Jays in the upper stretches of forest and Common Ravens, American Pipits, and White-throated Sparrows above the timberline.

Once at the top (where the average temperature is 27 degrees F), hold on to your hat. On average, Mount Washington has hurricane-force winds 100 days per year. On April 12, 1934, the wind gauge here recorded the highest wind ever measured on the planet (231 mph). This combination of brutal wind and cold is exhilarating to the person who drives to the summit but potentially fatal to the ill-prepared hiker. The trails above the timberline in the Presidential Range have claimed the lives of scores of hikers and skiers over the years. Climbers starting out in balmy weather at the trail heads

Above the timberline on Mount Washington

can encounter drastic and sudden temperature and weather changes and may succumb to hypothermia if not properly equipped. Hat, gloves, and jacket, as well as a hiking partner, are essential parts of a trip into the higher reaches of the White Mountains.

CONTACT White Mountain N.F., P.O. Box 638, Laconia, NH 03247; 603-528-8721. **HOW TO GET THERE** Rte. 112 (Kancamagus Hwy.), which bisects the area in an east–west path, is 65 miles north of Concord on I-93. Rtes. 302 and 16 service the Presidential Range in the eastern sector. **SEASONAL ACCESS** Year-round. **VISITOR CENTERS** Pinkham Notch V.C., Rte. 16 Box 298, Gorham, NH 03581; 603-466-2721. Mt. Washington S.P., P.O. Box D, Gorham, NH 03581; 603-466-3347; open mid-May–mid-Oct.

NEW HAMPSHIRE COAST

The 18 miles of New Hampshire that border the Atlantic, although a short coastline compared to those of neighboring Maine and Massachusetts, have some very fine natural habitats. A driving tour along Rte. 1A can cover many of the best areas in a day. High sum-

Odiorne Point State Park

mer brings most of the year's beachgoers, but also good shorebird viewing; at other times, crowds are virtually nonexistent.

Beginning just north of the Massachusetts border, Hampton Harbor (or Seabrook Harbor, as it is sometimes called) is a haven for shorebirds during migration. Scan the mudflats from a parking area just south of the Hampton Harbor Bridge. Hampton Beach, across the bridge, is crowded in summer, but attracts Horned Larks and Snowy Owls during winter months. The breakers located along the beaches for several miles to the north are the winter home of scoters, grebes, and loons; you can pull into the state park and state beach parking areas along the way. On some of the beaches, high-tide lines may be littered with washed-up seaweeds, shells, and flotsam and jetsam of varied description. Birds as well as beachcombers can often find much of interest here.

Horned Lark

Farther north is Odiorne Point State Park, arguably the single best tidepooling and birding stop along the coast. The park's Seacoast Science Center has marine life displays and educational programs for schoolchildren and adults. For birdwatchers, trails lead to a variety of habitats, including shrubby areas sometimes overflowing with birds during migrations. Hawk-watching can be good at peak flight periods.

Finally, consider an offshore adventure to the Isles of Shoals. Five miles out to sea, these nine islands are part Maine, part New Hampshire and have a fascinating history and good birding potential.

CONTACT Seacoast Science Ctr., Odiorne Pt. S.P., 570 Ocean Blvd., Rye, NH 03870; 603-436-8043. **HOW TO GET THERE** Rte. 1A provides access to the entire length of the N.H. coastline. The Isles of Shoals Steamship Co. (603-431-5500 or 800-441-4620) and the Audubon Society of N.H. (603-224-9909) offer boat access to the Isles of Shoals spring–fall. **SEASONAL ACCESS** Year-round. **VISITOR CENTER** Seacoast Science Ctr. is open year-round.

MONADNOCK STATE PARK   Jaffrey

Monadnocks are ancient, tough, isolated mountains that have survived erosion from all sides. Monadnock State Park protects the peak whose Abenaki name (meaning "mountain that stands alone") now describes all peaks of this type. Mount Monadnock (3,166 feet), the most imposing feature in southwestern New Hampshire, is the northern terminus of the Connecticut to New Hampshire Metacomet–Monadnock Trail and the southern terminus of the Monadnock–Sunapee Greenway. Miles of trails lead to the summit. The Cascade Link Trail offers a gradual ascent, with White Ash woodlands yielding to Yellow Birch and finally to Red Spruce as the climber ascends. Do not expect to find solitude here; with 100,000 visitors annually, Monadnock is said to be the second most frequently climbed mountain in the world (after Japan's Mount Fuji). All six New England states may be glimpsed from the summit on clear days.

CONTACT Monadnock S.P., P.O. Box 181, Jaffrey, NH 03452-0181; 603-532-8862. **HOW TO GET THERE** From Keene, drive east about 3 miles on Rte. 101, turn south on Rte. 124, and go about 9 miles, watching for state park signs. **SEASONAL ACCESS** Year-round; limited services Nov.–Mar. **VISITOR CENTER** Near main parking area and campground.

MOUNT CARDIGAN STATE PARK   Canaan

Nestled at the western edge of the lakes region of New Hampshire, not far from the Vermont state line, is Mount Cardigan State Park. Mount Cardigan—or Old Baldy, as it is often called by the locals—attains a height of 3,121 feet. The views of the surrounding countryside are

outstanding from the summit, where a solar-powered fire tower is also an attraction. Some 30 miles of trails wind up and around the mountain and offer great exercise and the possibility of rewarding wildlife and plant encounters. Watch and listen for Hairy and Downy Woodpeckers, White-breasted and Red-breasted Nuthatches, and Solitary and Red-eyed Vireos by day and Barred and Great Horned Owls by night. Many hikers use the Appalachian Mountain Club's lodge at Cardigan Reservation, just outside the eastern boundary of the park, as a base.

CONTACT Mt. Cardigan S.P., c/o N.H. Division of Parks and Recreation, P.O. Box 1856, Concord, NH 03302-1856; 603-271-3254. **HOW TO GET THERE** From Lebanon, drive 13 miles east on U.S. 4 to Canaan. Turn north onto Rte. 118; after 1 mile turn right onto the access road to the park. The AMC lodge and trails of the east flank are reached via back roads west of Newfound Lake and Bristol. **SEASONAL ACCESS** Mid-May–mid-Oct. is prime season; access restricted at other times.

SCIENCE CENTER OF NEW HAMPSHIRE AT SQUAM LAKES
Holderness

The 200-acre Science Center of New Hampshire is exactly in the middle of the state, in the Squam Lakes region, an area well utilized for outdoor adventure. The Science Center focuses on environmental activities, with two pontoon boats for lake-ecology and moonlight cruises, and four nature trails through varied habitats, including one to the top of Mount Fayal. One of the most popular walks is along the Gephart Exhibit Trail, where visitors can see and learn about live birds of prey, White-tailed Deer, Northern River Otters, Bobcats, Black Bears, and other local species.

While in the area, take time to explore more of Squam Lake, home to a dozen breeding pairs of Common Loons. The New England Forestry Foundation Association holdings southeast of Holderness (get directions at the Science Center) are great for birding.

CONTACT Science Ctr. of N.H. at Squam Lakes, P.O. Box 173, Holderness, NH 03245-0173; 603-968-7194. **HOW TO GET THERE** The center is located at the intersection of U.S. 3 and Rte. 113 in Holderness, 4 miles from exit 24 off I-93. **SEASONAL ACCESS** Programs are offered year-round. The Nature Store and live-animal exhibit trail are open May–Oct. **VISITOR CENTER** Adjacent to the parking area.

CONNECTICUT LAKES STATE FOREST
Pittsburg

The Connecticut Lakes area offers innumerable North Country sights and experiences: great trout and salmon fishing, first-class canoeing, numbers of Moose (and black flies), rare Black-backed Woodpeckers, spruce woods, bogs, Northern Pitcher Plants, and Mink Frogs. The 1,500-acre Connecticut Lakes State Forest is a rather narrow strip of woods on either side of Route 3, but the whole region is so rural that you need not confine yourself to the state forest for prime nature-viewing. A good map will prove invaluable. (Most of the side roads are privately owned and must not be blocked in any manner by your vehicle.) The main road runs beside First, Second, and Third Connecticut Lakes in succession from south to north. East Inlet and Scott Bog, to the east between Second and Third Lakes, are two of the most popular areas with birders. Fourth Connecticut Lake, the source of the Connecticut River, lies a rugged mile hike from the road on the Quebec border.

CONTACT Conn. Lakes S.F., c/o N.H. Division of Parks and Recreation, P.O. Box 1856, Concord, NH 03302-1856; 603-271-3255. **HOW TO GET THERE** Take U.S. 3 north from the White Mtns. to northernmost New Hampshire. **SEASONAL ACCESS** Year-round.

AUDUBON HOUSE AND SILK FARM
Concord

Woodland-blooming wildflowers are a highlight of a spring visit to the state Audubon Society 15-acre headquarters. Turkey Pond attracts waterfowl. **CONTACT** Audubon House and Silk Farm, Audubon Society of N.H., 3 Silk Farm Rd., Concord, NH 03301; 603-224-9909.

BEAVER BROOK ASSOCIATION
Milford, Brookline, and Hollis

The association manages 1,700 acres of properties in Milford, Brookline, and Hollis, and offers more than 500 educational programs yearly. **CONTACT** Beaver Brook Assoc., 117 Ridge Rd., Hollis, NH 03049; 603-465-7787.

FRANCONIA NOTCH STATE PARK
Franconia

The granite profile of Old Man of the Mountain and the 90-foot granite gorge walls of the Flume are two features that make this 6,786-acre park one of the most scenic places in the state. **CONTACT** Franconia Notch S.P., Rte. 3, Franconia, NH 03580; 603-803-5563.

GREAT BAY NATIONAL WILDLIFE REFUGE
Newington

Ospreys, Oldsquaws, and oysters are all part of the natural environment at this refuge, which protects almost 6 miles of undeveloped bay shore. **CONTACT** Great Bay N.W.R., 336 Nimble Hill Rd., Newington, NH 03801; 603-431-7511.

LAKE UMBAGOG NATIONAL WILDLIFE REFUGE
Errol

Leave the car behind: to see Lake Umbagog's nesting Bald Eagles and Common Loons, you will want to canoe some of the lake's more than 8,500 acres. **CONTACT** Lake Umbagog N.W.R., P.O. Box 280, Errol, NH 03579; 603-482-3415.

Lake Umbagog National Wildlife Refuge

MOUNT KEARSARGE
Warner and Wilmot

Winslow and Rollins State Parks share Mount Kearsarge, which has an auto route almost to the top and views from Vermont to the Atlantic Ocean. **CONTACT** Winslow S.P. and Rollins S.P., c/o N.H. Division of Parks and Recreation, SW Region, P.O. Box 123, Greenfield, NH 03047; 603-547-3373.

MOUNT SUNAPEE STATE PARK
Mount Sunapee

For the truly energetic, this 2,900-acre park is the northern terminus of the 51-mile Monadnock–Sunapee Greenway trail. For the rest of us, Mount Sunapee offers year-round chairlift rides to wonderful scenic views. **CONTACT** Mt. Sunapee S.P., P.O. Box 2021, Mt. Sunapee, NH 03255; 603-763-2356.

PARADISE POINT NATURE CENTER
East Hebron

Located on Newfound Lake, said to be the cleanest lake in New Hamphire, the center's 43 acres feature 2 miles of nature trails and offer interpretive programs. **CONTACT** Paradise Pt. Nature Ctr., Audubon Society of N.H., N. Shore Rd., E. Hebron, NH 03232; 603-744-3516.

PONDICHERRY WILDLIFE REFUGE
Jefferson and Whitefield

If you enjoy the pristine beauty and bizarre plant life of northern bogs, as well as American Beavers and Moose, this 300-acre refuge will thrill you. **CONTACT** Pondicherry W.R., c/o Audubon Society of N.H., 3 Silk Farm Rd., Concord, NH 03301; 603-224-9909.

RHODODENDRON STATE PARK
Fitzwilliam

A magnificent 16-acre stand of Rosebay Rhodendrons which blooms in June is the primary attraction here. **CONTACT** Rhododendron S.P., c/o Monadnock S.P., P.O. Box 181, Jaffrey, NH 03452; 603-532-8862.

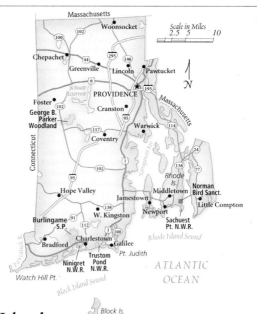

Rhode Island

With 22 state parks, five state beaches, and five national wildlife refuges, Rhode Island (total area 1,214 square miles) has surprisingly diverse natural history opportunities. In rural western Rhode Island among the oaks, maples, and pines live White-tailed Deer and Eastern Gray Squirrels, Pink Lady's Slippers and Indian-pipes, Mourning Cloaks and Eastern Commas. Jerimoth Hill, the state's highest elevation, rises 812 feet above sea level.

Narragansett Bay, in eastern Rhode Island, is the largest estuary in New England. Its convoluted shoreline makes up the larger part of the 420 miles of coast that the glaciers carved out along Rhode Island's margin. There are 35 islands in the bay; the largest, Rhode Island (formerly called Aquidneck Island), is home to Newport, Middletown, and Portsmouth. Many of the other islands have names that are whimsical (Hog, Hen, and Rabbit) or Puritanical (Patience, Hope, and Despair). All are worth exploring.

Rhode Island's south coast, from Point Judith west to Watch Hill Point, is backed by the Charlestown Moraine, a long, low mound of glacial sediment. Eight impressive coastal ponds are prominent features on the south shore. Mute Swans, Canada Geese, Ospreys, and multitudes of migrant, wintering, and resident birds, as well as other animals, depend on these refuges for shelter and sustenance.

Rhode Island's major river systems are the Pawcatuck, draining southwestern Rhode Island, and a series of five rivers flowing into Narragansett Bay: the Pawtuxet, Woonasquatucket, Blackstone, Seekonk, and Sakonnet.

BLOCK ISLAND

"Island of hope" and "one of the last great places" are phrases used by the Nature Conservancy to describe Block Island, which lies 12 miles off the Rhode Island coast. Its conservation-minded citizens have apparently decided that humankind can indeed

Mohegan Bluffs

coexist with nature to the benefit of both. Wild moorlands, sweeping bluffs and dunes, and salt ponds and marshes have been protected, and these are the drawing cards for visitors, who bicycle, watch birds, photograph, and enjoy the island's Victorian charm and natural beauty.

There are 28 miles of paved roads on the pear-shaped island's 11 square miles. Walking trails, including the Greenway, which winds from the center of the island to the south shore beaches, are popular. Highlands occur in the north and again in the south, where the dramatic heathland moors rise to 150 feet at the Mohegan Bluffs. Between the highlands, at the center of Block Island, is the imposing Great Salt Pond, which almost cuts the island in two.

Sandy Point

Visit Block Island at any season, but to see birds, it's best to come in the fall. Each year, the Audubon Society of Rhode Island has an early-October birding weekend, to coincide with the peak autumnal flights. Often the island's Northern Bayberry bushes and reed patches overflow with resting and feeding migrant songbirds, such as cuckoos, kinglets, and sparrows. Yellow-rumped Warblers can be a nuisance because of their sheer abundance. Other warblers include Cape May, Black-throated Green, and Palm, and perhaps the uncommon Orange-crowned, Mourning, or Connecticut. Raptors of many species—almost always including a number of Peregrine Falcons—can be numerous, especially on the island's southern half.

Butterflies, too, are a feature of the fall migration. Monarchs stream along in numbers each year, but there are occasional sightings of Cloudless Sulphurs and other southern strays to spice up the list. Seaside Goldenrod flowers are butterfly favorites.

CONTACT Block Is. Chamber of Commerce, 23 Water St., Block Island, RI 02807; 401-466-2982. **HOW TO GET THERE** Block Island may be reached year-round by ferry from Pt. Judith. Summer ferries run from Providence and Newport, New London, CT, and Montauk, NY. **SEASONAL ACCESS** Year-round. **VISITOR CENTER** The Old Harbor ferry landing has an information booth.

NORMAN BIRD SANCTUARY Middletown

Whether you are a youngster hurrying along looking for the next colored trail marker or an old hand casually admiring the scenery, this sanctuary will please you. Right from the entrance area, where Barn Owls reside in the water tower and Ruby-throated Hummingbirds dash about the field borders, you will be delighted.

Norman Bird Sanctuary, on 450 acres, has 7 miles of hiking trails, ranging in length from ⅒ mile to 1½ miles. The Red Fox Trail may produce a fox sighting. The Valley Trail passes through quiet beech, maple, and holly woods. The Hanging Rock Trail climbs to its namesake formation and overlooks Gardiner Pond, where Ring-necked Ducks, scaups, mergansers, and Canvasbacks flock in fall and winter. The major trails follow puddingstone ridges between Gardiner's and Nelson Ponds.

CONTACT Norman Bird Sanct., Audubon Society of R.I., 583 Third Beach Rd., Middletown, RI 02842; 401-846-2577. **HOW TO GET THERE** From Newport Bridge (Rte. 138), take the Middletown–Portsmouth exit. Turn left off the exit ramp, proceed east on Green End Ave. and turn right onto Third Beach Rd. The sanctuary is ¾ mile on the right. **SEASONAL ACCESS** Year-round. **VISITOR CENTER** Sanctuary Barn is located near the main parking area.

SACHUEST POINT
NATIONAL WILDLIFE REFUGE Middletown

Just southeast of the Norman Bird Sanctuary, on a short promontory, lies Sachuest Point National Wildlife Refuge, 228 acres of rocky shorelines, sandy beaches, freshwater and salt marshes, and grasslands. There are 3 miles of trails and three observation towers that provide easy viewing ac-

cess to all of the refuge, which is perhaps best known for its wintering flock of Harlequin Ducks. These marvelously patterned little seaducks are easier to see here than anywhere else in New England. The ducks, which may number more than 50, stick together in quite tight flocks, tend to stay close to coastal rocks, and often submerge en masse, so it sometimes takes a few minutes to locate them. Loons, grebes, and goldeneyes share the inshore waters with the Harlequins, while Short-eared and Snowy Owls frequent the open upland areas from fall through spring. Tautog, Bluefish, and Striped Bass occur all around the peninsula.

CONTACT Sachuest Pt. N.W.R., c/o Ninigret N.W.R., P.O. Box 307, Charlestown, RI 02813; 401-847-5511. **HOW TO GET THERE** From Norman Bird Sanct. drive south to Hanging Rock Rd., turn left on Second Beach Rd. (Sachuest Pt. Rd.) after 1.3 miles, and proceed to the refuge entrance. **SEASONAL ACCESS** Year-round. **VISITOR CENTER** Located at the parking lot.

BURLINGAME STATE PARK   **Charlestown**

Burlingame State Park (2,100 acres, 755 campsites) is an excellent place to brush up on bird songs. The mixed broadleaf woods ring in spring and summer with the flute-like choruses of Wood and Hermit Thrushes, the loud weeping of Great Crested Flycatchers, the pleasant rattle of Downy Woodpeckers, the staccato crescendoes of Northern Waterthrushes and Ovenbirds, and the sing-song patter of Yellow-throated and Red-eyed Vireos. Canada Mayflowers and many other flowering plants brighten the woodlands. The white, blue, and yellow trails circumventing Watchaug Pond provide an 8-mile circuit. The pond is good for watching migrant waterfowl. Bald Eagles occasionally spend the winter here.

CONTACT Burlingame S.P., 75 Burlingame Park Rd., Charlestown, RI 02813; 401-322-7337. **HOW TO GET THERE** From U.S. 1, take the King's Factory Rd. exit, drive north 3.2 miles, and turn left on Buckeye Brook Rd. Proceed .6 mile to a large dirt road on the left. Turn here and continue 1.5 miles to the north end of Watchaug Pond and the camping area. **SEASONAL ACCESS** Mid-Apr.–mid-Oct.

NINIGRET NATIONAL WILDLIFE REFUGE   **Charlestown**

Located more or less directly across the highway from Burlingame State Park, Ninigret National Wildlife Refuge protects Rhode Island's largest coastal pond and associated wetland and upland habitats, including swamps and grasslands. With 310 species recorded, it is

one of the premier bird-finding spots in the region. As much of the 407-acre refuge is the site of a former naval air station, expect a combination of asphalt and natural vegetation underfoot. The refuge is at its best in late summer and fall, when Ninigret Pond and nearby marshes attract great numbers of harriers, herons, egrets, gulls, terns, and shorebirds and the upland shrubs and fields harbor kinglets, vireos, warblers, blackbirds, and sparrows.

Across Ninigret Pond, the Ninigret Conservation Area has more than 2 miles of barrier beach. Access to the beach is via East Beach Road at the western end of the pond. In summer, parking is a problem by midmorning, so plan accordingly.

CONTACT Ninigret N.W.R., P.O. Box 307, Charlestown, RI 02813; 401-364-9124. **HOW TO GET THERE** The west entrance is along U.S. 1. To reach the east entrance, exit U.S. 1 on Rte. 1A, drive .5 mile, turn right at Ninigret Park entrance, and proceed to the end of the road. **SEASONAL ACCESS** Year-round. **VISITOR CENTER** Frosty Drew Nature Ctr. is located halfway along the road that connects the Ninigret Park entrance with the refuge's east entrance.

TRUSTOM POND NATIONAL WILDLIFE REFUGE

South Kingston

This 642-acre property has black-berries, raspberries, blueberries, wild grapes and cherries, even apples—great attractions for large numbers of animals, resident or migrant. The refuge's vertebrate list has 300 birds, 40 mammals, and 20 reptiles and amphibians, and hungry representatives of all three groups are always prowling the shrubbery looking for a meal. Trustom Pond is the only undeveloped coastal salt pond in Rhode Island, and the refuge that protects it is one of the outstanding wildlife viewing areas in New England. Nest boxes and pole platforms are heavily used by Ospreys, Wood Ducks, Purple Martins, and Eastern Bluebirds. The pond has up to 200 resident Mute Swans, and its waters shelter hordes of migrant and wintering ducks. During summer months, naturalists are on duty to lead walks or direct visitors to the best viewing areas.

CONTACT Trustom Pond N.W.R., c/o Ninigret N.W.R., P.O. Box 307, Charlestown, RI 02813; 401-364-9124. **HOW TO GET THERE** From U.S. 1, take the Moonstone Beach exit, drive south 1.1 miles, turn right on Matunuck Schoolhouse Rd., and drive .7 mile to the refuge entrance. **SEASONAL ACCESS** Year-round.

GEORGE B. PARKER WOODLAND

Coventry and Foster

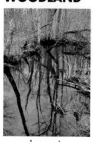

Visitors to Parker Woodland can ponder history and nature at the same time and place. Property of the Audubon Society of Rhode Island, the 690-acre woodland consists of two areas, the more-visited Coventry tract and the less-traveled Foster tract. The two areas are linked by a connector trail, and the six hours or so of walking trails that cross the woodland are well marked. Archaeologists have unearthed ample evidence of historical charcoal burning near the main entrance, and some 100 stone cairns—signs of long-gone inhabitants—are spread about along the trails under the broadleaf forest canopy. For the ornithologically inclined, Acadian Flycatchers, Worm-eating Warblers, and Canada Warblers are noteworthy breeding species. Turkey Meadow Brook bisects the Coventry tract from east to west.

CONTACT George B. Parker Woodland, Audubon Society of R.I., 1670 Maple Valley Rd., Coventry, RI 02816; 401-949-5454. **HOW TO GET THERE** From Providence, drive south on I-95 to Rte. 117. Proceed west about 12 miles along Rte. 117, turn right on Rte. 102, drive about 1.5 miles, turn right on Maple Valley Rd., and continue to the parking area, about 100 yards after the first house on the left. **SEASONAL ACCESS** Year-round. **VISITOR CENTER** Nature Ctr. located in converted barn in Coventry tract.

ARCADIA MANAGEMENT REGION — Hope Valley
One of Rhode Island's few remaining extensive areas that retain an un-spoiled, rural character, the 14,000-acre region offers ample botanizing and other outdoor pursuits. **CONTACT** Arcadia Management Region, Division of Forest Environment, Arcadia Hdqrs., 260 Arcadia Rd., Hope Valley, RI 02832; 401-539-2356.

BEAVERTAIL STATE PARK — Jamestown
Fall and especially winter offer fine birding here. Behind the pounding surf, impressive numbers of sea ducks, loons, grebes, and cormorants gather and feed in the park's 170 acres. **CONTACT** Beavertail S.P., c/o Goddard Memorial S.P., Ives Rd., Warwick, RI 02818; 401-884-2010.

BRENTON POINT STATE PARK — Newport
One of the many headlands along Rhode Island's south coast, 89-acre Brenton Point attracts surf casters (for Tautog and Bluefish) and birdwatchers (for Snowy and Short-eared Owls). **CONTACT** Brenton Pt. S.P., c/o Ft. Adams, Harrison Ave., Newport, RI 02840; 401-847-2400.

BUCK HILL WILDLIFE MANAGEMENT AREA — Chepachet
Ninety percent of the 2,049 acres here are woodlands. Wildlife watchers and hunters look for the White-tailed Deer, Red Fox, Wild Turkey, and Ruffed Grouse. **CONTACT** Buck Hill W.M.A., c/o R.I. Division of Fish & Wildlife, 4808 Tower Hill Rd., Wakefield, RI 02879; 401-789-0281.

GEORGE WASHINGTON MANAGEMENT AREA — Chepachet
The 8-mile Walkabout Trail, constructed by visiting Australian seamen in 1965, passes through Eastern Hemlocks and an Atlantic White Cedar swamp. **CONTACT** George Washington Management Area, c/o R.I. Division of Forest Environment, 2185 Putnam Pike, Chepachet, RI 02814; 401-568-6700.

GREAT SWAMP WILDLIFE MANAGEMENT AREA — West Kingston
The Great Swamp is an excellent bird- and butterfly-watching area. Gravel roads and trails provide access to various parts of the 3,349 acres. **CONTACT** Great Swamp W.M.A., c/o R.I. Division of Fish & Wildlife, 4808 Tower Hill Rd., Wakefield, RI 02879; 401-789-0281.

LINCOLN WOODS STATE PARK — Lincoln
This 687-acre park has some quiet corners where typical woodland plants and birds may be studied. Olney Pond harbors Hooded Mergansers and Wood Ducks. **CONTACT** Lincoln Woods S.P., 2 Manchester Print Works Rd., Lincoln, RI 02865; 401-723-7892.

POWDER MILL LEDGES WILDLIFE REFUGE — Greenville
Headquarters of the Audubon Society of Rhode Island, Powder Mill Ledges comprises groves of Eastern White Pine, a pond and brook, and an environmental resource center on its 100 acres. **CONTACT** Powder Mill Ledges W.R., Audubon Society of R.I., 12 Sanderson Rd., Smithfield, RI 02917; 401-949-5454.

SAKONNET POINT — Little Compton
This birding hotspot in southeastern Rhode Island, with nearby coastal ponds and offshore islets, is superb in fall and winter, particularly for raptors and waterfowl. **CONTACT** R.I. Division of Fish & Wildlife, 4808 Tower Hill Rd., Wakefield, RI 02879; 401-789-0281.

SWAN POINT CEMETERY — Providence
About 200 species of birds, from loons to sparrows, have been sighted here over the years. A tree and shrub guide locates hundreds of woody plants for the visitor to this 200-acre, park-like cemetery. **CONTACT** Swan Pt. Cemetery, P.O. Box 2446, Providence, RI 02906; 401-272-1314.

Vermont

The grand green hills and rolling farmlands of Vermont (total area 9,609 square miles) are New England's own pastoral symphony. Vermonters have worked hard to preserve their enviable natural heritage. Almost 80 percent of the state is forested, most commonly with Sugar Maple–dominated broadleaf woodlands. Vermonters tap half a million gallons of sap annually to supply maple syrup lovers.

Vermont has six primary physiographic regions. The *Green Mountains*, which run north to south and split into three separate ranges, are 160 miles long and include the highest peaks in the state; Mount Mansfield is the grandest at 4,393 feet. The *Taconic Mountains*, in southwestern Vermont, are an important source of limestone, marble, and slate. Between the Greens and the Taconics is the *Valley of Vermont;* as much as 8 miles wide, this limestone basin supports many plants usually not found in the state. The fourth region is the *Champlain Valley*, with the mildest climate in Vermont and flat, rich farmland. Lake Champlain itself is 125 miles long and up to 399 feet deep; its waters support a number of unusual and rare New England fishes, as well as two turtles, the Eastern Spiny Softshell and the Map Turtle, that don't otherwise occur in New England. The largest of Vermont's physiographic regions is the *Piedmont*, which spreads over much of the eastern half of the state and includes many lakes and the Mount Ascutney monadnock. Finally, there is the *Northeast Kingdom*, also known as the Northeastern Highlands— 600 square miles of primarily spruce bogs and northern Vermont wilderness.

Vermont has three major westward-flowing rivers. Otter Creek, Winooski River, and Lamoille River combine, south to north, to drain the Green Mountain runoff into Lake Champlain. In eastern Vermont, the White River flows southeast into the Connecticut River, which forms Vermont's entire eastern border.

Only one-third of Vermonters live in urban settings; like their state wildlife areas, they are well spread around the land. Vermont has 42 state parks, more than 60 state forests and wildlife management areas, one national wildlife refuge, and one very green national forest.

MOUNT MANSFIELD STATE FOREST **Stowe**

At the center of this 33,692-acre state forest, divided into two tracts, is Mount Mansfield, the highest peak in the state at 4,393 feet. To get to or near the top, drive the toll road, ride the gondola, or hike one of the many trails. People are always coming and going here, with wildflower enthusiasts and summer climbers giving way to autumn leaf peepers, who in turn yield to winter sports lovers. The 250-acre summit of Mount Mansfield is owned by the University of Vermont, which studies and protects this largest alpine area in the state. The remarkable vegetation here includes many small but handsome members of the heath family (low, multi-branched evergreen shrubs) and the predominant Bigelow's Sedge. These plants are both terribly hardy and terribly fragile, and cannot withstand being trampled, so please stay on the paths. Just below the alpine area is a fine krummholz woods zone.

CONTACT Mt. Mansfield S.F., c/o Dept. of Forests, Parks and Recreation, 103 S. Main St., S. Waterbury, VT 05671; 802-241-3655. **HOW TO GET THERE** From Stowe, drive north 9 miles on Rte. 108 and watch for Mt. Mansfield signs. **SEASONAL ACCESS** Year-round. The auto road is open late May–mid-Oct. (weather permitting). **VISITOR CENTER** Green Mountain Club (802-244-7037) naturalists available at summit of mountain and in Waterbury Center.

SMUGGLERS' NOTCH STATE PARK **Stowe**

This 4,000-acre parcel of Mount Mansfield State Forest has a forest of Yellow Birch, maples (Sugar, Red, and Mountain), and American Mountain Ash, plus a nice campground, summer ranger-naturalists, and the most breathtaking array of 1,000-foot cliffs, boulders, and ledges to tower over any Vermont roadside. Many visitors just stand and gawk. If you feel the urge to ascend, there are trails that will take you up to dramatic overlooks. Tread as lightly as possible here, for, as at the peak of Mount Mansfield, there are a number of rare and fragile plants growing in a precarious environment. The steep cliff walls, wet and cold, support plants of the aptly named Cold Calcareous Cliff Community. These include Alpine Woodsia, Marble Sandwort, Purple Mountain Saxifrage, and Butterwort. Peregrine Falcons have an aerie here and should not be disturbed during the nesting season.

CONTACT Smugglers' Notch S.P., 7248 Mountain Rd., Stowe, VT 05672; 802-253-4014 (summer); 802-479-4280 (winter). **HOW TO GET THERE** Drive 6 miles west of Stowe or 10 miles east of Jeffersonville along Rte. 108. **SEASONAL ACCESS** Season is from late May–mid-Oct.; during other seasons, call to make arrangements. **VISITOR CENTER** Contact station located 7 miles up Mountain Rd. from Stowe.

GREEN MOUNTAIN NATIONAL FOREST

Vermont is defined by the Green Mountains. They are the state's backbone, its lofty heights, and the source of its nickname. Stretching from the Canadian border to Massachusetts, they are home to rare alpine plants, pristine streams, towering cliffs, dramatic waterfalls, birds, insects, bears, and trees, trees, trees. The Green Mountain National Forest protects 350,000 acres in two major regions, one in southern Vermont and the other in the central part of the range. Together, they constitute half of the public land in the state. There are four wilderness areas in the southern section, two in the north.

Deerfield River

The Long Trail, maintained by Green Mountain Club members, runs the entire length of the mountain chain, with 125 miles crossing ridges in the national forest. Another 375 miles of hiking, biking, skiing, and snowmobiling trails are accessible from various points in the forest's borders. There are five developed campgrounds. Following are some of the many areas of interest in each of the two forest tracts. There are many others.

Southern Tract (Manchester Ranger District)

For most people, both the southern and the northern tracts of the forest are best explored by trail. The Appalachian and Long Trails share common ground in the southern part of the state and cover 72 miles of beautiful terrain within this district. A national forest brochure, available from the supervisor's office, lists 20 day hikes, ranging in difficulty from easy to demanding. Three day hikes are delineated in the Burn and Stratton Pond areas off Forest Road 6, near the center of the district, and a dozen more in the popular White Rocks National Recreation Area and vicinity in the northern reaches of the Manchester district. Two wilderness areas located in the northern part of the tract, Big Branch and Peru Peak, can be reached via Forest Road 10.

Expect to be charmed by the glorious mountain scenery and exhilarated by the sights and sounds of the forest at any season.

Campers may be awakened by the incessant *toot-toot-toot* of the diminutive Northern Saw-whet Owl or the booming *Who cooks for you?* notes of the vociferous Barred Owl. Woodpeckers, commonly heard and seen, include the huge Pileated Woodpecker, sometimes known as the Cock of the Woods. Watch for some of the region's squirrels: Eastern Chipmunks scramble about and dive into their trailside holes (those are not snake holes), Red Squirrels whir around in the conifers, and Northern Flying Squirrels cavort by night, squeaking and gliding about in their hardwood territories.

Northern Tract (Middlebury and Rochester Ranger Districts)

Routes 73 and 125 cross this district from east to west and provide good access to most of the area's forest roads and trail systems. The forest service has an introductory brochure describing 27 day hikes, again varying in length and difficulty. It is essential to hike prepared, even on a day trip. Always carry the most detailed map available, adequate food and water, and additional warm clothing and insect repellent, depending on the season.

Route 125 delivers the visitor to two popular trailheads. The Texas Falls Nature Trail, with a vertical rise of only 70 feet, is easily walked and provides fine views of the falls. The Robert Frost Interpretive Trail, to the west and also an easy walk, winds about a mile through forest and old fields, and is punctuated along its length by Frost poems mounted on signposts.

If you crave a wilder experience, hike north into the Bread Loaf Wilderness Area, where five peaks top 3,500 feet and the climb will burn off all the calories you can carry in your pack. Black Bears, White-tailed Deer, and Bunchberry live here, as well as Red-tailed Hawks and Common Ravens, which soar on the thermal updrafts. With a little patience and some decent binoculars you should be able to distinguish some of the region's finches: the plum-colored Purple, the vivid yellow-and-black American Goldfinch, the stripe-breasted Pine Siskin, the bizarrely beaked crossbills, and the elegant and relatively huge Evening Grosbeak.

Sugar Maple

CONTACT Green Mountain N.F., 231 N. Main St., Rutland, VT 05701; 802-747-6700. **HOW TO GET THERE** U.S. 7 and Rte. 100 run north–south along the western and eastern boundaries of the forest, respectively. Rutland is located between the two halves of the forest. **SEASONAL ACCESS** Year-round. **VISITOR CENTER** The forest supervisor's office in Rutland has free trail maps and general information on all aspects of the forest.

MISSISQUOI NATIONAL WILDLIFE REFUGE

Swanton

Where else in Vermont can the visitor find nesting Black Terns, a beautiful Silver Maple swamp, a White Oak floodplain forest, and summer skies alive with most of the state's species of bats? Tucked into the northeastern corner of Lake Champlain, a stone's throw from the Canadian border, Missisquoi is the only national wildlife refuge in Vermont. A canoe or kayak will enhance your visit, for this is a great place to see wetland animals and plants. American Beavers and Northern River Otters are common in the 6,000 acres here, as are several nesting heron species, including Great Blue Herons and American Bitterns. Fall waterfowl numbers usually peak at about 20,000. If you are boatless, walk the trails behind the headquarters building or scan the marshes and swamps from the roadside.

CONTACT Missisquoi N.W.R., P.O. Box 163, Swanton, VT 05488; 802-868-4781. **HOW TO GET THERE** From Burlington, travel north on I-89 about 25 miles to exit 1 at Swanton; proceed 2 miles west on Rte. 78. **SEASONAL ACCESS** Year-round, although some walking trails may be seasonally flooded.

DEAD CREEK WILDLIFE MANAGEMENT AREA

Addison

Bird life is the primary focus at this 2,858-acre area. Dead Creek is a tributary of Otter Creek, Vermont's longest stream. Its marshes and impoundments are the site of the biggest waterfowl management program in Vermont. Nesting birds include American Bitterns, Least Bitterns, Soras, and Virginia Rails—all secretive marsh dwellers, but early-morning or early-evening visitors, especially canoeists, can usually hear or glimpse them. Canada Geese and ducks of several species breed in numbers. This is one of the outstanding inland shorebird spots in New England in years of low water. In winter the fields are home to many raptors, owls, Horned Larks, and Snow Buntings.

For access by land, drive west from the headquarters building, cross Dead Creek Bridge, and immediately turn left at the Brilyea East access point. Park near the two ponds and start exploring.

CONTACT Dead Creek W.M.A., R.D. 1 Box 130, Vergennes, VT 05491; 802-759-2397. **HOW TO GET THERE** From Middlebury, drive northwest 8 miles on Rte. 23, turn left on Rte. 17, and proceed to Addison. The hdqrs. building is on the north side of Rte. 17, about 1 mile west of Addison center. **SEASONAL ACCESS** Year-round; avoid the area from mid-Oct.–mid-Nov. if you are not a waterfowl hunter.

GROTON STATE FOREST
Groton

Vermont's largest (25,000-plus acres) state-owned forest is located between Barre and St. Johnsbury at the southern edge of the Northeast Kingdom. There are more than 200 campsites, mostly in the northern half of the forest, and plenty of opportunities to get out and up into the forested hills. The nature center has two short loop trails and a longer trail to 700-acre Peacham Bog Natural Area, site of one of Vermont's largest Black Spruce–Tamarack bogs. Bring boots. Lake Groton has breeding Common Loons, while other forest lakes, including Osmore Pond and Marshfield Pond, have more solitude. Owl's Head, at 1,958 feet, is easily reached by a dirt road and short trail; a climb up 3,352-foot Signal Mountain to the south requires more planning and stamina. Moose, White-tailed Deer, Fishers, and American Beavers live here.

CONTACT Groton S.F., c/o Dept. of Forests, Parks and Recreation, 103 S. Main St., Waterbury, VT 05671; 802-241-3655. **HOW TO GET THERE** From Barre, drive east 15 miles on U.S. 302, turn north on Rte. 232, and watch for various forest parking areas on either side of the road. **SEASONAL ACCESS** Year-round. **VISITOR CENTER** Groton Nature Ctr. is located along the forest road at the north end of Lake Groton.

VERMONT INSTITUTE OF NATURAL SCIENCE AND RAPTOR CENTER
Woodstock

Small and easily covered, this a great place for a family outing and an introduction to Vermont nature. Start with the Raptor Center, where about 40 living but unreleasable birds of prey of 24 species—owls, eagles, falcons, and hawks—are exhibited in a series of enclosures. If you have ever seen distant hawks soaring over a fall hawkwatching spot or glimpsed an owl dashing across your car's headlight beams, you will appreciate how

much more majestic and handsome these birds are up close. After admiring the raptors, head out on either the Communities Trail or the Interrelationships Trail and find out how good an interpretive trail can be. Both are fairly easy walks and great learning experiences. The institute offers local and statewide natural history trips and other educational opportunities.

CONTACT Vermont Inst. of Natural Science and Raptor Ctr., R.R. 2 Box 532, Woodstock, VT 05091; 802-457-2779. **HOW TO GET THERE** From Rte. 4 in the center of Woodstock, turn southwest onto Church Hill Rd. (at St. James Episcopal Church), and drive 1.5 miles to the institute's entrance. **SEASONAL ACCESS** Year-round. **VISITOR CENTER** Offers displays, seasonal programs, and self-guided trails.

ASCUTNEY STATE PARK
Windsor

Mount Ascutney overlooks the south-central Connecticut Valley. The 2,000-acre park's skies are shared by watchful hawks and hang gliders. Miles of trails are maintained. **CONTACT** Ascutney S.P., Box 186, HCR 71, Windsor, VT 05089; 802-674-2060 (summer); 802-886-2434 (winter).

BOMOSEEN STATE PARK
Fair Haven

Abandoned slate quarries, near-pristine Glen Lake, and a series of Eastern Hemlock–Eastern White Pine woodland ridges are a few of the 365-acre park's attractions. **CONTACT** Bomoseen S.P., R.R. 1 Box 2620, Fair Haven, VT 05743; 802-265-4242 (summer); 802-483-2001 (winter).

BRIGHTON STATE PARK
Island Pond

This 150-acre park is an excellent base for exploring the Island Pond area, which has some of the finest boreal (northern) forest in the Northeast Kingdom. **CONTACT** Brighton S.P., P.O. Box 413, Island Pond, VT 05846; 802-723-4360 (summer); 802-479-4280 (winter).

CAMEL'S HUMP STATE PARK
Jonesville

At 4,083 feet, Camel's Hump is a good climb. The splendid mountain forest scenery in this 20,000-acre park makes the hike to the alpine summit a joy. **CONTACT** Camel's Hump S.P., c/o Vt. Dept. of Forests, Parks and Recreation, 111 West St., Essex Junction, VT 05452; 802-879-6565.

GREEN MOUNTAIN AUDUBON NATURE CENTER
Huntington

Come here for educational programs on everything from astronomy to zoology or hike one of the trails to the river or beaver pond on the 255-acre property. Maple sugaring is a spring highlight. **CONTACT** Green Mtn. Audubon Nature Ctr., 255 Sherman Hollow Rd., Huntington, VT 05462; 802-434-3068.

KILLINGTON PEAK
Plymouth

Killington Peak, at 4,241 feet, is at its most magnificent in the winter. A gondola can transport you to this roof of south-central Vermont. **CONTACT** Killington Peak, Calvin Coolidge S.F., Box 105, Plymouth, VT 05056; 802-672-3612.

MOLLY STARK STATE PARK
Wilmington

The views from the top of Mount Olga, located in this 148-acre park, are breathtaking during fall foliage season. **CONTACT** Molly Stark S.P., 705 Rte. 9 East, Wilmington, VT 05363; 802-464-5460.

QUECHEE STATE PARK
White River Junction

Quechee State Park

Vermont's most dramatic river gorge, 165 feet deep and over a mile long, Quechee Gorge is spectacular at any season. **CONTACT** Quechee S.P., 190 Dewey Mills Rd., White River Junction, VT 05001; 802-295-2990 (summer); 802-886-2434 (winter).

VICTORY BASIN WILDLIFE MANAGEMENT AREA
St. Johnsbury

Snowshoe Hares, Black Bears, and Moose (along the Moose River) are some of the inhabitants of this 4,970-acre wetland mosaic, known locally as Victory Bog. **CONTACT** Victory Basin W.M.A., c/o Vt. Dept. of Fish & Wildlife, 184 Portland St., St., Johnsbury, VT 05819-2099; 802-748-8787.

WILLOUGHBY STATE FOREST
St. Johnsbury

Glacial scouring thousands of years ago produced the 7,300-acre National Natural Landmark area of Lake Willoughby and the spectacular cliffs of Mount Pisgah and Mount Hor. **CONTACT** Willoughby S.F., c/o Vt. Dept. of Forests, Parks and Recreation, 184 Portland St., St. Johnsbury, VT 05819-2099; 802-748-8787.

The Authors

Peter Alden, principal author of this volume, is a naturalist, author, and tour guide who has lectured and led nature tours all over the world for Harvard's Friends of the Museum of Comparative Zoology, Massachusetts Audubon Society, Overseas Adventure Travel, Lindblad Travel, and many cruise lines. He has written books on North American, Latin American, and African wildlife. Alden lives in Concord, Massachusetts.

Brian Cassie, author of the habitats, parks and preserves, and other sections of this guide as well as general regional consultant, is a naturalist, teacher, tour leader, and the Director of Education for the North American Butterfly Association. He lives in Foxboro, Massachusetts.

Richard Forster, author of the insects species accounts, was the regional editor for National Audubon's ornithological journal American Birds, a staff ornithologist and tour leader for Massachusetts Audubon, and a distinguished naturalist. Forster, who died in 1997, is greatly missed.

Richard Keen, author of the weather and night sky sections of this guide, is a freelance science writer, nature photographer, and public speaker. He has published many books, articles, and photographs on the topics of meteorology and astronomy.

Amy Leventer, author of the geology and topography sections of the guide, is a visiting assistant professor at Colgate University's Geology Department. She has published many articles on geology and co-authored the *National Audubon Society Pocket Guide to the Earth from Space*.

Acknowledgments

The authors collectively thank the thousands of botanists, zoologists, and naturalists we have worked with over the years and whose books and papers provided a wealth of information for this first book in the series. The staff and members of the following organizations were most helpful: National Audubon Society, Massachusetts Audubon Society, Harvard's Museum of Comparative Zoology, Gray Herbarium and Arnold Arboretum, the Nature Conservancy, New England Wildflower Society, North American Butterfly Association, Nuttall Ornithological Club, and Brookline Bird Club. We also thank the staffs of the many federal and state land, game, and fish departments.

We thank all of the experts who contributed to each section of this book. Wayne Petersen of Massachusetts Audubon and Guy Tudor offered valuable advice on the species selection, Carter Gilbert of the Florida Museum of Natural History reviewed the fish species accounts, Wendy Zomlefer reviewed the plant species and wrote the flora introductions, Sylvia Sharnoff reviewed the lichen section, Gary Mechler reviewed the weather and night sky spreads, Chuck Keene reviewed many species photographs, and Rick Oches reviewed the topography and geology text. Thanks also go to the Massachusetts Maple Producers Association for information on maple sugaring, Jim Cantore and the Weather Channel for the fall foliage map, and Arnold Howe and Ken Reback, senior biologists at the Massachusetts Division of Marine Fisheries for information on overfishing Georges Bank. We also thank Jeff Stone of Chic Simple Design for initial editorial and design consultation.

Special thanks go to Alfie and Sally Alcorn, Dorothy Arvidson, James Baird, Jerry Bertrand, Bill Brumback, Richard Carey, Sarah Jane Cassie,

Linda Cocca, Kevin and Kristen Forster, Winthrop Harrington, Karsten Hartell, Elizabeth Kneiper, Vernon Laux, Chris Leahy, Dotsie Long, Janna Meyer, Larry Millman, Blair Nikula, Simon Perkins, Roger and Virginia Peterson, Noble Proctor, Barbara Pryor, Judy Schwenk, Jackie Sones, Guy Tudor, Dick Walton, and W. David Winter, Jr.

We are grateful to Andrew Stewart for his vision of a regional field guide encompassing the vast mosaic of New England's topography, habitats, and wildlife, and to the staff of Chanticleer Press for producing a book of such excellence. Editor-in-chief Amy Hughes provided fundamental conceptual guidance as well as constant encouragement and supervision. Series editor and main text editor Patricia Fogarty was the project's guiding light, and the success of the book is due largely to her considerable skills and expertise. Editors Miriam Harris and Pamela Nelson thoroughly examined and refined the flora and invertebrates sections, respectively. Editors Lisa Leventer and Holly Thompson made many valuable contributions to the project. Managing editor Edie Locke shepherded the book through the editorial process. Assistant editor Kristina Lucenko and editorial assistant and map researcher Michelle Bredeson provided boundless editorial support while they meticulously fact checked, copyedited, and proofread the book through all stages. Publishing assistant Karin Murphy and editorial intern Tessa Kale offered much assistance and support. Dan Hugos's editorial database helped keep track of the species lists and text.

Art director Drew Stevens and designer Vincent Mejia took 1,500 images and tens of thousands of words of text and created a book that is both visually beautiful and eminently usable. The design contributions of interns Anthony Liptak and Enrique Piñas and designer Areta Buk were invaluable. Howard S. Friedman created the beautiful and informative color illustrations. Ortelius Design made the detailed maps that appear throughout the book. The tree silhouette drawings were contributed by Dolores R. Santoliquido, and the animal tracks by Dot Barlowe.

Photo directors Zan Carter and Teri Myers and photo editor Christine Heslin sifted through thousands of photographs from hundreds of photographers in their search for the stunning images that contribute so much to the beauty and usefulness of this guide. They carefully chose the images that best represented each subject, and worked patiently with the authors, consultants, natural history experts, and the editorial and design teams. The team from Artemis Picture Research Group, Inc.—Linda Patterson Eger, Lois Safrani, Yvonne Silver, and Anita Dickhuth—brought considerable skills and experience to the task of researching and editing many of the species photographs. Permissions manager Alyssa Sachar facilitated the acquisition of photographs and ensured that all records and photo credits were accurate. Kate Jacobs, Leslie Fink, Jennifer McClanaghan, and intern Mee-So Caponi helped sort and traffic photographs and offered endless additional support.

Director of production Alicia Mills and production assistant Philip Pfeifer saw the book through the monumentally complicated production and printing processes. They worked closely with Dai Nippon Printing to ensure the excellent printing quality of these books.

In addition, we thank all of the photographers who gathered and submitted the gorgeous pictures that make this book a delight to view.

—Peter Alden, Brian Cassie,
Amy Leventer, Richard Keen

Picture Credits

The credits are listed alphabetically by photographer. Each photograph is listed by the number of the page on which it appears, followed by a letter indicating its position on the page (the letters follow a sequence from top left to bottom right).

Kevin Adams 140b, 148d, 159c, 161d, 162d, 163b & d, 168b, 171f, 172c, 174b, 176f, 177a, 178c & f, 179d

Gene Ahrens 19a, 425

Donna L. Allen 413a

Walt Anderson 142a

Peter Arnold
Jeff Rotman 235a

Frederick D. Atwood 29h, 33a, 44, 402a & b

Ron Austing 47a, 53a, 142b, 267a, 287a, 290b, 292a, 294a, 295d, 296a, 298c, 306c, 308c, 314a & b, 316b & c, 317a & b, 318a & b, 319a & b, 324a, 328a, 332a, 333b & c, 337c, 340b, 343a, 344b & c, 361b

Margaret Barnes & E. R. Degginger/ Color-Pic, Inc. 169b

Daniel F. Belknap/ University of Maine 21c

Steve Bentsen 299a, 317d

Fred Bruemmer 305c, 308d, 309b

Sonja Bullaty & Angelo Lomeo 11b, 97b, 103a, 104d, 105a, d & e, 106d, e, g & h, 107a, 109d, 111a, 114d, 115d & f, 119a & d, 120e, 122b & e, 423a

Gay Bumgarner 315d, 343c, 346e, 347d, 368b

Les Burdge 381a, 382a, 383b

George H. Burgess 251f

Scott Camazine 210d

Z. Carter 427b

David Cavagnaro 104c, 107b, 109e, 114a, 116e, 117g, 118a

Rick Cech 49a, 163c, 165c, 202a, 218b, 219c & e, 220a, b, c & d, 221b, c & e, 222a & c, 223a, b & e, 224b, c, d & e, 225d & e, 226a, b & d, 227a, b & c, 411b

Herbert Clarke 290d, 299c, 307d, 311c, 332b, 334a, 335d, 338a, 349d

John M. Coffman 206a, 208a, 264a, 272b

Eliot Cohen 27b, 99f, 115g, 156d, 378a & b, 381b, 390b, 391b, 405b, 406b, 408, 412a, 413b, 418a, 419a & b, 420a & b

Gerald & Buff Corsi/ Focus on Nature, Inc. 324b

Daniel J. Cox/Natural Exposures, Inc. 364b, 365a, 370a

Bob Cranston 254

Sharon Cummings 280b, 304e, 328b, 345a, 359a, 380c

Rob Curtis/The Early Birder 110c, 151d, 172a, 204c, 207b, 210e, 219d, 229c, 296c, 311b, 321d, 322b, 326a & c, 327e, 329b, 342c & d

Daybreak Imagery
Richard Day 270c

Larry Dech 86a, 89b, 91b & e

E. R. Degginger/ Color-Pic., Inc. 24c, 25b, d & f, 28b, 59c, 80c, 81a& b, 83c, 84, 87c & d, 89e, 90b & d, 91c, 96a, 97a & c, 98a & d, 99c, d & e, 100b, c, d, e, & h, 101a, c & d, 103c, 108a, 109c, 110f, 115a, 116b, 117f, 120a, 127e, 130c,

131c, 141b & d, 142e, 148b, 149b & e, 156e, 157e, 158d, 160b, 161b, 164f, 167a, 169c, 171c, 172e, 174c, 182e, 188b, 189, 190b & c, 193b, 194c, 196a & b, 197c, 202c, 204a, b & d, 207c & d, 208d & e, 210a, 211a, 212b & d, 216b, c, d & e, 217a, 220e, 223d, 225a, 227d & e, 229d, 230a, d & e, 244a, 258a, 259a, 261d, 264b, 267c, 271b, 272a, 274a, 308b, 315a & b, 318c, 346c

Phil Degginger/Color-Pic, Inc. 179b, 257a, 262a

Dembinsky Photo Associates
Gary Meszaros 245b, 354b
Jim Roetzel 363b
Carl E. Sams III 358a

Jack Dermid 21a, 292b, 353a, 356b, 387a, 401

Alan & Linda Detrick 126d, e, f, g, h & i, 146e, 166a, 175a

Townsend P. Dickinson 22b, 36a

Larry Ditto 286a

Christine M. Douglas 24b, 89d, 90c, 107d, 111e, 128c & e, 160a, 170a, 173b

Kerry Dressler 115b, 119c

Sidney W. Dunkle 200b, 201a & d, 203c & e

Harry Ellis 154d

Dennis Flaherty 121b

Donald Flescher 233b, 240a, 241b, 242d, 244c, 250a & b, 253c

Jeff Foott 258b, 287d, 289d, 298b & d, 368a, 374b

Index

Converting to Metric

Limited space makes it impossible for us to give measurements expressed as metrics. Here is a simplified chart for converting inches and feet to their metric equivalents:

	MULTIPLY BY
inches to millimeters	25
inches to centimeteres	2.5
feet to meters	0.3
yards to meters	0.9
miles to kilometers	1.6
square miles to square kilometers	2.6
acres to hectares	.40
ounces to grams	28.3
pounds to kilograms	.45
Farenheit to Centigrade	subtract 32 and multiply by .55

Prepared and produced by Chanticleer Press, Inc.

Founder: Paul Steiner
Publisher: Andrew Stewart

Staff for this book:

Editor-in-Chief: Amy K. Hughes
Series Editor: Patricia Fogarty
Managing Editor: Edie Locke
Editor: Miriam Harris
Contributing Editors: Lisa Leventer, Pamela Nelson
Assistant Editor: Kristina Lucenko
Editorial Assistant: Michelle Bredeson
Photo Directors: Zan Carter, Teri Myers
Photo Editor: Christine Heslin
Photo Research and Editing: Artemis Picture Research Group, Inc.
Rights and Permissions Manager: Alyssa Sachar
Art Director: Drew Stevens
Designer: Vincent Mejia
Design Interns: Anthony Liptak, Enrique Piñas
Director of Production: Alicia Mills
Production Assistant: Philip Pfeifer
Publishing Assistant: Karin Murphy
Illustrations: Howard S. Friedman
Maps: Ortelius Design

Series design by Drew Stevens and Vincent Mejia

All editorial inquiries should be addressed to:

Chanticleer Press
665 Broadway, Suite 1001
New York, NY 10012

To purchase this book or other National Audubon Society Fiel
Guides and Pocket Guides, please contact:

Alfred A. Knopf
201 East 50th Street
New York, NY 10022
(800) 733-3000

b